THE SUBLIME

A STUDY OF CRITICAL THEORIES
IN XVIII-CENTURY ENGLAND

BY
SAMUEL H. MONK

With a new Preface by the author

ANN ARBOR PAPERBACKS
THE UNIVERSITY OF MICHIGAN PRESS

First edition as an Ann Arbor Paperback 1960
Copyright © by The University of Michigan 1960

First published by the Modern Language Association of America in 1935

Published in the United States of America by
The University of Michigan Press and simultaneously
in Toronto, Canada, by Ambassador Books Limited

Manufactured in the United States of America

PREFACE

THIS book records in some detail the history of an idea—the sublime—during something more than a century of aesthetic and critical speculation in Great Britain. It isolates for study one aspect of a complex subject which includes theories of the beautiful, the picturesque, and the possibility of a standard of taste and which has important bearings on arts other than literature, notably painting and architecture. Moreover it describes some of the shifts that occurred in cultivated or merely fashionable taste during the eighteenth century, most notably in respect to the aesthetic enjoyment of wild and mountainous scenery and to the deployment in literature and painting of such intense emotions as rapture, awe, terror, and horror.

Twenty-five years ago I wrote: "The development of the sublime was a sort of Methodist revival in art." Today that statement seems to me, like most analogies, a good deal more clever than true. The Augustans of the late seventeenth and the earlier part of the eighteenth centuries, like their twentieth-century descendants, could enjoy quite different sorts of art or of natural scenery. If the articulate admirers of the vast in nature and of what the critic John Dennis called the "enthusiastic passions" in art were in the minority before the 1760's, they were none the less present; and that most typically reserved and reasonable of Augustans, Joseph Addison, as early as 1712 had found a place for the vast along with the uncommon and the limited, ordered, symmetrical, and unified "beauty" of current taste, among his "pleasures of the imagination." It is perhaps worth remarking that *Gulliver's Travels* and James Thomson's *Winter* were published in the same year (1726) and made their way together in popular esteem. But it is also useful to recall that after the 1740's (for reasons not unrelated to the subject of this book) *The Seasons* survived changes in taste and retained its popularity when *Gulliver's Travels* was becoming unacceptable to a great many readers who nonetheless acknowledged its brilliance. It seems to me preferable not to regard the cult of the sublime as a revolutionary movement outside of and against neo-classical standards of taste (though eventually it certainly helped to overthrow those standards), but rather as the other, the constantly present but before the 1740's not always eagerly visited, pole on which the world of eighteenth-century art turned.

Since the publication of this book in 1935, a number of scholars have published works that valuably supplement and occasionally correct my work. The most important of these, it seems to me, are Ernest Tuveson's article "Space, Deity, and the 'Natural Sublime'," *MLQ* XII (1951), 20–38; H.V.S. and Margaret S. Ogden's *English Taste in Landscape in the Seventeenth Century* (Ann Arbor, 1955); and Marjorie Nicolson's *Mountain Gloom and Mountain Glory* (Ithaca, 1959), which among them help to account on quite other grounds than those that I have suggested for the emergence of a taste for sublime scenery in late seventeenth-century Britain. Walter J. Hipple's *The Beautiful, the Sublime, and the Picturesque* (Carbondale, Illinois, 1957) is a rigorously conducted philosophical analysis of his subject. Finally, J. T. Boulton has provided us with a superb critical edition of Burke's *Enquiry* (London, 1958), perhaps the most influential discussion of sublimity produced in the eighteenth century.

Minneapolis   S.H.M.

CONTENTS

ERRATA

p. 23, l. 21, and note 47:   *For* Rhapsody *read* Rapsody.

p. 24, l. 26:   *For* Lanson *read* Lawson.

p. 25, note 54:   *For* Lanson *read* Lawson.

p. 73, note 26:   *For* January, 1747 *read* January, 1744.

p. 80, note 48:   *For* Lawrence *read* Laurence.

p. 87, l. 26:   *For* that *read* which.

p. 107, l. 26:   *For* Lanson *read* Lawson.

p. 107, note 16:   *For* Lanson *read* Lawson.

p. 124, l. 19:   *For* MacPherson *read* Macpherson.

p. 125, l. 1:   *For* or *read* of.

p. 168, l. 17:   *For* Freart *read* Fréart.

p. 168, note 8:   *For* Freart *read* Fréart.

p. 170, l. 28:   *For* Vice-Roy *read* Viceroy.

p. 173, l. 37:   *For* Freart *read* Fréart.

p. 189, l. 19:   *For* MacPherson *read* Macpherson.

p. 203, l. 25:   *For* Lorraine *read* Lorrain.

p. 205, l. 4:   *For* Macaulay's *read* Arnold's.

p. 212, l. 14:   *For* MacPherson *read* Macpherson.

p. 215, l. 30:   *For* Killegrew *read* Killigrew.

p. 239, l. 32:   *For* Freart *read* Fréart.

p. 242, l. 38:   *For* Lanson *read* Lawson.

p. 246, l. 5:   *For* Rhapsody *read* Rapsody.

p. 247:   *For* Chambray, Freart de *read* Chambray, Fréart de.

p. 248:   *For* Lanson, John *read* Lawson, John.

INTRODUCTION

A LL students of the eighteenth century are familiar with the fact
that during that period there was throughout Europe an immense
amount of speculation on æsthetic questions. This was true of Britain,
and although most of the British writers of this sort doubtless deserve
Croce's scornful epithet "scribblers," it is in such writings that one can
see expressed with varying degrees of completeness the tastes and artistic
values or confusion of values that find expression in the arts in England
during the years when neo-classicism was dominant and when it was in
decay. Under a great variety of titles, a great variety of men at one time
or other composed an essay or a book or a poem on taste or beauty or
sublimity or the pleasures of the imagination or the art of poetry, of
painting, or of music. Not everyone who wrote had something to say,
but on the part of both philosopher and connoisseur (and most fine gentlemen had a "taste") considerable interest was manifested in the questions
of why objects are beautiful and how those objects affect one. On the
part of philosophers this was probably due to the emphasis which
empiricism had placed on sensation, with the resultant interest in psychology of a rudimentary sort; as for the connoisseur, he was doubtless
merely following a fashion in philosophy in an age when cultivated leisure
permitted every gentleman to take pen in hand.

The result of this abundant speculation is a mass of material that has
never been systematically sorted and arranged. The great age of æsthetic theory was of course the nineteenth century, when German
thought predominated in England as elsewhere. Consequently the standard histories of æsthetic, such as Max Schasler's *Kritische Geschichte der
Aesthetik*, Heinrich von Stein's *Die Entstehung der Neuern Aesthetik*, and
Bernard Bosanquet's *History of Aesthetic* have perforce treated the
eighteenth century with a becoming brevity, out of respect for the
claims of proportion. In such general histories English thought necessarily commands only a small amount of space; the more important
thinkers are treated concisely and simply, individual ideas are discussed
but briefly, and the minor figures appear not at all.

Some interesting essays on eighteenth-century æsthetic exist, for example, Folkierski's *Entre le Classicisme et le Romantisme*, which is concerned mainly with Diderot, but which is a helpful book to the student
of the pre-romantic period; the introductory chapter of Basch's *Essai
Critique sur l'Esthétique de Kant;* numerous specialized treatises by Ger-

man students, such as Candrea's *Der Begriff des Erhabenen bei Burke und Kant*, or Hofmann's *Die Lehre vom Erhabenen bei Kant und seinen Vorgängern*, and numerous articles in the various learned journals, many of which are listed in the Appendix of Professor Draper's excellent *Eighteenth Century English Aesthetics: A Bibliography*. These are generally concerned with a study of thought in more than one country, or again considerations of space have forced the writers to restrict their observations to single men or single ideas.

There should be room, therefore, for a detailed study of one of the leading æsthetic ideas in eighteenth-century England. Beauty, sublimity, taste, imagination, and the picturesque are the most important of these ideas. Their rise, transformation, and progress are interesting and the complete history of any one of them should throw light upon the progress of taste, the change of values, and the gradual growth of critical and æsthetic theories in the period that lies between the flourishing of neo-classicism and the triumph of romanticism, or romanticisms (as Professor Lovejoy has taught us to say).

Such a study is undertaken here, and it has seemed wise to concentrate attention almost wholly upon England, at the expense of a broadly historical point of view. The writer is not unaware that thought throughout the whole of the eighteenth century was strikingly cosmopolitan, and that for the historian of ideas France and Germany are as important as England for him who would give a complete picture of the age. The aim of this book, however, is only to trace the history of one idea, the sublime, as it developed in England, and this can be done within a reasonable space only by the deliberate overemphasis that has been here employed.

But the task of carrying out a piece of narrowly specialized research is not necessarily easier because of its restricted field. Everyone is familiar with the fact that a mountain which seems perfectly shaped when seen from a great distance loses that shape and becomes a formless mass when one approaches its base. The same is certainly true of the history of ideas. It is possible to sketch in the general outlines, but closer inspection will reveal the complexity of a design that seemed at first to be quite simple and obvious. The danger, of course, is that the outline will be entirely obscured by close study. The history of an idea is complex because thought is organic, and every thought in every period is in some way conditioned by other thoughts. The difficulty, therefore, is that the history of an idea may tend to grow into the history of a period, and one is tempted to avoid this danger by tearing up the idea by its roots, dissociating it from the soil in which it has flourished, and presenting it, a withered fragment, to an unenthusiastic world. Certainly a study of the sublime in England comes very near being a study of English thought and arts, for we find the idea applied to rhetoric, to literature, to painting, to sculpture, to music, to biblical criticism, and to natural scenery; and it has its roots in the psychology and the philosophy of the times. If this volume errs, and it does err, it is rather in the human failure of not doing enough, than in the heroic attempt to treat the subject fully. I have attempted to find as many theories of sublimity as possible, and to summarize them clearly and truthfully, relating them incidentally to contemporary movements in literature; to follow out the history of the idea as it was applied to painting and to the enjoyment of natural scenery; and to view all of these theories as an important link in the chain of ideas that, through various transformations, connects organically the literature of the Augustan age with that of the age of Wordsworth.

The chaos of which Croce has complained in English æsthetic speculation in the eighteenth century does not diminish as one begins to explore what was written during that extremely prolific age. And this is especially true of writings on the sublime. When Martin Shee, in his *Elements of Art*, 1809, looked back over the field of English thought in the preceding century, he was impelled to attack the whole tradition of the sublime as "the insane point of the critical compass;" for, he says,

those who talk rationally on other subjects, no sooner touch on this, than they go off in a literary delirium; fancy themselves, like Longinus, "the great sublime they draw," and rave like methodists, of inward lights, and enthusiastic emotions, which, if you cannot comprehend, you are set down as un-illumined by the grace of criticism, and excluded from the elect of Taste.

There is much too much truth in this bit of satire. But although such writings may not throw much light on the perplexed problems of the philosophy of art, they are an excellent guide to a knowledge of what the eighteenth-century Englishman desired in art; and it is just because they give expression to "enthusiasm" that they are important as enshrining tastes and tendencies, inimical to the well-ordered and rational world that the neo-classical age had erected on the foundation of Cartesianism. Theories of beauty are relatively trim and respectable; but in theories of the sublime one catches the century somewhat off its guard, sees it, as it were, without powder and pomatum, whalebone and patches.

To reduce to any sort of order the extremely diverse and individualistic theories of sublimity that one finds in the eighteenth century is not easy. For instance, it has not been possible to write a "triumph" of the sublime in England; or to lead carefully up to a particular treatise and say, "Just here the sublime is transformed, with the following important results." Indeed, the chief problem has been the problem of organization. The necessity of imposing form of some sort has continually led to the danger of imposing what is essentially a false and artificial form. Once the process of categorizing ideas is begun, it is likely to become an end in itself and to give to the subject a symmetry that is entirely false. I have therefore grouped the theories together loosely under very general headings in an effort to indicate that there is a progress, slow and continuous, but that this progress is one of organic growth. Ideas in individual treatises often advance it imperceptibly.

The direction of this growth is toward the subjectivism of Kant. Based at first on the rhetorical treatise of Longinus as interpreted by Boileau, the sublime slowly develops at the hands of such writers as Dennis, Addison, Baillie, Hume, Burke, Kames, Reid, and Alison into a subjective or semi-subjective concept. *The Critique of Æsthetic Judgment* is a part of the *Critique of Judgment*. Though I refer to the English translation of that part, I believe it more correct to speak only of *The Critique of Judgment* here. Kant's *Critique of Judgment* is the great document that coördinates and synthesizes the æsthetic concepts which had been current throughout the eighteenth century. It was Kant who took the isolated discoveries of earlier thinkers and welded their fragmentary æsthetic together so as to create a truly philosophical system, and who, moreover, found a place in his larger system for æsthetic theories. The purpose of Kant's philosophy was to defend the existence of *a priori* concepts; all of his efforts are directed toward rescuing thought from the slough of scepticism into which he saw that the empiricism of Hume was bound to lead. In his æsthetic, as elsewhere, Kant's purpose constantly brings him to the justification of the *a priori* as against the merely empirical, a contention that rests upon his recognition of the fundamental volitional and intuitional characteristics of man, such as the absolute authority of the call of duty and the absolute character of the æsthetic judgment.

The "subjectivity" of Kant lies in the fact that he rests his whole thought in each of the critiques upon some such contention, which he takes to be absolutely incorrigible. This basic point of view led to his analysis of the powers and faculties of the human mind, for the fact that he had set himself the task of nothing less than a justification, in logic, in ethics, and in æsthetic, of the *a priori* judgment, and the fact that he recognized that its *a priori* character lay in the judging mind rather than in the object judged, made it inevitable that he should undertake an examination of the capacities of that mind.

Kant's subjective point of view has a certain kinship with modes of thought in the romantic era. In the preface to the second edition of the *Critique of Pure Reason*, Kant likens his assumption that objects must conform to our cognitions, rather than our cognitions to objects, to the Copernican revolution; and indeed the point of view that he takes does represent as great a change from methods of thought in the Enlightenment as is found in the difference between the Copernican and the Ptolemaic astronomy. That difference is reflected in a general way in the fundamental contrasts between the romantic age and the early eighteenth century. This is not to say that Kant created the romantic age, but that his philosophy and the art of the romantics are symptoms of a changed point of view, far too involved to be discussed here. Argument by analogy is confessedly weak, but the nature of this change can be indicated by saying that it is possible to maintain that there is a general similarity between the point of view of the *Critique of Judgment* and the *Prelude;* and that the *Prelude* differs from the *Essay on Man* in a manner vaguely analogous to the way in which the *Critique of Pure Reason* differs from *An Essay on Human Understanding.* But if we take Kant as a symbol of the new world and Locke as representative of the old, we still have not analysed and accounted for the differences between them.

It has become a truism that in the art and theory of the eighteenth century are to be found all or about all of the ideas and methods that we usually associate with that unhappy term *romantic.* Of late years it has been fashionable to set up, as a bogy to be explained away, the older conception of neo-classic art as merely cold and regular and decorous, and of the neo-classicist as a rule-bound pedant, intent on displaying his lack of taste and of the divine afflatus by grinding out frigid and absurd poems cut to the patterns of Horace and Boileau. Fortunately the time has come when to argue that case at all is merely to set up a straw-stuffed dummy in order to have the academic exercise involved in knocking it down. We can assume as true that in the pre-romantic period there are a gradual shift in emphasis and a change in taste that foretell to the twentieth-century observer the coming into prominence of the æsthetic standards that produced a Wordsworth, a Scott, a Byron, and a Keats.

The study of the sublime is of interest because it permits one to observe from a fresh point of view the gradual coming to domination of such standards as characterize the romantic age of English literature. M. Basch has pointed out[1] how Kant's theories of æsthetic, particularly of the sublime, are largely a synthesis, a reinterpretation, and a deepening of the kaleidoscopic æsthetic of the eighteenth century. It was given to Kant to bring order out of chaos, to express perfectly a philosophical system and an æsthetic that were exactly suited to the needs of his time. In his critiques are expressed the philosophical ideas which form the

[1] Victor Basch, *Essai Critique sur l'Esthétique de Kant* (Paris, 1927), pp. xxv, xxvi.

basis for the art of his time, and this is true even if a given artist was not familiar with his works. And just as eighteenth-century literature has as its unconscious goal, in the fulness of time, the literature of the early nineteenth century, so it may be said that eighteenth-century æsthetic has as its unconscious goal the *Critique of Judgment*, the book in which it was to be refined and re-interpreted.

If this is true, or if it is only a half-truth, the æsthetic of Kant becomes of importance at the outset of this study as the summary of all we have to say here. It would be unwise to embark on the confused seas of English theories of the sublime without having some idea as to where we are going. If, therefore, at this point we look at Kant's theory, it will then be easier to map our course and to take our bearings from time to time. Fortunately Kant's æsthetic is so well known that we can summarize briefly. Kant discusses the sublime in Part I, Book II, of the *Critique of Judgment*,[2] where he isolates the æsthetic experience, showing that the pleasure that we feel in the sublime and the beautiful does not result from any cognition by concepts, but presupposes a "judgment of reflection." It is connected with the mere presentation of the object. The æsthetic experience is therefore disinterested because it seeks to discover no knowledge of the object. Following the fashion of his century, he discusses æsthetic judgment from two points of view—the sublime and the beautiful. To paraphrase briefly:

Although points of agreement between the sublime and the beautiful exist (in so far as each is an æsthetic judgment), there are great differences. Beauty is concerned with limited objects, with forms; the sublime is to be found in objects that are limitless, that have no form, though they are always accompanied with a "super-thought" of totality. The beautiful, therefore, implies an effort of the *understanding*, the faculty that determines objects by specific conceptions; the sublime implies an effort of the *reason*, the faculty that seeks an unconditioned totality. Hence delight in the beautiful is associated with a representation of quality; in the sublime, with a representation of quantity. Pleasure in the beautiful arises from "a feeling of the furtherance of life," and is compatible with charm and a playful imagination; the feeling of the sublime is brought about by "a momentary check to the vital forces, followed at once by a discharge all the more powerful" for having been restrained. Therefore pleasure in the sublime is secondary, a negative pleasure, unlike the positive pleasure experienced in the beautiful.

[2] I have quoted and paraphrased the *Critique of Aesthetic Judgment*, tr. J. C. Meredith (Oxford, 1911), and have made free use of Basch's essay. Kant's tentative effort to discuss the sublime and the beautiful in his *Beobachtungen über das Gefühl des Schönen und Erhabenen* is of little value in view of the profounder analysis that he makes in his later work. How slightly Kant was known in England before Coleridge took up the task of discipleship in the early decades of the nineteenth century has been admirably shown by Dr. René Wellek in his *Immanuel Kant in England, 1793-1838* (Princeton, 1931).

In experiencing the sublime, the imagination seeks to represent what it is powerless to represent, since the object is limitless, and thus cannot be represented. This effort and this inevitable failure of the imagination are the source of the emotions that accompany the sublime, which achieves its effect by the opposition between the object and our faculties of knowledge; but beauty achieves its effect through their complete harmony. It is upon this lack of harmony between object and subject, upon the futile effort on the part of the imagination to grasp and to represent the formless, that Kant erects his theory of the sublime.

Turning to nature, Kant shows that, although it is possible to term objects of nature beautiful, it is impossible to consider them sublime, since all external nature is a totality of forms, and the sublime is essentially unlimited. It can only be said that objects of nature awaken the feeling of sublimity by the reaction of the mind to the object. Since reason constantly seeks an absolute whole, and no object sensuously presented can give such a whole, the sublime cannot be found in nature, but only in ideas of reason. To illustrate: even the ocean in a storm is not itself sublime, but terrible; nevertheless it can awaken feelings of the sublime in the mind because of its capacity for having ideas of reason and because such a mind can rise above sense, and "employ itself upon ideas involving higher finality."

There are two subdivisions of the sublime—the mathematical and the dynamic. In the discussion of these categories Kant explains more concretely the deductions summarized in the above paragraphs.

The sublime is the name given to what is absolutely great, and the absolutely great is "what is beyond all comprehension great"; it exceeds every definite quantity. Now the absolutely great has no standard outside itself to which it can be referred. Such greatness does not exist in nature, where all magnitudes are relative, but in our ideas. But all representations of phenomena—and nature is represented only thus—are limited and cannot yield an absolute conception of magnitude. Hence the sublime is to be found only in our own minds. Nevertheless, the imagination attempts to represent absolute magnitudes, and its failure indicates that reason demands and can conceive absolute totality, for we have an idea of it, although we cannot experience it. Hence the sublime "is that, the mere capacity of thinking which evidences a faculty of mind transcending every standard of sense." It will be observed that in the process of proving the sublime to be wholly subjective Kant appeals to our actual experience of sublimity to sustain his transcendental doctrines.

The estimation of magnitudes by means of numbers is mathematical; by means of the eye, æsthetic. There is no maximum possible to the mathematical estimation of magnitudes, since we can add units *ad infinitum;* but there is a maximum beyond which the imagination cannot represent magnitude. Hence, æsthetically a magnitude "in comparison with which all else is small" can be reached, but it is reached only by setting up an idea that transcends every possible representation, and thus the idea of the sublime is conveyed through an absolute magnitude. Magnitude is represented in a successive aggregation of units, and in this aggregation the mind advances without let or hindrance, guided by the understanding by means of concepts of numbers. And this can go on to infinity without producing the sublime. But when the voice of reason demands totality; when we seek in a single intuition to gather up the aggregates into one; when, in a word, we seek to realize by the reason this magnitude, we transcend every standard of sense and the feeling of the sublime is evoked. "When the size of natural objects is so great that the imagination spends its whole faculty of comprehension on it in vain, it carries our concept of Nature to a supersensible substrate (underlying both Nature and our faculty of thought) which is great beyond every standard of sense." Hence it is the constitution of the mind, not merely the object in itself, that must be studied if we are to understand the sublime. The emotion that accompanies this experience is reverence, or respect, since the reason imposes on us a law (the comprehension of an absolute totality) which as sensuous beings we cannot obey. Hence arises the mixed feeling of displeasure and pleasure, displeasure at the inadequacy of imagination to estimate absolute magnitude, and pleasure at the fact that the greatest faculty of sense, imagination, is in accord with reason in so far·as it makes the effort to attain to these ideas of reason.

The sublime sets the mind in motion. The motion is a vibration, a rapid alternation of repulsion and attraction produced by the same object. This is because imagination in the apprehension of the intuition is driven to the point of excess and is afraid of it, while the reason finds nothing excessive in the attempt to estimate the magnitude.

The dynamic sublime is found in nature represented as might, but as might that has no dominion over us. To be dynamically sublime, nature must be a source of fear, but not at the moment of æsthetic judgment. Overhanging rocks, thunderclouds and lightning, volcanoes, hurricanes, the stormy ocean, high waterfalls—in comparison with their might, our power of resistance is of no account. Hence they are fearful. But if we are safe from their menace, they become delightful because of their fearfulness. These objects awaken sublime feelings because, although the immensity and the energy of nature reveal our own physical limitations, we are aware that we have a faculty (reason) of estimating ourselves as independent of nature and superior to it. External nature is not sublime, but it awakens feelings of sublimity by challenging "our nature to regard as small those things of which we are wont to be solicitous . . . and hence to regard its might . . . as exercising over us and our personality no such dominion that we should bow down before it. . . ." Thus we are lifted momentarily above nature. Physically we may be dwarfed, but our reason remains undaunted, and the mind becomes aware of the sublimity of its own being. A high degree of culture is requisite to the experience of this feeling. Man must have a capacity for ideas, particularly for moral ideas, which are the foundation of the sublime.

In the foregoing paraphrase, abbreviated as it is, one can perceive at least the outlines of Kant's conception of sublimity. A few aspects of this theory should be kept in mind by him who would follow the progress of eighteenth-century ideas of the sublime.

1. Sublimity as an æsthetic concept is made entirely subjective; it is not a quality residing in the object, but a state of mind awakened by an object. A century of fumbling æsthetic speculation lies behind this statement. Until it became possible to turn from the object to the subject and to realize that in the æsthetic act the object is "colored by the imagination," and until interest centered definitely in the analysis

of the subject's experience—that is, until the question, "What effects do so-called sublime objects have on the mind and emotions of the subject?" became more important than the question, "What sublime qualities does the object possess?"—no steady progress in the æsthetic of sublimity was made. The growth of æsthetic toward a subjective point of view reaches its fulness in Kant.

2. Kant's assumption of the sublimity of only the great and the energetic aspects of nature is typical of the eighteenth century. His list of sublime objects—lightning, storms, mountains, water-falls, etc.—is found with variations throughout the age. Chapter x, "The Sublime in Natural Scenery," will discuss this aspect of the matter fully.

3. The idea so brilliantly explained, that pain as well as pleasure is found in the experience of the sublime, played a considerable part in eighteenth-century England. The disturbing effect of grandeur undoubtedly called attention to this idea, which was exploited fully by Burke, and which probably underlies the distinction that the century drew between the æsthetic of the beautiful and the æsthetic of the sublime. The sense of effort and of difficulty overcome which Kant puts to such good use in illuminating his notion of the moral import of man appears from time to time in the theories that we shall discuss.

But no single theorist that we shall treat became so genuinely philosophical as Kant. Most of the treatises on the sublime were written by connoisseurs and literary critics, and none of them goes very deeply into the subject. But the constant discussion kept if before the public, and the sublime played no inconsiderable part in transforming English theory and literature by attracting to itself diverse elements recognized as of value, even while it was acknowledged that they did not come within the compass of good taste as formulated by the rules.

CHAPTER I

LONGINUS AND THE LONGINIAN
TRADITION IN ENGLAND

ANY historical discussion of the sublime must take into account the
fountain-head of all ideas on that subject—the pseudo-Longinian
treatise, *Peri Hupsous*, known for over two centuries as Longinus, *On
the Sublime*. In a sense, the study of the eighteenth-century sublime is
the study of the Longinian tradition in England, although, as may be
supposed, the student will be led far away from the Greek critic's views.
Only by stretching the meaning of the term out of all conscience can
Longinus's treatise be considered an essay on æsthetic, but it is none
the less true that it was in *On the Sublime* that the eighteenth century
found ideas that motivated many of its children, important and unimportant, to attempt an analysis of the sources and the effects of sublimity,
and it was out of the interest in this analysis that there began to emerge,
early in the century, a concept that was truly, if rudimentarily, æsthetic.
Therefore, it becomes of some importance to look again at the treatise,
and if possible to see it as the eighteenth century habitually saw it.
We shall never entirely escape its influence as we progress through the
century, for certain ideas implicit in it become fundamental in eighteenth-century theories and criticism, and the tendency of the writer
of the period to seek support from the ancients will keep the name of
Longinus alive until well after 1800.

Since this is true, a summary, however brief, of *Peri Hupsous* becomes necessary. The best edition and translation is that of Mr. W.
Rhys Roberts, but to become familiar with the Longinian vocabulary of
our period, it seems best to quote from the translation of William Smith,
which appeared in 1739 and reached its fifth edition in 1800.[1] This was
the standard translation during the period in which Longinus attained
his greatest fame and influence.

Of course Longinus did not invent the rhetorical conception of the
sublime style; it is older than his essay.[2] Although Aristotle did not

---

[1] *Dionysius Longinus on the Sublime*, translated from the Greek, by William Smith,
D.D. The Fourth Edition Corrected and Improved. London, 1770.

[2] See G. L. Hendrickson, "The Origin and Meaning of the Ancient Characters of Style,"
American Journal of Philology, XXVI (1905), 249–290, to which I am indebted, as well as to
the introduction to W. Rhys Roberts' edition of Demetrius, *On Style* (London, 1927). For
a brief discussion of the whole matter see C. S. Baldwin's *Ancient Rhetoric and Poetic* (New
York, 1924), pp. 56–58.

draw a very clear distinction between the styles, his conception of language as pragmatic and dialectical or emotional implied styles suitable to each function. The idea that rhetoric is an instrument of emotional transport was dominant among the ancients, and the grand style, the purpose of which was to move, was an integral part of their rhetoric.

The three styles, familiar in the treatises on rhetoric of the sixteenth, seventeenth, and eighteenth centuries, did not make their appearance until Roman times. They arose out of the threefold definition of the function of oratory—*docere, conciliare, movere*—set forth in Cicero's *De Oratore* and *Orator*. Once Cicero had made this division, a style which was the *tertium quid* between the plain and the grand (the pragmatic and the emotional) inevitably came into being. The Ciceronian categories are *gravis* (*grandis, vehemens*), *medius*, and *subtilis* (*tenuis*), the great, the middle, and the plain. The important fact for us is that from its inception the grand style had as its purpose the awakening of emotion in the audience, for, as we shall see, this is the point of departure for the earliest eighteenth-century discussions of sublimity.

Other ancients wrote on the various styles. Demetrius finds that there are four sorts of style—the plain, the elevated, the elegant, and the forcible. The elevated is ornate, and is therefore diametrically opposed to the plain, with which it can never be united. Three ingredients, thought, diction, and appropriate composition, go to make up elevation.[3] Dionysius of Halicarnassus uses the more customary tripartite division into the austere, the smooth (or florid), and the harmoniously blended. Of the austere, which corresponds to the great style, he says that it is rugged, and even frequently harsh. It uses stately rhythms and long words in order to effect its end, which is "to suggest nature rather than art, and to stir emotion rather than to reflect character."[4] These ideas might have been developed to interesting conclusions, but Dionysius is intent on discussing the best order of words, and therefore rests content with a brief treatment of the grand style. Quintilian, in the third chapter of his eighth book, while discussing ornament (the principal element in the grand style) definitely connects the idea of sublimity with the ornate and the pathetic.[5]

It is evident that Longinus is well within the tradition of ancient rhetoric when he treats the sublime style as emotive in purpose and as capable of being expressed both in ornamental and in simple language.

---

[3] *On Style*, pp. 323–325.

[4] Dionysius of Halicarnassus, *On Literary Composition*, ed. W. Rhys Roberts (London, 1910), pp. 211–213.

[5] Quintilian, *Institutio Oratoria*, tr. H. E. Butler (London and New York, 1922), Loeb Classical Library, III, 211, 213, and 215.

The subject that he wrote on was an old question in rhetoric, and he
might easily have repeated the old formulæ and illustrated the old
figures that were conventionally regarded as being conducive to sublimity; he might have done this and no more. But he was at the same time
rhetorician and critic, and as a critic he saw more deeply into the nature
of art than did most of his fellows. His critical intuitions found their
way into his treatise, where they lay dormant until they became in a
later age and among a modern race, an influence in criticism and æsthetic
theory.

Nevertheless, his treatment of the subject is primarily rhetorical; the
essay is a discussion of style, and only incidentally does Longinus allow
his deeper perceptions to find expression. He states that his intention
is to show how the sublime in writing and in discourse (i.e., in literature
and in oratory) may be attained, and in so doing it is natural and
proper that he should devote much space to an analysis of the various figures of speech which were so important in ancient rhetoric. Fortunately, much of what he says on this subject need not delay us, for,
however interested the eighteenth century may have been in rhetoric,
it had nothing new to offer on the subject. The numerous treatises on
oratory and rhetoric are almost without exception no more than sum-
maries of Cicero, with Longinus and Quintilian thrown in, the whole
perhaps plagiarized from the work of some Frenchman. With this static
rhetoric we are in no way concerned. The abiding interest of Longinus
for the eighteenth century, and consequently for us, lay in his conception of the sublime that underlies sublimity of style and that is an
expression of a quality of mind and of experience. To write on the sublime
style is to write on rhetoric; to write on sublimity is to write on æsthetic.
The sublime style is a means to an end; sublimity is an end in itself.
It is the latent æsthetic aspect of *Peri Hupsous* that was Longinus's
contribution to eighteenth-century thought, and it is with that aspect
that this chapter deals.

The author begins by stating that "the *Sublime* is a certain eminence
or perfection of language,"[6] but he hastens to described the effect of the
sublime, which "not only persuades, but even throws an audience into
transport. . . . In most cases it is wholly in our power, either to resist or
yield to persuasion. But the *Sublime*, endued with strength irresistible,
strikes home, and triumphs over every hearer."[7] The test of the sublime
is in its effect. "For the mind is naturally elevated by the true *Sublime*
and so sensibly affected with its lively strokes, that it swells in transport
and an inward pride, as if what was only heard had been the product of

---

[6] *On the Sublime*, p. 3.   [7] *Ibid.*, pp. 3, 4.

its own invention."[8] This idea is important because it emphasizes the relation between the sublime and emotion; it transcends the realm of rhetoric and begins that analysis of the effect of sublime objects on the mind which is to lead later to an æsthetic concept of sublimity.

Energy enters into the Longinian sublime. *"That* . . . is grand and lofty,*[9]* which the more we consider, the greater ideas we conceive of it; *whose* force we cannot possibly withstand; *which* immediately sinks deep, and makes such impressions on the mind as cannot be easily worn out or effaced." There follows a statement which must have been welcome to the neo-classicists, for it brought the sublime into close relationship with their own theory of art: "In a word, you may pronounce *that* sublime, beautiful and genuine, which always pleases, and takes equally with all sorts of men."[10] Here is the *quod ubique, quod semper* of classical and neo-classical art.

Assuming that a natural ability to speak well must be a source of all sublime writing and discourse, Longinus enumerates five qualities that go to the creation of the sublime.

The *first* and most excellent of these is a boldness and grandeur in the *Thoughts.* . . . The *second* is call'd the *Pathetic,* or the power of raising the passions to a violent and even enthusiastic degree; and these two being genuine constituents of the *Sublime,* are the gifts of nature, whereas the other sorts depend in some measure upon art.[11]

These are the gift of nature, and cannot be attained through the technique of rhetoric. And it was on these two sources that the eighteenth century was to fix its attention. The emphasis on great thought led

[8] *Ibid.,* p. 21.

[9] Observe the synonyms that Smith uses for *sublime.*

[10] *On the Sublime,* pp. 21, 22.

[11] *Ibid.,* pp. 23, 24.—Perhaps it is necessary to call attention to the fact that in all eighteenth-century critical writings the term *pathetic* is used in its generic sense of "producing an effect upon the emotions," not necessarily the tender emotions. In his *Cyclopedia,* 1727, Ephraim Chambers defines the word as "something that relates to the passions; and particularly that is proper to awake, or excite them." Bailey's *Dictionarium Britannicum,* 1721, gives a similar definition, and adds that "pathetick Musick" is "very moving, expressive, passionate, capable of exciting pity, compassion, anger, or the like passions." This definition shows the broad application of the term. Parnell, in his *Essay on the Different Stiles of Poetry* (London, 1713), p. 21, distinguishes two sorts of pathetic:

> Here all the *Passions,* for their greater sway,
> In all the Pow'r of Words themselves array;
> And hence the soft *Pathetick* gently charms,
> And hence the Bolder fills the Breast with Arms.

Johnson does not record the modern specialized meaning of the term, but shortly after the publication of the *Dictionary* Owen Ruffhead defines it as "a term usually confined to such ideas, as raise in us an emotion of pity." *Life of Pope* (London, 1769), p. 339.

Longinus and his followers into a consideration of the mind that creates a work of art; the emphasis on emotion, in the hands of English critics, developed into a study of the effect of a work on the perceiving mind.

The three remaining sources—"*Figures* of sentiment and language,"— "a noble and graceful manner of *Expression*," and "The *Structure* or composition of all the periods, in all possible dignity and grandeur"[12]— are rhetorical, and as such are of minor interest historically, although, as we shall see, the tradition of a sublime style survived for many centuries, and even long after sublimity came to be a matter of major importance. But once the sublime was isolated as a quality of art, having its source in the mind of the artist and arousing an intense emotion in the mind of the reader or spectator, emphasis naturally tended to center on the first two sources, which were considered to be independent of and even to transcend artistic skill.

The question of the pathetic receives little attention, since Longinus had devoted to it a separate essay, now lost. Although he admits that the grand and the pathetic do not include each other, since many passions are "vastly different from grandeur, and are in themselves of a low degree; as lamentation, sorrow, fear," and although he declares that many grand and lofty objects and ideas raise no passion whatever, he none the less avers that "nothing so much raises discourse, as a fine *Pathos* seasonably applied. It animates a whole performance with uncommon life and spirit, and gives mere words the force (as it were) of inspiration."[13]

These hints form the nucleus of much that was written and thought in the eighteenth century as to the relation of the sublime to the pathetic. Although Longinus does not consider emotion as absolutely necessary to sublimity, he nevertheless habitually associates the two, since the orator's task was to persuade by affecting the emotions of his audience as well as by convincing their reason. The presence of emotion in art is the point of departure for the eighteenth-century sublime, and indeed the study of art as the evoker of emotion is perhaps even more characteristic of the æsthetic thought of the period than the study of the rules. The importance of Longinus's purely conventional and rhetorical ideas on the relation between the sublime and the pathetic becomes increasingly evident as the quantity of æsthetic speculation increases. The traditional view of the sublime as the strongly emotive quality of art, the sanction of a great Greek's authority for such a view, and the generally heterodox tastes of the British public and critics easily served to stretch the boundaries of the sublime far beyond the point which strictly neo-

[12] *Ibid.*, pp. 24, 25. [13] *Ibid.*, 25–27.

classic theory permitted. Longinus was to become the patron saint of much that is unclassical and unneoclassical, and eventually of much that is romantic, in eighteenth-century England.

A very few more of Longinus's remarks need be quoted, but these are of importance. *A propos* of elevation of thought, he declares: "the *Sublime* is an image reflected from the inward greatness of the soul. Hence it comes to pass, that a naked thought without words challenges admiration, and strikes by its grandeur."[14] The silence of Ajax in the eleventh book of the *Odyssey* is given as an example of this kind of sublimity, an example that is repeated *ad nauseum* in the eighteenth century. Once again we notice the emphasis on the creative mind and its thoughts rather than on technique and style; this idea was to help Boileau formulate his theory of the difference between *le sublime* and *le style sublime*.[15] It is in this connection that Longinus points out the sublimity of the Mosaic account of the creation.

In speaking of amplification—one of the rhetorical devices of the sublime style—Longinus expresses again, and very clearly, his conviction that sublimity in the last analysis is to be found in content rather than in the mode of expression.

But the orator must never forget this maxim, that in things however *amplified* there cannot be perfection, without a sentiment which is truly *sublime*, unless when we are to move compassion, or to make things appear vile and contemptible. But in all other methods of *Amplification*, if you take away the *sublime* meaning, you separate as it were the soul from the body. . . . *Sublimity* consists in loftiness, and *Amplification* in number; whence the *former* is often visible in one single thought; the *other* cannot be discerned, but in a series and chain of thoughts rising one upon another.[16]

The implication here is that there is a real distinction to be drawn between content and style, "the soul and body" of art. We shall see how this conception fares at the hands of Boileau.

Two utterances extremely important for the eighteenth-century were the praise of an erring and irregular genius as opposed to a mediocrity that attains correctness by merely following rules, and the recognition of sublimity in nature. Of the first, Longinus says:

I readily allow, that writers of a lofty and tow'ring genius are by no means pure and correct, since whatever is neat and accurate throughout, must be exceedingly liable to flatness. In the *Sublime*, as in great affluence of fortune, some minuter articles will unavoidably escape observation. . . . And for this reason I give it as my real opinion, that the great and noble flights, tho' they cannot every where boast an equality of perfection, yet they ought to carry off the prize, by the sole merit of their own intrinsic grandeur.[17]

[14] *Ibid.*, pp. 28, 29.
[15] See Chapter II.
[16] *On the Sublime*, pp. 62 and 63.
[17] *Ibid.*, pp. 136, 137; and 138.

These statements helped to support the method of criticism that weighed beauties against faults.[18] Horace had expressed the same idea less vividly in *Ars Poetica*, ll. 347–365, and the combined influence of the two critics was sufficient to inculcate the idea that great beauties can atone for small faults. Thus the emphasis of all the better critics of the eighteenth century falls on the discovery of beauties rather than the condemning of irregularities, and in England at any rate criticism by rules early began to fall into disrepute, and criticism by taste to come into vogue, for had not Longinus himself shown that true genius transcends the rules?

> Great Wits sometimes may gloriously offend,
> And rise to faults true critics dare not mend;
> From vulgar bounds with brave disorder part
> And snatch a grace beyond the reach of art,
> Which, without passing thro' the judgment, gains
> The heart, and all its ends at once attains.[19]

Addison, for example, obviously represents this method of criticism. His critique of *Paradise Lost*, despite the strong Aristotelian influence, is written throughout in the beauties-and-faults manner. Almost with the exactness of an accountant, he records Milton's beauties and his faults, credit and debit, and finally strikes a balance that leaves the poet rich in reputation. In *Spectator* 291, he speaks with displeasure of those critics who judge by "a few general rules extracted out of the French authors," and proceeds:

A true Critick ought to dwell rather upon Excellencies than Imperfections, to discover the concealed Beauties of a writer, and communicate to the world such things as are worth their Observation. . . .

And that Longinus is not far from his mind when he makes this statement is shown by his subsequent apology for the fact that he must point out some of Milton's faults:

I must also observe with *Longinus*, that the Productions of a great Genius, with many Lapses and Inadvertencies, are infinitely preferable to the works of an inferior kind of Author, which are scrupulously exact and conformable to all the rules of correct writing.[20]

It was this idea of Longinus that was to become the basis of so much liberal critical thought in eighteenth-century England. The theory of

---

[18] For helpful discussions of Longinus as a liberalizing factor in eighteenth-century critical thought see A. F. Clark, *Boileau and the French Classical Critics in England* (Paris, 1925), pp. 391–393; and H. G. Paul, *John Dennis: His Life and Criticism* (New York, 1911), pp. 124, 125.

[19] A. Pope, "An Essay on Criticism," l, 152–157. *Works*, II, 43. For the relation of Pope to Longinus, see Austen Warren, *Pope as a Critic and Humanist* (1929), pp. 11–13.

[20] *The Spectator*, ed. H. Morley (London, 1891), II, 298 and 299. See also Number 592.

original genius as developed by Young and Duff, the decline in the power of the rules and the rise of a realization of the validity of the individual impression, and the association of the sublime with these ideas—all of this is attributable in some degree to Longinus.

The other important idea is the discussion of sublimity in external nature, and the deduction, from man's ability to enjoy and to be moved by natural grandeur, of an innate greatness in human nature that instinctively responds to greatness in the external world. We shall see in a later chapter that at the time when Longinus was introduced into England by Boileau, there was little enthusiasm for natural sublimities, and there can be little doubt that *Peri Hupsous* played a small part in increasing the chorus of praise that the eighteenth century came to sing in honor of the wilder aspects of the external world. The passage in question is much too long to be quoted in full, but a summary will doubtless suffice to recall it to mind.

Man, says Longinus, was not created to be "a grov'ling and ungenerous animal," but was placed in this world to pursue glory. For this purpose nature planted in his soul an invincible love of grandeur, and a desire to emulate whatever seems to approach nearer to divinity than himself. "Hence it is, that the whole universe is not sufficient, for the extensive reach and piercing speculation of the human understanding. It passes the bounds of the material world, and launches forth at pleasure into endless space." Nature impels us to admire not a small river "that ministers to our necessities," but the Nile, the Ister, and the Rhine; likewise the sun and the stars "surprise" us, and Aetna in eruption commands our wonder.[21]

This summary has intentionally emphasized certain thoughts out of proportion to the amount of space that they occupy in *Peri Hupsous*. The greater part of the essay is concerned with style and the tricks of rhetoric. But from our point of view the ideas here quoted have importance. They form the starting point for the development of the eighteenth-century sublime. Much was read into them—doubtless much

---

[21] *On the Sublime*, pp. 145–147.—

Mighty rivers, the heavenly bodies, and volcanoes played a part in eighteenth-century sublimities. They awakened admiration and wonder in the breasts of man and woman before the century ended. In view of this fact it is worth noticing that when the sublime was given to England it was already associated with the external world, as well as with literature and with rhetoric. Especially interesting, in the light of Kant's theory, is the idea that the human understanding seeks to transcend the material world and to grasp infinity, and that the appreciation of sublimity is a token of the spiritual greatness of man. Is it not this idea which Kant expresses in his more technical language and which is, of course modified by his own philosophical system? At any rate the sublime at its very inception points inward to the mind and soul of man, and the eighteenth century will modify after its own fashion this rhetorical passage in which deep is said to cry unto deep.

more than Longinus meant—and much was taken from them, and some of them were to survive throughout our period.

The story of Longinus in England, his neglect in the seventeenth century, and his sudden rise to fame in the eighteenth, is known in a general way to most students of the criticism of that period. Rosenberg has demonstrated the enormous popularity of the Greek critic in the eighteenth century, and has taken a backward glance at the criticism of the seventeenth century;[22] but he has not made it his business to consider the history of the word *sublimity* before Boileau's translation in 1674 started the sublime on its long career as an æsthetic concept. We shall do so briefly, since the results are almost purely negative.

The first edition of Longinus appeared in 1554 at Basle. Franciscus Robertello was the editor. This was followed in the next year by the edition of Paulus Manutius, published at Venice. The third and last edition of the sixteenth century was that of Franciscus Portus, published at Geneva in 1569. In 1572 there appeared the first translation from the Greek—the Latin version of Pagano, published at Venice.[23] One would expect to find in England during the last half of the sixteenth century some traces of the interest that was being manifested in Longinus by Continental humanists, but one looks for them in vain.

Of course the three styles of Latin rhetoric had been known and practiced throughout the middle ages. This is no occasion for a disquisition on medieval rhetoric, and we need not multiply illustrations. A poet so learned as Chaucer certainly knew his rhetoric. It will be recalled that he wrote of the "heigh style."[24] The use of the word *high* in this metaphorical sense might seem to suggest the Greek *hupsos*, but there can hardly be any connection with Longinus. There is no doubt that Chaucer means no more than the ornate, rhetorical style, "your termes, your colours, and your figures," the *genus grande* of the Romans.[25] Spenser uses *sublime* only once and then in the sense of "proud."[26] He

---

[22] A. Rosenberg, *Longinus in England bis zur Ende des 18. Jahrhunderts* (Weimar and Berlin, 1917).

[23] For information as to the early editions of Longinus, I am indebted to Rosenberg's dissertation, pp. 1–19, and to Roberts' *Longinus on the Sublime* (Cambridge, 1899), App. D, pp. 247–261.   [24] *Canterbury Tales*, E, 18, 41, 1148.

[25] For an excellent description and discussion of the three styles of discourse inherited by the middle ages from ancient rhetoric, see C. S. Baldwin's *Medieval Rhetoric and Poetic* (New York, 1928), pp. 67–72. "The third, or great style," says Mr. Baldwin, "whether it be elegant or not, has for its distinguishing quality the force of emotional appeal" (p. 70). Thus in preaching and in oratory, the ancient sublime style survived. In poetic it became more concerned with questions of ornate form. For rhetoric in Chaucer's poetry, see Baldwin, pp. 284–301, and J. M. Manly's *Chaucer and the Rhetoricians*, Warton Lecture on Poetry, XVII (London, 1926), *passim*.   [26] *Faerie Queene*, V, VIII, 30, 4.

too knew the "lofty style,"[27] but there is no hint that he or his circle had any interest in the conception of the sublime as Longinus discusses it.

The earliest example of the use of *sublime* in connection with style listed in the *N.E.D.* is from A. Day's *English Secretorie*, 1586. He says:

We do find three sorts [sc. of the style of epistles] . . . to have bene generally commended. Sublime, the highest and stateliest maner, and loftiest deliverance of any thing that may be, expressing the heroical and mighty actions of Kings.

This shows clearly enough the use of the Latin term *sublimitas* to express the same idea that lies behind Chaucer's "heigh style" and Spenser's "lofty style." A new term has been applied to an old idea, but a conception of the sublime is as yet unborn. Apparently Longinus was of no importance to the sixteenth-century critics and poets. Mr. Gregory Smith is able to dismiss his influence in one short sentence: "From Longinus little or nothing has been borrowed."[28] There is no mention of his name in this period, or indeed for many years to come.

In 1612, appeared the second Latin translation of *Peri Hupsous*, by Gabriel de Petra. Rosenberg regards this version as the first real advance in the growth of Longinus's reputation. But it was not until 1636 that Gerard Langbaine translated the treatise into Latin and brought out at Oxford the first version made by an Englishman and printed at an English press. Although we have no evidence of the growth of interest in Longinus in the years preceding 1636, it is not unreasonable to conclude that Langbaine's translation was evoked by some sort of demand for a new Latin rendering of the treatise; but the critical writings of this period are still devoid of Longinian influence. Clark declares: "None of the Elizabethan or Jacobean critics (not even Ben Jonson) mention his [Longinus's] name or show any trace of his influence."[29] My own investigations have given me no reason to modify this statement.

In 1652 there appeared the first translation of Longinus into English; it was made by John Hall, and was entitled, *Peri Hupsous, or Dionysius Longinus of the Height of Eloquence rendred out of the originall by J. H. Esq.* Hall is the earliest of the moderns to show that he understood Longinus's purpose. In the dedication, he formulates for the first time in English the idea of the sublime.

It must therefore have somewhat I cannot tell how divine in it, for it depends not of the single amassing or embroidery of words, there must be in it, excellent knowledge of Man, deep and studied acquaintance with the passions, a man

---

[27] *Ruines of Rome*, XXV, 13, 14.

[28] Gregory Smith, *Elizabethan Critical Essays* (Oxford, 1904), I, lxxiv. See also D. L. Clark, *Rhetoric and Poetry in the Renaissance* (New York, 1922), pp. 62 and 67, where the same conclusion is reached.

[29] *Boileau and the French Classical Critics in England*, p. 368.

must not onely know very perfectly the agitation of his own mind, but be sure
and conversant in those of others. . . . And yet all this, without somewhat which
I cannot expresse, is but the smallest part that goes to the building up of such a
prodigy, there must be somewhat *Ethereal*, somewhat above man, much of a soul
separate, that must animate all this, and breath [*sic*] into it a fire to make it both
warm and shine.[30]

Hall is decidedly on the way to stating a conception of the sublime similar
to that formulated later by Boileau, but he does not get beyond this
fumbling and groping definition, and his words seem not to have provoked speculation on the subject.

One might reasonably hope to find a noticeable increase in reference
to Longinus from this time. Ninety-eight years had passed since the
editio princeps had been printed; in the meantime several editions had
appeared, and both a Latin and an English translation were in existence.
But the time had not yet come for Longinus to gain the ear of the
critical world, and we find his name mentioned seldom.[31] Milton himself, with all of his interest in the ancients, seems not to have felt
Longinus's charm. In his essay "Of Education," he mentions Longinus as
one of the teachers of "a graceful and ornate rhetoric," but that is all.[32]
It is a strange paradox that the most sublime of English poets should
not have caught from Longinus the suggestion of the sublime as the expression of ultimate values in art, beyond the reach of rhetoric and her
handmaidens, the rules, He did not; and it was left to the propounders
of an adolescent æsthetic in the next century to find in John Milton's
poems, not a "graceful and ornate rhetoric," but the supreme illustration of whatever particular type of the sublime they advocated.

This seems to have been the state of Longinus and the sublime in
England until after 1674. He was known, but was not often quoted, and
he had not yet become an authority.[33] *Sublime* was known and used
as an adjective, signifying physical or metaphorical height, and the
lofty or sublime style continued purely in the realm of rhetoric. The
substantive *sublime* in its æsthetic connotation had not yet come into
use. Our own investigations bear out Rosenberg's statement that between 1612 and 1674 Longinus and all that Longinus was later to stand
for meant little enough.[34]

[30] See the Dedication to the Lord Commissioner Whitelock.

[31] Thomas Blount quotes from Hall's version, and refers to Longinus occasionally. See
The Academy of Eloquence (London, 1653), pp. 47 and 65. But his own *Glossographia* (1656),
and Phillips's *A New World of English Words* (1658), define *sublime* simply as "height."

[32] *The Prose Works of John Milton*, ed. J. A. St. John (London, 1848), III, 473, 474.

[33] Rosenberg (p. 7) points out Davenant's borrowing from Longinus the statement that
Homer's gods are like men (*Preface to Gondibert*, 1650, Spingarn, II, 2), but it is a matter
of no importance here.   [34] *Longinus in England*, p. 7.

In his *Dictionary* (1755), Johnson defines the substantive *sublime* as "the grand or lofty style," and adds, *"The sublime* is a Gallicism, but now naturalized." In this sentence he epitomizes the history of that phase of criticism which we are discussing. The sublime came to England from France in Boileau's translation of Longinus (1674)—came with a certain accretion of æsthetic concepts that it had gathered from Boileau's *Préface.* It will be recalled that John Hall had translated *Peri Hupsous* as "the Height of Eloquence"; likewise Pulteney, the second translator of the treatise into English, adopted the title, *A Treatise of the Loftiness or Elegancy of Speech,* even though he translated not from the Greek but from Boileau's version. It was an anonymous translator who, in 1698, first translated *hupsos* by the Latin and Romance derivative, *sublime,*[35] although, as we shall see, the word was by that time established in critical usage.[36]

Boileau's translation was the turning point of Longinus's reputation in England and France. By the end of the century the two English translations referred to above had appeared, and as the next chapter will show, the sublime had become a subject of speculation. There is no reason to labor the proof of Longinus's subsequent popularity in England. Rosenberg has treated the subject at length, but it needs no dissertation come from Germany to convince even a casual reader of the criticism of the period that Longinus was a presence not to be put by.

The bibliographical evidence of his vogue is interesting. Two editions of the Greek text were brought out during the eighteenth century, and were many times reprinted. The one was by J. Hudson, published at Oxford in 1710, the other was that of Z. Pearce (London, 1724). Rosenberg gives the following list of the years in which editions of *Peri Hupsous* were printed: 1710, 1718, 1724, 1730, 1732, 1733, 1743, 1751, 1752, 1762, 1763, 1773, 1778, 1789.[37] This is an extraordinary number especially when we remember that Welsted's and Smith's translations appeared in 1712 and 1739, respectively; the first was reprinted with the translator's complete works in 1789, and the second reached its

---

[35] The translations in question are: *A Treatise of the Loftiness or Elegancy of Speech. Written originally in Greek by Longinus; and now translated out of the French by Mr. J. P.* London, 1680; and *An Essay on Sublime: Translated from the Greek of Dionysius Longinus Cassius the Rhetorician. Compared with the French of Sieur Despréaux Boileau.* Oxford, 1698.

[36] For the history of *hupsos* see Roberts, pp. 209, 210. The word has a variety of meanings, even in Longinus's essay. Roberts gives "elevation," "dignity," "grandeur," "eloquence" as the most important variations. The Latin words used to translate *Peri Hupsous* have been *de grandi sive sublimi orationis genere, de sublimi genere dicendi, de sublimitate.* The French naturally adopted the Latin word, which in turn, through Boileau's influence, drove out the native English *loftiness* or *height.*

[37] Rosenberg, p. 9.

fourth edition in 1770.[38] Moreover, Boileau's version went through eighteen editions in France, copies of which surely reached England, and
there were three translations of Boileau's translation in the editions of
his complete works which were englished in 1711–13, 1736, and 1752.[39]
It should not be overlooked that most of this interest in Longinus is
concentrated in the first half of the century.[40] Only five of the fourteen
printings mentioned by Rosenberg appeared after 1752; the third edition
of Smith's version is dated 1752, along with the last complete edition
of the translation of Boileau's works. In France, after 1747, Boileau's
translation had only two editions.

This remarkable interest in Longinus is symbolic of the power that
he exercised over the minds of eighteenth-century Englishmen. Pope's
eulogy in the *Essay on Criticism*, 1711, in which Longinus is praised as
being "himself the great Sublime he draws" (a *cliché* echoed from
Boileau),[41] is an expression of contemporary as well as personal opinion.
Rosenberg's dissertation mentions fifty-nine authors who show a knowledge of Longinus, and the list is far from being complete. Early in the
century the author of *Peri Hupsous* had become the delight of the critics,
as well as of the wits and would-be critics. As early as 1679, for that
matter, in *A True Widow*, Shadwell had satirized the sublime as a cant
phrase. Young Maggot, the conventional "Inns-of-Court Man who neglects his law and runs mad after wit," says of a play:

I saw it Scene by Scene . . . it breaks well, the *Protasis* good, the *Catastasis*
excellent; there's no *Episode*, but the *Catastrophe* is admirable; I lent him [the
author] that, and the Love Parts, and the Songs. There are a great many
Sublimes, that are very Poetical.[42]

Young Maggot reminds us of that member of the Club which is described
in the second *Spectator*, who belonged to the Inner Temple, and knew
more of Aristotle and Longinus than of Littleton and Coke.

In 1712, Steele could refer to the distinction between the true and the
false sublime quite as if Boileau's ideas were then general property;[43]
and in the same year Welsted published his translation, and in the Remarks which accompanied it, linked the names of Shakespeare and
Milton to the increasingly popular word *sublime*, an early example of

[38] W. T. Lowndes, *The Bibliographer's Manual of English Literature* (London, 1865),
III, I, 1395.

[39] *Boileau and the French Classical Critics in England*, p. 370.

[40] Two other translations are lost to us. One was by Edmund Smith, whose life Dr.
Johnson wrote; the other was by the Rev. Mr. McCarthy of Dublin. For a discussion of
these versions, see Rosenberg, pp. 12–15.

[41] Boileau, *Œuvres Complètes*, ed. A. Ch. Gidel (Paris, 1873), III, 437.

[42] *Works of Thomas Shadwell* (London, 1720), III, 122. The passage is quoted in the
N.E.D.   [43] *Spectator*, 350, April 11, 1712.

how Longinus served to supply reasons to justify tastes that were natural to Englishmen.[44]

Keen satire on the critical terms popular with the wits is found in James Ralph's *The Touchstone*, 1728. He says:

These Gentlemen [criticasters], at the Expense of much Labour and Birch, are whipp'd at School into bad Translations, false *Latin* and dull Themes; from thence they run the Gantlope through all the pedantick Forms of an University-Education; There they grow familiar with the Title-Pages of Antient and modern Authors, and will talk of *Aristotle, Longinus, Horace, Scaliger, Rapin, Bossu, Dacier*, as freely, as if bosom Acquaintance. Their Mouths are fill'd with the Fable, the Moral, Catastrophe, Unity, Probability, Poetick Justice, true Sublime, Bombast, Simplicity, Magnificence, and all the critical Jargon, which is learn'd in a quarter of an Hour, and serves to talk of one's whole Life after.[45]

The sublime was evidently frequently mentioned at the coffee houses, since Pope felt safe in using *Peri Hupsous* as the medium for his attack on the duncies preparatory to the publication of the *Dunciad*. The delicious parody of Longinus, *Peri Bathous, or the Art of Sinking in Poetry*, 1728, presupposes a familiarity with the treatise on the part of the town, and bears out other pieces of evidence that indicate that Longinus had come into his own.[46]

Swift had his fling at the sham critics in his *On Poetry: a Rhapsody*, 1733. He advises the youth who is bent on becoming a man of letters despite his native dullness to take up criticism, not poetry. The passage is too long to quote in full, but "our modern critic's jargon" is set forth in detail. The Dean concludes:

> A forward Critick often dupes us
> With sham Quotations *Peri Hupsous:*
> And if we have not read *Longinus*,
> Will magisterially out-shine us.
> Then lest with *Greek* he over-run ye,
> Procure the Book for Love or Money,
> Translated from *Boileau's* Translation,
> And quote Quotation on Quotation.[47]

---

[44] *The Works of Dionysius Longinus on the Sublime*, etc., tr. Leonard Welsted (London, 1712), pp. 145; 146; 147; 151; 154; 156; 160.

[45] [James Ralph], *The Touchstone*, etc. (London, 1728), p. 161.

[46] In his unpublished dissertation, *Alexander Pope's Art of Sinking in Poetry* (Princeton, 1932) Dr. Archibald Hart has made a thorough study of Pope's satire. He points out the close relation of *Peri Bathous* to Boileau's translation of Longinus.

[47] [Jonathan Swift], *On Poetry: A Rhapsody* (London, 1733), p. 16.—Satire on the use of the sublime as a cant term of the pseudo-critic continued at least into the 1750's. The word is a favorite with Dick Minim, the honest dullard of Johnson's creation, who established his fame as a critic by becoming an echo of coffee-house critiques. "Sometimes he is sunk in despair, and perceives false delicacy gaining ground, and sometimes brightens his countenance with a gleam of hope and predicts the revival of the true sublime." *Idler*, 61, *Works* (Oxford, 1825), IV, 330.

Longinus had evidently become the victim of a cult, and as the object of a constant lip-service he must have become a bore to the serious men of letters. Charles Lamotte was able to speak of him, in 1730, as one "whose Authority will be thought unexceptionable,"[48] and when any critic attains such fame he is a legitimate object of satire.

Though Longinus probably reached the height of his fame at about 1738, he nevertheless had to face no sudden decline in popularity and prominence. The interest in sublimity which emanated from his treatise kept his name alive, even after the sublime had grown into a concept far different from that found in *Peri Hupsous*. Rosenberg has given an incomplete, but a competent, account of Longinus's reputation. Longinus's name was on every one's tongue, and his influence in unexpected places. For example, Turnbull called in Longinus when he wrote on the theory of painting in 1740; Hurd in 1751, considered Longinus, together with Bouhours and Addison, "the most eminent, at least the most popular" of critics, and he found Longinus the "most instructive" of the three.[49] Longinus's voice was heard in the liberal criticism of Young and Duff, in whose discussions of original genius the Greek becomes a true enemy of the rules, and an ardent advocate of the licenses that inspired and untutored genius takes.[50] Smith's translation and Pearce's edition were used as school books in 1766;[51] young and earnest Mr. Gibbon read through *Peri Hupsous* in the autumn of 1762, and found it "valuable," "worthy of the best and freest days of Athens," pleasing, and astonishing.[52] As late as 1774 Mrs. Elizabeth Carter read Longinus because she "thought one must read Longinus," but gained little pleasure from following the fashion.[53] John Lanson thought that he could take a knowledge of Longinus for granted when he delivered his lectures to the students of Trinity College, Dublin, and a few years later the general interest in Longinus justified the publication of Greene's dull commentary

---

[48] Charles Lamotte, *An Essay upon Poetry and Painting* (London, 1730), p. 7.

[49] George Turnbull, *A Treatise on Ancient Painting* (London, 1740), pp. 76; 83; 84: etc.— Q. Horatii Flacci, *Epistola ad Augustum*, ed. Richard Hurd (London, 1751), pp. 99 and 101.

[50] [Edward Young], *Conjectures on Original Composition* (London, 1759). [W. Duff], *An Essay on Original Genius* (London, 1769).

[51] "A Catalogue of the School Books Now in General Use," *A Complete Catalogue of Modern Books* (London, 1766), pp. 91 and 92.

[52] Edward Gibbon, *Journal*, ed. D. M. Low (London, 1929), pp. 138, 139; 142. Gibbon has indicated clearly one reason for Longinus's success with the eighteenth-century mind. He says that hitherto he had known but two methods of criticizing a book—to analyze its beauties and to exclaim. "Longinus," he says, "has shown me a third. He tells me his own feelings upon reading it; and tells them with such energy, that he communicates them" (p. 155).

[53] Elizabeth Carter, *Letters to Mrs. Montagu*, ed. Rev. Montagu Pennington (London, 1817), II, 273.

on *Peri Hupsous*.[54] John Ogilvie declared in 1774 that Longinus has pre-occupied the province of the sublime, and that he is universally read and admired by readers of even the smallest classical knowledge.[55]

Such general and widespread fame, however, did not keep æsthetic speculation subservient to Longinus. It was rather as a critic than as a guide to æsthetic that Longinus was powerful. Speculation soon out-grew *Peri Hupsous*, which indeed is the point of departure rather than the guiding influence of theories of the sublime, especially after the middle of the century. Silvain had early complained that the Greek critic did not give a clear idea of the sublime,[56] and a similar dissatisfaction was felt by all the more important theorizers. Burke simply did not dis-cuss Longinus; Blair and Beattie complained of the dominatingly rhetorical character of *Peri Hupsous*;[57] and these are typical cases. Oc-casionally, as in the case of Stack,[58] Longinus found his defenders. As late as the first decade of the nineteenth century, so advanced a thinker as Richard Payne Knight could quote Longinus against Burke, as though he considered the Greek a weightier authority.[59] But despite the popu-larity of Longinus, and despite the reputation of *Peri Hupsous* among critics, speculation grew more and more purely æsthetic, and, so far as the sublime is concerned, Longinus's influence decreased as the century drew to a close. In 1829 it was possible for James Mill to speak with contempt of a work that had been one of the chief influences on the critical thought of the eighteenth century, and that was the source of the sort of speculation in which Mill himself was indulging when he con-demned Longinus.[60]

It is not difficult to explain the fact that Longinus rose to so lofty a position in the eighteenth century, after his neglect during the pre-ceding age. Hans Hecht, reviewing Rosenberg's dissertation, offers as a reason the ease with which *Peri Hupsous* could be employed in the in-terest of either side in the controversy of the Ancients and the Moderns,

[54] John Lanson, *Lectures Concerning Oratory*, Second Edition (Dublin, 1759), p. 59. [Richard Burnaby Greene], *Critical Essays* (London, 1770). Greene did not express a new or a singular idea when he said that Longinus was "the best of the ancients" (p. ii).

[55] John Ogilvie, *Philosophical and Critical Observations on the Nature, Character, and Various Specimens of Composition* (London, 1774), II, 161.

[56] Silvain, *Traité du Sublime* (Paris, 1732), p. 2.

[57] Hugh Blair, *Lectures on Rhetoric and Belles Lettres* (London, 1783), I, 59.—James Beattie, "Illustrations on Sublimity," *Dissertations Moral and Critical* (London, 1783), p. 605.

[58] Richard Stack, "An Essay on Sublimity of Writing," *Transactions of the Royal Irish Academy* (Dublin, 1787), I, 19–26.

[59] Richard Payne Knight, *An Analytical Inquiry into the Principles of Taste*, The Second Edition (London, 1805), p. 376.

[60] James Mill, *Analysis of the Phenomena of the Human Mind* (London, 1829), II, 192.

and the fact that Longinus offered a reputable authority for a love of such irregular writers as Shakespeare, Milton, and Spenser.[61]

Longinus did ride into fame on the crest of the controversy between the Ancients and the Moderns, as we shall see in the next chapter. He became an ally of either party, used now to defend the ancients, now to champion original and untutored genius. He is moderate, urbane, and eloquent, and his moderation discouraged dogmatism, his eloquence stirred enthusiasm, and he was sufficiently liberal in his opinions to appeal to eighteenth-century modernism. His high seriousness, his moral point of view, his insistence that the great poet is the good man, would be understood and valued in an age whose æsthetic had not yet divorced itself from the ethical point of view. In the last section of his treatise, Longinus accounts for the decline of genius in his age on the grounds that liberty no longer existed, and that only in a state of freedom can great art be produced—an opinion that would naturally commend itself to the English in an age when they complacently contrasted their own constitutional monarchy with the despotism that prevailed on the Continent, and when they prided themselves on the prevalence of individual liberty in the body politic. Moreover, Longinus's essay must have seemed a complement to the more analytical criticism of Aristotle and Horace, and must have been welcome, as Gibbon suggested, because of its impressioniatic and interpretive quality.

Finally, it may be said that Longinus was not needed in the seventeenth century, and that he had a very definite function to fulfil in the early years of the eighteenth century. An age that produced poets so different as Ben Jonson and Donne, Herrick and Crashaw, Carew and Herbert, Milton and Cowley, surely had no need for a theoretical defence of individualism in art. But when, shortly after the Restoration, the reaction against the decadent Donne tradition set in, and when, England after her experiment in political liberty, settled down to enjoy a comfortable and urbane enlightenment under a constitutional monarchy, the tendency was to regiment taste and the art of poetry under the rules which sought to control in the interest of neo-classicism.

But the English genius was never comfortable in the borrowed garments cut to the pattern of the rules. Despite the stand made by various poets and critics in their defence, clarity and correctness were exotic growths on English soil. There was an instinctive and uneasy feeling that the true destiny of English letters lay with Shakespeare and not with Horace and Boileau, and even when, say from 1660 to 1740, the ideas of neo-classicism were dominant, it is dangerous for the student to generalize as to the tastes and theories of the age. Of course no age is

[61] *Beiblatt zur Anglia*, XXXI (1920), 163.

unanimous in its tastes, and romanticism and classicism of one variety or another always exist side by side. The study of eighteenth-century criticism is in fact the study of the increasingly rapid disintegration of the neo-classical standards, and the re-emerging of a freer, more individualistic, and consequently more native theory of art. Longinus is not the cause of this disintegration, but it is none the less true that during the century *Peri Hupsous* was a sort of *locus classicus* for that type of critical thought which sought to combat and destroy the rules.

The case of Samuel Cobb is indicative of the process which united Longinus with those spirits who wished to justify the conception that the greatest art can be produced only by native genius expressing itself after its own manner, rather than in the tradition of Horace and Boileau. His was not a voice crying in the wilderness; he was no lone romanticist foretelling the advent of a Byron, but he was representative of the protest against the overemphasis of the rules, a protest that became vocal very early indeed, that, in fact, was never silent. And his use of Longinus is typical of the practice of those modifiers of the neo-classical tradition who contributed to its transformation as the century drew to a close. His language and ideas are very closely akin to those of Young more than fifty years later.

To study to be correct, he says in his A Discourse on Criticism, and the Liberty of Writing, 1707, "enervates the Vigour of the Mind, slackens the Spirits, and cramps the Genius of a *Free Writer*. He who creeps by the Shore, may shelter himself from a Storm, but is likely to make few Discoveries: . . ." The rules are "leading strings" to be laid aside by a mature genius in the interest of the expression of "a free generous, and manly Spirit." He concludes: "Let a Man follow the Talent that Nature has furnish'd him with, and his own Observation has improv'd, we may hope to see Inventions in all Arts, which may dispute Superiority with the best of the *Athenian* and *Roman* Excellencies."[62]

These statements are made on the authority of Longinus, and in protest against "a slavish Bigotry to the Ancients." In principle there is little here that Pope and Addison would not have agreed with; their own statements on the subject differ only in degree of emphasis. The importance of Cobb's Discourse for us is that it offers concrete evidence as to the promptness with which the ideas of Longinus were assimilated, and the ease with which they joined in the protest of the liberal criticism against a type of literature in essence foreign to the national tradition. Longinus came into favor because he could fill a need; he alone of the ancients could be used to support the idea of "the liberty of writing."

[62] Samuel Cobb, *Poems on Several Occasions* (London, 1710), The Third Edition. The pages of the Discourse are not numbered.

But the Longinus who is of value for this study is really the creation of Boileau, who called *Peri Hupsous* to the attention of his contemporaries, and who initiated speculation on the nature of the sublime in his *Préface* and in his *Réflexions*. The sublime that came into existence in 1674 was the offspring of two minds so startlingly unlike as those of the Greek critic and the author of *L'Art Poétique*. To that sublime we turn in the following chapter.

IT is an interesting and a curious fact that in the same year, 1674, Boileau gave to the world his *L'Art Poétique* and his *Traité du Sublime ou du Merveilleux dans le Discours Traduit du Grec de Longin*. The two works apparently make up his artistic confession of faith. Paradoxical as it may seem in the light of the future career of Longinus's ideas in England, it is nevertheless true that both in the *Préface* to the translation and in the *Réflexions* Boileau brought Longinus into his critical system. The paradox, to be sure, is only apparent; it was the later *interpretation* of Longinus, not *Peri Hupsous* itself that was heretical. Every man of taste in the neo-classic period was prepared to admit that there are effects in literature that cannot be obtained except through "strokes of genius." Boileau's *L'Art Poétique* is a complete expression of the neo-classic code.[1] As such it became one of the chief documents of the literary tories of the eighteenth century; as such it was one of the chief rationalizations of a type of art that the nineteenth century regarded as anathema. The translation of Longinus, taking quite a different course, was, throughout the neo-classic period in England, the center around which revolved many of the ideas that influenced poets to lay the old aside. Thus Boileau unwittingly set at work in the world two forces that eventually became mutually hostile. Viewed historically, his credo has the dual physiognomy of Janus.

By beginning with Boileau one does not necessarily imply that he rediscovered Longinus for his contemporaries. For instance, Rapin frequently referred to and quoted from Longinus, and had something to say about the sublime several years before 1674. His *Comparaison de Vergile et Homère*, 1668, *Comparaison de Démosthène et Cicéron*, 1670, and *Réflexions sur l'Usage de l'Eloquence de ce Temps*, 1672—this last was translated into English in the year in which it appeared[2]—all speak of the sublime. His *Réflexions sur la Poétique d'Aristote et sur les ouvrages des poètes anciens et modernes* was published in the same year as was Boileau's *L'Art Poétique*, and was translated immediately by Rymer.[3] It was extremely popular in England, and is so much at one with Boileau's doctrines that Clark finds it virtually impossible to disentangle and

[1] F. Brunetière, "L'Esthétique de Boileau," *Revue des Deux Mondes*, XCIII (1889), 662–685.

[2] Clark, *Boileau and the French Classical Critics in England*, p. 275, note.

[3] *Ibid.*, p. 276.

isolate the influences of the two critics.[4] The favor with which the *Ré-flexions sur la Poétique d'Aristote* met would naturally recommend the earlier works to the English critics. It thus seems probable that Rapin had some share in stimulating in England an interest in Longinus, although his discussion could not be so valuable for future speculation as was Boileau's. For dispite his observing that the sublime depends on what one says, on the grand images with which one says it, and on elevation of genius, rather than on brilliance of language,[5] he usually stresses the rhetorical aspects of the question. In addition, Boileau's importance lies not merely in the fact that he discussed the sublime, but also in the prominence which his own popularity gave to any work recommended by him.

Fortunately the accuracy and the merits of Boileau's translation are of no importance here. Despite the fact that modern scholarship has found Boileau inadequately equipped for the task of translating a style so difficult as that of the Greek rhetoricians, and has convicted him of taking unwarranted liberties with the text,[6] what matters for us is the fact that the eighteenth century found the translation highly satisfactory. The sins which Boileau committed against pure scholarship have their origin in the *mores* of the republic of letters as it existed in the seventeenth century, and if Dr. Johnson is right, the fact that the version found many readers justifies any liberties that the translator took with his author. William Smith expresses the opinion of the eighteenth century when he says that Boileau's translation is the first good one into any modern language, and that its elegance and spirit will never be surpassed.[7]

It is in his preface that Boileau first speculates on the nature of the sublime. He leaves no doubt in his reader's mind as to his enthusiasm for Longinus and his treatise. Although the work is a fragment, he says, enough remains "to make us conceive a great idea of its author."[8] He avers that "when he speaks of the sublime, he is himself very sublime,"[9] a neat turn of phrase that is to be echoed for many years in England.

Toward the end of the preface to the first edition Boileau presents his definition of the sublime as he understood it from Longinus's ideas. He points out that by *sublime* Longinus did not mean what orators call

---

[4] *Ibid.*, p. 275. For a discussion of Rapin's fame, see Clark, pp. 275–285.

[5] "Réflexions sur l'Usage de l'Eloquence de ce Temps en Général," *Œuvres* (La Haye, 1725), II, 15, 16.   [6] E. Egger, *L'Hellénisme en France* (Paris, 1869), II, 144, 145.

[7] Smith, *Longinus on the Sublime*, p. 5.

[8] Boileau, *Œuvres Complètes*, ed. A. Ch. Gidel (Paris, 1873), III, 436.

[9] *Ibid.*, III, 437. According to Gibert, Gabriel de Petra, whose translation of Longinus in 1612 was the second version to be made, had found Longinus sublime. See B. Gibert, *Jugemens des Savans*, etc. (Paris, 1713), I, 226.

the sublime style, but that extraordinary and marvellous quality (*cet extraordinaire et ce merveilleux*) which strikes in a discourse, and which enables a work to elevate, ravish, and transport (*qui fait qu'un ouvrage enlève, ravit, transporte*). The sublime style always requires elevated diction (*grands mots*), but the sublime can be found in a single thought, in a single figure, in a single turn of phrase (*tour de paroles*). An idea may be expressed in the sublime style, and if it be neither extraordinary nor surprising, it will not be sublime.

Proof of this idea is offered in a famous illustration. Longinus, it will be recalled, had pointed out the sublimity of the Mosaic account of the creation of light. Boileau paraphrases: *Le souverain arbitre de la nature d'une seule parole forma la lumière.* This is an example of the sublime style, but it is not sublime, since it contains nothing "marvellous." But, *Dieu dit: Que la lumière se fasse, et la lumière se fit*—this is truly sublime, because in what Boileau calls *un tour extraordinaire d'expression* there is described vividly the instantaneous obedience of the creation to the Creator. Boileau concludes that we must understand by *sublime*, in Longinus's treatise, "the extraordinary, the surprising, and . . . the marvellous in discourse."[10]

Boileau is here elaborating on Longinus's hint as to the possibility that a single word, thought, or action can express the sublime, but he states the distinction between the rhetorical sublime and the sublime of content and spirit more clearly and at greater length than anyone had previously done. The examples which he gives make this distinction quite obvious. The difference lies not only in diction, although the grandiose language of the first sentence is a part, and a traditional part, of the sublime style. There is a subtler contrast between the two. The first is a simple statement that God made light, and although it is expressed in all the finery of language Boileau found nothing in it to call sublime. The second is vivid: *Dieu dit: Que la lumière se fasse;* and there follows instantly the fulfilment of the divine command and a revelation of the omnipotence of God. An overwhelming sense of vastness and power, the imaginative apprehension and expression of a great cause and a great effect, shine through the simple and lucid language. The very contrast between the striking event and the matter-of-fact language in which it is recorded serves to make the statement effective. Boileau, following Longinus, perceived the sublimity of these words and proceeded to generalize from them, deducing that the greatest thought in simple language is the highest form of the sublime, since the thought operates directly and with no let or hindrance to the reader's mind, filling it with awe

[10] *Œuvres Complètes*, III, 442.

and awakening emotions of a very intense kind. Thus at one blow the sublime is severed from rhetoric and becomes art, a matter of the revelation of a quality of thought and the emotions which that quality, vividly presented, evokes.

The power of the sublime to awaken strong emotions is explicit and implicit in all that Boileau says on the subject. The sublime is described as the extraordinary, the marvellous, the surprising; it elevates, it ravishes, it transports. One has only to follow these words and their definitions through *Le Dictionaire de l'Académie Françoise*, 1694,[11] to discover how strongly emotional Boileau's language is. One or two definitions will suffice. *Merveilleux* means "admirable, surprising, astonishing" (*admirable, surprenant, estonnant*). It is defined in regard to poetry as "that part of the fable that causes admiration," and *admiration* carries with it the generic meaning of "wonder." *Estonner* signifies figuratively "to cause to tremble through some great, some violent emotion," *esbransler* (the definition of *estonner*) expresses the idea of violent shaking. The sublime must *strike*, and its effect is said to be that it elevates, ravishes, and transports. These emotions are suggested in Longinus's conception of the sublime in oratory, but they sorted ill, at least theoretically, with the self-possessed, urbane art that the neo-classicists valued and that was an expression of the attitude toward life that Pope so neatly expressed when he remarked that "fools admire, but men of sense approve." Transfer them into painting, poetry, and nature, and glorify them as the products of the greatest art, as the eighteenth century did, and eventually they will change the face of the arts.

Boileau's terms may be vague and unsatisfactory, but they indubitably tell us that the sublime, apart from the sublime style, must be a great thought and that it must awaken strong emotions in the reader or the audience. This is the new, the eighteenth-century, sublime for which Boileau is responsible. The zeal with which he took up Longinus and his ideas suggests that even the great formulator of the neo-classic code felt the need of a higher sort of art and stronger emotions than the rules could produce.

But he was not long permitted to hold his opinions in peace. He soon became involved in quarrels in which he used Longinus to good advantage, and in the course of which he expanded his definition and illustrated his ideas more fully. During these controversies he came more and more to insist on simplicity of style and diction as essential to sublimity, and therefore more completely to separate the sublime from the field of rhetoric. It will be necessary to follow these quarrels which

[11] These definitions are taken from the reproduction of the edition of 1694, ed. Paul Dupont (Paris, 1901).

gave prominence to Longinus and made the sublime one of the burning questions of the day.

In 1694 Boileau published nine *Réflexions Critiques sur quelques Passages du Rhéteur Longin*. They were a part of the opening fire of the battle of the Ancients and the Moderns, and were aimed against Charles Perrault, whose poem, *Le Siècle de Louis le Grand*, read before the Academy on January 27, 1687, had given offence to Boileau by claiming that the moderns could equal the ancients in art and in knowledge. Moreover, in order to defend himself, Perrault had begun to write his *Parallèle des Anciens et des Modernes*, 1688–98, in which he went even further in his attack on the ancients. Boileau's nine *Réflexions* are a sarcastic and witty attack on Perrault's learning and judgment, in which nine quotations from Longinus serve as battering rams with which to demolish the stronghold of the heretic. Thus Longinus came to lend a hand in the famous literary war.[12]

It was the second controversy that forced Boileau to defend his views as to the nature of the sublime. In 1679 Pierre-Daniel Huet maintained in his *Demonstratio Evangelica* that Longinus was wrong in claiming sublimity for Genesis 1, 3, since the style is too simple to express the sublime.[13] In 1683 Boileau took up the challenge in the revised *Préface* of the new edition of the *Traité*. Huet, in the same year, addressed a letter to the Duc de Montausier in which he enlarged on his opinion, bringing to bear on the question his knowledge of Hebrew and Hebrew syntax, and attempting to show that the particular turn of phrase which had seemed sublime to Boileau is common in biblical style, that the thought of the sentence is not sublime, and that it would be inartistic to begin a book at the height of the sublime. This last argument presumably infers that a book dictated by the Holy Spirit cannot err in taste. This letter did not find its way into print until 1706, when it was published by Jean le Clerc in the tenth volume of his *Bibliothèque Choisie*,[14] interspersed with the approving comments of the publisher. Boileau regarded this as an attack upon himself (as indeed it was, although not unprovoked); and pretending not to believe that Huet had written the letter, he answered le Clerc in the tenth, eleventh, and twelfth *Réflexions*, published posthumously in the edition of 1713, with

[12] For a full account of this and other controversies of a similar nature see M. H. Rigault, *Histoire de la Querelle des Anciens et des Modernes* (Paris, 1856).

[13] P. D. Huet, *Demonstratio Evangelica*, etc., tertia editio (Paris, 1690), Propos. IV, Cap. II, pp. 65, 66.

[14] *Bibliothèque Choisie* (Amsterdam, 1706), X, 211–260. For le Clerc's replies to Boileau and Renaudot, see *Bibliothèque Choisie*, XXVI, 64–112. Perrault's response can be found in *Mélange Curieux des Meilleures Pièces Attribuées à M. de Saint-Evremond* (Amsterdam, 1726), I, 471–516. The controversy grows very tiresome.

an *Advertissement* by l'Abbé Renaudot. In these essays Boileau defends
his theory, gives other illustrations, and, in true controversial manner,
tends more and more to insist on simplicity of expression for the sublime.

He begins by attempting to refute Huet's argument that, had Moses
opened his account of the creation in the sublime style,

> he would have sinned against all the rules of art, which requires that a beginning
> should be simple and without affectation: which is very true, but which does not
> exclude the sublime, since the sublime is not opposed to simplicity, and since at
> times nothing is more sublime than simplicity itself.[15]

It is in support of this opinion that he points out the sublimity of the
"Qu'il mourût" of old Horace, and the

> Moi,
> Moi, dis-je, et c'est assez,

of Medea,[16] examples of the sublime from Corneille that are frequently
repeated in French and English criticism, and that are infallible signs of
Boileau's influence. Both of these passages share to some degree the
qualities of the biblical sentence around which the controversy raged.

There is evidence that Boileau had reflected carefully on the nature
of the sublime since he had written his *Préface* of 1674, for in the tenth
Réflexion he states explicitly the part that energy plays in the sublime.
So far is elevated diction from being the essence of the sublime that one
of the passages (the description, from Herodotus, of Cleomenes hacking
himself to pieces) quoted by Longinus is sublime because of *la petitesse
énergique des paroles;*[17] and he proceeds: "One perceives there a certain
energetic power which, emphasizing the horror of the thing that is recounted, is somehow sublime."[18]

Huet had found four sorts of sublimity—the sublime of words, the
sublime of expression, the sublime of thought, and the sublime of things.
The first is purely rhetorical and consists of grand and beautiful diction;
the second depends only on the arrangement of words which in another
order would stir no emotion; the third is dependent on a sympathy between author and reader, orator and audience, spirit taking fire from
spirit; the last depends entirely upon dignity and grandeur.[19] Boileau
does not argue against the premise, but he refuses to accept the deduction that the passage from Genesis is not sublime. Accepting Huet's
categories, he maintains that the words of Moses illustrate each one,
and that they are therefore an excellent example of sublimity.[20]

---

[15] *Œuvres Complètes*, III, 405.
[16] *Ibid.*, III, 406, 407.
[17] The phrase defies translation.
[18] *Œuvres Complètes*, III, 409.
[19] *Bibliothèque Choisie*, X, 246.
[20] *Œuvres Complètes*, III, 416, 417.

In his twelfth and final *Réflexion*, Boileau ceases arguing, and attempts a new definition of the sublime. It is not exactly a logical development from the tenth *Réflexion*, but it is a good antidote to the effect of words spoken in the heat of controversy. It shows, moreover, that, although he had redefined the word *sublime* for French criticism, he had not broken entirely with the past.

The sublime is a certain power of discourse which is calculated to elevate and to ravish the soul, and which comes either from grandeur of thought and nobility of sentiment, or from magnificence of words, or from a harmonious, vivid, and animated turn of phrase; that is to say, from one of these regarded separately, or —and this is the perfect sublime—from the three joined together.[21]

This is, in effect, a repetition of the four sublimities that Huet had named (the sublime of objects being omitted), and is much more in the true Longinian tradition than was the earlier definition. In the first place it is restricted to discourse; this is of a piece with the exclusion of the sublimity of objects, and shows that Boileau had no concern with—even, perhaps, no appreciation of—natural grandeur. Longinus had spoken of wonder in the presence of vastness in nature, but Boileau does not seem to have responded to the suggestion. For the rest, in this definition, magnificence of words, and harmonious, vivid, animated expression are given an equal place with grandeur of thought; they are admitted to be sublime in their own right, always providing that the soul be elevated and ravished. This position is much less an innovation than were the earlier, more independent and positive ideas.[22]

In spite of this modification of his views the total impression that one derives from all that Boileau wrote on the subject is that the sublime is essentially related to thought that it is independent of rhetoric, and that it has a strong emotional effect. For thirty-five years Boileau had preached simplicity of language as the chief means of expressing sublimity, and this doctrine could but result in emphasis on greatness of conception and the emotional effect of the sublime, rather than on the form of expression. No posthumous modification of this view could eradicate the memory and the effect of those years of controversy. The English critics, at least, seized on the ideas of content and emotional effect, and virtually ignored Boileau's retreat to a more conventional position. In 1721, only eight years after the publication of the last *Ré-*

[21] *Ibid.*, III, 430.

[22] No wonder La Bruyère, in the midst of this controversy, found himself far from satisfied with the definitions of the sublime. In 1689 he wrote: "What is the sublime? It seems that it has not been defined. Is it a figure of speech? Is it born of figures of speech, or at least of certain figures? Does every *genre* of writing receive the sublime, or are only great subjects capable of it?" (*Œuvres*, ed. G. Servois [Paris, 1912], II, I, 143, 144.)

flexion, Bailey, in his *Dictionarium Britannicum*, defined the sublime in a sentence that is simply a paraphrase of Boileau's first definition.

It is not difficult to find reasons to account for Boileau's eager defence of simplicity. Reacting, in common with all his fellows both in France and in England, from singularity in language and the preciosity of mid-seventeenth century writing, and believing in clarity as one of the cardinal virtues of thought and style, it was natural that he should insist that language be simple. How else should good sense be expressed? He states this dogma metaphorically:

> Un style si rapide, et qui court en rimant,
> Marque moins trop d'esprit que peu de jugement.
> J'aime mieux un ruisseau qui sur la molle arène
> Dans un pré plein de fleurs lentement se promène,
> Qu'un torrent débordé qui, d'un cours orageux,
> Roule, plein de gravier, sur un terrain fangeux.[23]

Simplicity is the narrow gate through which the sublime enters into Boileau's system of poetry. He says:

> Soyez simple avec art,
> Sublime sans orgueil, agréable sans fard.[24]

Good sense and sublimity are not incompatible.

> Quelque sujet qu'on traite, ou plaisant, ou sublime,
> Que toujours le bon sens s'accorde avec la rime.[25]

Apparently his own predilection in favor of simplicity led him to seize on Longinus's statement that the sublime can exist, and most often does exist, without ornate style. From the quarrels that followed the enunciation of this doctrine, there emerged a new idea of the sublime, which severed it from rhetoric. It is the first theory on the subject in modern Europe. Whoever read the French version of *Peri Hupsous*, read also the *Préface* in which, speaking as one having authority, Boileau endowed the word *sublime* with new significance. The idea that the sublime is not a matter of style opened the way for investigations into the inner quality of great art, into the experiences of artist and reader when the one perceives a sublime object and the other experiences a great work of art. It was a step away from Longinus. In the years that followed Boileau's death, the distance that separated theories of the sublime from the Greek critic grew progressively greater.

Indeed, Boileau having pointed the way, others were not long in thinking for themselves, and in finding Longinus far from satisfactory

---

[23] "L'Art Poétique," I, 165–170; *Œuvres Complètes*, II, 304.
[24] *Ibid.*, I, 101, 102; *Œuvres Complètes*, II, 295.
[25] *Ibid.*, I, 28, 29; *Œuvres Complètes*, II, 286.

in his treatment of the sublime. Boileau was to witness the beginning of the development of theory away from Longinus in the treatise which young Silvain sent him in 1708. The story of Boileau's indifference, of Silvain's discouragement, and of the ultimate publication of the essay in 1732 has been told elsewhere,[26] and need not be repeated here. If one can offer any excuse for Boileau's rudeness to a young author, it must be that an old and a busy man might well have shrunk from reading and commenting on the appallingly long manuscript which Silvain, in his enthusiasm, had written.

Silvain's *Traité du Sublime* seems to have enjoyed no fame. It received a few unfavorable reviews in France[27] and was occasionally referred to by French critics. The Chevalier de Jaucourt's article on the sublime in the *Encyclopédie*, for instance, quotes a few sentences from Silvain, but the *Traité* exercised no influence on his own definition, which is taken word for word from the *Principes de la Littérature* of l'Abbé Batteux, 1747–48, and is expanded with phrases and ideas from Boileau.[28] Indeed the treatise seems to have been virtually unknown, although toward the end of the century, Sulzer, with characteristic German thoroughness, unearthed if from its obscurity.[29] Silvain is mentioned by no English critic or writer on æsthetic, and consequently has no real connection with this book. Yet Silvain may be used here to indicate the whole advance that was made in attaining an æsthetic conception of the sublime in France during the first half of the eighteenth century. The question seems not to have interested the French as it did the English, and a reading of Boileau's *Préface* and Jaucourt's article in the *Encyclopédie* will prove how sterile the interim was for such speculation in the land that had given the modern sublime, in a rudimentary form, to the world.

The importance of the *Traité*, then, lies in its being anti-Longinian and anti-rhetorical in purpose, and in the few semi-æsthetic concepts that close scrutiny will reveal. It is as an indication of a tendency rather than as an influential document that we shall glance at Silvain's neglected essay. To claim with Michiels that Silvain discovered Kant's sublime[30] is to be guilty of an enthusiasm dangerous to truth. What

[26] See Alfred Michiels, "La Théorie de Kant sur le Sublime Exposée par un Français en 1708," *Revue Contemporaine*, III (1852), 447–465; and V. Bouillier, "Silvain et Kant, ou les Antécédents Français de la Théorie de Sublime," *Revue de Littérature Comparée*, VIII (1928), 242–257.

[27] *Memoirs de Trévoux*, Paris (September, 1733), pp. 1802–1826; *Le Pour et Contre* II (1733), 284–288; *Ibid.*, XI (1737), 74–86.

[28] See the article *Sublime* in the *Encyclopédie* and Batteux, *Principes de la Littérature*, Cinquième Edition (Paris, 1774), III, 219.

[29] See the bibliography appended to the article *Erhaben*, in J. G. Sulzer's *Allgemeine Theorie der Schönen Künste* (Leipzig, 1786).   [30] Michiels, III, 450.

is true is that, like many other theories of the sublime in the eighteenth century, Silvain's shows some resemblance to Kant's, but that is because Kant, despite his difficult technical language, is really writing out of the eighteenth-century tradition, and thus has sources (perhaps unknown to him) in common with other writers. In this case the common source is Longinus. Bouillier's estimate is much more just; while recognizing the vast difference between the objective method of Silvain and the subjectivism of Kant, a difference that Michiels tended to minimize, he nevertheless admits that the *Traité* has value as being the closest approach to an æsthetic theory of the sublime that eighteenth-century France can show.[31]

Silvain is far from feeling satisfied with Longinus's treatment of the sublime, and his long condemnation of *Peri Hupsous* is in effect also a condemnation of Boileau's *Préface* and *Réflexions*. Perhaps this did not please the tyrannous old dictator who had made Longinus's reputation. At any rate the *Traité* opens and closes with an attack on Longinus, because, in Silvian's opinion, his ideas are vague, and he confused the sublime with its opposite, with ordinary grandeur of discourse, with the pathetic, and with rhetoric. Silvain saw quite clearly that rhetoric is not æsthetic, although he had no name for the latter.[32]

Because of his discontent with *Peri Hupsous* and because of his conviction that the sublime is somehow of great importance, Silvain undertook to reconsider the problem. It is amusing to observe that although he seeks to escape Longinus, he does not succeed. His is the first of many instances of how eighteenth-century theorizers constructed a system on one idea that Longinus had expressed. Indeed the relation of Longinus to most of the independent thinkers on the sublime in the first half of the eighteenth century can be summed up in the words of Emerson's Brahma: "When me they fly, I am the wings." For somehow Longinus is rather subtly diffused throughout the æsthetic thought of that era.

Silvain's treatise is an extension of the Longinian idea that grandeur in discourse is a direct reflection of grandeur in the human soul. An idealistic conception of the greatness of man runs through the whole book, and this idealism is the rock on which Silvain's barque splits, for it impels him to flee the Scylla of rhetoric by running full against the Charybdis of morality. It is this fact that converts the *Traité* into many hundreds of pages of irrelevance. The danger lurks in his opening remark that no part of rhetoric is so clearly connected with the moral as is the sublime: nothing can so impress man with his own natural

[31] Bouillier, VIII, 252.

[32] Silvain, *Traité du Sublime à Monsieur Despréaux*, etc. (Paris, 1732), pp. 2–5 and 380–431.

greatness as can the experience of the sublime, "not only because it elevates the soul, and fills it with a noble pride, that comes from virtue and magnanimity, but because it makes us recognize that this marvellous sublime which ravishes us, has its principal source in our hearts." Man's innate love of grandeur in external objects is witness to his own grandeur and to the fact that he seeks in the external world the grandeur which is latent in his own soul. In experiencing the sublime the soul forms a noble opinion of itself, not, as Longinus holds, because it imagines that it has produced the object contemplated, but because it becomes aware of its own nobleness and greatness. Hence Silvain declares that he writes his treatise to urge men to cultivate a taste for that which elevates the soul, since this experience will constantly remind man that "after God, he is himself the sole object worthy of his care."[33]

On this ground Michiels seeks to prove Silvain's discovery of Kant's sublime,[34] but surely such a claim overshoots the mark. The doctrine that there is a correspondence between the grandeur of the soul and the grandeur of the ideas which the soul can entertain is at least as old as Plato; it is expressly stated in *Peri Hupsous;* and it is found frequently in the essays on the sublime in England for ninety years before Kant wrote. To find in Kant a certain natural adherence to traditional thought is more just than to make for an obscure French treatise so high a claim. A definite approach to the ideas of Kant is present in Sylvain's statement that the sublime has its chief origin in our hearts. But Silvain's treatment is not the subjective method of Kant; it is rather almost wholly the rhetorical method of Longinus. Sublimity is conceived as a quality residing in the object, whereas Kant takes pains to prove that no object can be sublime. None the less, Silvain has taken up an important idea, and has advanced a step toward the creation of an æsthetic. His moral proclivities prevented his concentrating on the psychological aspect, as the English soon began to do.

If Silvain could complain that Longinus's treatise is almost purely rhetorical, a modern can claim with equal justice that the *Traité* is a mingling of ethics and rhetoric. A great part of it is given over to praise of man and to proof that the sublime is the image of high virtue, and much space goes to a hair-splitting discrimination between the sublime and the sublime style. No mention is made of the other arts, and the sublimity of nature is barely touched on. Despite all this, the treatise is important because it marks the first step taken in France away from the Longinian-Bolevian sublime and because of its dim perceptions of the æsthetic implications of some of Longinus's ideas.[35]

[33] *Ibid.*, pp. 6–8 and 23.   [34] Michiels, III, 450, 457, 458.

[35] Bouillier says, "Apart from Silvain, the French eighteenth century did not examine

Silvain's definition of the sublime is long and clear, and it indicates
how little he himself had escaped the rhetorical point of view. He begins
with the usual "extraordinary turn of phrase," but, as we shall shortly
see, he seeks to explain, on grounds other than those of rhetoric, the
origin of this vivid expression and its effect on the hearer. Noble images
are the sign of noble feeling, elevating the soul above its ordinary ideas
of grandeur and inspiring it with admiration, ravishing it, and giving
it a high idea of itself.[36] This noble imagery he describes as vivid and
animated, and characterized by a singular vivacity—qualities which
differentiate the language of the sublime and the ordinary language of
judgment and reflection.[37] In the last analysis, Silvain is distinguishing
the vital and creative language of art from the less expressive language
of ordinary prose. The former demands that the speaker should himself
be moved before he moves others, an obligation which does not hold for
rhetoric. The point which Silvain reiterates is that it conveys the idea of
the object and the emotions that the object arouses more clearly than
any other sort of language could do, and thus it fulfills the end of the
sublime, which is not to move the passions, to teach or to convince, but
to "elevate the soul," one might almost say, to intensify experience.[38]

Admiration, the characteristic effect of the sublime, is the natural and
inseparable result of extraordinarily grand objects, and is the emotion
that elevates the soul. Joy and pleasure always accompany admiration,
thus distinguishing it from astonishment, which is accompanied by the
depressing emotions of fear and sadness, and hence is not sublime. This
emotion gives the soul a noble opinion of itself, by revealing its kinship
with the grandest objects and ideas that the world affords. Thus arises
Silvain's two-fold division of the sublime—the sublime of images, based
on grand objects, and the sublime of sentiments, based on the noblest
sentiments of the heart of man.[39]

Sublime images turn out, as in Genesis 1, 3, to be simply descriptions
of great power. It is disappointing to find that Silvain nowhere shows
desire to analyse the effect of natural objects on the emotions. All of
his examples come from literature, or from anecdotes from history. These
images seem to be regarded as an artistic shorthand for the expressions
of emotions caused by sublimity; they have a dual significance, being on
the one hand the crystallization of emotions that the artist feels (Silvain
always speaks of the "orator"), and on the other the agent for stirring
similar emotions in the reader. Thus the "audience" sees the image only

---

or even understand the question of the sublime," VIII, 252. My own study of the sublime
in France, from Boileau to the *Encyclopédie*, bears out this generalization.

[36] *Traité du Sublime*, p. 14.   [37] *Ibid.*, pp. 15, 16.
[38] *Ibid.*, pp. 18, 19.   [39] *Ibid.*, pp. 22–25 and 32.

in the impression that the object has made on the orator; and the orator, vividly experiencing the grandeur of the object, impresses by his "extraordinary turn" both the image of this grandeur and the image of the emotion that he feels.[40] We are here at least on the threshold of the problem of æsthetic communication.

The sublime of sentiments Silvain finds to be the ultimate expression of the grandeur of man, and consequently to be nobler than the sublime of images. This grandeur, which consists primarily in being elevated by magnanimity above the fear of death and above all passion, elevates the soul and expresses itself in the same manner as does the sublime of images. Admiration is its effect; its object is man himself; its cause is enthusiasm, which Silvain justifies in a manner similar to Shaftesbury's in *The Moralists*.[41]

We can pass over most of Silvain's second book, in which he distinguishes the sublime from the grand, from the perfect, and from forceful demonstration. From what he has said of the sublime of sentiments, one is not surprised that he should hold that the sublime and the pathetic are different and often opposed qualities. The pathetic is the communication of passions, and Silvain has a puritan's distrust of these enemies of the reason. Christianity and reason condemn them; it is not virtuous to abandon oneself to them. How can nobleness or grandeur exist without virtue, or the sublime without nobleness and grandeur? Passions degrade man to the level of the beasts, and man is great only when he rises above them. All of this runs counter to Silvain's conception of the sublime, and he scornfully relegates the passions to a lower order of art, reserving for the sublime the pure serene of a higher sphere of existence.[42]

Finally, Silvain insists on the distinction between the sublime style and the sublime. Grand diction does not always make the sublime; it is rather akin to false eloquence. One can be eloquent on slight themes, which offer nothing capable of elevating the soul. All that is sublime is eloquent, for it consists of great ideas expressed in vivid language, but all that is eloquent is not sublime.[43]

All of this, one may say, leads nowhere. And yet it would not be fair to condemn the *Traité* outright. In this verbose book we see how Boileau gave an impulse to the study of the sublime, and how that study leads to the freeing of the concept from some of the trammels which bound it so long as it remained linked to rhetoric. Silvain took a step along the road that the English were to travel. No mention is made of beauty; indeed, it remained for the English to separate the sublime from the beautiful, as well as to reconcile the sublime and the pathetic. Silvain

[40] *Ibid.*, pp. 27–76.
[42] *Ibid.*, pp. 257–350.
[41] *Ibid.*, pp. 77–208.
[43] *Ibid.*, pp. 355–379.

is vaguely aware of the subjective nature of the æsthetic experience; his preoccupation, at least to some extent, is with the sublime as the expression and the evoker of emotions that represent the grandeur of the soul of man. The English, in speculation less austere and puritanical, more concerned with psychology than with the moral point of view, were to develop during the next half century an analysis of the emotional aspect of the question.

CHAPTER III

THE SUBLIME AND THE PATHETIC

THE close relationship between French and English criticism during the last decades of the seventeenth century, made any literary event in the one country of some importance to the other. The controversy between the Ancients and the Moderns had elevated Longinus to a position of eminence in France, and had brought the sublime into critical discussions. One may justly infer that Boileau's praise and use of *Peri Hupsous* created an interest in Longinus across the channel. Rosenberg and Clark have shown that Longinian influence was conspicuously absent from Dryden's criticism until shortly after 1674, and that five years after the publication of Boileau's translation, Dryden declared: "Aristotle with his interpreters, and Horace, and Longinus, are the authors to whom I owe my lights."[1] The weight of such authority as Boileau's and Dryden's was certain to bring the ideas of *Peri Hupsous* not only into prominence but into fashion. One may be confident that, after the two great critics of the age had recognized the value of Longinus, the lesser critics would take him up.

Of Longinus's effect upon Dryden's criticism in general we shall have nothing to say. Our concern is only with sublimity.[2] As one should suspect, the heightened or lofty style is a concept familiar to Dryden in his earliest essays. His theory of the diction proper to tragedy and heroic poetry was consistently based on the ancient conception of the high style, with its figurative language and its emotional effect; when he adopts the "gallicism" *sublime*, he does not really change his point of view. He held no theory of the sublime, but occasionally he seems to use the term in a manner analogous to that of Longinus. Lucretius, for

---

[1] *Longinus in England*, pp. 20, 21; *Boileau and the French Classical Critics in England*, p. 369. The nature of this influence is fairly evident, although of course not revolutionary. It is most clearly seen in the *Preface to Troilus and Cressida*, 1679. See *Essays*, ed. W. P. Ker (Oxford, 1900), I, 186; 220, 221; II, 85.

[2] Dryden never consistently substitutes *sublime* for *elevation* and *high*. His concern in the matter is almost wholly with the sublime style as the most expressive vehicle for the passions. See *Essays*, I, 18; 104, 105; 113, 114; 186 and 190; 220, 221, 224, and 227; 247 and 248; II, 165. The conception of tragedy as pathetic and of the pathetic style as figurative and "high," opened the way for some of the satire in *The Rehearsal*, in which the "new kind of Wits" are described as "fellows that scorn to imitate nature; but are given altogether to elevate and surprise." Bayes exclaims rapturously over some fine bit of rhodomantade, "Is not that good language now? Is not that elevate?" [George Villiers, Second Duke of Buckingham], *The Rehearsal* (London, 1672), pp. 2 and 34.

instance, is said to possess a "sublime and daring genius" from which
proceeds his lofty verse; and Milton is granted "a true sublimity, lofty
thoughts."[3] But despite Dryden's recognition of the necessity of sup-
porting an ornate and pathetic style with great thoughts, and his association of sublimity with "daring" genius, he seems never to have regarded sublimity as a subject for speculation. His importance is due
rather to his sanctioning Longinus and adopting him as a guide, than
to his formulating any definite concept of the æsthetic implicaticns of
the sublime. That he gave an impulse to a critical investigation of sublimity by his praise of Longinus can scarcely be doubted.

The word rapidly passed into the current critical vocabulary, and
was well known before the eighteenth century began. Hobbes considered
"Elevation of Fancie" to be " the greatest praise of Heroique Poetry,"
for "in Fancie consisteth the Sublimity of a Poet, which is that Poetical
Fury which the Readers for the most part call for." But this sublimity
must of course be restrained by judgment and must be discreetly used.[4]
The epic continued to be the sublime *genre* throughout the eighteenth
century, but the sublime was to break more and more from the shackles
of judgment. Sir William Temple connects the sublime with the amazing,[5] a partnership that continued as long as the sublime endured, and
that is indicative of the habit of regarding the sublime as affecting the
stronger emotions. William Wotton wrote a Longinian passage on the
value of liberty in inspiring genius and elevating the souls of men, in
the course of which he cast a scornful glance at the rules.[6] But none
of these Restoration critics seriously attacked the problem of the sublime. That remained for a very serious man indeed—John Dennis.

The eighteenth century opened, then, with Longinus established, along
with Aristotle and Horace, as an arbiter of critical opinion; his rise to
great popularity was only a few years in the future. The high style of
which the ancient rhetoricians had written, as we have seen, had not
been forgotten during the Middle Ages or the Renaissance, and had, by
1700, been rechristened the sublime style. The word was common property among the critics, and connoted perfection, grandeur, the ultimate
excellence, or any other idea of strong approbation so long as dignity
was also implied. But Boileau, as all the world knew, had read in
Longinus that the sublime is a quality of art that does not depend for

---

[3] *Essays*, I, 260, and II, 109. See also *Ibid.*, I, 179 for praise of Milton as sublime.

[4] Thomas Hobbes, "Preface to Homer's Odysses," 1675, Spingarn, *Critical Essays of the
Seventeenth Century* (Oxford, 1909), II, 70.

[5] Sir William Temple, "Essay on Poetry," 1690, Spingarn, III, 81.

[6] William Wotton, "Reflections on Ancient and Modern Learning," 1694, Spingarn,
III, 211, 212.

its existence on fine words and rhetorical devices. He had insisted that it is above rhetoric, and lives really in the grandeur of a great artist's thoughts, that it conveys emotions, that it is recognizable by its sudden overwhelming effect, and he had agreed with Longinus that it is the product of genius not of rules.

What was the eighteenth century to make of this? The French were to rest content with Boileau's statement of the case, for their interest continued strongly centered on the rules. But the English were naturally more metaphysical, and would hardly be disposed to let the matter rest where Boileau had left it. Two concepts at least would interest them—the pathetic and the failure of the rules to achieve the sublime; the one because English literature had always been a literature of feeling and emotion rather than of intellect, the other because the rules were never really acclimated among a people who genuinely loved Shakespeare, and who found their literary ideal in his works rather than in more "correct" poetry, however loudly the Rymer's might rail. Moreover, Locke's *Essay on Human Understanding* had inaugurated a sort of psychology, by seeking to explore the mind by an analysis of experience. What more natural than that the English should apply the empirical method to the discussion of the sublime, and should seek to analyse the effect of the sublime on the minds and emotions of men?

Thus the eighteenth century saw various critics and philosophers take up the idea of the sublime where Boileau had left it, and develop it through a series of phases into an æsthetic concept of the first importance. The first and most interesting of these theories that we meet in the early years of the eighteenth century comes, oddly enough, from one of the minor critics of the age, Pope's sworn enemy and the target of many of that poet's barbed shafts of satire—John Dennis, who early manifested an interest in the sublime, not only in regard to natural scenery, but to theory as well. Before the end of the seventeenth century he had outlined his ideas, carrying the inquiry far beyond the region in which Longinus and Boileau had wrought, by investigating the emotional responses of individuals who experience the sublime. Boileau, following Longinus, had tried to ascertain the quality in art which may be called sublime, and had indicated generally the effect of this quality; Dennis was the first Englishman to see that if anything of value was to be learned, the inquiry must take into account not only the nature of the sublime object, but its effect also, i.e., the subjective element.

Dennis declared his intention of investigating the nature of genius, which he considered to be "nothing but a very common Passion, or a complication of common Passions." This beginning is characteristic of Dennis's view of art. His interest is always in the emotional; he can explain poetry and genius on no other ground than the passions. Thus he draws a parallel between the emotions that accompany happiness in life and those that are the result of felicity in writing. In life, when anything lucky occurs, we experience a transport of joy, which is followed by an exaltation of the mind, and frequently by astonishment. So with a fine thing in art; the soul is transported by the consciousness of its own excellence, and amazed by the view of its own surpassing power.

Now it is very certain that a man in transport, and one that is lifted up with pride and astonish'd, expresses himself quite with another air, than one who is calm and serene. Joy in excess as well as rage is furious. And the pride of Soul is seen in the expression as well as in the mien and actions, and is the cause of that Elevation, which *Longinus* so much extolls, and which, he says, *is the image of the greatness of the mind*.[7]

Thus, under the guidance of the great Greek, Dennis is led to reduce art to the expression of passion, and to maintain that the highest art—the sublime—is the expression of the greatest passion. The sublime and the pathetic begin their long journey in each other's company. It is noticeable, also, that Dennis is the first of many writers to recognize with Longinus, in the experience of the sublime, that sense of the greatness of the human soul which Kant uses in his analysis of the sublime.

In 1701 Dennis published what Paul, his biographer, regards as his most important work—*The Advancement and Reformation of Modern Poetry*. Its sequel, *The Grounds of Criticism in Poetry*, published in 1704, was originally planned as a more extensive work which was to be his *magnum opus*, and was to contain "a Criticism upon our most Celebrated English Poets deceas'd." This work never saw the light of day, since only about seventy subscriptions were taken.[8] Of all Dennis's writings the two books with which we are concerned are his most original. They appeared shortly after the death of Dryden and before the ascendency of Pope during the brief interregnum in the realm of criticism when Dennis was known as "the Critic."[9] They brought him a modest fame, some notoriety, and the gibes of the Martinus Scriblerus Club.

In these books Dennis stands out with startling vividness from his contemporaries. In *The Advancement and Reformation of Modern Poetry* he builds up a theory of poetry based entirely on emotion, thus carrying out to some degree the plan which he had earlier announced. Hamelius gives him first place in his chapter *Anfang der Aesthetik* and does not

---

[7] John Dennis, *Remarks on a Book entituled, Prince Arthur, an Heroick Poem*, etc. (London, 1696), Preface. In the same passage Dennis defines genius as "the expression of a Furious Joy, or Pride, or Astonishment."

[8] Paul, *John Dennis*, pp. 49, 50.

[9] *Ibid.*, p. 108.

hesitate to classify him as a romanticist.[10] Such terms are dangerous, and we have learned not to dub a man romantic because he praised Milton or admitted emotion into his theory of art. But in spite of the fact that, taken in its totality, Dennis's criticism is quite neo-classic in method, Hamelius is not mistaken when he finds something new in these two books, and in calling attention to Dennis's departure from the strait and narrow path of criticism as practiced by his contemporaries. Dennis himself boasted of "the Newness and Boldness of the Positions" which he held.[11]

Paul has discussed the criticism of Dennis and its relation to the various schools and movements of the early eighteenth century—a none too simple task, for Dennis's life was long and active, and his criticism is correspondingly many-sided. It is sufficient here to call attention to his religious, moralistic point of view, which Paul is inclined to attribute to the influence of Milton, and to his fondness for Longinus, which will shortly become evident.[12] It was in *Three Hours after Marriage* that Pope and Gay satirized Dennis's discipleship of Longinus by representing the critic as "Sir Tremendous Longinus."[13] Certainly the name of Longinus is frequently found in Dennis's criticism; it is evident that he was very much under the influence of *Peri Hupsous* and that he prided himself on his knowledge of that treatise.

Dennis, like Boileau, brings Longinus to the fore in connection with the Ancients and the Moderns. The aim of *The Advancement and Reformation* is to offer a middle ground whereby neither party need lose out irrevocably. In his second, third, and fourth chapters, Dennis proves that the ancients did not surpass the moderns either because of "external advantages" or "internal advantages," but that they derived their greatness from the nature of their subjects. He proposes a scheme whereby the moderns may equal the ancients in those kinds of poetry in which they have hitherto had the disadvantage. Dennis's opinion that "Passion is the Principal thing in Poetry,"[14] leads to his formulated definition: "Poetry then is an imitation of Nature by a Pathetick and Numerous Speech."[15] He elaborates this view at considerable length. Passion he finds more essential to poetry than harmony, for harmony is merely the "instrument" of poetry, but passion distinguishes its very nature and character.

[10] P. Hamelius, *Die Kritik in der englischen Literatur des 17. und 18. Jahrhunderts* (Leipzig, 1897), p. 79.

[11] Epistle Dedicatory, *Advancement and Reformation* (London, 1701).

[12] *John Dennis*, p. 140.   [13] *Ibid.*, p. 91:

[14] Epistle Dedicatory, *Advancement and Reformation*.

[15] *Ibid.*, p. 23. Dennis's claim that this is the first definition of poetry is characteristic of his boasting.

For therefore Poetry is Poetry, because it is more passionate and sensual than Prose.[16] A discourse that is writ in very good Numbers, if it wants Passion can be but measur'd Prose. But a discourse that is every where extremely pathetick, and consequently every where bold and figurative, is certainly Poetry without Numbers.[17]

The timeworn doctrine of imitation is here, and the idea of figurative language as the proper expression of strong emotions—both old and respectable in Dennis's time. But despite the outward garb of conventional language, despite the discouraging confusion of poetry and rhetoric, Dennis's definition is out of harmony with prevailing opinion by virtue of the emphasis that it lays on the strong emotions, which he finds to be the distinguishing feature of poetry. It matters little that he adds that the function of emotion in poetry is to facilitate the two great ends of pleasing and instructing;[18] the fact remains that the idea of the *furor poeticus* is more prominent in Dennis's system than in that of any other critic of his day.

There follows the distinction, so important for Dennis's system, between ordinary passion and enthusiasm.

I call that ordinary Passion, whose cause is clearly comprehended by him who feels it, whether it be Admiration, Terror, or Joy; and I call the very same Passions Enthusiasm, when their cause is not clearly comprehended by him who feels them.[19]

This statement is extremely awkward, and standing alone would mean little. He goes on to explain that an object and the idea of an object produce the same emotions, and that some ideas "latently and unobserved by us, carry Passion along with them."[20] All of this seems to be an attempt to account for that sense of wonder in the presence of the vast that plays so important a part in the eighteenth-century sublime. In the *Grounds of Criticism* one finds this statement, in which Dennis redefines his terms:

Enthusiastick Passion, or Enthusiasm, is a Passion which is moved by Ideas in Contemplation, or the Meditation of things that belong not to common life. Most of our Thoughts in Meditation are naturally attended with some sort and some degree of Passion; and this Passion, if it is strong, I call Enthusiasm.

This enthusiasm is contrasted with ordinary emotion ("Vulgar Passion"), which is described as "that which is moved by the Objects them-

[16] The similarity of this phrase to Milton's "simple, sensuous, and passionate" is too close to be accidental. Dennis knew and quoted from the essay on education in the "Epistle Dedicatory" to the *Advancement and Reformation*.

[17] *Advancement and Reformation*, p. 24.   [18] *Ibid.*, 24, 25.

[19] *Ibid.*, 26. Later (on p. 30) Dennis defines poetical enthusiasm again as "a Passion guided by Judgment," whose cause is not clearly comprehended by us.

[20] *Ibid.*, pp. 30 and 31.

selves, or by the Ideas in the ordinary Course of Life."[21] To illustrate his meaning, he says that the sun, mentioned in ordinary conversation, suggests "a round flat shining Body, of about two foot diameter." But occurring to the mind in meditation, it suggests "a vast and glorious Body, and the top of all the visible Creation, and the brightest material Image of the Divinity."[22]

Despite the obvious handicap of a lack of vocabulary, it is clear that Dennis has perceived the distinction between practical emotion and æsthetic emotion, between phenomena as revealed by sense and phenomena as expressed in art. True, his concern with emotions obscures the issue, but he is certainly on the way to an æsthetic when he distinguishes between what Croce calls the theoretical and the practical.

It should be observed, also, that in this, the earliest theory of the sublime in England, the author turns to association to explain the æsthetic experience. Associationism was to become one of the chief elements in æsthetic during the whole century, but neither Hartley nor Alison was responsible for its presence in the philosophy of taste. As soon as men began to look within themselves for explanations of questions of æsthetic, they found that some psychological theory was necessary if they were to understand the creation and the enjoyment of beauty and sublimity. Association presented itself to every observer, and was found to a certain extent in Locke, so that long before it became the explanation of all knowledge, it was used to account for the increment that art adds to experience.

Upon this enthusiastic passion Dennis seeks to found the sublime. The sixth chapter of *The Advancement and Reformation* is meant to prove "That Passion is more to be deriv'd from a Sacred Subject than from a Prophane one;" and the rest of the book is intended to show that only in their sacred poetry did the ancients excel the moderns. The poetry of the "Graecians" and the Romans failed with the decay of their religions. Let the modern poet but drink of Siloa's brook, and no longer will he have to yield to the ancients. This is Dennis's scheme for advancing and reforming the poetry of his day. Milton serves as an example of the greatness of religious poetry, and the pages of the book are strewn with passages from *Paradise Lost*. But Milton is not the only authority summoned to help Dennis prove his point, for Longinus is plainly the chief influence on the critic's mind. Almost all the examples of sublimity that Longinus gives, Dennis remarks, have as their basis religion and its emotions.

---

[21] "Grounds of Criticism in Poetry," *The Select Works of John Dennis* (London, 1718), II, 423.   [22] *Ibid.*, p. 424.

Once launched on the subject of Longinus, Dennis naturally finds his way to a discussion of the sublime. He begins by stating that enthusiasm is made up of the passions, admiration, joy, terror, and astonishment, the first giving elevation, "that Pride which exalts the Soul at the conceiving a great Hint;" the second giving transport; and the third vehemence.[23] Elevation, transport, and vehemence were, in one form or other, to be concomitants of the sublime for many a day. They were found in the Longinian sublime, as interpreted by Boileau, and many decades later were used by Kant in his analysis of sublimity. They indicate the strongly emotional concepts that were habitually associated with the sublime, and that helped to centralize, in one idea, forces that always were considered to transcend the rules and to lie outside the realm of pure technique and within the reach only of genius.

How Longinus pointed the way to the analysis of the subjective element in æsthetic is shown in Dennis's account of his sublime.

He takes great pains to set before us, the effects which it produces in the Minds of Men; as, for example, that it causes in them admiration and surprize; or noble Pride, and a noble Vigour, an invincible force transporting the Soul from its ordinary Situation, and a Transport, and a fulness of Joy mingled with Astonishment. These are the effects that *Longinus* tells us that the Sublime produces in the minds of men. Now I have endeavoured to shew what it is in Poetry that works these effects. So that take the Cause and the Effects together, and you have the Sublime.[24]

When these words were written, Longinus was relatively a new force in English criticism. We therefore discover in them something of the point of view of a man who was reading him freshly. The striking thing to Dennis is that Longinus analysed the effects of the sublime on the soul. This statement would seem to support the idea that Longinus had some share in the founding of an æsthetic concept of the sublime; that he sought to turn criticism away from the rules, to turn men's minds away from the dogmas of the ancients, and to set them to analysing their own emotions in the presence of grandeur and beauty. By investigating the emotions consequent to sublimity, men began to learn that art is a matter, not of the rules, but of the individual's response to an object or an experience, and this knowledge led them gradually to that subjective view of art out of which an æsthetic was evolved. Incidentally the habit of studying the emotional effect of art was certain to emphasize the belief that the individual emotion is more valid than all the rules, and such a belief firmly held and clearly understood produces the poetry of a Wordsworth not of a Pope. Although he never forgets that poetry should teach and improve, Dennis nevertheless emphasizes the

---

[23] *The Advancement and Reformation*, p. 34.   [24] *Ibid.*, p. 47.

emotions, because instruction comes after the reader has been moved.[25]
The greater poetry—epic, tragedy, and ode—has as its basis poetic enthusiasm, which is evoked by religion. To Dennis, this is also the sublime emotion.

In the *Grounds of Criticism* Dennis attempted to systematize and expand some of these ideas, and in this book are found his ideas of the sublime. Remembering that Dennis is discussing epic, tragedy, and ode,
genres that are based on enthusiasm; that enthusiasm is emotion aroused
by the ideas of things that do not belong to common life, considered in
contemplation, emotion whose cause is not clearly perceived; and that
the sublime is found only in poetry which contains this enthusiasm, we
may consider his theory.

There are six "Enthusiastic Passions"—admiration,[26] terror, horror,
joy, sadness, and desire.[27] They are strongest when they have their
origin in religious ideas.[28] The two emotions that Dennis discussed at
length are admiration and terror; if he had finished *The Grounds of
Criticism* he would have treated of the others, but the failure to obtain
subscribers cut short his work. It is regrettable, in the light of future
developments, that we have none of his opinions on the relation of horror
to the sublime.

Dennis gives a list of objects that arouse admiration, an emotion
evoked by "the Sight of a strange Object, or the Relation of one."[29] They
are ideas of God, of his works, such as angels and the great phenomena
of the material universe—the heavens, the sun, the moon, the stars—
and the divine virtues in man—temperance, justice, fortitude.[30] The effect of ideas of God is described in Longinian language, and agrees with
the older conception of the sublime. Great elevation must be produced
by great admiration, which exalts and lifts up the soul, and fills it with
wonder.[31] This is of course the proof that Dennis offers to uphold his
theory that religion is the source of the greatest poetry. The association
of the power and vastness of the universe with strong emotions brings
into Dennis's theory objects that are found in conjunction with sublimity from Longinus to Kant.

---

[25] Dennis professes to admire Greek tragedy above the modern, because, as he says,
"I am more delighted and instructed by the former; and that for this very reason, because
I am more mov'd by it; For I find by experience that I am no further pleas'd nor instructed
by any Tragedy, than as it excites Passion in me." Epistle Dedicatory, *Advancement and
Reformation.*

[26] Of course Dennis uses *admiration* in a sense different from the modern usage. Bailey,
in 1721, defined *admire* as "To behold with wonder, to be surpriz'd at, or wonder greatly."

[27] "The Grounds of Criticism," *Works*, II, 423.

[28] *Ibid.*, II, 425.   [29] *Ibid.*, II, 423.

[30] *Ibid.*, II, 429–447.   [31] *Ibid.*, II, 434.

The sublimity of terror is more interesting, both in itself and in view of the part that terror is to play in the sublime during the whole century. For some reason the æsthetic of terror interested the eighteenth-century Englishman. In a sense it is the æsthetic of the ugly, for neither the ugly nor the terrible is agreeable. It is in this connection that the English show their independence. The paradox of the pleasure of pain held great attraction for them, and French neo-classicism offered no explanation. The problem was attacked through the sublime by Dennis, and during the whole century it remained in the sphere of sublimity. This is an historical fact of some importance, for terror is the first of several qualities that, finding no very happy home in the well-planned, orderly, and carefully trimmed domain of neo-classicism, sought and found refuge in the sublime, which constantly gathered to itself ideas and emotions that were to be prominent in the poetry and prose of the romantic era.

Of terror Dennis says that if it be rightly managed, no emotion "is more capable of giving a great Spirit to Poetry"; for it is seldom found alone, but is usually "complicated with Admiration. For everything that is terrible, is great at least to him to whom it is terrible."[32] There follows a novel passage, which must be fully quoted. The common emotion of terror is

a Disturbance of Mind, proceeding from an Apprehension of an approaching Evil, threatening Destruction or very great Trouble either to us or ours. And when the Disturbance comes suddenly with surprize, let us call it Terror; and when gradually, Fear. Things then that are powerful, and likely to hurt, are the Causes of Common Terror, and the more they are powerful, and likely to hurt, the more they become the cause of Terror; which Terror, the greater it is, the more it is joined with Wonder,[33] and the nearer it comes to Astonishment: Thus we have shewn what Objects of the Mind are the Causes of Enthusiastick Terror. . . .

He adds that the greatest enthusiastic terror is derived from religious ideas, for since the more objects are powerful and likely to hurt, the greater terror their ideas produce, the most terrible idea is that of an angry God.[34] And he bases this capacity for feeling terror on the instinct of self-preservation.[35]

"Everything that is terrible, is great at least to him to whom it is terrible;" "a Disturbance of the mind proceeding from an Apprehension of an approaching Evil"—here is a new note. Dennis is no psychologist, and certainly he is no æsthetician, but surely in those phrases we have

---

[32] *Ibid.*, II, 450. "The terrible . . . is exceedingly proper for epick Poetry, as being in its own Nature sublime and grave, and majestick," *Remarks on Prince Arthur*, p. 187.

[33] "We name those things wonderful, which we admire with fear." *Works*, II, 437, 438.

[34] *Ibid.*, II, 450, 451.   [35] *Ibid.*, II, 461.

a crude attempt at both psychology and æsthetic. To use Burke's phrase Dennis is "turning the soul in upon itself." In view of his expressed interest in the sensations of mingled terror and pleasure that he felt in crossing the Alps,[36] it becomes apparent that Dennis had an empirical interest in sublimity.

After establishing the origin and the effect of terror, Dennis cites Longinus as proof of his views, alleging that all of the examples of the sublime in *Peri Hupsous* are ultimately based on that emotion.[37] Sappho's ode is an obvious exception, but Dennis does not mention it. This naturally leads to a discussion of the sublime, in which the critic seeks to prove that Longinus errs in admitting the occasional independence of the sublime and the pathetic. "Common Passion" it may lack, but it can never exist where "Enthusiastick Passion" is lacking, "for the sublime is nothing else but a great Thought, or great Thoughts, moving the Soul from its ordinary Situation by the Enthusiasm which naturally attends them." Dennis is convinced that he has discovered an inconsistency in *Peri Hupsous*, for the total impression that Longinus gives is that the sublime

does not so properly persuade us, as it ravishes and transports us, and produces in us a certain Admiration, mingled with Astonishment and with Surprize, which is quite another thing than the barely pleasing, or the barely persuading; that it gives a noble Vigour to a Discourse, an invincible Force, which commits a pleasing Rape upon the very Soul of the Reader; that whenever it breaks out where it ought to do, like the Artillery of Jove, it thunders, blazes, and strikes at once, and shews all the united Force of a Writer.[38]

Dennis's sublime is made of stern stuff. Ultimately, however he might dress it in the conventional critical language of his decade, it could never harmonize with an art whose spirit was *nil admirari*. The strongest emotions are its effect; it negates reason, and transcends rules. Dennis establishes the sublime beyond the sphere of that moderate urbanity which was the ideal of Augustan literature. But it is important to remember that he did so without apparently disrupting the system. The canonization of Longinus by Boileau and Dryden had left the way open for the introduction into the neo-classic system of ideas and forces which eventually were to play an important part in its destruction. The best testimony of the need that the English felt for such ideas as Longinus's is the zeal with which they adopted and spread them. Dennis's treatment of *Peri Hupsous* is typical; he has seized on one or two statements and has expanded them, building a theory on them, and forcing Longinus to conform to his views. Paul is right in seeing the influence of Boileau's *Préface* in the passage just quoted, for the "ravishes

---

[36] See below, p. 207.   [37] *Works*, II, 459.   [38] *Ibid*., II, 455, 456.

and transports" is obviously from that critical essay; but Dennis is original in respect to the value which he attaches to powerful emotion in art and particularly in the sublime.

The critic asserts that all the examples of sublimity that Longinus uses are impregnated with terrible ideas, and that terror gives to writings all the qualities that make them sublime. There follows a list of objects that inspire this emotion. They are:

Gods, Daemons, Hell, Spirits and Souls of Men, Miracles, Prodigies, Enchantments, Witchcraft, Thunder, Tempests, raging Seas, Inundations, Torrents, Earthquakes, Volcanos, Monsters, Serpents, Lions, Tygers, Fire, War, Pestilence, Famine, etc.[39]

This is an interesting list. By 1740 poetry was full of terror and horror. The graveyard school was to make good use of hell, spirits and souls of men, thunder, tempests; the ruin-poetry often enough used witchcraft and enchantments, ghosts, and serpents; the descriptive and excursion poets were fond of storms, raging seas, inundations, earthquakes, volcanoes, lions, and tigers; and in Dennis's own day there were poems on death and plague. Their association, thus early, with the sublime casts some light upon the aims of these poets.

This is Dennis's view of the sublime. With its insistence on strong emotion it goes beyond Longinus, and is certainly quite different from Boileau's theory, for Dennis is willing to subordinate all qualities to emotion. In view of the prominence of terror, both in later theories of the sublime and in much of eighteenth-century literature, the most interesting aspect of Dennis's treatment of the sublime is his introduction of that emotion. Dennis's influence is known to have been slight,[40] but he was certainly read, and if he helped to strengthen the cause of emotions in art, he has contributed his share to the history of English literature. But his interest in the sublime, with its powerful emotions and overwhelming effects, left him no time to consider the beautiful, or to make the inevitable separation of the two categories. As a matter of fact, his sublime is simply the highest beauty, not a separate experience, different from one's perception of the beautiful. The distinction of first establishing the sublime as a separate category, is due to Addison, although he may not have realized the significance of what he had done.

The break was unavoidable, for the sublime became more and more a thing apart from neo-classic beauty. That this was inevitably the case is indicated by the opinion of St. Evremond in his "A Discourse upon

[39] *Ibid.*, II, 459, 460.

[40] Even Paul, who is bent on doing his best for Dennis, is forced to admit the slight influence that Dennis's criticism exercised. Gildon, Giles Jacob, and Blackmore make up the far from impressive list of those who praise him.

the Word *Vast*," which he read to the gentlemen of the French Academy in 1677, before the sublime became a popular concept. The term *vast*, he says, is never complimentary. *Great* signifies perfection, but *vast* is always a reproach. It is the lack of proportion involved in the term that he objects to. A just and regulated Extent makes the *Great;* an immoderate Grandeur makes the *Vast*." There is a disagreeable excessiveness in the word *vast*, and it is closely related to the terrible, of which he evidently does not approve. Vast things differ from "those that make an agreeable Impression." Among the disagreeable objects that he cites as being vast are many of the objects that later win the approval of the eighteenth century as sublime: vast solitudes, that inspire horror; vast houses; vast gardens, that "cannot have that Agreement which proceeds from Art, or those Graces which Nature might afford;" vast forests; vast plains, rivers, whose extent the eye cannot behold with pleasure; savage countries. The term, he declares, means almost the same thing as "spoiled" and "ruined."[41] This is undoubtedly the neo-classicist's point of view. Such objects present no gentle unity in variety to awaken agreeable sensations in a cultivated mind. Johnson's inability to appreciate the wild grandeur of Scotland, his scornful "Norway, too has noble wild prospects; and Lapland is remarkable for prodigious noble wild prospects," are cases in point. But it is exactly such objects as St. Evremond finds unbeautiful and disagreeable, and such scenery as Johnson disliked, that were to be assimilated into the sublime and that were to rise into favor as the century wore on. They were not considered beautiful by the just standards of taste, but as their æsthetic significance came to be perceived they won for themselves a place in eighteenth-century taste, but a place that was considered to be outside and above and apart from the beautiful.

Beauty came to include, generally speaking, those qualities and gentle emotions that neo-classic art sought to embody; *sublimity* might contain anything else that seemed susceptible of giving æsthetic pleasure provided that it was grand enough and might conceivably "transport." When the century was half spent, Montesquieu wrote a brief passage on the sublime in which he shows that he felt the opposition between it and contemporary canons of taste. He laments the loss of the sublime and an appreciation of sublimity among the French, and he blames this state of affairs on "this new philosophy, which tells only of general laws," and which, speaking only of "pure understanding, of clear ideas, of reason, of principles," neglects imagination and allows a taste for poetry to die out.[42] General laws, clear ideas, and reason certainly play

[41] Marguetel de St. Denis (St. Evremond), *Works* (London, 1700), III, 323-325.
[42] C. de S. Montesquieu, *Pensées et Fragments inédits* (Bordeaux, 1899-1901), I, 221, 222.

the leading rôle in orthodox neo-classic criticism; no more distinct impression of the opposition between the sublime and eighteenth-century art at its most typical can be found. It is rather remarkable that Montesquieu saw so accurately into the relation of art to the prevailing philosophy, and that he saw the chief weakness of the neo-classical system. The sublime in England permitted the existence both in theory and in fact of those elements which Montesqueiu missed in the French poetry of his day; and it becomes increasingly powerful as the century wears on.

It is right and proper that Addison should have performed the necessary service of separating the sublime from the beautiful. His relation to Longinus has been discussed by Rosenberg,[43] who has no difficulty in demonstrating the influence of *Peri Hupsous* on Mr. Spectator; indeed, Rosenberg regards Addison as barely second in importance to Boileau himself as a popularizer of Longinus among the English. In his conception of the nature of genius, his adherence to the beauties-and-faults method of criticism, and in his frequent use of the word *sublime*, Addison confesses his discipleship.

In his criticism, the word occurs with such frequency as to preclude the possibility of its always having a very definite meaning, though it may be said that Addison holds somewhat loosely to the emotional conception that characterized the sublime in his day. Thus, as early as 1694, in his *An Account of the Greatest English Poets*, Milton is signalized as the sublime poet, in terms that were soon to be *clichés*. His verse is said to be bold and sublime, to be arrayed in majesty, to strike with terror and delight, and to be "above the critic's nicer laws,"[44] the last a thoroughly Longinian and sublime trait. The Alps had awakened a similar response in Addison,[45] as had the Coliseum, which he describes in rather ludicrous lines:

> an amphitheater's amazing height,
> How fills my eye with terror and delight.[46]

The papers on Milton in the *Spectator* continue to emphasize the sublimity of *Paradise Lost* and of the epic *genre* in general. With rather wearisome frequency they aver that the poem is "great and astonishing," that "it raises and astonishes," that "it raises and ennobles."[47] And from

---

[43] Rosenberg, pp. 40–54.   [44] *Works*, Bohn Standard Library (London, 1903), I, 24, 25.
[45] See below, p. 207.   [46] "A Letter from Italy," *Works*, I, 33.
[47] *The Spectator*, ed. H. Morley (London, 1891), II, 385, 456, 478.—In the same year in which Addison criticized *Paradise Lost*, Leonard Welsted's translation of Longinus appeared. In the "Remarks on Longinus," Welsted uses Milton, Shakespeare, and Spenser to illustrate Longinus's meaning. See *Works of Dionysius Longinus*, pp. 144–189.

this time on there were few who doubted that Milton was the sublime poet of the English race. All of this is far from being a theory of the sublime, but Addison finally attempted æsthetic speculation in his papers *The Pleasures of the Imagination*. It is in them that he makes his contribution to the subject of the sublime. They are the first sustained piece of writing on æsthetic in eighteenth-century England. Addison considers questions of taste as they are related to all the arts and to the appreciation of natural scenery; he brings the whole discussion under the head of the imagination, treating the arts as directly related to the imagination; and he tries to explain our perceptions of beauty and the pleasure that we take in the beautiful on the basis of what psychology the philosophy of Locke provided. Addison's papers, though necessarily superficial, are none the less of importance by virtue of their being the first effort in the century to build up a real æsthetic.

Addison considers the pleasures of the imagination as they arise from the great, the uncommon, and the beautiful. It is here that there is at least an implied difference between the sublime and the beautiful, but it must be borne in mind that the two categories did not become mutually exclusive until many years after Addison wrote. Addison certainly conceives of grandeur and beauty as qualities residing in objects, and often in the same objects. For instance, he says: "But there is nothing that makes its Way more directly to the Soul than *Beauty*, which . . . gives a Finishing to any thing that is Great or Uncommon." And again: "The fancy is still more pleased the more it finds of these Perfections [the Great, the Uncommon, the Beautiful] in the same Object."[48]

Greatness is identical with sublimity, but Addison prefers not to use the latter term, probably because of its association with rhetoric and purely critical writings. The effect of greatness is virtually that of sublimity; certainly, in a general way, it is akin to the effect of Kant's sublime. The objects that have this quality are "the Prospects of an open Champaign Country, a vast Desert, a huge Heap of Mountains, high Rocks and Precipices, or a wide Expanse of Waters," in which is found the "ruder kind of Magnificence" that characterizes the stupendous in nature. The æsthetic explanation of the effect of mass and space is that Our Imagination loves to be filled with an Object, or to grasp at any thing that is too big for its Capacity. We are flung into a pleasing Astonishment at such unbounded Views, and feel a delightful Stillness and Amazement in the Soul at the Apprehension of them. . . .[49]

---

[48] *Spectator*, No. 412, II, 718 and 719.—In his "Inquiry Concerning Beauty, Order," etc., Hutcheson refers specifically to *Spectator* 412 when he declares: "*Grandeur* and *Novelty* are two Ideas different from *Beauty*, which often recommend objects to us." *An Inquiry into the Original of our Ideas of Beauty and Virtue* (London, 1725), p. 78.

[49] *Spectator*, No. 412, II, 717.

The essential elements of this analysis of the æsthetic apprehension of mass and space were to appear again and again in theories of the sublime—the aspiration of the imagination to grasp the object; the preordained failure, and the consequent feeeling of bafflement; and the sense of awe and wonder. Various men were to use this pattern with varying significance, but it is essentially the sublime experience from Addison to Kant. Nothing could better indicate Addison's independence of the rhetorical tradition than the fact that he sublimated the emotional element of the experience. The emotions are there, as the words *astonishment* and *amazement* show, but Addison had advanced beyond the simple transport of the Bolevian sublime to a conception of the æsthetic experience in which emotion was only one of the elements.

Addison attributes to natural objects more power to please the imagination than to art,[50] but of all the arts architecture best expresses the great, and consequently is best able to move and to astonish. This is because it deals in mass. Speaking of a large church, Addison says:

everything that is Majestic imprints an Awfulness and Reverence on the Mind of the Beholder, and strikes in with the Natural Greatness of the Soul.[51]

In reading such a statement, one naturally looks back to Longinus and forward to Kant. Of course Addison prefers classic to Gothic architecture because the one is conceived and executed in a great, and the other in a mean manner, since the multiplicity of ornament in Gothic buildings is conducive to a sense of pettiness.

In a later paper, Addison returns to the subject of greatness:

This has suggested to me the reason why, of all Objects that I have ever seen, there is none which affects my Imagination so much as the Sea or Ocean. I cannot see the Heavings of this prodigious Bulk of Waters, even in a calm, without a very pleasing Astonishment. But when it is worked up in a Tempest, so that the Horizon on every side is nothing but foaming Billows and floating Mountains, it is impossible to describe the agreeable Horrour that rises from such a Prospect.[52]

In natural objects, then, vastness and rude magnificence and energy seem to Addison equivalent to the sublime, and consequently to awaken strong emotions. It was well for æsthetic speculation that at this juncture a man so eminent as Addison should have taken the sublime out of the field of literature and applied it to other arts as well as to nature. "Pleasing Astonishment" and "agreeable Horrour" are phrases that indicate the pleasure that Addison, and his age, took in the stronger emotions which they came to associate with the sublime, and incidentally they point to Addison's own experiences in the Alps, when he found that

[50] *Ibid.*, No. 414, II, 723.   [51] *Ibid.*, No. 415, II, 727.
[52] *Ibid.*, No. 489, III, 229.

he could enjoy a landscape so unbeautiful as that of Switzerland, even when it filled him with horror. The sublime emerged from Addison's hands, definitely related to nature, to mass, and to space, and with the usual accretion of emotional effects which the age liked to find in sublimity. After Addison had written, it was no longer likely that anyone should say with Trapp, "Whatever, indeed, is *sublime*, is *beautiful*."[53] The grand and the beautiful were gradually differentiated, and interest began to center very slowly in a psychological study of the effect of grand objects, rather than merely the effect of grand ideas. It was only thus that an æsthetic of sublimity could come into existence, and it is thanks to the reputation of Addison and the enormous popularity of the *Spectator* that the sublime became an important idea in the philosophy of taste and in an investigation of the pleasures of *imagination*, not of rhetoric. No change was visible overnight, and fully to understand the progress of the idea we must glance rapidly at some other, unrelated theories of æsthetic.

An additional impetus had been given to æsthetic speculation by Shaftesbury in his *Characteristicks*, in which, as the upholder of a rather Platonic theory of beauty, he kept alive a view of art not wholly reconcilable with neo-classicism. Unfortunately he did not discuss the sublime,[54] but we shall have occasion to observe that *The Moralists*, 1709, and the *Miscellaneous Reflections*, 1711, dwell on the value of enthusiasm, and thus reinforced the cause of emotionalism in art and in life, while, at the same time, they provided a philosophical basis for the appreciation of the natural world.[55] In 1715, Jean Pierre Crousaz, later to become famous in England through his attack on Pope's *Essay on Man*, had introduced the theory that we have a *feeling* for beauty, that our æsthetic judgments are not judgments at all, but simply a matter of feeling, which is accompanied by pleasant emotions that arise from the heart. Sentiment reaches directly and without delay the same conclusion as to the beauty or ugliness of an object as would reason if time were given for reflection.[56] This is distinctly a change from the judgment of art by rules and by reason; the way had been prepared for such a theory and its far-reaching inferences when the neo-classicists themselves were forced to admit the failure of the rules after a certain point. Pope's "grace beyond the reach of art" is distinctly said "to gain the heart,

[53] Joseph Trapp, *Lectures on Poetry* (London, 1742), p. 115.—Trapp was Professor of Poetry at Oxford from 1708–1718. The lectures were published three times in Latin. The tone of the lectures is quite Longinian, and shows Trapp's familiarity with Boileau.

[54] But see *Characteristicks* (London, 1711), I, 242, 243, for a brief statement of Shaftesbury's disapproval of the sublime style.   [55] See below, pp. 208, 209.

[56] J. P. Crousaz, *Traité du Beau* (Amsterdam, 1724), pp. 11 ff., and 170, 171.

and all its ends at once attain." The Longinian tradition, and especially the sublime, were from the first capable of being easily blended with such a theory, for the sublime was a matter rather of feeling than of the rules.

Crousaz's feeling for beauty became a definite "sixth sense" in l'Abbé Du Bos's *Réflexions Critiques sur la Poésie et sur la Peinture*, 1719,[57] a book that is in part concerned with the emotional significance of art. Du Bos attacked empirically the paradox of the pleasure derived from the image of suffering in art, and reached the conclusion that the emotion which art awakens is an end in itself, a pleasure necessary to achieve relief from the monotony of life.[58] The effects of painful and terrible objects or spectacles are not good; but art satisfies the need for emotion and prevents evil consequences by providing us with the emotional stimulation without the disturbance of mind that the reality would bring about. Finally, Francis Hutcheson reinterprets Shaftesbury's æsthetic, and develops the doctrine of the internal sense by which we perceive beauty.[59] The tendency of all these isolated speculations is to emphasize the subjective element in the æsthetic experience, and to bring more and more into prominence a vague sort of sensationalism, a theme that is to recur more loudly in mid-century speculation. The idea of the internal sense particularly prepared the way for the psychological investigation of the æsthetic experience that is so important during the last half of the century.

But we must return to the sublime, which grows by no such leaps and bounds as the last few paragraphs would indicate. In 1735 there was published an essay by Hildebrand Jacob, entitled "How the mind is rais'd to the Sublime." Although of little importance from the point of view of theory, it may be used conveniently at the end of the present chapter to indicate general trends in taste and the widening scope of the sublime in the third decade of the century. Jacob agrees with Dennis that enthusiasm is the foundation of the sublime in art, but not every one is capable of attaining this lofty emotional state.[60]

A *Mind* truly *disposed* for the *Perceptions* of that, which is *great* and marvelous, whether in nature or in art, is a product of nature and cannot be attained through

[57] J. B. Du Bos, *Réflexions Critiques sur la Poésie et sur la Peinture* (Paris, 1719), II, 305 ff. The book was translated by Thomas Nugent in 1748. For an excellent study of Du Bos's rather important work, see A. Lombard, *L'Abbé Du Bos, un Initiateur de la Pensée Moderne* (Paris, 1913). [58] *Réflexions Critiques,* I, 1–11.

[59] Francis Hutcheson, *An Inquiry into the Original of our Ideas of Beauty and Virtue,* Treatise I. Du Bos had written of this sixth sense. *Réflexions Critiques,* II, 305 ff.

[60] The following summary is made from the pages of the essay as it was published in the *Works of Hildebrand Jacob,* Esq., etc. (London, 1735), pp. 421–426. The essay was translated *in toto* in *Le Pour et Contre,* XIX (1740), 183–192.

study. All the *vast*, and *wonderful Scenes*, ... which the *Universe* affords, have this *Effect* upon the *Imagination*.

These scenes are all vast prospects, but especially the ocean, both in a calm and in a storm, the rising and the setting of the sun, and the stars; dreadful precipices, great ruins, and caverns work similar effects. Magnificence in architecture, the sight of large armies, and vast assemblies of people cause sublime enthusiasm. "The *Charms* of Beauty, or the *Resemblance* of beautiful *Persons*, and Things in fine *Statues*, or *Paintings*" inspire us with this ardor. The sense of hearing operates in the same way, notable examples being the sound of cataracts, the roaring of the sea, the noise of tempests, thunder, and the clash of arms. Three quotations from Milton illustrate this last observation.

SHAKESPEARE was no less susceptible of this *Poetic Enthusiasm*, as his *Enchantments*, *Fairy* Way of Writing, *Spirits*, and *Creatures* of his own formation may testify. The *Easterns* swore by the *Coming on* of *Night;* by the *Whistling* of the *Winds;* by the *Hour* of *Evening*, etc., and by their bold *Metaphors*, and figurative *Style*, we find, they were more than any other People addicted to *Sublimity* of *Expression*.

Other source of sublimity are the power of rhythm and of music; oratory; the passion of love; prayer; superstition; and strange convulsions of nature. By way of conclusion, Jacob adds to this list terror, compassion, "with all that relates to the pathetic;" the heroic deeds and sentiments of great men; reflections on the ruins of time; the contemplation of death, and of the formation and final dissolution of all things.

One wonders as one reads this list how anyone at all capable of enthusiasm managed to get through an ordinary day, without being perpetually elevated to the true sublime; but amusing and heterogeneous as it is, it none the less bears witness to the rapid expansion of the sublime to the point where it included many ideas and objects that play a considerable part in English literature from the time of Thomson. Despite the glances that Jacob throws toward the rhetorical sublime, he none the less holds with Dennis that the sublime can exist only when the mind has responded in a strongly emotional manner to the object or idea contemplated. In addition to this semi-subjective point of view we observe a preponderance of objects from nature as well as a sensitiveness to the mysterious charms of ghosts and enchantments that looks forward to the pre-romanticism of the mid-century. A fairly large group of emotions is allowed by him to contribute to the sublime—love, the joy of intoxication, horror, terror, and melancholy. And the inclusion of the sense of hearing widens the scope in a manner that suggests Burke.

It was the sublime that helped to release this flood of emotionalism into the æsthetic theory of the period. Two years before Jacob wrote his essay, a scornful article on the English taste for sensationalism and horror in tragedy was published in *Le Pour et Contre*. The author called attention to the ferocity of the stories that delight the English on the stage. "It is thence that an English Sophocles or Euripides borrows his ideas of the sublime." The fabulous plots are devoid of characters or manners; the heroines are all fools, and the heroes all kill themselves. Add to this some ghosts, a funeral, and the account of a battle, and you have an English tragedy.[61] The emotionalism of the English sublime as reflected in English literature was evidently puzzling to the more correct critics across the channel. Jacob, although an almost unknown figure, none the less sums up the development of the sublime through the third decade of the century.[62]

[61] *Le Pour et Contre* (1733), I, 71, 72.

[62] Of course all writings on the sublime were not typical of any orderly development. The rhetorical sublime occurs frequently, as for example, in the *Gentleman's Magazine*, v (1735), 252, 253; 358-360; 461-463; in the anonymous *Rhetoric, or the Triumphs of Oratory Delineated* (London, 1736), pp. 37-44; in Edward Manwaring's *Institutes of Learning: Taken from Aristotle, Plutarch, Longinus*, etc. (London, 1737), pp. 8, 9; 16-20; in Henry Pemberton's *Observations on Poetry, Especially on the Epic* (London, 1738), pp. 151-155; and in John Holmes's *Art of Rhetorick* (London, 1739), of which Part II is a summary of Longinus's ideas on sublimity, with illustrations from *The Seasons*. This book seems to have been popular; the British Museum Catalogue lists four editions in the eighteenth century, and three in the nineteenth century. It must have been of service in popularizing Longinus, even though its nature is mainly rhetorical.

CHAPTER IV

THE SUBLIME IN TRANSITION

THE years between 1735 and 1756, when Burke published his epoch-making *Enquiry*, produced only two complete theories of the sublime, but they are of some importance for our study. The relative silence of theorizers implies no lack of interest in the subject, for it was during these years that Longinus attained his greatest popularity, and consequently that the sublime was prominent in the minds of critics. Editions of *Peri Hupsous* appeared in 1730, 1732, 1733, 1743, and 1752; Smith's translation was published in 1739, and Boileau's translation was englished in 1736 and 1752. It is difficult not to see some sort of causal relationship between this interest in Longinus and the writings of the Wartons, Young, and Hurd, during the last years of the fifth and the early years of the sixth decades of the century; for these writings are essentially a revision of the neo-classic system in terms of originality and imagination, the two qualities that Longinus had sponsored from his first appearance on the scene.

The word *sublime* continued to hold a place in the vocabularies of the critics and the criticasters. Armstrong felt impelled to satirize it in the contemptuous couplet:

> But hear their Raptures o'er some specious Rhime
> Dub'd by the musk'd and greasy Mob sublime.[1]

The term was so generally known that Fielding was able to construct a novel on the true and false sublime in human nature, and to draw an analogy between the sublime in art and the sublime in character.[2]

Much of a minor nature was written and thought on the subject during these years. David Hume's *Treatise on Human Nature*, 1739, first claims out attention. From the outset, Hume discarded the old concep-

---

[1] [John Armstrong] *Taste: an Epistle to a Young Critic* (London, 1753), p. 9. A gloss on this passage is furnished in a pseudonymous work of Armstrong, in which he remarks, "Noise and Bluster is what passes for Sublime with the great Majority of Readers. . . ." "Launcelot Temple," "Of Turgid Writing," *Sketches: or Essays on Various Subjects* (London, 1758), p. 11.

[2] Henry Fielding, Preface to "Jonathan Wilde," *Miscellanies* (London, 1743), xxvii–xxix. Fielding had earlier used the false sublime as a means of satirizing heroic tragedy, in the last paragraph of the Preface to the *Tragedy of Tragedies*, 1731. His use of the term for comic effects in *Tom Jones* is familiar to every one.

tion of beauty as a quality residing in objects.[3] On the contrary, he holds
that beauty and deformity are based on the opposing sensations, pleasure and pain; these sensations have their cause in the order and construction of the parts of an object, which, through the constitution of
our nature, or through custom and caprice, awaken in us the one emotion
or the other. "Pleasure and pain, therefore, are not only necessary at-
tendants of beauty and deformity, but constitute their very essence."
Beauty thus becomes "a form which produces pleasure," and "all the effects of these qualities must be deriv'd from sensation." We shall notice
this sensationalistic interpretation of beauty, or rather of the æsthetic
experience, later, when we come to Baillie. It completely subjectivizes
beauty, and Baillie will later subjectivize sublimity.

But Hume is careful to emphasize that the pleasure is purely disinterested; it arises from a perception of utility and convenience in the
structure of the object, but this utility is in no way related to the subject;
it is merely, one might say, an impersonal recognition of the functional
perfection of an object, the knowledge that it is complete and at least
latently purposive.[4] A realization of the disinterestedness of æsthetic
pleasure is all too rare in the first half of the century. One can never be
sure that Dennis's fear, for example, is not merely physical fear, which
is not æsthetic, and the same doubt arises in regard to other writers.
Hume, as one would expect, thinks clearly and philosophically on the
subject.

In the *Treatise* beauty and sublimity are not opposed; indeed Hume
does not use the word *sublime* at all, but his *greatness* is obviously the
same thing. Greatness, he tells us, "whether successive or extended, enlarges the soul, and gives it a sensible delight and pleasure." Since beauty
gives pleasure also, it would seem that Hume has not taken Addison's
hint as to the difference between the two, but has preferred to conclude
that the great is simply a larger beauty. It is beauty accompanied "with a
suitable greatness."

Several problems concerning the sublime occupy Hume's attention.
Why, he asks, does a great distance increase our esteem and admiration
for an object? In other words, why does distance lend sublimity? He
decides that whenever a distant object is presented to the imagination,
we reflect on the "interspers'd distance," and thus conceive a great idea
which awakens æsthetic pleasure.

[3] An interesting general discussion of some of the more prominent aesthetic theories of
the eighteenth century both in England and in France may be found in Folkierski's *Entre
le Classicisme et le Romantisme* (Paris, 1925). See pp. 46–52 for a statement of Hume's
subjective theory of taste.
[4] David Hume, *Philosophical Works*, ed. Green and Grosse (London, 1874), II, 95, 96;
and 150, 151.

But as fancy passes easily from one idea to another related to it, and transports to the second all the passions excited by the first, the admiration, which is directed to the distance, naturally diffuses itself over the distant objects.[5]

Thus by a cumulative process of association distant objects awaken sublime emotions in the soul. We have here an early and an interesting effort to analyse psychologically the experience then called sublime.

Again, Hume takes up the problem of the influence of height and depth on the imagination. Any great elevation of place "communicates a kind of pride or sublimity of imagination," while a sublime imagination "conveys the idea of ascent and elevation." In running from low to high, the imagination finds an opposition, which the soul is eager to meet and overcome. The soul is ready to ascend, even if it does so with great difficulty, and thus the fancy is impelled to soar to heights above the "natural stream of thoughts and conceptions."

This aspiring progress of the imagination suits the present disposition of the mind; and the difficulty, instead of extinguishing its vigor and alacrity, has the contrary effect of sustaining and encreasing it.

Hence virtue, genius, power are associated with height and consequently with sublimity. Vast objects and the difficulty of conceiving them elevate the mind, and enable it to overcome the opposition of which this difficulty is an expression.[6] The part that difficulty plays in the experience of the sublime reminds us of Kant.

In comparison with many essays on sublimity in the eighteenth century, Hume's remarks are incomplete enough, but they are none the less new departures, for they are concerned in the main not with the object *qua* object, but with the experiences of the mind that perceives the object. Hutcheson had carried the subject into the sphere of the subjective by establishing the sixth sense, but he had been powerless to analyse the experience because he lacked a psychology. Hume began the application of psychology to the discussion of the sublime which Baillie was to carry on in the next decade and which Burke was to take to exhaustive lengths. Such speculation forms an oasis in the midst of the more conventional consideration of the sublime and the pathetic. But other brief passages in several writers point to the same general development during the earlier years of the century.

Isaac Hawkins Browne, in 1739, first clearly opposed the beautiful and the sublime, while keeping both qualities well within the boundaries of neo-classic art; the sublime that he shows us has had its wings clipped and shorn, and has been made duly subservient to the neo-classical idea of nature. The soul of beauty, according to *An Essay on Design and Beauty*, is design, which is the love of order that "from NATURE springs."

[5] *Ibid.*, II, 210.   [6] *Ibid.*, II, 212, 213.

NATURE the Power of Harmony displays,
And Truth and Order shine thro' all her Ways.

Art, the imitator of nature, is the imitator of nature's universal order,
for human wit "But copies out the Plan by Nature writ." The element
of design in nature, which makes different parts harmoniously agree,
when carried over into art creates beauty, which is the product of genius
and skill, and

which depends
On the fair Aptitude of Means to Ends.
Parts corresponding, if devoid of this,
Are affectations all, and Emptiness.

Of course there is no reason to comment on the orthodox neo-classicism
of this view of nature and its relation to art.[7] Such a conception of
beauty necessarily minimizes the value of the highly imaginative, the
passionate, the original, the individualistic, all elements of the sublime
as it had been developed in England. It is therefore natural that Browne
should be aware of an inherent difficulty in harmonizing beauty and
sublimity. He states the opposition more boldly than clearly:

Reverse of this, the true Sublime attains
The noblest Purpose by the simplest Means:

But the element of design, even in the sublime, must always be apparent.

unless due Boundaries be plac'd,
Oft will the *Simple* swell into the *Vast:*
Vast, where the Symmetry of parts a-kin
Lies too remote, and is but dimly seen.[8]

This insistence on symmetry and the consequent distrust of the vast is
quite out of harmony with later theories which tend to regard the idea
of the infinite as the sublimest of all ideas. But the strict neo-classicist
preferred unity in variety to the suggestion of the infinite; this was one
reason for the preference of Greek and Roman buildings to Gothic cathedrals, in which the relation of part to part and parts to whole is not easily
grasped at one *coup d'œil.* Nature, itself, our poet goes on to say, is never
really "Vast, or misshapen, or irregular," for all of the parts are pro-
portioned to the "All-Seeing Mind." Hence, since art is "bounded by
Perception still," the sublime must seek that great simplicity, which

Bestows
An awful Stillness, and sublime Repose.

[7] For an excellent recent discussion of the relationship of neo-classicism to the rationalism of the Enlightenment, see Arthur O. Lovejoy, "The Parallel of Deism and Classicism,"
Modern Philology, XXIX (1932), 281–299.

[8] We are reminded of the passage from St. Evremond quoted in the preceding chapter.

> Great without Pomp, and finish'd without Toil,
> Such as the Plans of ANGELO and BOYLE.

Vastness oppresses, but the sublime fills the mind; and intricacy must
be avoided, for "all is *Gothic*, which is intricate." But even a writer who
values symmetry as the "Bright Emmanation of Intelligence" cannot
avoid making the usual exception for the "Wit sublime" (Pindar is the
example) who may "nobly err" and

> Rise in Disorder to a glorious Height:
> And with Contempt of just, tho' vulgar Arts,
> Rear up illustrious, incoherent Parts: . . .[9]

No clearer example could be found of how the sublime was instinctively
felt to be something beyond the sphere of neo-classic beauty. With all
of his effort to discipline this lawless quality and to subjugate it to
harmony and proportion, our author is unable to avoid granting some
license to "great wits." So long as art was conceived to be an imitation
of nature, and so long as nature was regarded as the orderly, harmonious,
universal regularity of the divine mind, there was no place for the sublime of nature and of original genius. One of the missions of the sublime was to help art to escape from the neo-classicist's nature, and to
establish it on a conception of nature that included the very irregularity
and vastness from which the orthodox speculation of the Enlightenment
instinctively shrank.

In the notes to William Smith's translation of Longinus, also published in 1739, we return to ideas that are more typical of the general
development of the sublime than are those of the author of *An Essay on
Design and Beauty*. Smith's was in no sense a revolutionary mind, nor
did he seek to use *Peri Hupsous* in a revolutionary manner, but in view
of the four editions of his version that were published in the eighteenth
century, one can be certain that his habit of illustrating Longinus's dicta
by passages from the older English poets must have been of influence in
shaping popular taste and in connecting the sublime with poetry that
obviously did not fulfil the requirements of the neo-classical standards.

Longinus had illustrated the various aspects of sublimity with passages from Homer and Demosthenes, and other great writers of antiquity. Smith, following Welsted, and to some extent Addison, added
in his notes quotations from Milton and Shakespeare, and thus helped
to relate the two greatest English poets with the very ancients them-

---

[9] [Isaac Hawkins Browne] *An Essay on Design and Beauty* (Edinburgh, 1739), pp. 1–4;
6; 10. The same conception of beauty had been expressed by Robert Morris: "Beauty, in
all Objects, springs from the same unerring Law in Nature, which, in *Architecture*, I would
call Proportion. The just Union and Concordance of the Parts, in an exact Symmetry,
forms the whole, a compleat Harmony. . . ." *Lectures on Architecture* (London, 1734), p. 81.

selves. He considers the storm scenes from *Lear* to be sublime because they are painted with "judicious horror" and "add solemnity to terror."[10] The æsthetic of terror interested Smith as it did many of his contemporaries and successors. He explains that there is a "serious turn, an inborn sedateness in the mind, which renders images of terror grateful and engaging." The gloomy and the solemn can be made to produce "agreeable sensations." He continues:

It is not the blue sky, the chearful sun-shine, or the smiling landskip, that gives us all our pleasure, since we are indebted for no little share of it to the silent night, the distant howling wilderness, the melancholy grot, the dark wood, and hanging precipice. What is *terrible*, cannot be described too well; what is *disagreeable*, should not be described at all, or at least should be strongly shaded.[11]

The habit of relating the sublime to the terrible throughout this period prepares for Burke's theory, and is surely related in some way to the prevalence of this emotion in the graveyard and ruin poetry of the same decades. It should be observed that Smith values terror in art because of its ability to awaken "agreeable sensations." This view of the function of art is typical of the age of sensibility, which produced charnel-house poetry, sentimental gardens, and later that more emotion-provoking *genre*, the gothic novel. It is a far cry from the pure serene of Homer and Virgil to the deliberate sensationalism of much mid-century art, but thanks to the traditional association of the sublime and the pathetic, agreeable sensation could be brought into the sublime, and in some cases could be made its sole basis.

Thus slowly the stronger emotions group themselves under the ægis of Longinus, and along with them go ghosts and darkness and storms and mountains—in short any ideas or objects that the age chose to find terrible. But the delicate intellectual walls of neo-classicism could not long endure the pounding of violent emotions; theory had to be broadened to include these emotions. This was done in essays on the sublime, which grew steadily away from the stricter neo-classical point of view. The art and the theory of the mid-century are foreshadowed when Smith and his contemporaries bring into the fold of the sublime such an un-neo-classic author as Shakespeare, and such startlingly emotional passages as the murder-scene in *Macbeth* and the appearances of the ghosts of old Hamlet and Banquo. Supernatural terror had no place in a rational art or a rational life; on the contrary it kept alive throughout the eighteenth century emotional and imaginative qualities that were to be used by the poets of the romantic era.

The illustrations from Milton add nothing qualitatively to what Dennis, Addison, and Welsted had said, although Smith must have

[10] *On the Sublime*, pp. 58, 59, note 3.   [11] *Ibid.*, p. 34, note 5.

played some part in spreading the gospel of Milton's sublimity; but it is amusing to find Milton embalmed in commentaries on a treatise whose value he seems to have missed, and to observe how Longinus came to bolster up and increase the English poet's growing popularity and to make "the word *Miltonic* mean sublime."[12] Smith's lack of originality in pointing out the sublimities of Shakespeare and Milton does not take away from the service that he must have done for English taste, for the passages that he selected from the older poets were for the most part those that were least neo-classical in spirit and execution, and it was well to have them related to so authoritative a piece of criticism as *Peri Hupsous*, in a version extremely popular throughout the whole century.

Other occasional remarks and scattered bits of writing might be reported if space permitted. The fragmentary correspondence between West and Ashton, schoolboy friends of Gray and Horace Walpole, in which the nature of the sublime is argued, bears witness to the growth of popular interest in the subject. West's letter is incomplete, but one gathers that he held views derived directly from Boileau, and it is against such a conception that Ashton protests. He takes the position that the sublime is "a proper and lively representation of the grand images and aspects of Nature," and he refuses to equate sublimity with good writing alone, averring that the ideas of eternity, immensity, and "unbounded Prospects" are the true sources of the sublime. He witholds assent to West's proposition that the sublime is a species of the pathetic, maintaining that the reverse is true, and that in many instances the sublime has nothing to do with passion, but appeals rather to the imagination and the understanding.[13] In his insistence on grandeur and on the sublimity of external nature, and in his determination to carry the discussion of the sublime away from mere literary expression, Ashton is typical of his age. He does not give us a theory, but he helps to indicate the direction in which the sublime was moving.

The same is true of Hurd's notes to Horace's *Ars Poetica* and *Epistola ad Augustum*, in which Hutcheson's theory of the "sense" of beauty is prominent. Beauty is carefully distinguished from the pathetic, on the grounds that it affords only "*calm* pleasures," and yet the æsthetic value of the pathos is fully recognized.[14] In view of the close relationship be-

[12] The reputation of Milton in the eighteenth century is well known, thanks to Dr. Havens. For other references to Milton as a sublime poet see his *Influence of Milton on English Poetry* (Cambridge, 1922), pp. 8, and 8, note 3; 13, note 2; 16; 17; 18; 19; 21; 24; 36; 37. These among others.

[13] *The Correspondence of Gray, Walpole, West, and Ashton*, ed. Paget Toynbee (Oxford, 1915), Letters 132 and 126, pp. 352–354, and 328–332. Both were written in 1740.

[14] Q. Horatii Flacci, *Ars Poetica. Epistola ad Pisones*, ed. Richard Hurd (London, 1749), pp. 50, 51.

tween the sublime and the pathetic in this period, it is instructive to see how beauty tends more and more to be relegated to the domain of the simple, the harmonious, the unified, and the calm, while the pathetic-sublime grows steadily to include unbeautiful ideas and objects and the more turbulent emotions. For Hurd at any rate, thanks to the Hutchesonian sense of beauty, the sublime, "and every other species of excellence in universal poetry, is the object not of *reason* but sentiment; and can be estimated only from its *impression* on the mind, not by any speculative or general rules."[15] Such ideas as this, besides marking the increasing dislike of the rules, prepare us for the emergence of a more subjective view of sublimity in the works of Burke and his successors, a development that was certain to take place once the theories of Hutcheson and other sensationalists became current. But we must pass on to larger game.[16]

We have seen that Addison first separated the sublime and the beautiful, and that Browne had regarded them as opposites. Akenside, more effectually than either of these two, definitely established the two categories in the public mind, in his poem *The Pleasures of Imagination*, 1744. The great popularity of the poem is familiar to all students of the century; it was read by everyone who made any claim to taste, and wherever it went it must have carried the contradistinction between the sublime and the beautiful, just as the modern novel has carried a vague and vulgarized Freudianism into the uttermost parts of the literary world. Addison and Akenside, between them, did a thorough job. The poem is confessedly based on Addison's essays on the same subject, but since it is in verse it is as speculation considerably vaguer and less satisfactory than its original. The truth of Dr. Johnson's observation that "The words are multiplied till the sense is hardly perceived; attention deserts the mind, and settles in the ear,"[17] does not facilitate the task of analysing Akenside's thoughts; but in the profusion of poetic diction, there may be discovered some ideas that should be recorded.

The lines that deal with the sublime are obviously paraphrased from the thirty-fifth chapter of Longinus's treatise.[18] So, in a less exact manner, is a part of Addison's *Spectator* 412, the second of the papers on

---

[15] *Epistola ad Augustum*, p. 98.

[16] Attention may be called to Charles Avison's consideration of the relation of music to the passions, particularly to *terror*, and to his explanation of the enjoyment of terror as resting on a sense of security. No mention is made of the sublime, but the problem is essentially the same as that attacked by Burke, who uses the same word, *delight*, for the sensation of terror æsthetically perceived. *An Essay on Musical Expression*, The Second Edition (London, 1753), pp. 5, 6, note.   [17] Samuel Johnson, *Works*, VIII, 473.

[18] This was pointed out by J. C. Collins in "Longinus and Greek Criticism," *Studies in Poetry and Criticism* (London, 1905), p. 216.

The Pleasures of the Imagination. Akenside undoubtedly drew directly from Longinus,[19] but it was from Addison that he derived his categories, "the sublime, the wonderful, the fair."[20] In fact, there is little or no difference between Akenside's treatment of the sublime and Addison's treatment of the great. Both associate sublimity with the wild and the vast in nature,[21] but where Addison leaves one in some doubt as to the exact provinces of beauty and sublimity, Akenside is clear and distinct. Beauty is personified, and is addressed as a maiden who

> For ever beamest on th'inchanted heart
> Love, and harmonious wonder, and delight
> Poetic.[22]

Her haunts are calm and peaceful—ripe autumn scenes or the Vale of Tempe. She is graceful, gentle, mild, radiant, and she inspires love,[23] but more important than this, Akenside definitely related beauty to the useful, the good, and the true.

> Does beauty ever deign to dwell where health
> And active use are strangers? Is her charm
> Confess'd in aught, whose most peculiar ends
> Are lame and fruitless? Or did nature mean
> This awful stamp the herald of a lye; . . . ?
>
> . . . Thus was beauty sent from heav'n
> The lovely ministress of truth and good
> In this dark world: for truth and good are one
> And beauty dwells in them, and they in her,
> With like participation. . . .
> . . . Truth enthron'd with her coelestial twins
> The undivided part'ners of her sway
> With good and beauty reigns.[24]

The sublime is quite another matter. Following Longinus's lead, Akenside sees in it an earnest of man's immortality; his great soul is

---

[19] Compare Longinus's "Nor do we view the tiny flame of our own kindling (guarded in lasting purity as its light ever is) with greater awe than the celestial fires, though they are often shrouded in darkness; . . ." (Roberts's translation, p. 135), with Akenside's

> Who but rather turns
> To heav'n's broad fire his unconstrained view,
> Than to the glimm'ring of a waxen flame . . . ?

The Pleasures of Imagination (London, 1744), Book I, ll. 174–176.

[20] Addison speaks of "the great, the uncommon, the beautiful."

[21] Professor Manwaring has discussed Akenside's poem in her *Italian Landscape*, pp. 111, 112.

[22] *Pleasures of Imagination*, Book I, ll. 278–280, p. 25.

[23] *Ibid.*, Book I, ll. 287–335, pp. 25–28.

[24] *Ibid.*, Book I, ll. 350–354, 372, 376, 415–417; pp. 30, 31, 33.

not content with the petty, the finite, but is always yearning for the infinite. There is an affinity between the spirit of man and the vastness of nature, and this affinity is a symbol of man's divine origin and his ultimate attainment of perfection. Vastness in natural objects is the sublime. Hence man ignores a small flame, and turns instinctively to the greatness and splendor of the sun; hence no man would turn aside from a grand view of the Nile or the Ganges in order to

> . . . mark the windings of a scanty rill
> That murmurs at his feet.

Vast scenes, vast expanses of sky, "the flying storm," "the vollied lightning," the sun and the other stars, the empyrean itself—these are sublime objects and sublime ideas, and as such are quite distinct from the softer and more gentle beauty. The sublime is awe-inspiring in its magnitude, its energy, its terror. While beauty is related to virtue and use, the sublime is related to infinity, to immortality, to the divine in man. When nature is beautiful she is "serene;" when she is sublime she is arrayed "in vast, majestic pomp."[25]

The distinction is made even clearer in the revised version of 1772, where the wonderful is omitted, and beauty and sublimity are thrown into direct contrast; but although, after Akenside, the sublime was generally felt to be a separate category of the æsthetic experience, opposed to the beautiful, it remained for Burke in the next decade to develop this opposition to its fullest and to establish it as a completely articulated æsthetic idea. It should be noticed also that Akenside kept in circulation, so to speak, the Longinian idea of the analogy between the vastness of the sublime and the vastness of the soul of man, an idea that, despite radical differences, plays a considerable part in Kant's *Critique of Judgment*. Noteworthy, also, is Akenside's emphasis on the sublimity of the natural world. In this he was not original, but it may be remarked in passing that from about 1745 theorists became prone to draw deductions about the sublime from natural objects and to apply their feelings through analogy to the arts.

The fourth decade of the century produced only two complete theories of the sublime, but both are worthy of attention as indications of what is to follow. Both take us back to the question of the sublime and the pathetic, although they reach different conclusions. But in these essays we take a long step forward toward an æsthetic conception.

Dr. John Baillie's[26] *An Essay on the Sublime*, published posthumously in 1747, in its less original portions derives from Longinus, and where

---

[25] *Ibid.*, Book I, ll. 151-221 and 438-442, pp. 17-21 and 34.

[26] Little seems to be known of Baillie. His name is not found in the *D.N.B.* Ralph Strauss records the publication by Dodsley of his play, *The Married Coquet*, on April 8, 1747, and

it is thus conventional it expresses the traditional views of earlier writers; but despite the unmistakable Longinian flavor of occasional passages, the *Essay* is avowedly written to clarify and expand what Baillie, in common with several of his predecessors, regarded as the confused and inadequate account of sublimity given in *Peri Hupsous*, which is dominated by the idea of "Perfection of Writing in *general*."[27] After recording the usual generalizations, such as that the sublime "is peculiar to a Genius noble, lofty, comprehensive" and that it affects powerfully and instantaneously, he begins his analysis, whereby he intends to distinguish sublimity from the pathetic and the figurative. His treatment of the matter is to some extent psychological, and it is because of this fact that the *Essay* assumes importance. Associationism and Locke's conception of the mind's receiving knowledge through sensation about make up Baillie's psychology, but, in view of the predominatingly psychological approach of the last half of the century, it is enough to give him value as a pioneer.

Baillie frees himself from all rhetorical preconceptions, and attacks the problem through an analysis of the sublime in nature, for he maintains that the sublime in writing is a description of the sublimity of the external world, "painting to the *Imagination* what *Nature* herself offers to the *Senses*." The analysis of the sublime in writing can be made through argument by analogy from the sublime in nature.[28] From this time, the æsthetic perception of the natural world plays an important part in treatises on the sublime, thanks to the influence of Longinus, Dennis, Addison, and Akenside.

Baillie very nearly evolves the idea of empathy when he declares that when one sees a grand object he is "affected with something which as it were extends his very Being, and expands it to a kind of Immensity." Thus arises that "exalted Sensation," that recognition by the soul of its own vastness which is the source of the exaltation and pride that are integral parts of the sublime. As it is unnecessary to say, this idea

---

of the *Essay* on April 20 of the same year. See *Robert Dodsley* (London and New York, 1910), p. 333. The *Biographia Dramatica* states that he was one of the "physicians to St. George's Hospital, and also physician to the English army in Flanders. He died of a spotted fever at Ghent, in December, 1743." See D. E. Baker, *Biographia Dramatica*, etc. (Dublin, 1787), I, 9. The date of his death seems to be correct, since it agrees with the appearance of Baillie's name in the list of deaths in "The Monthly Chronologer," *The London Magazine* (January, 1747), p. 49.

[27] Hurd expressed the same dissatisfaction with Longinus a few years later. See *Epistola ad Augustum*, pp. 99–101. It was inevitable that, as speculation began to take on the appearance of æsthetic, Longinus should seem out of date, but the fact that the sublime grows away from *Peri Hupsous* in no way injured the reputation of Longinus, as we have seen. [28] *Essay on the Sublime*, p. 3.

is essentially Longinian, and is not only expressed in, but is implicit throughout the Greek treatise. Baillie would call sublime only those objects that so operate on the mind, and they have one absolutely essential quality—vastness. The list that he gives of vast objects is the conventional one of the age—large prospects, vast extended views, mountains, the heavens, and the ocean. There follows an important passage in which the Longinian idea is translated into the language of sensationalist psychology, to emerge as a rudimentarily æsthetic concept.

But as a *Consciousness* of her [the soul's] own *Vastness* is what pleases, so nothing raises this Consciousness but a *Vastness* in the *Objects* about which she is employed. For whatever the *Essence* of the *Soul* may be, it is the *Reflections* arising from *Sensations* only which makes [sic] her acquainted with Herself, and know her *Faculties*. Vast objects occasion vast Sensations, and vast sensations give the Mind a higher Idea of her own Powers—small scenes (except from Association . . .) have never this Effect; . . . the *Soul* is never filled by them.[29]

There enter into this paragraph several concepts which should be pointed out. In the first place, Baillie is founding his theory on sensations. There is no talk of the intellect or of a sixth sense; the æsthetic perception of sublimity rests wholly upon sensation as it is directly stimulated by the sublime object. The immediate perception of sublimity is achieved through the immediate and direct sensation which the object, either in nature or in art, stimulates. Such a view is an advance beyond that which conceived of a mythical sense for perceiving beauty, and abstracted it into a concept so vague and ambiguous as that inherent in the earlier theories of taste. It was a notable moment when these intervening æsthetic agents were swept aside, and the investigator was left with the object and the perceiving mind for his data, for only when this happened could the subjective view which was to characterize thought toward the end of the century be attained. Heretofore there had been a tendency to regard the sublime as a quality residing in objects, having objective reality like the primary characteristics of matter. The idea lingered on for a long time, but from 1747, interest began to be centered in the exploration of the subject rather than the description of the object. When the interest of thinkers turned to sensation and the emotions consequent to sensation, the first step had been taken toward that subjectivity fully developed in the *Critique of Judgment*.

The second idea is that of association, which, as everyone knows, was to become the dominant psychological theory of the century. Hutcheson had used it to explain the diversity of men's æsthetic judgments, and, as we have seen, Hume had made considerable use of it; other writers such

[29] *Ibid.*, pp. 4–7.

as Dennis and Hurd had hinted at its usefulness. Baillie takes it up, and employs it as others were to do in order to account for the sublime effect of objects which in themselves are not vast or grand.

It is noteworthy also that Baillie insists on the fact that vastness is a necessary quality in objects that elevate the soul. We recall St. Evremond's condemnation of the word, and the efforts of Browne to maintain proportion and harmony in the sublime. Baillie has no such compunctions. To the neo-classicist the vast may have seemed ugly and formless, but Baillie will restrict the sublime in no such manner. And because of this divorce between neo-classic beauty and the sublime, he comes near to an æsthetic of mass and space.

Although vastness is the principal characteristic of sublime objects, Baillie finds that "a certain degree of uniformity and novelty are [sic] also requisite." Uniformity enables the imagination to conceive the whole from a glimpse of a part. This process of reconstructing the object *ex pede Herculem* conveys "the vastest *Sensation*" under circumstances which could not otherwise produce the sublime. Uniformity thus becomes of great æsthetic value.

For what a different Conception must the Soul have of herself, when with the greatest *Facility* she can view the greatest Objects, and when with *Pain* she must hurry from part to part, and with *Difficulty* acquire even an incomplete View? . . . When an Object is *vast*, and at the same time *uniform*, there is [sic] to the *Imagination* no Limits to its Vastness, and the Mind runs out into *Infinity*, continually *creating* as it were from the *Pattern*.[30]

These remarks are surely of value in the development of the sublime. They stress the inner workings of the mind, they admit the value of illusion, they turn the soul in upon itself and regard the sublime not so much as an abstract quality in objects as the sensations and emotions and perceptions of the individual. It is curious that Baillie should consider difficulty to be derogatory to the sublime. Burke, Kant, and others were to stress the element of pain and difficulty *overcome* in the apprehension of vast objects, but Baillie maintains that when the mind perceives infinity with ease, and then only, sublime sensations arise.

Baillie is quite unorthodox when he considers the relation between the sublime and the pathetic. He finds that the two qualities have nothing to do with each other because the sublime composes the mind and bestows on it "a solemn *sedateness*" by filling it with "one large, simple, and uniform *Idea*, . . . one simple, grand *Sensation*." Admiration, arising from the uncommon, is the one passion that constantly accompanies the sublime.[31] Fundamentally, then, Baillie stands apart from the eighteenth-century tradition of the sublime as it developed from Boileau to Burke.

[30] *Ibid.*, pp. 8, 9.　　　　[31] *Ibid.*, pp. 10, 11.

That the sublime strikes, ravishes, transports, had been the starting point for many theorists, and had resulted in the general admission of the pathetic into the sublime. Baillie will none of this. If the idea is vast it fills the mind to the exclusion of emotion and all else; it results in a pure serene. But when Baillie states these opinions, he is speaking theoretically and is concerned with the *essence* of sublimity alone. He admits freely the difficulty of abstracting sublimity from emotions.

In nature, then, the sublime is made up of vastness, uniformity, and novelty, and these qualities beget "vast sensations" that fill the mind and give the soul a feeling of elevation and serenity as she realizes her greatness. Having thus isolated and analysed the sublime, Baillie proceeds to study by analogy the sublime of the passions, but it is not the passions that one *feels*, but the passions that one contemplates in others that he discusses. Passions can produce "an exalted and *sublime Disposition*" only when their objects are universally allowed to be sublime, for only then can the Imagination be "thrown into large *Prospects*, and extended *Scenes* of *Action*."[32] Not only are heroism, power, desire for fame, universal benevolence, and patriotism regarded as sublime, but desire for honor, and the wholly immoral "ravaging conqueror" may become sublime, so long as the object aimed at is vast and great.[33] All of this is quite dull, but at the end of this section of his book, he presents for the first time an analysis of the sublime that shows some awareness of the emotional complexity that plays so large a part in later theories.

Perhaps the chief fault of writers on the sublime during the first half of the eighteenth century is their habit of over-simplifying the æsthetic experience, of attempting to find the *one* sublime emotion or quality. Baillie is not guilty of this particular error. He is interested in the complexity and the apparent paradoxes that make up the sublime. Thus, the sublime dilates and elevates the soul, while fear sinks and contracts it; yet both are felt upon viewing what is great and awful. The explanation is that the two opposing states "succeed each other by such infinitely quick Vicissitudes, as to appear instantaneous." Moreover, the same idea, thanks to association, can produce the opposite kinds of sublimity. The idea of an angry God, for example, creates the emotion of sublime terror; the idea of a benign God awakens "the joyous sublime." The sublime predominates, but it is modified by emotions, depending upon the associations that are awakened at any given moment. These various emotions occasion a confusion of ideas and sensations; the grand may mingle with the pathetic, and the pathetic may be mistaken for the sublime. Nevertheless there is no real reason for confusion if the natures of the two are closely examined, for the sublime fills the mind with a solemn sedateness and the pathetic agitates it by "crouding into the Thoughts a thousand different Objects, and hurrying the mind into various scenes."[34]

Sublimity in the other arts is not neglected by Baillie. Averring that æsthetic pleasure ("delight") arises from "a certain *Harmony* or *Disposition* of . . . Parts" or from association, he considers the sublime in architecture, painting, and music. The theory of association often obscures rather than illuminates æsthetic. It was a necessary phase in the development of a psychological point of view, but it often obstructed the attainment of a purely æsthetic consideration of line, mass, and form by introducing extraneous, and nonæsthetic ideas. This is clearly shown in Baillie's discussion of architecture. Having promulgated a theory of sublimity based on vastness, he might easily have progressed to an æsthetic of mass and line in buildings. But no; association gives sublimity to architecture by introducing the ideas of riches, grandeur, and power, which, together with "the Imagination of *Strength* and *Durableness*," create sublime sensations. In painting sublimity consists in representing passions and grand objects. In music "grave" sounds, when the notes are long, are sublime, for they affect the ear as extended prospects do the eye.[35] In Baillie's essay, the scope of the sublime is considerably widened. Although he separates it from the pathetic, he none the less carries the discussion into the realm of psychology, and achieves the first important theory that bears any resemblance to æsthetic.

The subjective point of view which Baillie takes is held somewhat less emphatically by Robert Lowth, the successor of Joseph Spence as Professor of Poetry at Oxford,[36] in his *Praelectiones de Sacra Poesi Hebraeorum.* The question of the sublimity of the Hebrew poets and of the New Testament is almost as old as Christianity itself. The fourth book of St. Augustine's *On Christian Doctrine* is a vigorous defence of the Bible from those enemies of the faith who attacked the divine inspiration of the New Testament by pointing out the barbarous Greek in which it is written and its lack of eloquence in the ancient sense of that word. Those "ill-taught men who think our authors contemptible; not because they do not possess, but because they do not display, the eloquence which these men value so highly" rouse the Bishop of Hippo to claim that "all

---

[34] *Ibid.*, pp. 31–33.   [35] *Ibid.*, pp. 35–39.

[36] Lowth held this position from 1741 to 1750, during which time he read his famous lectures. They were first published in 1753, and first translated by Gregory in 1787. Remarkably learned for their day, they established the reputation of their author as an erudite man and a sound critic, and helped to secure him the many bishoprics which he held. See the account of his life in the *D.N.B.*

those powers and beauties of eloquence" are to be found in the sacred writings, as well as an eloquence peculiarly the property of the inspired men who wrote them down from the dictate of the Holy Spirit. Augustine quotes examples of the great style from both the prophets and from St. Paul.[37] The question from the outset was a serious one, on which rested the very authority of the Bible and of the Church. The controversy continued sporadically, even into the period that we are studying. Thus Henrie Leslie, writing of the authority of the scripture in 1639, says:

> Wee give credite unto her Report; but when we peruse it, and consider the divinity of the matter, the sublimity of the style, the efficacy of the speach, we are fully perswaded that the same is from *God* indeed.[38]

A score of years later, Robert South attempted to prove that in the Bible we have not only a body of religion, but a system of rhetoric as well, and that only an atheist could fail to see the sublimity of the sacred writings.[39] In 1725 Anthony Blackwell wrote a defence of the sublimity of the Bible, in which the Longinian sublime played a considerable part. He adopts Boileau's interpretation of Longinus, declaring that the sublime is "just, grand, and marvellous Thought." It strikes like lightning; it may employ all the ornaments of language, yet it "needs none of 'em"; translation cannot mar it; it creates ecstasy and transport; and it is beyond "cavil and criticism."[40] This sublime he finds *par excellence* in the writings of the Old Testament authors, which he seeks to show are more sublime than the works of the Greeks. The words of Jesus, when "he chides the sea, and hushes its boisterous waves into an immediate calm" surpass the sublimity of "the most majestic figures in Longinus." And although he professes to find all styles employed in the Bible, he insists that it is the greatness of thought that gives sublimity to the Bible, and that the sacred authors could dispense with the artificiality of rhetorical figures, because they had "innumerable advantages from the dignity of their subject, and the grand consequences of their doctrines."[41]

In the mid-eighteenth century, sublimity came forward once more in religious controversy in the rather amusing warfare that was carried

---

[37] Aurelius Augustine, *Works*, ed. Rev. Marcus Dods (Edinburgh, 1871–1876), IX, 124–167. [38] Henrie Leslie, *A Treatise of the Authority of the Church* (Dublin, 1639), p. 20. [39] Robert South, *Forty-Eight Sermons*, etc. (London, 1715), IV, 30–32.

[40] Anthony Blackwell, *The Sacred Classics Defended and Illustrated*, etc. (London, 1725), pp. 276–277. Cf. the much later volume by "Courtney Melmoth" (S. J. Pratt), *The Sublime and Beautiful of Scripture* (London, 1777), which is based on Longinus's five sources of sublimity.

[41] *The Sacred Classics Defended*, etc., pp. 1, 2; 2–8; 248, 249; 278; 285; 295–319; 345. The same point of view is adopted by Philip Dodridge in *A Course of Lectures on the Principal Subjects of Pneumatology, Ethics, and Divinity* (London, 1763), p. 370.

on between Warburton and Conyers Middleton, with Thomas Leland barking at Warburton's heels like an excited terrier, and Hurd defending Warburton with all his vehemence. Middleton claimed that the gift of tongues lasted only one day, and that the apostles could not speak all languages, and he cited as evidence their "utterly rude and barbarous" Greek. Warburton, finding this a heretical insinuation that the scriptures were not inspired, tried to prove that sublimity is "accidental and arbitrary, and depends on custom and fashion," and that the simplicity of the New Testament in no way prevents its being sublime, as the language of God should be. Leland joined the fray with an attack on Warburton's conception of eloquence and sublimity, and diverted the controversy from matters of doctrine to a discussion of the relation of simplicity and the pathetic to the sublime.[42]

But these doctrinal disputes were not the only means by which attention was called to the sublimity of the Bible. It will be remembered that Longinus himself had connected the sublime with biblical literature in his use of Genesis i. 3 as an illustration of that elevation which accompanies high thinking, and that Boileau's controversy with Huet and Le Clerc had, as we are too inclined to say today, given publicity to the sublimity of the Mosaic account of the creation. The pious were only too eager to discover sublimity where *a priori* it should most likely exist— in the writings of the men who were under the direct inspiration of Jehovah. Moreover, the Hebrew poets *are* sublime, if the word has any validity at all,[43] and it is therefore not strange that once men became concerned with sublimity, they should have been impressed with the abundance of that quality in the Psalms, Job, and the writings of Isaiah.

It would be futile to multiply examples of an opinion that is expressed almost unanimously by critics and æstheticians throughout the whole century. It may find pious expression, as in the case of Henry Felton, who finds the "Sublime Majesty" of the "Sacred Penmen" unthinkable save as coming from the spirit of God;[44] or of Shaftesbury, who holds that sacred subjects cannot be well treated in poetry, since no mortal

[42] Conyers Middleton, "An Essay on the Gift of Tongues," *Miscellaneous Works* (London, 1755), II, 395 ff. William Warburton, *The Doctrine of Grace*, etc. (London, 1763), I, 1–89. Thomas Leland, *Dissertation on the Principles of Human Eloquence*, The Second Edition (Dublin, 1765), pp. 38–72. [Richard Hurd] *Letter to the Rev. Dr. Thomas Leland* (London, 1764), *passim*.

[43] Coleridge once said: "Could you ever discover anything sublime in our sense of the term, in the classic Greek literature? Sublimity is Hebrew by birth." *Table Talk and Omniana*, ed. T. Ashe (London, 1884), p. 174. Wordsworth held the same opinion. See E. F. Carritt, *Theory of Beauty* (London, 1923), p. 220.

[44] Henry Felton, *A Dissertation on Reading the Classics, and Forming a Just Style*, Fifth Edition (London, 1753), pp. 90–93.

poet can rise to the sublime requisite to the subject, an opinion which Dr. Johnson was to express years later.[45] The critic may simply state as an accepted fact that the Bible is the sublimest of books.[46] It may find fanciful expression as in the case of Joseph Warton's supposed translation of a manuscript of Longinus, in which the Greek critic is represented as maintaining with enthusiasm the superior sublimity of the poetry of the Old Testament to that of the greatest of the Greeks.[47] Or again Longinus's approval of Genesis I. 3 may be used to prove that the sublime is not incompatible with simplicity, but on the contrary is closely allied to it.[48] And all of this continues to be said throughout the century.

It may be assumed, then, that when Lowth informed the young Oxonians in his opening lecture that the mind can conceive nothing more "elevated, more beautiful, or more elegant" than Hebrew poetry, "in which the almost ineffable sublimity of the subject is fully equalled by the energy of the language and the dignity of the style"[49]—when Lowth made this statement, none of his listeners could have been impressed by the novelty of the ideas expressed. If in lecturing learnedly on Hebrew poetry the future Bishop of London was introducing an innovation, he was not so original in his insistence on the sublimity of the Old Testament poets.

In his first lecture, Lowth traces the origin of poetry to religion, and since the purpose and the end of the Hebrew poetry is religious, he has no difficulty in proving on these grounds that it is more natural and perfect, more noble and elevated, than Greek poetry. Poetry, he says, is an art derived from nature alone, and to be attributed to the more violent "affections," "the nature of which is to express themselves in an animated and lofty tone, with a vehemence of expression far remote from vulgar use." These affections are expressed with impetuosity; "they burst forth in sentences pointed, earnest, rapid, and tremulous; and the style is adapted to the emotions that are expressed. This is particularly true of admiration and delight, the passions that are excited by religious contemplation."[50] There is a kinship (though there is no proof of direct

[45] Anthony Ashley Cooper, "Advice to an Author," *Characteristicks, etc.* (London, 1711), I, 359. J. E. Brown, *Critical Opinions of Samuel Johnson* (Princeton, 1926), pp. 226–229.
[46] [John Newbery], *The Art of Poetry on a New Plan* (London, 1762), I, 22. Hugh Blair, *Lectures on Rhetoric and Belles Lettres*, I, 61, 62. Joseph Priestley, *A Course of Lectures on Oratory and Criticism* (London, 1777), pp. 162, 163.
[47] *The Adventurer*, No. 51, Tuesday, May 1, 1753; and No. 57, Tuesday, May 22, 1753.
[48] Lawrence Sterne, Sermon XLII, *Works* (London, 1823), III, 397–402. [J. Stedman], *Laelius and Hortensia* (Edinburgh, 1782), p. 98. John Ward, *A System of Oratory*, etc. (London, 1759), II, 174.
[49] Robert Lowth, *Lectures on the Sacred Poetry of the Hebrews*, tr. G. Gregory (London, 1787), I, 37.   [50] *Ibid.*, I, 161, 162.

influence) with Dennis in the view that emotion is the source of poetry, that the strongest emotions are those that arise from religion, and that hence they produce the finest poetry.

Turning to sublimity, Lowth reverts to Longinus, and draws the conventional distinction between the sublime style, and "that force of composition, . . . which excites the passions, and which expresses ideas at once with perspicuity and elevation," regardless of ornate language.[51] No very clear idea of the nature of the sublime emerges from Lowth's remarks; he is as vague as if he had used the time-honored phrase, *le je-ne-sais-quoi*. Nevertheless, for convenience he considers sublimity from three points of view—the sublime of expression, of sentiment, and of passion. The last is by far the most interesting; his views on the first two may be condensed briefly.

The diction of prose, according to Lowth, differs from that of poetry in so far as the one is the language of reason, cool, temperate, and humble, while the other is the language of emotion, impetuous, vivid, energetic, and often elevated. A psychological explanation is sought.

The mind, with whatever passion it be agitated, remains fixed upon the object that excited it; and while it is earnest to display it, is not satisfied with a plain and exact description; but adopts one agreeable to its own sensations, splendid or gloomy, jocund or unpleasant. For the passions are naturally inclined to amplification; they wonderfully magnify and exaggerate whatever dwells upon the mind, and labour to express it in animated, bold, and magnificent terms.[52]

Rhetoric still lays a hand on æsthetic, but not so heavy a hand as it once had done. These emotions and their "amplifications" are derived from the rhetoricians, but Lowth uses them to explain the effects which Wordsworth was to refer to the imagination when he spoke of throwing over objects "a certain colouring of the imagination." They are using different words to describe the same process—artistic creation.

The result of this action of the emotions is the use of imagery and extraordinary expressions. When Hebrew poetry is sublime, its expression takes the form of concise and abrupt forms of verse; boldness of figures; spirited, vehement, and perplexed forms of expression; crowded and abrupt sentences; force and impetuosity; bold and magnificent expressions; animation and energy.[53] Lowth sums up the matter of the expression of sublimity when he says that Hebrew poetry "consists of sentences, pointed, energetic, concise, and splendid; that the sentences are truly elevated and sublime, the language bright and animated, the expression and phraseology uncommon."[54]

So much for the outward show. The sublime of sentiment, one dis-

[51] *Ibid.*, I, 307.   [52] *Ibid.*, I, 309.
[53] *Ibid.*, I, 314; and 316, 317.   [54] *Ibid.*, I, 325.

covers, is equivalent to Longinus's "grandeur of conception." It is the spirit that informs the sublime of language, and the two are separable only theoretically. Lowth defines this aspect of sublimity somewhat vaguely, as proceeding from boldness of spirit and elevation of soul, and displaying itself in the sublimity of the subject, in the choice of adjuncts, and in the splendor of imagery with which all of this is illustrated.[55] He calls to mind the much-discussed creation of light, and explains that its sublimity depends on the quick comprehension of the divine power which an accumulation of fine phrases would prevent.[56] All of this is thoroughly Bolevian, and by Lowth's time commonplace.

A more interesting idea is expressed when Lowth deals with the sense of difficulty that follows the attempt of the imagination to apprehend a great thought. When immense ideas are expressed simply, the greatness of the subject stands out more clearly, and the imagination labors to comprehend what is beyond its power of comprehension. This ineffectual endeavor demonstrates the sublimity of the object.[57] Baillie would have none of this idea, but Burke and Kant were to use it effectively.

In view of the fact that Lowth believes that poetry takes its rise from emotion, it is not surprising that his lecture on the sublime of the passions should prove the best part of his discussion. Poetry, he repeats, is the "effect of mental emotion;" it is the result of the effect of agitated passions "upon the mind and body, upon the imagination, the senses, the voice, and respiration."[58] Here Lowth touches on a curious problem— the relation of art to the whole human mechanism, physical and mental. Burke was to follow out this scheme of inquiry several years later, and in so doing was to relate æsthetic to psychology, once and for all. Lowth might very well have carried this idea to interesting conclusions; as it was, the subject of his lectures held him fast to criticism, so that it is only in scattered passages that one is led to suspect that he was aware of problems that his contemporaries were to discuss.

Despite his critical point of view, Lowth nevertheless manages to penetrate somewhat into the effect that sublime objects have upon the perceiving mind. Poetry, he says, is an imitation, and the most agreeable of all imitations is that of emotion, which awakens an instantaneous response, as no other description can.

Hence that sublimity, which arises from the vehement agitation of the passions, and the imitation of them, possesses a superior influence over the human mind; whatever is exhibited to it from without, may well be supposed to move and agitate it less than what it internally perceives, of the magnitude and force of which it is previously conscious.[59]

[55] *Ibid.*, I, 346–348.   [56] *Ibid.*, I, 350.
[57] *Ibid.*, I, 353.   [58] *Ibid.*, I, 356.   [59] *Ibid.*, I, 368, 369.

Confused this statement is, but it bears witness to a willingness to regard sublimity not so much as a quality of the object as an effect on the subject. The mention of magnitude and force shows us how traditional was Kant's two-fold division into the mathematical and dynamic.

Lowth's explanation of æsthetic pleasure is unoriginal and disappointing.[60] In another place he is more informative. Hitherto, critics had for the most part separated the sublime into categories: the pathetic sublime, and the sublime that has no relation to the pathetic. Lowth insists on the distinction between the sublime and the pathetic, but admits "a kind of affinity or connexion."

> The pathetic includes the passions which we feel, and those which we excite. Some passions may be expressed without any thing of the sublime; the sublime also may exist, where no passion is directly expressed; there is, however, no sublimity where no passion is excited.[61]

This is a nice distinction; its value lies merely in the fact that it once more unmistakably points toward the subjective point of view, for it considers the effect of an object rather than its actual nature.

Five emotions accompany sublimity—admiration, which is its "efficient cause," and joy, love, hatred, and fear.[62] The discussion of these emotions is brief and of little value. But it must be observed that Lowth follows the spirit of the age in discussing the relation of the sublime to the pathetic.

The very aim of the lectures precluded the possibility of developing a thorough æsthetic system. They are criticism, and criticism can become an æsthetic only inferentially, for it is essentially an analysis by the reason of things created, and not an investigation through experience of the nature of artistic creation and æsthetic perception. If Lowth is less interesting than Baillie, his remarks are none the less typical of how the sublime developed through its traditional association with the pathetic into a concept that called for an analysis of the subject and the feelings and emotions that he experiences when he judges æsthetically.

---

[60] He finds that the "exquisite sensation of pleasure" which the imitative arts produce arises "partly from the contemplation of the imitation itself; partly from the consciousness of our own felicity, when compared with the miseries of others; but principally from the moral sense. Nature has endued man with a certain social and generous spirit; and commands him not to confine his cares to himself alone, but to extend them to all his fellow creatures; to look upon nothing which relates to mankind as foreign to himself." *Ibid.*, I, 370, 371. [61] *Ibid.*, I, 371–374.

[62] *Ibid.*, I, 377–387. Cf. Lowth's poem, "The Genealogy of Christ, as it is Represented on the Last Windows of Winchester College Chapel":

> Thy strokes, great Artist, so sublime appear,
> They check our pleasure with an awful fear.

Pearch's *Collection of Poems* (London, 1783), IV, 77.

CHAPTER V

BURKE'S *ENQUIRY*

DURING the first half of the eighteenth century, as we have seen, theories of sublimity were all more or less derived from Longinus, although there was a general opinion that *Peri Hupsous* was inadequate in its methods of analysing the æsthetic experience. The preoccupation of critics and theorists such as Dennis, Jacob, and Lowth with the relation of the sublime to the pathetic bears witness to the continuation of the rhetorical tradition. They would, perhaps, never have studied the question had not the rhetoricians of antiquity and of their own age based much of the persuasive power of their art on the emotions which the great style evokes. Such a description as Quintilian gives of the effect of Cicero's defense of Cornelius is typical. He says that it was "the sublimity, splendour, the brilliance, and the weight of his eloquence that evoked such clamorous enthusiasm."[1] Boileau had reinforced the conception of the sublime as primarily emotive in his much-paraphrased "*enlève, ravit, transporte*," and the writers of manuals of oratory and rhetoric, both in France and in England, took over the word *sublime* and kept alive the conception that it represents a device for persuading through the emotions. Longinus lent himself as readily to this point of view as he did to that expressed in the nascent æsthetic of England.[2] It is against a background of rhetoric, then, that the sublime begins to emerge, and it is no matter for surprise that it should take on a certain coloring from its origins. It was only in the works which we have studied that the sublime began to free itself from rhetoric.

But Boileau had made it possible to consider the sublime apart from the high style, and it was this that the English began to do. The difference between the rhetorical sublime and the pathetic sublime of the early eighteenth-century theorists is largely that in the one emotions have a practical value, to persuade against the will and the reason of the audience, and in the other they are regarded as the source of æsthetic pleasure. In the latter case, the sublime can be sought in all the arts, and the ques-

[1] *Institutio Oratoria*, VIII, iii, Vol. III, 213.

[2] It would be useless to quote from all of these works, for all of them say the same thing with damnable iteration. A few references, cited almost at random, can suffice. Le Clerc, *Parrhasiana*, Done into English by . . . (London, 1700), pp. 9, 16, 85; Gibert, *Réflexions sur la Rhetorique* (Paris, 1705), pp. 37, 38; Fénelon, *Dialogue Concerning Eloquence in General*, tr. Wm. Stevenson (London, 1722), p. 16; Rollin, *De la Manière d'Enseigner et d'Etudier les Belles Lettres*, Seconde Edition (Paris, 1728), pp. 103, 104; *Rhetoric* (London 1736), p. 41; *Traité de l'Eloquence* (Paris, 1752), pp. 54, 55.

tion of why certain objects and certain subjects give pleasure can be approached. When the emotions that the sublime traditionally awakened could be regarded as an end in themselves, rather than as a means to an end, an æsthetic theory was possible.

The preoccupation with emotions on the part of theorists was in every way healthful. The latent danger of the neo-classical theory (almost always, in England, only latent) was a too great standardization of literature under the current theory of a universalized nature, and a tendency to overemphasize the value of reason in art. The sublime came as a justifiable category into which could be grouped the stronger emotions and the more irrational elements of art. The speed with which theorists assimilated under the Longinian sublime the emotions of terror, horror, and ecstasy, and the vast and more overwhelming aspects of the natural world bears witness to the need which was felt for a method of making respectable the more un-neo-classical elements of art.

Moreover, an interest in the emotional *effect* of objects definitely pointed to the individual response rather than to a code of externally applied rules as an æsthetic norm. The problem to be considered gradually came to be by what means objects in nature and art arouse pleasurable emotions, not to what degree a work of art follows the rules. Thus these early theories of the sublime consider the nature of sublime objects and the emotional responses that they awaken, and tend to stand midway between an objective and a subjective point of view. The lack of an adequate psychological method is apparent in all the men whose work we have considered, but Addison, Hume, and Baillie at least partially succeeded in creating an æsthetic of the sublime.

But though their method may be different from that of Longinus, almost all their ideas can be traced back to *Peri Hupsous*. The astonishment that the sublime awakens, the expansion and elevation of the soul when brought face to face with grandeur of thought or grandeur of scenery, the analogy between the effect of the vast in nature and of the sublime in art had all been suggested by Longinus. In working out their theories, these early writers cleared much ground, emphasized the important ideas in the Longinian discussion of sublimity, and in the case of Baillie clearly indicated the method of analysis that was to be followed in the more fruitful years after the middle of the century.

It was in an effort to correct the confusion and ambiguity of discussions of beauty and sublimity that young Burke undertook his investigation of the subject. The preface to the first edition[3] of the *Philosophical*

---

[3] I refer to the edition published by Dodsley in 1757. The question of the date of the *Enquiry* is puzzling. All of Burke's biographers name 1756 as the year in which it appeared. In *Notes and Queries*, CXLVIII (Jan. 31, 1925), 80, Mr. F. A. Pottle called attention to

Enquiry into the Origin of our Ideas of the Sublime and Beautiful called
attention to the fact that "no exact theory of our passions, or a knowledge of their genuine sources" existed. Moreover, Burke had observed
that the ideas of the sublime and the beautiful were frequently confounded, and that even Longinus had "comprehended things extremely
repugnant to each other, under one common name of the *Sublime*." The
only escape from this "extremely inaccurate and inconclusive" reasoning
seemed to him to be

from a diligent examination of our passions in our own breasts; from a careful
survey of the properties of things which we find by experience to influence those
passions; and from a sober and attentive investigation of the laws of nature, by
which these properties are capable of affecting the body, and thus of exciting
our passions.[4]

This declaration indicates with sufficient clarity the point of view which
Burke takes. He breaks with tradition in so far as he can, and sets out to
make an original investigation of the nature of the beautiful and the sublime. But he carries over from the past several ideas. He holds (although
we shall see that at times he almost escapes from the idea) that sublimity in some way depends on qualities residing in the object, but his
analysis leaves ample room for a psychological and even a physiological
investigation of the origin of the æsthetic experience. Moreover, he
brings with him the idea of a relation between æsthetic and the pathetic,
which largely predetermines his definitions. Finally the vagueness of past
speculations impels him to that thorough and minute analysis which
characterizes his work, and which leads him into statements that are
often absurd. But despite absurdities that are patent, there are interesting passages in the *Enquiry*, and viewed historically it is certainly one

---

several facts which seem to indicate that the correct date is 1757. The most impressive of
these facts are the failure of the contemporary periodicals to mention the book in the
monthly "catalogue of new books" during 1756, and the appearance of all reviews of the
Enquiry in 1757. On page 140 of the same volume of *N. and Q.* two answers to Mr. Pottle
were printed. One gave reason for further doubt as to the existence of the edition of 1756;
the second stated baldly: "I have myself seen and perused a copy of the 'Philosophical
Enquiry into the Origin of our Ideas of the Sublime and Beautiful' dated 1756." Unfortunately, Mr. Theodore Prince, who makes this statement, did not see fit to be more
specific. For further reasons for rejecting the earlier date see Helen E. Drew, "The Date
of Burke's *Sublime and Beautiful, M.L.N.*, L (January, 1935), 29–31.

[4] [Edmund Burke], *A Philosophical Enquiry into the Origin of Our Ideas of the Sublime
and Beautiful* (London, 1757), pp. v–vii There is a well-authenticated tradition that the
Enquiry was begun when Burke was a student at Trinity College, Dublin, and that, in
its earliest form, it was read before the Club which he founded and sponsored. See A. P. I.
Samuels, *The Early Life, Correspondence and Writings of Edmund Burke* (Cambridge, 1923),
pp. 136, 137; 141. Burke states that it was completed four years before he published it
(*Enquiry*, p. vii).

of the most important æsthetic documents that eighteenth-century England produced.

The keystone of Burke's æsthetic is emotion, and the foundation of his theory of sublimity is the emotion of terror. We have observed how often in the first half of the century terror was related to sublimity, and have suggested that there is doubtless a connection between the taste for terror in the graveyard and descriptive poets and a desire to attain the sublime. It was Burke who converted the early taste for terror into an æsthetic system and who passed it on with great emphasis to the last decades of the century, during which it was used and enjoyed in literature, painting, and the appreciation of natural scenery. For this reason, even if the *Enquiry* had no importance as a treatise on æsthetic, even if it had not influenced Kant,[5] it would be of value as a study in taste.

There is reason to believe that Burke shared the fashionable tastes for ruins and melancholy and terror that found expression in the literature of his youth and early manhood, when the *Enquiry* was taking shape. His early love of the more horrid scenes of *Macbeth*[6] bears witness to such a taste. A letter to his friend, Shackleton, written on January 25, 1745/6, shows us how early this taste was formed, and points the way to the *Enquiry* in a vivid manner. He describes a flood in Dublin.

It gives me pleasure to see nature in these great though terrible scenes. It fills the mind with grand ideas, and turns the soul in upon itself.[7]

In this one sentence we find an epitome of Burke's theory of the sublime—terror fills the mind with great ideas, and the soul delights in the experience. Like Wordsworth, Burke seems early to have sought "that beauty that hath terror in it."

The *Enquiry* was taking shape between the years 1747 and 1756. These and the immediately following years make up a period of transition and growth in English literature. They were years of changing values and new points of view, years in which the emotions and imagination began to destroy the perfect balance and harmony which neo-classic art had sought in theory, at any rate, between the different elements of the poetic act. Creative art led the way, and theory, ever a laggard, followed behind in the fifth and sixth decades of the century. The need of

---

[5] For a discussion of Burke's influence on Kant see George Candrea, *Der Begriff des Erhabenen bei Burke und Kant* (Strassburg, 1894); H. J. Hofmann, *Die Lehre vom Erhabenen bei Kant und seinen Vorgängern* (Halle, 1913).

[6] Expressions of young Burke's admiration for the murder scene and the witch scenes from *Macbeth* can be found on Samuel's *Early Life*, pp. 100, 101; 168.

[7] *Early Life*, p. 84. It is amusing to compare with this passage a similar "sublime" flood described by the terror-loving Anna Seward, in a letter to Miss Wingfield, May 21, 1795. *Letters* (Edinburgh, 1811), IV, 62.

rationalizing the increasingly emotional art of the mid-century was met by such works as Hogarth's *Analysis of Beauty*, 1753, the first volume of Joseph Warton's *Essay on the Genius and Writings of Pope*, 1756, Young's *Conjectures on Original Composition* and Gerard's *Essay on Taste*, both of 1759, and Hurd's *Letters on Chivalry and Romance*, 1762. Burke's *Enquiry* is not the least important of these attempts to explain the age to itself.

Since Burke's sublime is based on terror, it may not be amiss at this point to take a brief glance at the part that the terrible was playing in poetry at about the time that he was writing the *Enquiry*. Such an account as can be given here must necessarily be no more than a reminder of the relation between Burke's theory and the general tendencies of the age. The presence of terror and horror in the poetry of the first half of the eighteenth century is familiar to all students of that period, and needs not to be labored here.[8] The poetry of the graveyard and of the ruined castle or abbey comes readily to mind to illustrate the emotionalism of the third, fourth, and fifth decades of the century. Whether the poet retires to a graveyard or to a ruin, his aim is usually the melancholy one of ruminating on the inconstancy of all sublunary things, a truism which is emphasized and driven home by such horrid descriptions as those of bodily decay or restless ghosts. With degrees of emotion varying from the "white melancholy" of Gray to the black despair and at times almost uncontrolled terror and horror of Blair, the graveyard poetry sought to turn men's thoughts from health to death, from the cheerful light of day to the horrors of the grave, and in so doing it developed into an instrument for awakening the strong emotion which the mid-century enjoyed. There is no need to quote examples here.

But supernatural and charnel-house terrors were not the only ones at the disposal of the poets. Thomson filled each successive edition of *The Seasons* with increasingly long passages which aimed at evoking terror before the vast and destructive forces of nature. Such imitators of Thomson as Mallet and Savage went considerably beyond their master in the use of volcanoes, storms, plagues, and wild beasts; but a few quotations from *The Seasons* will serve to illustrate how terror in nature was exploited. Summer presents to the reader a picture of "the Savage Race," "the Tyger darting fierce," "the lively-shining Leopard," "the keen Hyena, fellest of the Fell."

[8] Many discussions of this poetry exist. See Amy Louise Reed's *The Background of Gray's Elegy* (New York, 1924); Eino Railo's *Haunted Castle* (New York, 1927); Haferkorn's *Gotik und Ruine* (Leipzig, 1924); J. W. Draper's *The Funeral Elegy and the Rise of English Romanticism* (New York, 1929). For a discussion of the æsthetic of terror in the romantic period, see Mario Praz, *The Romantic Agony* (London, 1933), pp. 25–50.

> These, rushing from th' inhospitable Woods . . .
> Innumerous glare around their shaggy King,
> Majestic, stalking o'er the printed Sands.[9]

The terror-evoking description of the sharks[10] is too well known for quotation, as are also perhaps the picture of the shepherd struck by lightning,[11] and the storm in the desert.[12] Among other horrors in *Summer*, is the plague, which is described in great detail, and which ends with the picture of the empty streets

> . . . with uncouth Verdure clad,
> And rang'd at open Noon, by Beasts of Prey,
> And birds of bloody Beak; while, all Night long,
> In spotted Troops, the recent Ghosts complain,
> Demanding but the covering Grave. . . .[13]

Perhaps the most terrible image in the *Seasons* is that of the starving wolves

> Cruel as Death, and hungry as the Grave!
> Burning for Blood, bony, and gaunt, and grim! . . .

They descend from the mountains,

> And pouring o'er the Country, bear along,
> Keen as the North-Wind sweeps the glossy Snow . . .
> Rapacious at the Mother's Throat they fly,
> And tear the screaming Infant from her Breast . . .
> But if, appriz'd of the severe Attack,
> The country be shut up, lur'd by the Scent,
> On Church-Yards drear (inhuman to relate!)
> The disappointed Prowlers fall, and dig
> The Shrouded Body from the Grave; o'er which
> Mix'd with foul Shades, and frighted Ghosts, they howl.[14]

Here the terrors of the destructive forces of nature mingle with the shudder of the graveyard mood.

There is no doubt that these are "sublime" passages, and that they are sublime because of the terror which they are intended to provoke. We recall how Dennis had introduced this particular emotion into the sublime, and how Jacob had given a long list of sublime objects, many of which became the stock-in-trade of the graveyard and descriptive poets. But we need not rely on conjecture, for we have Thomson's own ideas on the subject. Writing to Mallet in regard to *The Excursion*, he urges him to confound his confusion by the introduction of sublimities:

[9] James Thomson, *The Seasons*, ed. Otto Zippel (Berlin, 1908), Summer, D, 912–938.
[10] Summer, D, 1013–1025.
[11] *Ibid.*, D, 1103–1168.   [12] *Ibid.*, D, 959–979.
[13] *Ibid.*, D, 1052–1092.   [14] Winter, E, 389–413.

Eruptions, earthquakes, the sea wrought into a horrible tempest, the abyss amidst whose amazing prospects, how pleasing must that be of a deep valley covered with all the tender profusions of Spring. Here if you could insert a sketch of the deluge, what more affecting and noble? Sublimity must be the character of your piece.[15]

And he tells Mallet that *The Excursion* displays "an inimitable mixture of animated simplicity and chastised sublimity," approving especially the line: "Shrieking witches in the desert—at the dead of night," and the passage

> . . . or to invert the year
> And bring wild Winter into summer's place,
> Or spread brown Night and tempest o'er the morn.

"This is Poetry," he exclaims; "this is arousing fancy—enthusiasm—rapturous terror."[16]

As a rule, in neither the graveyard nor the descriptive poetry did the emotion exist for its own sake. In the poetry of death, the purpose of terror was to prepare the mind for whatever moralizing the poet might choose to indulge in; in the descriptive poetry, terrible aspects of nature helped to show the greatness of the Creator and the inscrutability of His ways. Once this emotion was introduced into prose fiction, however, its moralistic purpose was soon lost, and it came to be the primary consideration. The gothic novel exists almost purely for the sake of evoking pleasant terror.

Before Burke published his *Enquiry*, fiction had begun to borrow mood and material from the contemporary poetry of terror. In 1753, Smollett introduced into *Ferdinand Count Fathom* a scene which, as has been frequently remarked, contains many of the elements of the gothic novel—a storm, a forest, banditti, a blood-stained corpse, the suggestions of a ghost, a hair-breadth escape.[17] In these chapters the sole desire of the author seems to be to stir strong emotion in the reader. Later in the book, when he recounts the visit of Renaldo to the supposed tomb of Monimia, Smollett borrows from the graveyard poets the mood and the properties of the scene. Darkness, silence, a lonely church, a clock striking midnight, an owl screeching from the ruined battlements, a glimmering taper, a tomb—all are crowded into one paragraph in order to pack it with emotive ideas.[18] In such scenes the emotion comes to be the important factor, to be enjoyed in and for itself.

---

[15] Peter Cunningham, "James Thomson and David Mallet," *Miscellanies of the Philobiblon Society* (London, 1857–58), IV, 30.

[16] *Ibid.*, IV, 21; 24, 25.

[17] [Tobias George Smollett], *The Adventures of Ferdinand Count Fathom* (London, 1753), I, 122–135.   [18] *Ibid.*, II, 236, 237.

It was this emotion—already widespread in theory and in art—that Burke came to strengthen and to place definitely and finally in the theory of art. The prevalence of terror perhaps accounts for some of the favor with which the *Enquiry* met, while certainly the *Enquiry* did much for the cause of the appreciation of terror in both art and nature. That Burke was not by nature incapacitated for sharing the tastes of his contemporaries is shown in a letter to Matthew Smith, written shortly after he came to London, in which he refers to *Il Penseroso* as "the finest poem in the English language" and imagines that it was composed "in the long resounding aisle of a mouldering cloister or ivy'd abbey."[19]

It is now time to turn to the *Enquiry* itself, and to analyse its chief ideas; this in spite of the fact that even today it is a not unfamiliar piece of writing.[20] The whole system is based on the antithesis of pain and pleasure, the one being the foundation of the sublime, the other of the beautiful. Hume, it will be recalled, had taken pain and pleasure as the effects of the ugly and the beautiful, and it may be said that in general this was the point of view of the first half of the century. Burke is interested in the fact that we can derive pleasure even from pain when we judge æsthetically, and in introducing pain as the basis of sublimity, he opens the way for the inclusion of ideas and images in art that had hitherto been considered as lying properly outside the sphere of æsthetic pleasure. The emotions of pleasure and pain Burke associates with the ideas of self-preservation and society (1, 6) and he makes them respectively the bases of the sublime and the beautiful. The relation between self-preservation, pain, and the sublime, he sums up in the following words:

Whatever is fitted in any sort to excite the ideas of pain, and danger, that is to say, whatever is in any sort terrible, or is conversant about terrible objects, or operates in a manner analogous to terror, is a source of the *sublime;* that is, it is productive of the strongest emotion which the mind is capable of feeling. . . . When danger or pain press too nearly, they are incapable of giving any delight, and are simply terrible; but at certain distances, and with certain modifications, they may be, and they are delightful,[21] as we every day experience (1, 7).

[19] *Early Life*, p. 221.

[20] The text from which I have quoted is that of the second (revised) edition, London, 1759. In order to avoid a superfluity of footnotes, such as defaces so much of this book, it has seemed expedient to take advantage of Burke's rather minute division of his essay into sections, and to refer to them, rather than to pages. The reader will be able to refer conveniently to the context in any edition that happens to be at hand.

[21] A note is needed on Burke's use of the word *delight*. He distinguishes between positive pleasure, which has an existence independent of pain, and that pleasure which arises from the removal of pain. It is this latter sensation that Burke terms "delight." Thus actual pain is kept out of the æsthetic experience.

Beauty, on the other hand, is social, and rests primarily on love and its attendant emotions (I, 8–17). No one had sought heretofore such a final and clear-cut distinction between the sublime and the beautiful, although, as we have seen, Addison and Akenside had contrasted them. Burke's æsthetic dualism has all the latent dangers of a too-exact pigeon-holing. Neat as it is in theory, it is none the less an awkward splitting of the æsthetic experience; that it came to be considered unfortunate is shown by the invention, late in the century, of a third category, the picturesque, which had to come into existence in order to give those objects that are neither beautiful nor sublime (in Burke's sense of the words) a local habitation and a name.[22] And the picturesque, by its very existence, bears witness to the influence of the *Enquiry* in æsthetic thought during the rest of the century.

In attempting to establish an æsthetic system on the "passions," and in relating it ultimately to bodily states, Burke takes a long step in the direction of realism. He is honestly interested in ascertaining how objects affect us, rather than in discussing, on the basis of preconceived ideas inherent in the neo-classic system, how they ought to affect us. He turns his back upon the work of artists and other critics, because he believes them to be too imitative, too traditional, too divorced from experience. Holding that "the true standard of the arts is in every man's power" (I, 19), he deliberately closes his mind to the dicta of the past, forgets Longinus, Boileau, *et al.*, and attempts the somewhat heroic task of building up a system on his own observations of his physical and mental being. For this reason, Burke is original as none of his predecessors had been, and the *Enquiry* marks a new departure in æsthetic thought.

In the second main part of his treatise, Burke is occupied wholly with a discussion of sublime objects and their effect. The great and sublime in nature cause the passion which Burke, in common with his age, called astonishment. In a definition that seems to be a paraphrase of Dr. Johnson's explanation of the word in his dictionary, Burke says that astonishment is "that state of the soul in which all its motions are suspended with some degree of horror." He goes on to point out that in such a state "the mind is so entirely filled with its object, that it cannot entertain any other, nor by consequence reason on that object which employs it." Thus the sublime, in its highest degree, "hurries us on by an irresistible force." The inferior effects of the sublime are admiration, reverence, and respect (II, 1).

Of all passions, fear has most power "to rob the mind of all its powers of acting and reasoning," and in this regard it resembles pain in all its action. Any object that threatens danger to man may produce the sublime,

[22] See below, pp. 156 ff.

even small objects. Thus, unlike many theorists, Burke does not restrict the sublime to the grand; the emotion produced, not the object
that produces it, is the important factor in Burke's æsthetic. For this
reason, a wide expanse of plain is less sublime than an equally wide expanse of ocean, for we are accustomed to associate peril with the sea.
"Indeed," he says, "terror is in all cases whatsoever, either more openly
or latently, the ruling principle of the sublime" (II, 2). This recognition
of the function of association in our æsthetic perceptions was familiar
in speculation before Burke's day; Dennis, Hutcheson, Hume, and
Baillie had all employed it, and Hartley had only recently erected a
system of psychology on that idea alone. But Burke is careful in his use
of association, and as we shall see, refuses to follow Hartley in adopting
it as the sole explanation of our mental processes. He helps, however, to
establish it definitely in speculation against the time when Alison ex-
ploits it fully. The idea that the sublime is completely irrational had been
common since the ancients discussed the high style, but it should not
be overlooked that in this, the most popular treatise of the century, ir-
rationality is given what is at least a pseudo-scientific basis, and is passed
on to the preromantic period, where it helps prepare the way for the
overthrow of what Wordsworth calls "the meddling intellect" and
Keats, "the dull brain."

There follows a classification of ideas that are sublime and an explanation of the sublimity of each. They are obscurity, where darkness and
uncertainty arouse dread and terror (II, 3); power, where the mind is
impelled to fear because of superior force (II, 5); privations, such as
darkness, vacuity, and silence, which are great because they are terrible
(II, 6); vastness, whether in length, height, or depth, the last being the
most powerful source of the sublime (II, 7); infinity, or any object that
because of its size seems infinite (II, 8); difficulty—that is, any object
that seems to owe its existence to a vast expenditure of labor and effort
(II, 12); and magnificence (II, 13).

This is an interesting list. With the exception of power, none of these
ideas would have been very much at home in neo-classic art. The age in
which, as Austin Dobson puts it,

> . . . Phoebus touch'd the Poet's trembling Ear
> With one supreme Commandment, *Be thou Clear*,

was not an age to domicile the obscure in its art. It was a social art,
and in its more characteristic moments preferred town and court to
Burke's privations. It was, as we have seen, an art that sought proportion and that disliked the vast. It preferred the concrete and the bounded
to the infinite, and it sought to give the impression of ease and urbanity,

not of difficulty. This is not to attempt to convert Burke into a sort of philosophical Byron, but only to indicate that in the *Enquiry*, under the caption of the sublime, tastes that are not strictly compatible with neo-classic theory take up their position in a treatise that was extremely popular throughout the rest of the century, for the very reason that it chimed in so well with tastes that were to become dominant as the century drew to a close.

It is in relation to obscurity that Burke says: "A clear idea is therefore another name for a little idea" (II, 4). This repudiation of clarity is especially important when we remember that Burke considered the sublime to be the highest domain of art, for it removes the greatest art from the atmosphere in which neo-classicism lived and moved and had its being. In his fifth *Méditation* Descartes had said: "*Toutes choses qui je connais clairement et distinctement sont vrais.*" Hence French neo-classicism had preferred the *School of Athens* to the *Last Judgment;* hence deism, the typical religion of the neo-classical enlightenment, had stripped Christianity of its miracles; hence the truths which neo-classic art had sought to incarnate were clear and universal truths; and hence precision and proportion were regarded as valuable æsthetic qualities in all the arts. Burke's objection to clarity, his insistence on the essential pettiness of ideas that the reason can grasp, arises from his preoccupation with the non-rational element in art. "It is one thing to make an image clear, and another to make it affecting to the imagination," he avers (II, 4), and he sustains his opinion by pointing out the greater emotive value of a verbal description as opposed to a drawing of the same scene, and the influence of music in arousing feeling without the aid of images. Such a position is clearly at variance with the standards of Augustan art, and it represents an advance toward that element in romantic art that manifests itself in half-lights, suggestions, and mystery. Much of that mood is expressed in the passage from Job that Burke quotes in this connection:

In thoughts from the visions of the night, when deep sleep falleth upon man, fear came upon me and trembling, which made all my bones to shake. Then a spirit passed before my face. The hair of my flesh stood up. It stood still, *but I could not discover the form thereof;* an image was before mine eyes; there was silence; and I heard a voice: Shall mortal man be more just than God? (II, 4).

This evoking of awe through mystery is very much akin to the "sublimity" of Ossian and to many passages in the romantic poets.[23]

It is in discussing magnificence that Burke makes what Folkierski has claimed to be his chief contribution to æsthetic.[24] A profusion of splen-

---

[23] Compare Coleridge's opinion: "Poetry gives most pleasure when only generally and not perfectly understood." *Anima Poetae*, ed. E. H. Coleridge (London, 1895), p. 5.

[24] *Entre le Classicisme et le Romantisme*, pp. 96, 97.

did or valuable objects, he says, is magnificent. The "starry heavens" afford an example, and their number is the explanation of the fact that they always excite ideas of grandeur. "The apparent disorder augments the grandeur, for the appearance of care is highly contrary to our ideas of magnificence" (II, 13). The idea derives ultimately from Longinus's statement that a great genius, like a wealthy man, can afford to be careless, but its strict application to the practice of art would have been an innovation indeed. Once disorder is admitted into art, classic beauty, whose very essence is order, harmony, and proportion, is no more. Simplicity (which we found Boileau advancing as an appropriate dress for the sublime, and whose value Burke fully recognizes) was an essential element in neo-classical art, and cannot exist side by side with a magnificent disorder. It is true that Boileau had written of the ode:

> Son style impétueux souvent marche au hazard:
> Chez elle un beau désordre est un effet de l'art;[25]

but this disorder is merely a trick employed by a cunning craftsman who wishes to simulate the supposed disorder of the Pindaric ode. Burke's disorder produces "an appearance of infinity,"; else "you will have disorder only, without magnificence" (II, 13), so that there is evidently a distinction to be drawn between Boileau's "beau désordre" and Burke's "magnificent disorder." It is only fair to point out that the suggestion of the value of disorder is made very timidly, and is so qualified as to be almost revoked as soon as it is uttered, for Burke says that this kind of grandeur is "to be very cautiously admitted" because of its difficulty, and because "in many cases this splendid confusion would destroy all use, which should be attended to in most of the works of art with the greatest care" (II, 13). This statement is a sensible qualification of what must have seemed an anarchistic idea in æsthetic, but it does not obscure another instance of Burke's unorthodox tastes.

The remainder of Part II can be briefly summarized. Brilliant light, such as the direct light of the sun striking the eye, light moving with celerity (lightning), and quick transitions from light to darkness, or from darkness to light are sublime, but darkness is more productive of sublimity than is light, as quotations from Milton illustrate (II, 14); "sad and fuscous colours, as black and brown, or deep purple" belong to the same category, and bright colors are opposed to it because they militate against that "melancholy kind of greatness" which is the sublime (II, 16).[26] Excessively loud and regularly recurring sounds, low, tremulous,

---

[25] "L'Art Poétique," Canto II, *Œuvres Complètes*, II, 316.

[26] Burke's taste in scenery is prophetic of the cult of wild nature that was to grow up in the next decade: "An immense mountain covered with a shining green turf is nothing, in this respect, to one dark and gloomy; the cloudy sky is more grand than the blue; and night more sublime and solemn than day" (II, 16).

intermitting sounds, and inarticulate cries of pain or fear in beasts and in man evoke fear, and consequently operate on the soul as does the sublime (II, 17, 18, 19). Even the senses of smell and of taste play their part in producing these emotions; excessive bitters, or intolerable stenches(!), if they are not associated with mean ideas, create states of mind analogous to the sublime (II, 21). It is in this part of the *Enquiry* that one smiles to perceive how Burke's thesis is running away with him.

In Part IV Burke attempts to explain psychologically and physiologically, the effect of the ideas discussed in Parts I and II, so as to reach the "efficient cause" of the sublime, and it is at this point that he seems most original. Whatever one may think of his deductions, no one can deny that in seeking to observe the physiology of beauty and sublimity, in going beyond the passions to the body, and in bringing the whole organism into the æsthetic experience, Burke showed remarkable "modernity" of thought. Blake, the apostle of imagination and inspiration, was to feel "Contempt and Abhorrence" for the *Enquiry*,[27] as he would have felt for most modern psychology, for in Burke's essay there is shadowed forth the materialistic implication of twentieth-century psychological investigation, the method that seeks a physical explanation even for art itself.[28] The empirical method of Burke's thought is seen in his statement: "When we go but one step beyond the immediate sensible qualities of things, we go out of our depth" (IV, 1). He is therefore compelled to restrict his inquiry to sensation and its physical and emotional effect.

Burke uses association to explain the effect of objects, but the measure of his disagreement with the Hartleian psychology is shown in his refusal to explain all mental processes by that principle, preferring, as he does, to find when possible an explanation in the natural properties of the object and their physical effect upon a sense organ (IV, 2).[29]

---

[27] See the marginalia in the British Museum's copy of the second edition of the *Works* of Reynolds, I, 282. In Blake's opinion the *Enquiry* mocks inspiration and vision, his "Element," and "Eternal Dwelling place."

[28] See Francisco Mirabent's *La Estética Inglesa del Siglo XVIII* (Barcelona, 1927), pp. 118, 119.

[29] It is not easy to trace Burke's indebtedness to the psychology of his time. The general method is, of course, that of Locke, whom Burke has constantly in mind, and with whom he differs on occasion (I, 3 and IV, 3). To Hume he may have been indebted, although here, too, specific borrowings are hard to find. The similarities which one can discover—such as their common opinion that there is no greater punishment that a man can suffer than perfect solitude—prove exactly nothing (see Hume's *Philosophical Works*, II, 150). Burke's habit of regarding sensation as caused by the vibration of the nerves finds its parallel in Hume's writings, in which the mind is compared to a stringed instrument, whose vibrations gradually decay (*Philosophical Works*, II, 140); and in Hartley's explanation of the continuation of the sense impression after direct stimulation has been removed as due to the vibrations of "Infinitesimal medullary Particles" (*Observations on Man*, I, 9–11). Burke

Arguing from the fact that pain and fear affect the body in much the same way—that is, they cause a violent contraction of the muscles and a tenseness of the nerves—Burke concludes that he is justified in treating the sensation and the emotion together, observing the distinction that pain operates on the mind through the body, and terror on the body through the mind (IV, 3). It follows that sublime objects must work their effect by causing such a tension and such a contraction in the subject, either through their natural properties or through association (IV, 5). But there remains the question as to why such an effect, which should be and which often is disagreeable, should in art and sometimes in reality prove capable of producing delight. The answer, which is suggested by Du Bos's statement that a state of rest and inactivity is disagreeable, is that as exercise is healthful for the body so it is good for the "finer organs" on which and by which the imagination acts.

... if the pain and terror are so modified as not to be actually noxious; if the pain is not carried to violence, and the terror is not conversant about the present destruction of the person [that is, if it can be regarded theoretically], as these emotions clear the parts, whether fine or gross, of a dangerous and troublesome encumbrance, they are capable of producing delight; not pleasure, but a sort of delightful horror, a sort of tranquility tinged with terror; ... Its object is the sublime. Its highest degree I call *astonishment;* the subordinate degrees are awe, reverence, and respect ... (IV, 6, 7).

On this basis Burke explains why visual objects of great dimensions are sublime. Light from an object striking the retina causes tension and vibration, and when the object is large, this continued effect produces a state very like that which causes pain, and consequently produces an idea of the sublime. If the eye moves from one to another small and diversified object, it experiences an instant of relaxation, but if the object is both simple and vast, the eye (and therefore the mind) does not arrive readily at its bounds, and has no rest, since the image is everywhere the same. Hence the impression of an "artificial infinite" is created by a large and unified object which throws the retina into a state of tension and impresses itself so vividly on the mind that an idea of the sublime is suggested (IV, 9, 10, 13). The same reasoning is followed in regard to sounds (IV, 11, 12).

It is thus that Burke arrives at the conclusion that beauty and sublimity act directly on the nervous system through sense impressions.

---

uses this bit of knowledge to show how a large, but uniform, building can create the impression of infinity on the senses. There are other minor, but equally unimpressive, parallels between Hartley and Burke, who, in the main, disagree too much to have much in common. About all that one can say is that Burke seems to have studied the physiology and the psychology of his day.

He removes the perception of the beautiful and the sublime from the realm of judgment, where the French neo-classicists had sought it, as well as from the realm of sentiment where some of his immediate predecessors had found it. Crousaz had referred æsthetic judgment to "sentiment," Du Bos had invented a "sixth sense," and Hutcheson had used the term "internal sense." These were vague ideas, but they all presupposed a separate faculty by which men perceive æsthetic values. Burke turned his back on these older theories, and had recourse to a sensationalism that has the advantage of being simpler and clearer. Moreover, although he cannot, by the very nature of his reasoning, refer beauty and sublimity to the perceiving mind alone, as Kant was to do and as Hume had already done, he does, perforce, concentrate most of his attention on the effect rather than on the qualities of objects. As we have seen, small objects may be regarded as sublime if they create terror, and even the ugly may be associated with sublimity if it is "united with such qualities as excite strong terror" (III, 21). This opinion represents a certain awareness of the supreme value of the individual impression, and is a step toward the abolition of purely objective formulæ in the labelling and consideration of æsthetic experiences.

The reviewers received the *Enquiry* kindly enough.[30] Burke's boast that his subject has led him "out of the common course of discourse" (I, 4) is well borne out by the dicta of the critics. The *London Chronicle* declares that the *Enquiry* gave "criticism a face that we never saw it wear before;"[31] Goldsmith, writing for the *Monthly Review*, dwells on the novelty of Burke's method, and points to the innovation therein when he says that the author "rejects all former systems, and founds his philosophy on his own particular feelings;"[32] the anonymous reviewer of the *Critical Review* mentions the same fact, and Arthur Murphy makes Burke's originality the point of a rather ill-humored attack.[33] But although in the main the essay was favorably received, the critics were unanimous in stating that Burke had attempted to restrict the sublime too closely when he excluded all emotions but terror from its sphere,[34] and Murphy demonstrates the hold that Longinus had on the thought of his

[30] See Herbert A. Wicheln's "Burke's Essay on the Sublime and its Reviewers," *JEGP*, XXI (1922), 645–661. The article is a study of the relation between the reviews and the changes and additions that Burke made in the second edition.

[31] *The London Chronicle, or Universal Evening Post*, II (1757), 52.

[32] *Monthly Review*, XVI, 473.

[33] *Critical Review*, III, 316; Johnson's *Works* (1787), X, 199, 200. Murphy's review was erroneously ascribed to Johnson by Sir John Hawkins, and was published by him in his edition of the complete works. For Boswell's denial of Johnson's authorship, and his ascription of the review to Murphy, see *Life*, I, 310.

[34] See, for example, Goldsmith's views, *Monthly Review*, XVI, 475, note.

time when he contrasts the *Enquiry* with *Peri Hupsous*, very much to the advantage of the Greek treatise.[35]

For nearly half a century the *Enquiry* continued in high favor with the public, no matter how often æstheticians might dissent from its views. Perhaps Burke's early biographer, Charles McCormick, does not much overestimate the popularity of the book when he declares that "the author was universally allowed to have surpassed LONGINUS in precision, and Addison in depth and comprehensiveness. . . ."[36] Certain it is that Burke had provided the age with an idea of sublimity that suited nicely its increasingly sensational tastes, and that could easily be comprehended by those who were uninitiated into the deeper mysteries of philosophy. One of the most important phases of its influence will be pointed out in a later chapter.

Dr. Johnson considered it "an example of true criticism,"[37] and in Reynolds' opinion it was an "admirable treatise."[38] But Burke was not dependent on praise from members of his own coterie. Blair, although he refused to limit sublimity to terror, did not hesitate to borrow from the *Enquiry*,[39] and in this respect he is typical of his fellow theorists, who seldom succeeded in ignoring Burke, even when they wrote from a totally different point of view. Quite late in the century, Richard Stack was to find the essay "in most respects perfectly just, in all its parts beautifully ingenious,"[40] and Gregory, the translator of Lowth's lectures, was to speak of the author of the *Enquiry* as one "whose taste and imagination will be respected as long as the English language exists. . . ."[41] In 1792, the reviewer of Hickey's *History of Painting and Sculpture* could repeat the Burkean idea that terror is the "chief ingredient of the sublime,"[42] and as we shall see, the *Enquiry* regained something of its early fame in the controversy over the picturesque that was in progress as the century came to its end. But certainly the prettiest compliment that Burke was paid is to be found in John Bennett's *Letters to a Young Lady on a Variety of Useful and Interesting Subjects*. The author describes one of those model young people who appear so often in the improving books of the eighteenth century. She retires to a garden, where "she indulges all the luxury of her taste," and then she reads the *Enquiry*, and thereby

[35] Johnson's *Works* (1787), x, 207.

[36] Charles McCormick, *Memoirs of the Right Honourable Edmund Burke*, Second Edition (London, 1798), p. 29.

[37] James Boswell, *Life of Johnson*, ed. G. B. Hill (Oxford, 1887), II, 90.

[38] Sir Joshua Reynolds, *Works*, ed. Edmond Malone (London, 1798), I, 282, note.

[39] *Lectures*, I, 55.

[40] *Transactions of the Royal Irish Academy*, I, 4.

[41] *Lectures*, I, 302, 303, note.

[42] *Analytical Review*, XIV (1792), 165.

seems "more *beautiful* and more *sublime*, than the admired work of that well known and admired author."[43]

But none the less the treatise lost prestige as the century drew to a close. Something of this decline in fame is heralded by Plumer's fatuous attack in 1772,[44] but although the actual popularity of the book seems to decrease, its influence continued, and the book is always to be reckoned with even during the early nineteenth century. Dugald Stewart recorded his opinion that Burke's was the best of the eighteenth-century essays on sublimity,[45] and Edward Mangin borrowed copiously from the *Enquiry* when he constructed his theory of the sublime.[46]

But the work which had influenced so powerfully English æsthetic thought and taste during its formative years, and which had shaped some of Johnson's thoughts on poetry,[47] was ultimately to be regarded coldly, as when Coleridge dismissed it as "a poor thing."[48] But it had done its work by turning the attention of theorists to the sensations and the psychological influences that accompany and determine the æsthetic experience, and by helping to spread the cult of romantic terror throughout the literature of the era that just precedes the rise of romantic art.

[43] John Bennett, *Letters to a Young Lady* (Warrington, 1789), II, 59.

[44] [F. Plumer], *A Letter from a Gentleman to his Nephew at Oxford* (London, 1772), *passim*.

[45] Dugald Stewart, "On the Sublime," *Philosophical Essays* (Edinburgh, 1810), p. 344.

[46] [Edward Mangin], *Essays on the Sources of the Pleasures Received from Literary Compositions* (London, 1809), pp. 51 ff.

[47] Surely, when in *Rasselas*, Johnson says: "To the poet nothing can be useless. Whatever is beautiful; and whatever is dreadful, must be familiar to his imagination; he must be conversant with all that is awfully vast or elegantly little"; (*Works*, I, 221)—surely here he is thinking of the *Enquiry*.

[48] *Table Talk and Omniana*, p. 54.

CHAPTER VI

THE SEVENTEEN-SIXTIES: SUBLIMITY, PSYCHOLOGY, AND ORIGINAL GENIUS

BURKE'S *Enquiry* is in many respects representative of its decade, a decade of transition from the stricter ideas of neo-classicism to that individualism and freer interpretation of beauty and other æsthetic ideas which we are in the habit of regarding as characteristic of the romantic in art. Theories and tastes which, during the Augustan age, were well controlled and only latent, however much they may have worked to modify the opinions of individual writers, began in the fifth decade of the century to find positive and well-organized expression, and during the following decades they assumed a vitality that contrasts vividly with the moribund and decadent cult of neo-classical standards. If the first generation of romantics gave the *coup de grâce* to the outworn æsthetic and criticism of their literary ancestors, they were merely wielding weapons forged for them during the last half of the century.

The extreme instance of the new point of view is perhaps Edward Young, the Young of *Conjectures on Original Composition*, who, like Moses, was destined to point the way to a promised land which he himself was never to inherit save in imagination. For Young's essay is essentially a challenge to the neo-classical tradition, a spirited demand that, in the words of Johnson, authors and critics should distinguish between "what is established because it is right, and what is right because it is established," and, scorning the "meddling ape, *Imitation*," should trust to the innate genius which is the heritage of artists and the sole interpreter of beauty to man. The novelty of Young's *Conjectures* consists not so much in what is said as in the emphasis with which it speaks and the disinclination that it shows to hedge original genius about with the safeguard of the rules and the restraint of good sense.[1]

Young fully develops his theory of original genius, to which and to which alone he ascribes the ability to seize that "something beyond Prose reason," those "Mysteries. . . not to be explained, but admired."[2]

---

[1] In his *Edward Young's Conjectures on Original Composition in England and Germany* (Americana Germanica, No. 28, New York, 1917), Martin W. Steinke traces back into earlier criticism most of the ideas that Young expresses. All of his parallels are not convincing, but many of them are valid enough to demonstrate that Young is not so original as he might seem to the uninitiated. See also Paul Kaufman's "Heralds of Original Genius," *Essays in Memory of Barrett Wendell* (Cambridge, 1926), pp. 189–217.

[2] *Conjectures*, p. 28.

The nature of this grace beyond the reach of art is set forth in Longinian language which hints at the parentage of the *Conjectures* and which leaves no doubt in one familiar with the critical thought of the preceding fifty years that Young is saying that the servile following of the rules can never produce sublime art, and that the free interpretation of original genius is the sole source of what he terms elsewhere "unexampled excellence."[3]

Learning we thank, Genius we revere; That gives us pleasure, This Gives us rapture; That informs, This inspires; and is itself inspired; for Genius is from Heaven; Learning from Man.[4]

In this sentence Young goes far beyond Longinus, who had merely pleaded for the recognition of beauties which are attained by transcending the rules, and who was perfectly ready to state formulæ for the creation of that rhetorical sublime with which he was chiefly concerned.

The two "unlearned" or original geniuses whom Young selects for examples are Shakespeare, of course, and Pindar, poets who had served the English critics for instances of the sublime from the very first, though in what sense the author of the highly wrought *epinikia* could be called unlearned is not at once clear.[5] It is when one recalls Dryden's *On Dramatic Poesy* and the formless pindaric of Cowley that one is able to perceive that in both instances Young is uttering a commonplace.

The effect of the *Conjectures* was to strengthen the relation between sublimity, or, if you will, the highest beauty attainable in art, with the ideas of originality, freedom, individuality of interpretation, and trust in the present rather than in the past. In so doing, Young seems a thinker far in advance of his age, but his is only an exaggerated expression of tendencies already at work in the mid-century.

---

[3] Steinke derives eleven passages from *Peri Hupsous*. Some of the parallels seem far-fetched, but certainly, both directly and indirectly, the *Conjectures* derive in large part from Longinus.   [4] *Conjectures*, p. 36.

[5] Young is speaking conventionally when he makes Pindar into a genius who scorned the rules. The French neo-classicists regarded the Pindaric ode as the noblest and the only legitimately irregular form of lyric poetry, and it easily came to be associated with the Longinian sublime, because it apparently scorned the rules, and succeeded, in Boileau's words, in making "*un beau désordre*" into "*un effet de l'art.*" (Boileau, "Discours sur l'Ode," *Œuvres Complètes*, III, 3–11.) Pindar, says Boileau on page 5, "afin de mieux entrer dans la raison, sort, s'il faut ainsi parler, de la raison même, évitant avec grand soin cet ordre méthodique, et ces exactes liaisons de sens qui ôteroient l'âme à la poésie lyrique." It scorns reason and produces transports. Cf. Pope's *Temple of Fame*, ll. 210–221.

The Wartons were busily at work on similar ideas. Joseph had already called into question the claims of Pope to be a genius of the highest rank, by asserting that he lacked the sublime and the pathetic, which he regarded as "the two chief nerves of all genuine poetry," and by declaring that "a spirited and glowing imagination, '*acer spiritus ac vis*'," not reason and correctness, are the sources of the "transcendentally sublime."[6] Much has already been written and said on this passage. That it is illustrative of a change of taste is obvious. From the 1750's on, sublimity, imagination, original genius, fire, enthusiasm, in their current connotations, play an increasingly important part in criticism. Neo-classic taste begins to disintegrate, and the sublime does its share in removing from English art that particular balance and grace which the century at its best attained. Many remarks of an incidental nature, scattered through the writings of Warton, indicate his conception of sublimity and his more "romantic" tastes. Spenser, Milton, and Shakespeare are the only English poets who are sublime;[7] Dante's poem is sublime and original;[8] the *Iliad* has more of the sublime than the *Odyssey*, because it is distinguished for "the perpetual tumult and terror that reign through [it];" in the *Iliad* Homer "resembles the Nile, when it descends in a torrent that deafens and astonishes the neighboring inhabitants;" and its spirit and sublimity are due to the fact that when we read it "we are placed amidst the rage of storms and tempests."[9] All of this helps us to understand why Warton found Pope lacking; his taste was for the art of another age than the Augustan.

[6] It is noticeable that this passage occurs in the dedication to Young of the *Essay on the Writings and Genius of Pope* (London, 1756), I, v. Evidently the older poet was recognized as a leader of the new taste even before he chose to speak out. Warton's estimate of Pope's poetry provoked in the next decade an answer from Owen Ruffhead, in his *Life of Pope*. He evidently considered Warton rather wild, for he says of him that he "inherited the sublime Taste of *Martinus Scriblerus* who required every thing to be in the buskin or florid style," a manifestly unfair statement of Warton's position. In reference to Warton's highly esteemed sublime and pathetic, Ruffhead says: " . . . in these kinds of poetry, nature is generally represented in the *outré*. The imagination loves to be flattered, and it always pictures to itself something more grand and more extraordinary, than is ever met with in reality; and there is always something in every scene, which falls short of the perfection it aspires to. This propensity is favourable to poetic enthusiasm, and is what gives a peculiar relish to the sublime and pathetic. But to be extravagant requires less skill than is usually imagined and to describe nature in her genuine character, is perhaps the greatest effort of art." *Life of Pope* (London, 1769), p. 340.—These opinions show how, by 1769, the sublime had outgrown the neo-classic conception of nature and how a conservative critic could distrust it. Ruffhead may have been thinking of Blair's sublime Ossian rather than of Warton's *acer spiritus ac vis*.

[7] *Essay*, I, xi.   [8] *Ibid.*, I, 257.   [9] *Adventurer*, 80.

Thomas Warton was also busily at work applying the term *sublime* to poets and poems that were at odds with the neo-classical tenets. In the postscript to his work on the *Faerie Queene*, 1754, he says that in the products of the gothic imagination, "magic and enchantments . . . store the fancy with those sublime and alarming images, which true poetry delights to display;" and again, that after the publication of Fletcher's *Purple Island*, "a poetry succeeded, in which imagination gave way to correctness, sublimity of description to delicacy of sentiment, and majestic imagery to conceit and epigram."[10] The sublime that could be applied to the orations of Demosthenes was certainly different from that which described the *Faerie Queene*.

Early in the next decade a more positive statement of the mid-century creed was made by Hurd in his famous *Letters on Chivalry and Romance*, and here again the sublime was called upon to play a part. It will be recalled that Hurd was attempting to demonstrate the superiority of Gothic poets to "all others who have succeeded them," and their equality (at least) to the great ancients. To do so required a new definition of nature. In his earlier *On the Idea of Universal Poetry*, Hurd had maintained that poetry is actually free from the constraints of an *a priori* conception of nature, because its purpose is

not to delineate truth simply, but to present it in the most taking forms; not to reflect the real face of things, but to illustrate and adorn it; not to represent the fairest objects only, but to represent them in the fairest lights, and to heighten all their beauties up to the possibility of their natures; nay, to *outstrip* nature, and to address itself to our wildest fancy, rather than to our judgment and cooler sense.

In a passage that is based on Bacon's statement that poetry "submits the shows of things to the desires of the mind," he maintains that because of something "sublime and elevated" in the mind of man, it overlooks the obvious and familiar appearances of things, and "feigns to itself other and more extraordinary; such as correspond to the extent of its own powers."

All of this, at first glance, seems to be only a harking back to the classical conception of art as a representation of a higher perfection

---

[10] *Observations on the Faerie Queene of Spenser*, The Second Edition (London, 1762), II, 268 and 111. Although certainly no "Goth," Johnson was later to deny sublimity to the metaphysical poets, in a familiar passage from the Life of Cowley. Their wit kept them from attempting "that comprehension and expanse of thought which at first fills the whole mind, and of which the first effect is sudden astonishment, and the second rational admiration." Sublimity is produced by "aggregation," and great thoughts are always general. The attempt to find and express the novel, and the analytical method of the metaphysicals militate against their sublimity. Their conceits break up nature, exactly as a prism dissects a sun-beam. *Works*, VII, 16, 17.

than nature has achieved, a mere description of poetry as an "ideal" art, mingled with an echo of Longinus. But Hurd at once colors his ideas with "romantic" tints, for he attributes to this cause the fact that poetry deals in "atmospheres and invocations," that it peoples creation with new and living forms, and that it "calls up infernal spectres to terrify, or brings down celestial natures to astonish, the imagination."[11] This comes much nearer Shakespeare's poet, whose eye is in a fine frenzy rolling, or Shelley's dreamer, creating "shapes more real than mortal man," than it does to the nature-bound poetry of Boileau.

One is therefore prepared for Hurd's emphatic approval of "Gothic superstition" as "more amusing, as well as more awakening to the imagination" in his better known *Letters;* and for his declaration that Shakespeare possesses "a terrible sublime (which not so much the energy of his genius, as the nature of his subject drew from him), . . ." and which manifests itself in his witches and fairies. The superiority of the "Gothic enchantments" to the mythology of the ancients is boldly claimed, and is stated to be due to the fact that they are "more sublime, more terrible, more alarming" than the classic deities.[12] It is evident that Hurd's sublime is no mere offspring of a "bold" rhetoric, but that it is made of soul-shaking terror. It must be regarded as symptomatic of the taste that was to hail Ossian with rapture as sublime.

Passing over Hurd's extremely important formulation of "Gothic unity" as opposed to neo-classical unity, we must consider his conception of nature. The tenth letter is devoted to the question of poetic truth. The poet must indeed follow nature, but not that nature which is merely the sum of the "known and experienced course of affairs in this world"; for "he has a world of his own, where experience has less to do, than consistent imagination." Poetry that deals with men and manners and that seeks to move the passions must follow nature, but "the more sublime and creative poetry," which is addressed principally to the imagination, "has no need to observe those cautious rules of credibility so necessary to be followed by him, who would touch the affections and animate the heart."[13]

Here is change indeed. The neo-classical critic at his most neo-classical had always scorned the gothic fancies, while he inconsistently permitted the use of the classical machines as elegant and as sanctioned by the great ancients. But if he permitted this use of the "marvellous,"[14] he

---

[11] Richard Hurd, *Works* (London, 1811), II, 8, 9.

[12] *Letters on Chivalry and Romance*, ed. Edith Morley (London, 1911), pp. 109, 110; 111. See also, p. 117.   [13] *Ibid.*, pp. 137–139.

[14] On the part that the "marvellous" played in neo-classical theory and its relation to *vraisemblance,* see René Bray, *La Formation de la Doctrine Classique en France* (Paris,

none the less insisted on a measure of *vraisemblance*. Hurd, having been given the proverbial inch, takes the proverbial mile, and elevates the gothic marvellous to the highest height of poetry, finding it natural and truthful since nature and truth are simply consistency with the newly approved and wonder-working "imagination." And all of this is sublime. Here we see the sublime arrive at one of the stages of its journey. From being a florid style that ravishes and transports, it has been meta-morphosed into an order of poetry that is far removed from the ideal art of the neo-classicist. From the first, carrying latently un-neo-classical elements, it has become the depository of ideas and emotions that are definitely "romantic." Imaginative truth, not the rules, is the sole test for poetry, and imaginative truth, even when it contains the impossible, is sublime. The early theorists who had used the sublime as a category for those elements in the art of their day that pleased despite their being somewhat unorthodox, had wrought toward ends that the knew not of. The sublime was strongly entrenched in mid-century theory. It could now become the vantage point from which to carry on the critique of the older order. With the *Letters on Chivalry and Romance* and the advent of Ossian, so far as taste goes the sublime had become a powerful factor in pre-romanticism.

And Burke's *Enquiry* in its turn contributed to the new movement. Whatever one thinks today of the method, it cannot be denied that at least Burke undertook his inquiry in the spirit of independent investi-gation. We hear no talk of beauty as unity, variety, proportion, and regularity; he does not confuse rhetoric and art; he does not seek sub-limity by way of the well-beaten path that led through Boileau to Lon-ginus. He, too, is standing aside from tradition, is eager to study the problem realistically, and consequently he boldly takes the discussion into the realm of the psychological and the physical. The crudeness of the attempt may be excused by recalling Burke's youth and the dif-ficulty of pioneering; its influence, throughout the next half-century, is somewhat more difficult to explain. With all of its crudity and super-ficiality it went deeper into the subject than any previous treatise had done, and its orderly analysis must have recommended it to an age that loved the scientific. In addition, the *Enquiry* offered a sublime that the age was soon to exploit to the fullest—the sublime of terror. It chimed in nicely with developments in taste, was itself a symptom and a con-tributing cause of this development. The love of Ossian and of the more terrible aspects of nature would have come under any circumstances, but their coming was made somewhat easier by the presence of Burke's

1927), pp. 231–238. The recognized inferiority of magic to pagan deities is discussed, pp. 235, 236.

theory of sublimity and the work of such critics as the Wartons, Young, and Hurd. The sixth decade of the century witnessed a renewed application to æsthetic problems, mainly in the Burkean manner of psychological analysis. Much ground was cleared; much was thought and written that need never be thought and written again. The 1760's are important in the history of English æsthetic; they now claim our attention.

Indeed, so rich is the decade in critical and æsthetic documents that one is rather embarrassed by a superfluity of material to which to refer. Before turning to the chief documents of the period, we had best consider in a few paragraphs some of the shorter and less important writings on the sublime. It is well to glance at the small fry lest we get the impression that the longer treatises are typical of all speculation during the decade. Although it is indisputable that the more serious treatises are important in view of the innovations that they introduce in theory and in taste, it is also true that older ideas lingered on.

John Ward's *A System of Oratory*, 1759, is derived, quite naturally, from the rhetoricians, and Longinus appears frequently in Bolevian dress. There is much talk of sublime sentiments and sublime thoughts and sublime style, as is right and proper in a system of oratory. The book is composed of lectures delivered at Gresham College during Ward's tenure of a professorship, from about 1720 to 1758.[15] The fact that they were published and sold bears witness to the interest of the age in rhetoric and to the apparently infinite capacity of the eighteenth-century reader to endure repetition, for Ward says nothing that had not been said before. The same is true of another professor's lectures, which reached a second edition in the same year—John Lanson's *Lectures Concerning Oratory*, to which reference has been made in a previous chapter.[16]

But it was not the academic mind alone that continued working in the old grooves. Oliver Goldsmith wrote on eloquence in *The Bee*, November 17, 1759, and equated eloquence with the pathetic, and the pathetic with the sublime. He maintained that there is no such thing as a sublime style, since "eloquence is not in the words but in the subject."[17]

Nothing more exciting can be learned from *The Art of Poetry on a New Plan*, 1762, which has been dubiously attributed to John Newbery. There

[15] *A System of Oratory*, Lectures XXXVIII and XXXIX, II, 129-193.

[16] *Lectures*, pp. 59-67; 326-327. Lanson was professor of Oratory and History in Trinity College, Dublin. The first edition appeared in 1758; a third, in 1760.

[17] "Of Eloquence," *The Bee* (London, 1759), pp. 195-198. "On the Study of the Belles-Lettres," formerly attributed to Goldsmith, discusses tropes and figures as a source of the sublime, an idea thoroughly Longinian and directly opposed to the view held in *The Bee*. For the proof that Goldsmith did not write these papers, see Caroline Tupper's article, *PMLA*, XXXIX (1924), 325-342. My reference is to Goldsmith's *Works*, ed. J. W. M. Gibbs (London, 1884), I, 335-338.

is much talk of Longinus, of elevated thoughts, of the three sorts of style, of transports, of the sublimity of the Bible, Homer, and Milton, of epic, tragedy, and ode, but nothing new can be learned. It is a good summary of the most commonplace thoughts of the preceding eighty years, but it is uninteresting for that very reason. The same author's *Circle of the Sciences*, published somewhat earlier, is equally a *pot-pourri* of the past, for here he is frankly concerned with rhetoric. It is full of Longinus's ideas, and its chief interest lies in the fact that along with the Bible and Milton, the storm from Thomson's *Summer* is quoted as an illustration of the sublime.[18]

Our last minor character has considerably more reputation in æsthetics, although his value for us is slight. Daniel Webb wrote much, but said little, on the arts of painting, poetry, and music. In regard to poetry, he distinguishes the sublime and the beautiful on the grounds that the one "transports," the other "delights," and he attributes the sublime to the choice of great circumstances and "the rapid succession of those circumstances."[19] This is dull enough, but his attempt to apply sublimity to music is somewhat more interesting.

The passion of the eighteenth century for reducing all knowledge to a well-defined unity (in Batteux's words, *les beaux arts réduits à un même principe*) led naturally to the application of the principles of one art to another. It was the great heresy of the age, and Lessing did something to extricate the arts from this confusion. Webb naturally approached the problem with the idea that music and poetry are "sister arts," and that what is true for one is true for the other. After stating that in music we are transported by sudden transitions (which, one assumes, is analogous to the rapid succession of great circumstances that creates the sublime in poetry), "by an impetuous reiteration of impressions," and that we are delighted by "a placid succession of lengthened tones"—a succinct description of the sublime and the beautiful in music—he goes on to say that "a growth or climax in sounds *exalts* and *dilates* the spirits, and is therefore a constant source of the sublime," and that the converse is true, a descent being "in unison with those passions which depress the spirits."[20] No art is more difficult to write of than music, as Webb proves by example, if not by precept. His conviction that ascending notes affect the mind in a manner analogous to a soaring height is ingenious, and ought perhaps to be true, but like many analogies it breaks down. Such a method of argument is typical of the age.

[18] *The Art of Poetry on a New Plan*, I, 20–43; II, 71–74; [John Newbery], *The Circle of the Sciences*, The Fourth Edition (Dublin, 1770), III, 109–120.
[19] Daniel Webb, *Remarks on the Beauties of Poetry* (London, 1762), p. 87.
[20] *Ibid.*, p. 89.

The traditional view that pride is the source of the pleasure that arises from the sublime and that pride has its origin either in "a conscious superiority in ourselves" or in the contemplation of greatness in external objects, finds its place in Webb's theory. His discussion of terror probably has some connection with Burke. He finds that it is related to the sublime, and that its effect is due to "the enlargement of its images, and the vehemence of its impressions." Music is capable of arousing terror, as, of course, is poetry, but music cannot cause painful emotions, a fact that does not exclude terror, since, although it is founded on pain when it is real, it can be attended with pleasure in art if it is associated with sublimity; only in excess are terror and similar emotions painful—a statement that in its totality seems to mean little enough.[21]

Finally, Webb declares that in the sublime, "such images as are in motion, and which, by a gradual enlargement, keep our senses in suspense" are most interesting. This would seem to account for the sublimity of music, in which the suspense from note to note, and the cumulative effect of tones, serves, as does a series of images in poetry, "to exalt us above ourselves." But there are more important and interesting theories of sublimity that call for our attention

In 1758, Alexander Gerard submitted to the Edinburgh Society an essay on the much-mooted subject of taste, and won thereby a prize and some fame. The first edition appeared in 1759, and there was sufficient interest in the matter to call forth a second edition in 1764. The essay combines individual speculation with what might almost be called "research," for Gerard seems to have read carefully the works of his predecessors, his indebtedness to whom he is sedulous to acknowledge. Longinus, Hutcheson, Shaftesbury, Baillie, and Hume, among others find places in his footnotes, but it is possible that he did not know Burke's *Enquiry;* at least he does not acknowledge such an acquaintance, natural as it seems that he should have read the latest book on the subject.

Gerard refers taste to the "powers of the imagination," with which man is endowed by nature. These powers are in turn based upon the supposed existence of *"internal* or *reflex senses,* supplying us with far more delicate perceptions than any which can be properly referred to our external organs." The indebtedness to Shaftesbury and Hutcheson is too obvious to require any mention, and bodes ill for the reader who might expect a sudden break with the past after Burke. Taste is then divided into its integral senses—novelty, sublimity, beauty, imitation, harmony ridicule, and virtue—the catchwords of æsthetic before Gerard's day.[22]

---

[21] [Daniel Webb], *Observations on the Correspondence between Poetry and Music* (London, 1769), pp. 8, 9; 16; 25; 30; 51, 52.

[22] Alexander Gerard, *An Essay on Taste*, The Second Edition (Edinburgh, 1764), pp. 1, 2.

Beauty is discussed largely from the point of view of Hogarth, and Gerard rings the changes on the terms unity, variety, proportion, fitness, etc. It is sufficient for our purpose to notice that beauty is said to be largely intellectual, sublimity largely emotional. In view of the rising tide of gothicism, it is interesting to observe that Gerard denies to "works in the gothic taste" any claim to beauty, since they lack proportion and simplicity.[23] Such opinions are helpful in placing a man in relation to the general tastes of his age.

Baillie's conception of quantity and amplitude in conjunction with simplicity as the source of the sublime becomes the foundation of Gerard's system, and his first task is to explain why quantity or grandeur produces sublime emotions. To do this he does not have recourse to a minute psychological and physiological analysis such as Burke had employed, but to a more general terminology and, one observes, to a more conventional one. In comprehending a large object, the mind expands itself, and is filled with one sensation, whose effect is "a solemn sedateness" and "silent wonder and admiration." This expansion requires a definite effort on the part of the mind, analogous to the effort of overcoming an obstacle, the effect of which is an exhilaration that is a concomitant of the experience of the sublime. The sense of power gained by this successful effort leads the mind to imagine itself identified with the object in its totality, and this is the source of that "noble pride" and "lofty conception of its own capacity" that Longinus too casually considers to be the source of the sublime, whereas, in truth, it is only the last phase of the experience.[24] Perhaps it is the resemblance of these opinions to Kant's that causes one to feel that, for all his talk of internal senses, Gerard is somehow saying more than Burke was able to say in his *Enquiry*.

The necessity of simplicity in a sublime object is the natural deduction from the "one grand sensation" that fills the mind, for obviously two dissimilar objects or qualities can hardly cause one grand sensation. Moreover, in a simple object the view of one part can readily suggest the whole, and thus enable "fancy to extend and enlarge it to infinity, that it may fill the capacity of the mind."[25]

It will be seen that in his account of the sensation of sublimity, thanks to Baillie's influence, Gerard keeps the subject well within that half-subjective, half-objective sphere into which Burke and others had carried it, though he wisely avoids the error of being over-specific, a mistake into which Burke easily fell. In fact, he seems much nearer the Kantian than the Burkean sublime, for his formulation of the experience of the sublime in terms of a mingling of pain and exhilaration at once calls

[23] *Ibid.*, pp. 34, 35.   [24] *Ibid.*, pp. 11, 12.   [25] *Ibid.*, pp. 13, 14.

to mind Kant's treatment of the will working itself free from the shackles of space and time, and in admitting "noble pride" as one of the accompanying emotions, he is simply passing down to the next decades the idea that joy, too, is a part of the sublime. But all of this, in 1759, is latent and inferential only; by far the greater part of the *Essay* is taken up with other matters.

The rest of the discussion of sublime taste is concerned with the sublimity of objects that lack grandeur, or of moral qualities that are not objects at all. To do this, Gerard adopts the new, and not yet fashionable, psychology of association, systematized by Hartley in 1749, but also evident in the writings of Hume, from whom Gerard acknowledges that he borrows. This section of the essay is perhaps most germane to the present inquiry, since it is an instance of the increasing tendency to approach the matter from within, rather than from without.

How may objects that lack extension come to be regarded as sublime? Length of duration, prodigious numbers of things similar, eternity, moral qualities such as heroism, magnanimity, contempt of power and wealth, patriotism—these are certainly not large objects.[26] The answer is twofold. In the first place, passions are always considered in relation to their causes, their objects, and their effects, and since these are often connected in some way with quantity, they may render a passage sublime.

What wonder that we esteem heroism grand, when, in order to imagine it, we suppose a mighty conqueror, in opposition to the most formidable dangers, acquiring power over *multitudes* of nations, subjecting to his domain wide *extended* countries, and purchasing renown, which reaches *to the extremities* of the world, and shall continue *through all the ages* of futurity?[27]

Or again, whatever excites in the mind a sensation or an emotion similar to that excited by vast objects, is regarded as sublime. Thus the raging of the sea in a storm or the noise of thunder is sublime, because each inspires "an awful sedateness." This is much the same as saying that an object is sublime because it is sublime, for Gerard totally neglects the important inquiry as to why the rolling of thunder should produce an awful sedateness. It is in this connection that terror enters Gerard's æsthetic. Terror is sublime because it "always implies astonishment, occupies the whole soul, and suspends all its motions."[28] Moreover, objects may become sublime if their causes are sublime, for effects take on a definite coloring from their causes. Great and simple objects seem created by a great force and *at one impulse*. This helps suggest a certain

[26] The full and thorough discussion of the sublimity of moral virtue leads one to suspect the presence of that serious young man, M. Silvain.

[27] *Essay*, pp. 14, 15.

[28] *Ibid.*, p. 16.

sublimity in natural phenomena, which share in the greatness of their omnipotent creator and controller.[29]

The second explanation of the sublimity of small objects, or objects that lack extension, rests on association. It is at this point that Gerard is most genuinely psychological.

It is the nature of association, to unite ideas so closely, that they become in a manner one. In that situation, the qualities of one part are naturally attributed to the whole, or to the other part.[30]

Hence, if the object *suggests* the idea of grandeur, it too becomes sublime to the perceiving mind. This explains the origin of the grandeur that we attribute to objects that have descended from great antiquity. Gerard could well have afforded to expand this idea, but he chose to pass on, leaving association to be completely theorized into æsthetic by his fellow-countryman, Archibald Alison. He himself was content merely to echo Hume.

More interesting is the use of this principle to explain sublimity of style, which "arises, not so much from the sound of the words; though that doubtless may have some influence, as from the nature of the ideas which we are accustomed to annex to them," as well as from the character of the persons among whom they are commonly used.[31] This statement bears witness to the dimming of Longinus's star, and to the ascendency of psychology over rhetoric. Hume, Baillie, and Burke mark successive steps away from the Longinian conception of sublimity. With less and less frequency had the father's name been on the lips of the children. Hume it was who gave the signal that the time had come to adopt a psychological method, and this step once taken, the sublime came into the sphere of the æsthetic. Gerard is sensitive to the new influences; so much is he a part of his age that he passes over the high style without a word. No mention is made of diction; little is said of tropes.[32] Genesis 1.3, is silently ignored, to take little part in controversy again, until science, in a later age, endowed it with a notoriety far different from its Longinian fame.

Association is used to explain sublimity in the fine arts. Architecture may of course create actual grandeur, but even so the principal source of its sublimity is association, "by which the columns suggest ideas of strength and durableness, and the whole structure introduces the sublime ideas of the riches and magnificence of the owner."[33] In the mimetic arts sublimity is due entirely to suggestion and association, and conse-

---

[29] *Ibid.*, p. 18.   [30] *Idem.*   [31] *Ibid.*, p. 19.

[32] This should be qualified, however, by pointing out that Gerard recognizes the value of metaphors, comparisons, and imagery in suggesting sublime associations by introducing the ideas of grand objects. *Ibid.*, p. 25.   [33] *Ibid.*, p. 21.

quently to illusion. In music it is due to long notes, and to the imitation of the passions.[34]

By now the reader is well aware of how much Gerard owes to Baillie, a debt that is apparent in almost everything that he says. But it is only fair to state that the *Essay on Taste* is clearer and better organized than the *Essay on the Sublime*, and that if Gerard has lifted many ideas he has also acknowledged the borrowing. Baillie's essay seems to have been forgotten, and it was well that his ideas should be interpreted anew by a writer who was destined to be read as Baillie was never read, for the simple reason that he published his book at a time when æsthetic subjects were popular. It is as a transmitter of ideas, rather than as an original document, that the *Essay on Taste* is here important.

The psychological method was continued by Henry Home, Lord Kames, in his *Elements of Criticism*, 1762, which represents an effort to follow the path marked out by Burke. The book went through many editions and attained fame, although Johnson enjoyed a joke at its expense. No treatise on sublimity written after 1762, which purported to take into account the previous treatment of the subject, failed to give due attention to the views of Lord Kames.

The cause of all emotions and passions in the human mind is some quality in an object perceived.[35] External objects awaken in us either pleasure or pain, and we seek no explanation of this fact other than the presence of the object[36] whose qualities determine the presence of pain or pleasure in the perceiving mind. The ideas of objects—i.e., objects imagined—cause the same, but fainter, emotions as those caused by the actual presence of the object. In this statement, Kames draws a distinction between artistic experience and the experience of actuality, a distinction that Burke had drawn in his well-known example of a theatre emptied by a report of the execution of a famous criminal in a nearby square (I, 15). This distinction is further emphasized by his explanation of the difference between a passion and an emotion. Pure emotions are never followed by desire; when they are, they become passions. Here again Kames recognizes two methods of regarding objects—the æsthetic and the practical. In conformity with the thought of his age, he translates

---

[34] *Ibid.*, pp. 20–27.

[35] [Henry Home], *The Elements of Criticism* (Edinburgh, 1762), I, 45, 46 ff. This and the immediately following statements are taken from Section I of the chapter on the causes of emotions and passions. I am aware that in subsequent editions Kames revised rather freely, but nothing of importance to the present discussion was added or deleted. I therefore quote from the first edition.

[36] By "object" Kames means not only external objects, but moral qualities, such as courage, benevolence, wit, etc. *Ibid.*, I, 47, 48.

the æsthetic experience into terms of emotion pure and simple, but like Croce, he recognizes the difference between the disinterested enjoyment of an object and that enjoyment which calculates the *use* of the object, and thus prevents the perception of beauty. It is in such statements as this that one can perceive the emergence of an æsthetic point of view.

Kames's interest in emotions leads him to point out that the terms "pleasant and agreeable" and "painful and disagreeable" are not two sets of synonymous expressions, since it is obvious, to look no further, that painful emotions are far from being consistently disagreeable and unpleasant. The conclusion that he reaches is that *agreeable* and *disagreeable* denote qualities that adhere to objects and that are applicable to them as they are perceived; on the other hand, *pleasant* and *painful* denote emotional states prevailing in the person who perceives. Now, while an agreeable object always causes pleasure, and a disagreeable object always causes pain, that pleasure need not always be pleasant, and that pain may be pleasant and the source of enjoyment.[37] None of this is new, but it served to hold æsthetic speculation in the path that Hume and Burke had trod, and it helped to keep alive certain fundamental questions that were discussed from time to time throughout the century.

It is thus the *emotions* of grandeur and sublimity that Kames discusses, after he has dealt with beauty—for he naturally preserves the well-established categories. He begins with an even clearer foreshadowing of the idea of empathy than Baillie's. It is stated very amusingly in a passage which emphasizes the inherent response of man to "great and elevated" objects, classes which are to be distinguished, "not only in the internal feeling, but even in their external expression." Hear him further.

A great object dilates the breast, and makes the spectator endeavour to enlarge his bulk. This is remarkable in persons, who, neglecting delicacy in behaviour, give way to nature without reserve. In describing a great object, they naturally expand themselves by drawing in air with all their force. An elevated object produces a different expression. It makes the spectator stretch upward and stand a tiptoe.[38]

An age when good breeding and delicacy were in conflict with empathy must have been full of repressions.

It is obvious that Kames's conception of the sublime is very much governed by etymology. The Latin "height of style" has simply lost its prepositional modifier, and has been adapted to the physical world, a process that results in the classification of the emotional response to great objects as "grandeur," to elevated objects as "sublimity." In making this distinction Kames restricts sublimity as rigidly as did Burke.

[37] *Ibid.*, I, 129.   [38] *Ibid.*, I, 265.

To these terms Kames gives both an objective and a subjective signification. "They generally signify the quality or circumstance in the objects by which the emotions are produced; sometimes the emotions themselves."[39] Obviously our author is not inclined to over-emphasize the importance of the perceiving mind in the æsthetic experience. Into his proof that the emotions of grandeur and sublimity are pleasant emotions we need not go; it is simpler to concede the point, and to proceed to an examination of his application of these emotions to the field of art.

The ideas of grandeur and elevation are carried over into art as metaphors, and thus give rise to the sublime in art. When an emotion, no matter what its cause, resembles an emotion of grandeur or elevation, it is called by the same name, and the reverse is true of petty and low emotions. It is thus that the phrases, "an elevated genius," "a great man," "a low action," come to have validity. The same is true of sentiments and expressions; hence the sublime of poetry, which consists merely of ideas that awaken emotions similar to those awakened by grand and elevated objects.[40]

This view gives rise to a rule for reaching the sublime in art:

To put in view those parts or circumstances only which make the greatest figure, keeping out of sight every thing that is low and trivial. . . . The mind, from an elevation inspired by important objects, cannot, without reluctance, be forced down to bestow any share of its attention upon trifles.

It is by virtue of the poet's taste in selecting only such incidents and such objects as, taken as a whole, can create most vividly the desired effect, that poetry can move and take possession of the mind as actual events never do. In other words, art is capable of being more sublime than life.[41]

Here is that insistence upon content that is characteristic of much popular criticism in the century. The value of intense experience and unhampered expression seems to have been little considered in an age that was fond of giving rules and formulæ for the creation of art. It was only by working on some such assumption as that expressed by Kames that Miss Seward, for example, could have regarded the poems of Hayley as sublime, or indeed could have used the adjective with the prodigal carelessness with which she bestowed it on anything that deals with large or terrific objects and that happened to take her fancy. The mind, it is assumed, responds automatically and consistently to certain classes of objects; introduce these objects into a poem or a painting and you have the sublime. If it is objected that this is a caricature of what is most often a merely unconscious assumption, it can be granted,

[39] *Ibid.*, I, 266.   [40] *Ibid.*, I, 266, 267.   [41] *Ibid.*, I, 288, 289.

but the assumption is too often present, and is a symptom of the malady that produced much bad poetry in the eighteenth century.

Kames gives a word of warning as to the limits of sublimity. Grandeur and simplicity produce their strongest effects within certain bounds, and are lessened by virtue of excess or deficiency. An object that can be taken in by the eye at one view produces the most striking effect; if it is too large for this purpose it tends to distract rather than to satisfy the mind. The case holds for elevation. The greater the elevation, the smaller the object may appear, until finally it may vanish from sight. Elevation produces its most powerful effect when the object is seen clearly.[42] This is the physical analogy of the true and the false sublime in art. It is a clear witness to Kames's neo-classical prepossession for clarity and proportion. The true sublime, "circumscribed within proper bounds . . . inchants the mind and raises the most delightful of all emotions."[43]

The last aspect of the discussion that calls for notice is also connected with Kames's neo-classical taste. Following in the footsteps of Boileau, Pope, and Longinus, he declares that whereas in small objects and in beauty, regularity is required and order necessary to the arrangement, "in advancing gradually from small to great, regularity and order are less and less required." The *bulk* of the objects seen in any extended natural landscape are not well ordered, and although most are beautiful "a rugged rock or barren heath" is in itself disagreeable. Yet we enjoy such a scene, which swells the heart "to its utmost bounds" and raises strong emotions of grandeur.

The spectator is conscious of an enthusiasm, which cannot bear confinement nor the strictness of regularity and order. He loves to range at large; and is so inchanted with shining objects, as to neglect slight beauties or defects. Thus it is that the delightful emotion of grandeur, depends little on order and regularity. And when the emotion is at its height by a survey of the greatest objects, order and regularity are almost totally disregarded.[44]

Kames is nowhere more traditional than in his admission of irregularity into great beauty. The passage is an obvious extension of similar ideas in Longinus, Boileau, Pope, and all their descendants. It is merely an admission of the validity of Boileau's "*brave désordre*" when applied to natural scenery. Nevertheless, such conventional repetition and emphasizing of these old ideas were doubtless valuable in aiding the rapidly growing appreciation of the unbeautiful in nature to find a sure footing in popular taste. Kames follows his masters closely when he applies the same principle to art, adding as Pope had done, that order and regularity ought to be governing principles in all works of art, and citing

[42] *Ibid.*, I, 281.   [43] *Ibid.*, I, 285.   [44] *Ibid.*, I, 297, 298.

Longinus to the effect that "In works of art we have regard to exact proportion; in those of nature, to grandeur and magnificence."[45] One comes to believe in the value of mere repetition in extending the horizons of eighteenth-century thought. Certainly the constant reiteration of Longinus's high regard for the beauties beyond the rules, and its association with sublimity served throughout the century to keep an ever-increasing element of liberal thought in the minds of English critics and æstheticians.

In the same year in which Kames published *The Elements of Criticism*, Joseph Priestley was adding to his multifarious activities that of being tutor in the Languages and Belles Lettres at the Academy at Warrington. His discourses, soundly based on tradition, were published years later as *A Course of Lectures on Oratory and Criticism*.[46] The title is misleading, for Priestley was not concerned primarily with repeating the canon of rhetorical rules as handed down by the ancients. The first page of his preface informs us that the lectures were published "partly with a view to the illustration of the doctrine of the *association of ideas*," and this gives them an interest that their title would never suggest.

The relation of associationism to æsthetic is one of considerable importance. It would be an error to trace all associationistic tendencies in discussions of taste and beauty and sublimity to Hartley, for like other important thinkers, Hartley did not so much invent as systematize his doctrine, which is really too obvious to require invention, and had long been recognized as a leading principle of psychology. We have had occasion to observe the use of this principle in æsthetic very early in the century. In Hartley's system it becomes *the* principle and *the* explanation of all mental phenomena, and as such it represents a real advance beyond Locke's more general and reflective position, for associationism, as expounded by Hartley, gives a physical basis for thought, and, as is well known, is full of an implied necessitarianism, one of the more revolutionary doctrines of the coming age. It was therefore well calculated to suit the purposes of the Godwins and the young Coleridges of the closing years of the century.

Now associationism appears in æsthetic years before Hartley published his *Observations on Man*, in 1749. Hume had used it, as had Hutcheson before him; Burke was aware of its power, and Gerard had used it freely in his explanation of taste, and in neither Burke nor Gerard can one be sure of any ideas derived directly from Hartley. The consideration of the sublimity of small objects led naturally to the discovery of

---

[45] *Ibid.*, I, 299.

[46] The book was published in London in 1777. Priestley was a propagandist of the Hartleian psychology. See his *Hartley's Theory of the Human Mind* (London, 1775).

the helpfulness of association, and the proverb *de gustibus* cried aloud
for the application of some such idea to explain the diversity of taste.

No such doubt as arises in the mind when one considers the case of
Burke can possibly exist in regard to Priestley, who, converted to the
Hartleian psychology, set about spreading the gospel in his lectures, the
first system of æsthetic that is acknowledged to be founded on the *Observations*. Others were to follow—Alison, for instance—and everyone
knows that Hartley's theory lay behind the psychological elements in
Lyrical Ballads. It is therefore worth while to notice Priestley's lectures,
for they emphasize the slow drift in the sixties toward the formation
of an æsthetic based mainly on the mind that perceives, and not on the
objective qualities of a work of art.

Priestley definitely discards the Hutchesonian theory of internal
senses which perceive beauty and distinguish between the various "objects of taste," and adopts the Hartleian view that

these sensations consist of nothing more than a congenio or combination of ideas
and sensations, separately indistinguishable, but which were formerly associated
either with the idea itself that excites them, or with some other idea, or circumstance, attending the introduction of them.[47]

This is a radical change, a final break with the vagueness of such theorists
as Du Bos and Hutcheson, and a definite advance beyond Hume, Burke,
and Gerard, whose methods are carried to their logical conclusion by
means of definitely formulated scientific ideas.

The resemblance between Gerard's and Priestley's views is so close
that it would be futile to summarize in detail the latter's discussion of the
sublime, which may be briefly described. The sublime is a combination
of pleasurable and painful effort as the mind "enlarges itself to conceive
a great object" and realizes that it has accomplished the feat. Simplicity
is an indispensable quality of sublime objects, since the mind must be
capable of taking in the object as a whole. Sentiments and passions
become sublime, "if they relate to great objects, suppose extensive views
of things, require great effort of the mind to conceive them, and produce
great effects."[48]

When objects lack extension, the principle of association explains
their power to affect the mind in a manner analogous to sublimity. In
this case it is "the *causes*, the *adjuncts*, or the *effects* of these things,
that fill and charm the soul." Thus a palace seems more sublime when
one considers the labor, the expense, and the length of time necessary to
erect it. Ruined buildings and cities increase in sublimity when one
associates with their appearance the time that has elapsed since they

[47] *Lectures*, pp. 72, 73.
[48] *Ibid.*, pp. 151, and 153, and 154.

were built, and their pristine magnificence.[49] In this manner Priestley proceeds with his illustrations of the complexity of the sublime and the value of that half-realized borderland of associated ideas that color our experience both in art and in life.

He excludes terror from the sublime, for he insists that that emotion is composed of two sensations, fear and grandeur, to the latter of which only is due whatever of the sublime one may observe in terrible objects; for, he explains, when we are safe from all harm, the sight of a monstrous beast, or a storm at sea, presents only the pure sublime, that arises from size and not from fear. If pleasure is felt in such a situation it arises from a knowledge of our own safety; indeed, it cannot arise from fear, since that emotion is always painful. Now the pure sublime cannot create so painful an emotion as is felt from fear, for like Gerard and Baillie, Priestley holds that the sublime "tends to fix the attention, and to keep the mind in a kind of *awful stillness*."[50]

These views are used to uphold Boileau's conviction that simplicity of language is necessary for sublimity in writing, for "the *plainest terms* are the most favourable to the sublime, as they exhibit the most just and the strongest idea of the subject."[51] In such terms there is little danger of false and "low" associations, and through such language the true sublime can shine without let or hindrance.

Priestley's chief contribution to the discussion, then, is not so much a body of new ideas, as the fact that he applied definitely the psychology of Hartley to problems of taste. In both his ideas and his association-ism he is not unlike Gerard, but in his "modern" approach to the subject he is a good example of the increasing tendency to take æsthetic problems into the mind of man and to look more carefully at the effect than at the object. It is true that, properly speaking, the *Lectures* belong to the last years of the next decade, but they have been introduced here in order to emphasize the ferment of æsthetic thought that makes the 1760's so important for our discussion.

In his chapter on sublimity, Priestley had spoken of "the simple and sublime Ossian," and in so doing had indicated another tributary that at this juncture flowed into the every-increasing stream of the sublime. The theory of original genius, the patent artificiality of polite life and letters, the renewed interest in the "Gothic" past, and the fashionable sensibility that at times seems to have bordered on sensationalism—all of these forces had prepared the way for Ossian and had assured a good reception to the supposed works of an untutored genius who had lived in an age of simple and warlike virtues, and whose love of sentiment and strong emotion, of fainting maidens and midnight ghosts, and all

[49] *Ibid.*, 157, 158.   [50] *Ibid.*, 158–162.   [51] *Ibid.*, p. 160.

the claptrap of an age that delighted in the emotional "kick" were more than a strange coincidence.

The Ossianic poems merged with the sublime as soon as they appeared,[52] and although their reputation was enhanced by the already existing theories, they strengthened certain tendencies clearly manifest in the taste of the men who were writing on æsthetic problems. For if the sublime is terror, what can be more terrible than the ghosts of Ossian? If it is grandeur, what can be more grand than the armies and their battles, or the nobility and the high-thinking of Ossian's heroes and heroines? If it is energy, what can be more energetic than the winds and the storms that blow and roar through Ossian's lays and epics, what more intense and energetic than the expression of passion in the dark words and the bright deeds of the ancient heroes? If sublimity resides in words, what can be more lofty than the diction and style of the poems, a style so oddly akin to the grand style of the King James version of the Bible? So reasoned—or might have reasoned—the critics who accepted the Ossianic remains as genuine products of antiquity, as indigenous British epics, and who found in them the pleasure that arises when taste is thoroughly satisfied. But if for a while the chorus of praise was loud, it must not be forgotten that Johnson was convinced that the poems could have been written by "many men, many women, and many children."

One of the chief defenders of Ossian was Hugh Blair, Professor of Rhetoric and Belles Lettres at the University of Edinburgh. To him we must give considerable space, for, although his actual contribution to æsthetic is slight, the mass of material that he accumulated around the sublime and the evidently "romantic" quality in his thought render his lectures valuable in estimating the changing taste of the sixties.

Blair's theory of sublimity and taste (the two are rarely separated in the sixties, or even later) was probably influenced by Ossian. He began reading lectures at Edinburgh in 1759, and his preface tells us that the lectures which he published in 1783 had been read constantly for twenty-four years.[53] The lectures, then, would probably have been read in their final form by 1762, when Blair took the chair of Rhetoric and Belles Lettres, and would thus have been in the process of formation about the time of the appearance of the Ossianic poems. That these poems were in his mind when he wrote on taste, beauty, and sublimity, is clearly evident from the fact that his ill-advised critical dissertation on Ossian,

---

[52] The review of *Fingal* in the *Annual Register*, 1761, for example, dubs the poems sublime, points out resemblances to Homer and Milton, and speaks of their "rare and irresistible union of the pathetic and the terrible," IV, 276–286.

[53] *Lectures*, I, 3, note.

published in 1763, was originally a part of the Belles Lettres lectures.[54]

Blair shows himself reactionary to the extent of basing taste on an internal sense; perhaps *reactionary* is not the correct word, when one considers that he was writing only shortly after Gerard, whom he mentions along with D'Alembert and Du Bos; but he also shows a knowledge of Hume, Burke, and Kames, and seems to prefer not to follow them into the more modern view of taste.[55] He refuses to distinguish between sublimity and grandeur, but finds a difference between sublimity in objects and in art, a distinction that one is glad to find made frequently during this period. His description of the "impression of sublimity" is quite conventional; admiration, expansion and elevation of the mind, wonder and astonishment, awe, and solemnity, "even approaching to severity," but withal, delight—it is of this stuff that Blair makes his sublime.[56]

In external objects the simplest form of grandeur is found in the vast and boundless prospects of nature, for all vastness produces the impression of sublimity. Infinity is the ultimately sublime idea; great height and depth are more sublime than great length. Thus plains, the heavens, and the ocean are sublime, and thus a mountain or a tower are more sublime than a plain.[57]

Then follows the statement that nonspatial objects may be sublime. The inference is that vastness is not the sole source of the sublime; loud sounds—thunder, the noise of cannon and of cataracts—are equally capable of impressing the mind with great ideas. It is in this connection that Blair offers his contribution to the subject. "In general we may observe, that great power and force exerted, always raise sublime ideas: and perhaps the most copious source of these is derived from this quarter." Hence the grandeur of earthquakes, fires, storms, thunder, volcanoes, for "nothing is more sublime than mighty power and strength. A stream that runs within its banks, is a beautiful object; but when it rushes down with the impetuosity and noise of a torrent, it becomes a sublime one."[58]

Surely at this point we are carried forward toward the romantic fondness for the wilder aspects of nature, a fondness which this very decade was to crystallize. Byron on Lake Leman, longing to merge his soul with the storm, Shelley praying to be made one with the west wind—are not these extreme expressions of the attitude of mind that finds in vast power the source of the highest imaginative experience that comes to man? Vastness and height are qualities that may impress any man—the average man, or the spiritual child of *Sturm und Drang;* but Burke's terror

[54] [Hugh Blair], *A Critical Dissertation on the Poems of Ossian, the Son of Fingal* (London, 1763), p. 3.

[55] *Lectures*, I, 16, 17, note.   [56] *Ibid.*, I, 46.

[57] *Ibid.*, I, 46, 47.   [58] *Ibid.*, I, 47, 48, and 55, 56.

and Blair's power, these are progenitors of an emotion that was to become one of the dominant motifs of English poetry before the nineteenth
century attained its majority. It is not without significance that Blair,
while rejecting Burke's too restricted view of the sublime, nevertheless
drew on the *Enquiry* for ideas throughout his lectures. The two face
squarely toward the future.

The various ideas attached to Blair's thesis are equally romantic.
All "ideas of the solemn and awful kind, and even bordering on the terrible" assist the sublime. His examples are darkness, solitude, silence,
a hoary mountain, a solitary lake, an aged forest, a cataract, night, deep
bells—all the paraphernalia of Ossianic poetry, the cult of nature that
was rapidly increasing in popularity, and the shadowy moods of terror
that were to find crude expression in the novels of Ann Radcliffe and
consummate expression in *Christabel*.[59]

Burke is called in to substantiate the value of obscurity in creating
the sublime.

In general, all objects that are greatly raised above us, or far removed from us,
either in space or time, are apt to strike us as great. Our viewing them, as through
a mist of distance or antiquity, is favourable to the impression of Sublimity.

With Burke's example before him, Blair finds the step from obscurity to
disorder easy to take, and concludes that "exact proportion of parts"
regularity, limitation, are inimical to the sublime. A great mass of rocks,
he says is more capable of striking the mind with grandeur if they appear "thrown together by the hand of nature with wildness and confusion" than if they seem to have been "adjusted to each other with the
most accurate symmetry."[60] In another place our author is even more
emphatic:

The gay and the beautiful, will appear to more advantage in the midst of smiling
scenery and pleasurable themes. But amidst the rude scenes of nature, amidst
rocks and torrents and whirlwinds and battles, dwells the sublime. It is the
thunder and the lightning of genius. It is the offspring of nature, not of art. It is
negligent of all the lesser graces, and perfectly consistent with a certain noble
disorder. . . . For the sublime, is an awful and serious emotion; and is heightened
by all the images of Trouble, and Terror, and Darkness.[61]

Here is a thorough breaking away from the code of neo-classicism; here
is the final result of Longinus's toleration of beauties that transcend
rules; here is the rationalization of the newly acquired love of wildness

[59] *Ibid.*, I, 48, 49.
[60] *Ibid.*, I, 50–52. It is difficult to see the connection between obscurity and power.
Blair is simply giving way to his tastes and letting his theory go, without much effort to
correlate the two by the means at hand—the doctrine of association.
[61] *Critical Dissertation*, p. 68.

in natural scenery, of the newly fashionable fondness for literature
created before the age of rules, of the new-fangled appreciation of Gothic
architecture,[62] of the increasing desire of the mid-eighteenth century to
escape from itself. This passage is more anti-neo-classical than its parent
in Burke's *Enquiry*. Moreover, it is a total negation of the value of art,
in Pope's sense of the word. "Bring out number, weight, and measure
in a year of dearth," William Blake was to write in *The Marriage of
Heaven and Hell*. "Poetry is the spontaneous overflow of powerful feeling," Wordsworth was to declare in 1800. "The sublime is the offspring
of nature, not of art, "says Blair in 1763, echoing Young's earlier and
similar dictum. These creeds are alike in tone, though what Blair would
have said by way of scorn and disapproval had he been confronted with
a copy of *Songs of Innocence* or *Lyrical Ballads* is not difficult to guess.

The fourth lecture, The Sublime of Writing, merits only a passing
notice. Like Priestley and other writers, he harps on simplicity of style,
discarding all rhetorical devices, and distinctly parting ways with Longinus, who, in his opinion, was no authority on the sublime. One quotation will give the key to his ideas on the subject. The sources of the
sublime, he says, are to be looked for in nature, and not in tropes.

It must come unsought, if it comes at all; and be the natural offspring of a strong
imagination. . . . Whenever a great and awful object is presented in nature, or
a very exalted affection of the human mind is displayed; thence, if you can
catch the impression strongly, and exhibit it warm and glowing, you may draw
the Sublime. These are its only proper sources.[63]

The "sublime style" is dismissed as a very bad one, totally unrelated
to the true sublime, for sublimity lies in thought, not in words, "and
when the thought is truly noble, it will for the most part, clothe itself
in a native dignity of language."[64]

Here, if Blair's words had been heeded, would have died the rhetorical
sublime; but, as we have seen, Greek rhetoric was not yet to lose its
hold on English style, and tropes and figures were to be talked of for
many years to come. Blair's decade, however, witnessed not only an increase of interest in the psychological approach to the sublime, but a
corresponding decrease of interest in the old high style. Blair was at one
with all of his contemporaries who thought æsthetically when he ruled
out of court the concepts out of which had grown the whole discussion.

In an amusing passage, Blair expresses the eighteenth-century idea
of a golden age when nature held free sway and when original genius
flourished. The ancients were the most sublime poets, for "the early

[62] Blair finds that "A Gothic cathedral raises ideas of grandeur in our minds by its size,
its height, its awful obscurity, its strength, and its durability." *Lectures*, I, 52.
[63] *Ibid.*, I, 75.   [64] *Ibid.*, I, 76, 77.

ages of the world and the unimproved state of society, are peculiarly favourable to the strong emotions of sublimity."[65] The "genius" of these men turned easily to astonishment and admiration, and unrestrained by the artificiality of society, they expressed themselves boldly and without affectation. The Bible, Homer, and Ossian are examples offered as proof,[66] the last two being instances of original genius, the darling of the moment.

The Ossianic poems are the perfect example for illustrating Blair's theories, and as such he discussed them in the *Critical Dissertation* already referred to, which became an inevitable appendix to eighteenth-century editions of Ossian. It is unnecessary to urge the value of a document that relates an important work to the idea of sublimity and helps us to understand the popularity of a book which is at once an indication of changing tastes and an earnest of a new order that during the next forty years was to establish itself at the expense of the older traditions.

Blair's criticism is at once exclamatory and reasoned. His admiration of Ossian is sincere, and is all the more strong because the poems are the specific expression of his general critical canon. It would be interesting to know whether MacPherson's poems formed Blair's theories, or whether they came as a godsend to provide him with an apt illustration. The question is perhaps as futile as the quarrel of the Big-endians and the Little-endians, and must not be speculated on; in all probability Blair's taste was a sort to approve of *Fingal*, and the poems both answered a need and furnished an instance.

At any rate, Blair finds Ossian's poetry distinguished for tenderness and sublimity, and in a long comparison with Homer, of the sort so dear to the eighteenth century, he points out that Ossian is sublime in respect to a solemn and awful grandeur, elevation, and astonishment; that he excels in the sublimity of his descriptions and sentiment, and that in regard to the pathetic and dignity of sentiment, he surpasses Homer himself.[67] By virtue of his being an untutored genius, Ossian is naturally inclined to sublimity, for the Rousseauistic simplicity of his times, as we have seen, made for sublime thought and expression, and guaranteed that the poet should neglect "accuracy and correctness; artfully connected narration; exact method and proportion of parts," all, of course, signs of "art" and enlightenment, and by that token inimical to the sublime.[68]

Both in sentiment and in descriptive powers is Ossian preëminently sublime, and his "simplicity and conciseness" help to make him more so. We need not quarrel with Blair's admiration for the sentiments of Fingal

[65] The similarity of this view to Wordsworth's theory of poetic diction is obvious.
[66] *Lectures*, I, 60–63.   [67] *Critical Dissertation*, p. 23.   [68] *Ibid.*, p. 68.

and Oscar, but shall look at what is or more interest—his opinions of Ossian's scenery,

A discussion of the relation of scenery to the sublime must be postponed until a later chapter. Here it will suffice to say that, although Thomson had dealt in natural sublimities in the earlier decades of the century, it was not until about the time of Ossian's poetry that the sublime in scenery took a strong hold on the taste of the public. There is, moreover, a clear difference between the landscape of *The Seasons* and and that of Ossian. As Professor Manwaring has demonstrated, Thomson's landscapes are very much influenced by painting; they are carefully composed, and if they seem wild, it is because of the presence of "an artful wildness that perplexes the scene." But in the Ossianic poems all is wild and stormy and by no means picturesque. It is therefore of some interest to pause here to follow Blair's criticism of Ossian with care.

One of Ossian's virtues, according to Blair, is that he strikes one note and maintains it throughout his poems, every detail serving to enhance the dark grandeur of his sentiments and actions. Blair is very much aware of the harmony that exists between the scenery and the emotional tone of the poems. What are the ingredients of this scenery? "The extended heath by the sea-side; the mountains shaded with mist; the torrent rushing through a solitary valley; the scattered oaks, . . ." these are felt to be the harmonious background for the sublime events and characters of the Gaelic poems.[69]

In his *Critical Dissertation* Blair gives many examples of sublimity in Ossian. Two that are typical of the rest will be useful to the discussion.

They came over the desart like stormy clouds, when the winds roll them over the heath: their edges are tinged with lightning: and the echoing groves foresee the storm.[70]

He rushed, in the sound of his arms, like the terrible spirit of Loda, when he comes in the roar of a thousand storms, and scatters battles from his eyes. . . . He sits on a cloud over Lochlin's seas: his mighty hand is on his sword, and the winds lift his flaming locks. . . . So terrible was Cuchullin in the days of his fame.[71]

The elements of these sublime images form a curious list: the desert, stormy clouds, winds, the heath, lightning, tempests, seas. The list can be extended by gleaning from other passages that Blair cites for praise. Night, torrents, fitful blasts of wind, the dim, setting moon, mountains in a storm, thunder—these from some half-dozen excerpts. And a similar

[69] *Ibid.*, p. 21.

[70] "The War of Inis-Thona," *The Works of Ossian, Son of Fingal.* The Third Edition (London, 1765), I, 155. *Critical Dissertation*, p. 58.

[71] "The Death of Cuchullin," *Ibid.*, I, 213. *Critical Dissertation*, p. 61.

list may be found in the *Lectures*.[72] Not only the objects themselves, but the manner in which they are presented, are sublime. Blair's standard for sublime description requires that the object "must be set before us in such a light as is most proper to give us a clear and full impression of it; it must be described with strength, with conciseness, and simplicty."[73] For only in this way can the "imagination be seized at once."[74]

It is of no small consequence to the cause of romantic scenery that it should come to be representative of the sublime in the external world. The prominence of the sublime in philosophical inquiry, its unrivalled position as the ultimate emotional and æsthetic experience, its popularity as a catchword, as a bit of the prevailing critical jargon, would be of great service in the cause of spreading the cult of nature. Ossian's strange exotic wildness and his obscure, terrible glimpses of scenery were in essence something quite new. Pope and his generation had talked of nature, but they meant the nature of Isaac Newton's well-regulated cosmic machine; or at most the carefully controlled nature of the early landscape garden. Thomson had declaimed about nature, but he had been sedulous to compose his scenes with a view to their pictorial merit. Ossian's images were far from being "nature methodized." His imagination illumined fitfully a scene of mists and mountains and blasted heaths, as artificially wild as his heroines were artificially sensitive; to modern eyes they resemble too much the stage-settings of melodrama. But in 1760, his descriptions carried with them the thrill of the genuine and of naïvely archaic.

It is certainly true that Blair was not the first person to see sublimity in natural objects. But until about 1760, except with a relatively small number of people, the idea had not "taken." Then Ossian came, was seen, and conquered. The consensus of opinion was favorable to the poems. Their wide-spread popularity helped to make general a taste that was slowly coming into existence and that had already been prepared for by a multitude of forces that were silently at work. Ossian was a sublime, original genius. As such, he would be read and valued, and as such he would become a guide to the beauties of storms and mountains and the ocean and the wild, uncultivated heath. Everyone who read, read Ossian; nothing could have been more on a level with the taste of the age. Most readers found there what they sought—sentiment, and a new and mysterious kind of beauty. "Does he make his readers glow, and tremble, and weep?" asked Hugh Blair, rhetorically. The general answer was emphatically affirmative. And so, imperceptibly the Ossianic poems contributed toward converting Britons, nay, Europeans, into enthusiastic admirers of nature in her wilder moments. The Greeks and

[72] See above.   [73] *Lectures*, I, 60.   [74] *Critical Dissertation*, p. 48.

the Augustans were slowly pushed into the background. Rousseau and Ossian began to rival Aristotle and Homer, for Rousseau, at this time, was beginning to gain the ear of Europe and to tell them of the beauties and sublimities of Alpine scenery. The day of Dr. Syntax was at hand; and Syntax, kindly soul, is a voice crying in the wilderness, making straight the way of William Wordsworth.

It is probably not without significance that Johnson, who always regarded the poems of Ossian with scorn, never acquired a taste for the wild and uncultivated in landscape. Writing of the Scotch Highlands he says:

They exhibit very little variety; being almost wholly covered with dark heath, and even that seems to be checked in its growth. What is not heath is nakedness. . . . An age accustomed to flowery pastures and waving harvests is astonished and repelled by this wide extent of hopeless sterility. The appearance is that of matter incapable of form or usefulness.[75]

Although it is impossible to argue that *because* Johnson did not like Ossian he did not like the Highlands, it is none the less true that, as we shall see in a later chapter, a taste for the one generally accompanied a taste for the other, and even when due allowances have been made for the physical handicaps and æsthetic shortcomings that stood between the Doctor and the appreciation of such scenery, we may still find a certain symbolic value in his sturdy resistance to two popular fads.

One more quality of the poems of Ossian must be observed. The ancient poet, says Blair, heightens the "astonished imagination" with "sublimely terrible circumstances."[76] What these circumstances are, is not far to seek. The answer is "ghosts." Supernatural visitations are as frequent in Ossian as in an Elizabethan revenge tragedy. They are the source of that "solemn and awful grandeur," which Blair contrasts with Homer's "impetuosity and fire." Ossian sings:

The groan of the people spread over the hills; it was like the thunder of night, when the cloud bursts on Cona; and a thousand ghosts shriek at once on the hollow wind.

Blair exclaims: "Never was an image of more awful sublimity employed to heighten the terror of battle."[77] To us the passage may seem the mere Fee, fie, foh, fum of literature, but the Professor of Rhetoric and Belles Lettres at the University of Edinburgh, and his contemporaries with him, were impressed. For here Ossian's imagination becomes transcendent and employs the supernatural, susceptibility to which continued a vestigial sort of existence in the background of the minds of even the

[75] [Samuel Johnson], *Journey to the Western Islands of Scotland* (London, 1775), p. 84.
[76] *Critical Dissertation*, p. 61.
[77] *Ibid.*, p. 58.

most enlightened men of the age of reason, ever ready to be invoked into life by the magic wand of poetry.

Most of the ghost passages that Blair quotes as proof of Ossian's superiority to Homer in this kind of writing are declared or implied to be sublime.[78] There is no reason to quote them; anyone who has read the poems will easily call some of them to mind. They are said to "harrow up the soul,"[79] and are obviously of that sublimity which is strengthened by being mingled with terror. Thus ghosts, long a favorite with the eighteenth-century poets of melancholy, became associated with sublimity, to await the coming of Mrs. Radcliffe, who wrote novels almost entirely composed of material that at one time or another had been considered sublime.[80] Blair has no doubt as to the sublimity of Ossian's ghosts:

If the engagement of Fingal with the spirit of Loda, in Carric-Thura; if the encounters of the armies, in Fingal; if the address to the sun, in Carthon; if the similes, founded upon ghosts and spirits of the night . . . be not admitted as examples, and illustrious ones too, of the true poetical sublime, I confess myself ignorant of this quality of writing.[81]

In another passage relative to Ossian's sublime, Blair brings together a list of objects by which Ossian's poetry is characterized. It is of help in showing us for what the poems were valued.

The Sun, the Moon, and the Stars, Clouds and Meteors, Lightning and Thunder, Seas and Whales, Rivers, Torrents, Winds, Rain, Snow, Dews, Mists, Fire and Smoke, Trees and Forrests, Heath and Groves and Flowers, Rocks and Mountains, Musick and Songs, Light and Darkness, Spirits and Ghosts; these form the circle, within which Ossian's comparisons generally run.[82]

And thus Ossian for a time became the poet *par excellence* of nature and the supernatural.[83] His gloomy, wild scenery helped prepare the way for the outburst of enthusiasm for the sublime in nature during the next decades; his ghosts blended easily with the earlier ghosts in poetry to help adjust the public taste for the reception of the gothic novel.

[78] *Works of Ossian.* Crugal's ghost in "Fingal," *Ibid.*, I, 32 and 34; Trenmor's ghost in "The War of Caros," *Ibid.*, I, 143, 144; Fingal and the spirit of Loda, in "Carric-thora," *Ibid.*, I, 277–279. *Critical Dissertation*, pp. 34–37.   [79] *Critical Dissertation*, p. 35.

[80] It will be recalled that some of Shakespeare's ghosts had been taken for examples of sublimity in the earlier years of the century.

[81] *Critical Dissertation*, p. 68.   [82] *Ibid.*, p. 53.

[83] Another witness to the impression made by Ossianic scenery is John Gordon, Archdeacon of Lincoln, whose anonymous pamphlet, *Occasional Thoughts on the Study and Character of Classical Authors* (London, 1762), contains a long comparison of Homer and Ossian, in which Homer fares badly, particularly in respect to the delineation of external nature. Gordon quotes many passages from Ossian, and if we may judge from his use of italics, he valued the dark, wild scenes most of all, but he nowhere uses the word *sublime*. See pp. 90 ff.

In this process the sublime acted as a catalytic agent. It is, of course, true that Blair's opinions represent the extreme of adulation. They found opponents enough, as everyone knows, but although in their superlatives they are not wholly typical of public taste in general, it is none the less true that Ossian, the sublime poet, won the day for a time.

The whole business is ironically summed up by "Castor" in his Essay on Ossian, written in 1796.

... he astonishes with his multiplicity of heroes, and his direful descriptions of objects. In many passages, one meets with a strange incoherence of confusion, too sublime indeed for the human mind to comprehend. ... The reader, in almost every page, finds nothing but heroes strutting in armour, warriors flouncing to battle, winds roaring, streams tumbling, storms raging, blue-eyed maids fainting, and woods and rocks echoing to the clang of arms, and shouts of conquerors; objects too sublime for regularity, and too poetic for modern conception.[84]

This is the cynicism of a later age; we shall leave Ossian in full possession of his sublimity.

Blair, then, plays a considerable part in helping to create the taste for Ossian. As a theorizer on the sublime he is disappointing. There are contradictions in his lecture that are not worth pointing out, but that show none the less that he had not evolved a clear æsthetic system. He quite neglects to consider the problems of beauty and sublimity from the psychological point of view, remaining, on the whole, content to repeat the *clichés* of his predecessors.[85] And yet Blair is an important figure, for in his lectures is reflected much of the changing taste that goes to make up pre-romanticism.

Another lengthy contribution to the question, "Illustrations on Sublimity," was written at some uncertain date during this decade, by James Beattie, author of *The Minstrel* and Professor of Moral Philosophy and Logic in Marischal College. Perhaps it is chiefly memorable for the fact that Beattie derives *sublime* from *super limas*, "above the slime or mud of this world,"[86] but we must consider it for reasons other than its etymological aberrations. It is, for instance, one of the least original essays on the sublime, but for that very reason it becomes of use as a summary of its decade. The usual attempt to show the effects of the sublime in nature, the usual emotions, and the usual causes for them are brought forward and are then transferred by analogy from nature to art, and even to moral excellence.[87]

[84] *European Magazine*, XXIX (1796), 304.

[85] He does make some interesting remarks on beauty, which, he maintains, is not to be sought in the object, but "in the structure of the eye," which determines our pleasure in color and our ideas of beauty. *Lectures*, I, 82.

[86] *Dissertations*, p. 606.

[87] *Ibid.*, pp. 606–613.

It is rather characteristic of this period that Beattie should concern himself with the æsthetic of horror, and it is significant that he treats æsthetic horror in connection with the sublime, for soon the gothic novel was to begin its popular career. This pleasing, agreeable horror, which "may be infused into the mind both by natural appearances and by verbal description," is justly considered to be the product of objects that are sublime—vast caverns, deep and dark woods, overhanging precipices, a stormy sea, descriptions of ghosts and enchantments, all the stock in trade of the poetry of melancholy and the tale of terror. Beattie can offer no satisfactory explanation as to why horror is accompanied with pleasure; he merely states that there is a certain pleasure to be derived from the gratification of the curiosity that events tinged with horror awaken, and he falls back upon a vague reference to the Aristotelian catharsis.[88] True to the *Zeitgeist*, he finds "the most perfect models of sublimity" in the works of nature. The most immense works of man are as nothing before the mighty phenomena of the natural world, "so that without the study of nature, a true taste in the sublime is absolutely unattainable." Nevertheless, art can produce the true sublime—music, when it inspires "elevated affections;" architecture, "when it is large and durable, and withal so simple and well-proportioned as the eye can take in all its greatness at once;" painting, when it reveals great qualities in men, or "imitates" sublime natural objects.[89]

Poetry has five sources of sublimity—great sentiments that elevate the mind, grand images, horror, ability to awaken great and good affections, and descriptions of passions that give elevation to character.[90]

As for style, it is sublime only when it "makes us conceive a great object, or a great effect, in a lively manner; and this may be done, when the words are very plain and simple." In the pages that follow much is borrowed from Longinus,[91] but it need not be repeated here.

One more writer must find a place in this chapter—W. Duff, the author of *An Essay on Original Genius*, 1767. The subject has broadened and taken form since the time of Edward Young. Duff's conception of the nature of an original genius is put more distinctly than Young's. After all, an original genius had appeared on the scene, and the name of

[88] *Ibid.*, pp. 615–617. About this same time Dr. Aikin and his daughter, afterwards Mrs. Barbauld, were considering the same question, and were reaching the conclusion that pleasure enters very little into the experience of horror, but that "We rather chuse to suffer the smart pangs of a violent emotion than the uneasy cravings of an unsatisfied desire." J. and A. L. Aikin, *Miscellaneous Pieces, in Prose*, London (1773), p. 123.

[89] *Ibid.*, pp. 617–619.   [90] *Ibid.*, pp. 620–627.

[91] *Ibid.*, pp. 629–647. Rosenberg apparently did not know "Illustrations on Sublimity," for he states that Longinus had little influence on Beattie. (See *Longinus in England*, pp. 145, 146.) The reverse is true.

Ossian had been boldly placed beside that of Shakespeare and Homer. It is not surprising that the decade which opened with a plea for originality, should, before its close, witness the publication of a book which sought to vindicate the value of nature over art.

Duff considers the source of genius to be imagination, which, like Shelley, he regards as the foundation of all the arts and sciences, although his definition of imagination is far from Shelleian.[92] Original genius, which is characteristically regarded as genius in the highest degree, is "that NATIVE and RADICAL power which the mind possesses, of discovering something NEW and UNCOMMON in every subject on which it employs its faculties."[93] In other words, it is the ability to see the world æsthetically, as opposed to the knack of writing by rules.

Fortunately, not everything that Duff says on the subject is grist to our mill, but a few opinions should be observed. The sublime is "the proper walk" of a great genius, ᵗhe only sphere worthy of its powers. Such a genius always attempts "to grasp the most stupendous objects" and consequently takes a greater delight in "the rude magnificence of nature" than "the elegant decorations of art," for the latter causes only pleasure, but the former "throws the soul into a divine transport of admiration and amazement" which fills the mind and inspires dread and religious awe. "Irregular Greatness, Wildness, and Enthusiasm of Imagination" are the qualities that distinguish original genius.[94]

Duff associates with original genius "that native grandeur of sentiment which disclaims all restraint, is subject to no certain rules," and he thus accounts for the "irregular greatness" apparent in the work of such a man as Shakespeare.[95] An original genius turns naturally to "the contemplation of the Grand and Wonderful, in nature or in human life," and the lofty ideas that "dilate and swell his Imagination" cannot find

---

[92] Duff defines imagination as "that faculty whereby the mind not only reflects on its own operations, but which assembles the various ideas conveyed to the understanding by the canal of sensation, and treasured up in the repository of the memory, compounding or disjoining them at pleasure; and which, by its plastic power of inventing new associations of ideas, and of combining them with infinite variety, is enabled to present a creation of its own, and to exhibit scenes and objects which never existed in nature." *Essay*, p. 7.

[93] *Ibid.*, pp. 86–87.   [94] *Ibid.*, pp. 150–152; 162.

[95] Two years after the publication of the *Essay*, Mrs. Elizabeth Montagu took up the defense of Shakespeare against Voltaire. Like all her coterie she was distinctly susceptible to fads and fashions in critical thought. It is therefore not surprising to find that she considers Shakespeare an original genius, and that she pleads the cause of such a writer who leaves the beaten track and "strike[s] boldly into the pathless sublime." It is better to err so, than to "follow the cautious steps of timid imitators." Genius, she declares, is ill-adapted to following rules; it lays down its own rules. Nor is it more surprising to find that she regards Shakespeare's "praeternatural beings" as sublime. [Elizabeth Montagu], *An Essay on the Writings and Genius of Shakespeare* (London, 1769), pp. 8 and 137.

expression in words. Thus the regularity and obscurity of such writings are due to the weakness of language, a weakness that is evidence of the greatness of soul of an original genius.[96]

Again and again Duff says that lawlessness, irregularity, "unequal and disproportionable grandeur," wildness of imagery, scenery, and sentiment are characteristics of the work of original genius.[97] And this sort of poet possesses enthusiasm, inspiration, which are "the soul of Poetry."[98] Gothic architecture is offered as an example of the power of original genius to create by "spontaneous effort" the vast and the wonderful, and to do it in ignorance of all rules.[99] This power is generally associated with a Rousseauistic state of nature, of which a long description is given; he who will may read it.[100]

In view of Duff's two hundred eighty-two pages in praise of an art that is not created according to the rules, it is a bit difficult to take very seriously his dutiful declaration that rules dictated by good sense and the ages are "what ought never to be violated." If his essay means anything, it means the exact opposite, and his great example of original genius was a stock illustration of the power of an imagination unhampered by rules; for doubtless the reader has suspected that theory has not run ahead of taste. Duff's model is Ossian, who once again exhibits his hold over the imagination of this decade.

In the much later *Critical Observations*, which may as well be mentioned here as elsewhere, Duff discusses again original genius, this time under the various aspects of its manifestation—invention, description, sentiments, etc.,—and draws a long comparison between the only three complete original geniuses, Homer, Ossian, and Shakespeare. It is frankly a sequel to the *Essay* and need not detain us, although it is amusing to see how grudgingly Duff grants Homer superiority in sublimity over Ossian on one page, only to throw the whole matter into doubt on the next. It is the address to the moon in "Carthon" that causes Duff to waver, but he finally contents himself with saying that it, at least, is superior to anything in the *Iliad*.[101]

These years, then, become of real importance in the story of the sublime, which so neatly illustrates various aspects of taste. The emphasis on the subjective element in the æsthetic experience is continued in the habitual seeking of a psychological explanation for the effects of sublime objects. In this respect, Gerard, Kames, and Priestley are important, because they erect a system of emotions and passions and

---

[96] *Essay*, pp. 163–165.   [97] *Ibid.*, pp. 166–168.   [98] *Ibid.*, p. 171.

[99] *Ibid.*, pp. 256, 257.   [100] *Ibid.*, pp. 265–267.

[101] W. Duff, *Critical Observations on the Writings of the Most Celebrated Original Geniuses in Poetry* (London, 1780), *passim*. See especially the summary, pp. 184–188.

associations by which they seek to explain that lofty experience in the face of both nature and art which time had taught them to call sublime. But other forces were also at work. Original genius in theory and in practice was setting a premium on a new sort of art, an art that took little cognizance of the ancients and their rules; and the sublime, from the first friendly to greater freedom of expression, became the natural domain of this new freedom, justified in theory by Young, Blair, and Duff, in actuality, by Ossian. Moreover, the theoretical opposition of nature and art, with nature leading the field, served to rationalize the fondness for wild nature and the emotions that are conventionally aroused by it. Thus there grew up simultaneously a taste for the sublime in nature, and a theory for justifying that taste. It is no cause for wonder that the sixties saw the first appearance among sensitive souls of the passion for the terrific that plays a large part in the correspondence of the Blue Stockings.

CHAPTER VII

THE FINAL PHASE

THE psychological study of æsthetic problems, which characterized the decade immediately following Burke's *Enquiry*, reached its ultimate stage in the last decade of the century, when Archibald Alison published his theory of taste. It is impossible to trace any consistent growth of Alisonian doctrines in the æsthetic of the last half of the century, other than to show, as we have done, the constant habit of examining the responses of the individual when confronted with sublime and beautiful objects, and the tendency to employ associationism to account for æsthetic judgments. In view of the really enormous amount of speculation on the nature of the sublime and beautiful, any given period must perforce be full of totally irrelevant essays either by gentlemen who attempted little beyond the mere repetition of what had already been written, content like schoolboys to repeat what they had learned, or by theorists who were bent on offering something quite new and who consequently do not contribute to the general evolution of the idea, but who may be interesting in themselves. This is particularly true of the last three decades of the century, through which there runs a steady production of essays that mark the path that æsthetic takes in its course to maturity, but that are, in many cases, mere isolated and individual attempts to define æsthetic terms. Fortunately, few of these essays need be discussed in detail here; but, since this chapter will traverse thirty years of speculation, it is not out of place to indicate the varied *obligati* that were improvised for the main theme by various writers. Some of them are not unworthy of a passing notice.

The course of the sublime never did run smooth, since at any moment a writer might seek to deny validity to all that had been written and thought on the subject, and to revert to older ideas and tastes. Such an effort was made by Percival Stockdale, who, irritated by Joseph Warton's essay on Pope, wrote a splenetic and lively book, *An Inquiry into the Nature, and Genuine Laws of Poetry*, in which he not only attempted to uphold the reputation of the great Augustan, but did not hesitate to cast aspersions on the new taste which attributed sublimity to such poetry as Pope seldom attempted to write and to such emotions as he only occasionally desired to arouse.[1] The defense of Pope is oc-

---

[1] If for nothing else the book would be memorable for its dedication to Lord George Germaine. I cannot forbear quoting from it: "These are the motions which dictated this address to your Lordship:—not my gratitude, as an Englishman, for the progress, or rather

casioned by Warton's question, "What is there transcendentally Pathetic or Sublime in Pope?" Stockdale answers at length, referring to the Prologue to *Cato*, to "Many parts of the Essay on Man," and particularly to Warburton's estimation of the address to Bolingbroke which concludes the *Essay on Man*, and which, the Bishop had maintained, was a perfect illustration of Longinus's five sources of sublimity.[2] He then turns his attention to Warton, who, he declares, has a "vitiated and insatiable taste," which is stimulated only "with the *transcendentally* sublime." For such critics Stockdale has only contempt, and on them he pours the phials of his wrath.

If you can only astonish Them, They will immediately pronounce you sublime. In sentiment, give them all the extravagance, and madness of ill-imagined passion. In painting, let all your figures be grotesque; let all your colouring be Chinese. Give them a huddle, and a crash of objects; the gardens of Sir William Chambers;—the very Advertisements of a Langford;—the very Poetry of the Wartons.[3]

Such is the scorn of an old-fashioned taste for the "new art" of the late eighteenth century. It is obvious that the "Gothick souls" of the age of transition, who in theory were founding sublime art on strong emotion and in practice were pouring these emotions into an art that dealt with ruins and ghosts and knights and enchantments were anathema to a man whose tastes were loyal to the calmer art of a saner age, and it is amusing to realise that our own age, while it would hesitate to use Longinus as a measuring rod, or even to utter the word *sublime*, would none the less listen more sympathetically to Stockdale than the majority of his contemporaries could do, for by this time emotional art was sweeping all before it.

John Stedman is much more in harmony with the new spirit when he declares that the best method of examining the sublime is to attend to its effects on the mind, and that these effects may be reduced to the sensations of "surprise, wonder, astonishment; fear, awe, horror," although he manages to sit on two stools by adding the older emotions of complacency, pleasure, admiration, reverence, and astonishment.[4] He is at odds with Burke, refusing to separate the sublime from the beautiful; when calm, the air, the stars, the ocean are both beautiful and sub-

---

continuation, of our unconstitutional, sanguinary, and destructive continental war, over which *you* preside; not very auspiciously to your political reputation.—I pay this homage to the polite scholar, and to the orator,—not a particle of my respect is intended for the Minister." Percival Stockdale, *An Inquiry into the Nature, and Genuine Laws of Poetry*, etc. (London, 1778), pp. v, vi.

[2] *Ibid.*, pp. 124, 125. See also Pope's *Works*, ed. William Warburton (London, 1751) III, 147–151, note.

[3] *Inquiry*, pp. 128, 129.   [4] *Laelius and Hortensia*, p. 93.

lime, but in a storm these same objects become only gloomily sublime.
Nor will he grant Burke's demand that the sublime be always attended
with obscurity, which is suitable only when terror is the chief concomitant of the experience. His interest, however, is chiefly given to that
"branch of the sublime which excites in the mind ideas of power, and
impresseth us with awe, melancholy, or horror," and he is in no doubt
as to the sources of this species of sublimity—the stormy sea is the symbol of them all.[5]

Nathan Drake's preoccupation with the æsthetic of fear and horror
and his habitual association of these emotions with the sublime are
equally typical of the period. Coming as he does in the last decade of
the century, he offers a convenient summary of the more popular nature of the discussion and provides a convenient link between the sublime and the gothic novel. Like Burke, Beattie, the Aikins, and others
he writes at some length on the subject of fear and horror in art, and
develops ideas which virtually form a theory of the tale of terror.

Drake is thoroughly a part of his age in his interest in the emotional
effect of wild scenery, which he finds harmonious with grief and melancholy (an idea on which Mrs. Radcliffe worked) and provocative of a
desire for contemplation. These ideas are supported by quotations from
Alison, the popular æsthetician of the day.[6]

As one might suspect, this taste for sublime scenery goes hand in
hand with an admiration for Ossian, "that melancholy but sublime Bard
of other times," and for "Gothic superstition" in general. Indeed, Drake
has a more than casual fondness for ghosts. He is convinced that the
"enchanted forest of Tasso, the spectre of Camoens, and the apparitions
of Shakespeare" are sublime, and he ventures to predict that if at any
time poets abandon those "romantic legends," the sublime will cease to
exist.[7] Such tastes naturally impel him to consider the sources of the
pleasure which his age took in "objects of terror," which, he knows full
well, may be too horrid to give pleasure. For the artist who can treat
terror so as to prevent its being too painful he has unlimited praise. The
greatest works of art are those which,

approaching the brink of horror, have yet, by the art of the poet or painter, by
adjunctive and pictoresque embellishment, by pathetic, or sublime emotion, been
rendered powerful in creating the most delightful and fascinating emotions.

Two names are offered as instances of this greatest of all art—Dante,
in the episode of Ugolino, and Mrs. Radcliffe, "the Shakespeare of Ro-

[5] *Ibid.*, pp. 93–95; 41.
[6] Nathan Drake, *Literary Hours* (London, 1798), pp. 48; 50–52.
[7] *Ibid.*, pp. 88 and 93.

mantic Writers."[8] The strange tastes of the eighteenth century never correlated two names more ill assorted, not even Drake himself when he classes Collins, Pindar, and Gray as sublime, and declares that *The Bard* "so wildly awful, so gloomily terrific" is greater than anything by Pindar.[9] His formula for a sublime ode should surely be recorded. It must possess

all the higher beauties of poetry, vastness of conception, brilliancy of colouring, grandeur of sentiment[;] the terrible and the appalling must combine, and with mysterious energy alarm and elevate the imagination. A lighting of phrase should pervade the more impassioned parts, and an awful and even dreadful obscurity, from prophetic, or superhuman energy, diffuse its influence over the whole.[10]

It is statements such as these that convince one that Burke's sublime was important in shaping tastes that were destined to overthrow the neo-classical art of the eighteenth century.

Satire is always a helpful guide to the fashionable and prevailing ideas of any age, and as likely as not it sums up an era with a certain not untrustworthy exactness, for its presence presupposes on the one hand that certain tendencies have taken recognizable shape, and on the other that a certain dissatisfaction exists which enables the satirist to stand aside from his age and view it objectively. For this reason we may accept Joseph Fawcett's *The Art of Poetry* as a convenient, if exaggerated picture of the state of art in the year preceding the publication of *Lyrical Ballads*. The poem has much to say about the sublime, and it forms one more link in the chain of evidence that binds the tale of terror to the theory of Burke. Fawcett cautions the would-be poet that he must avoid the true sublime and its powerful emotions, since

> The courtly reader's finely structur'd eye
> See only coarseness in sublimity.

But if he would be popular, he must follow the new fashion and create a sublime composed of "solemn shadows" and "the majesty of mystery."

---

[8] *Ibid.*, pp. 245-249. In Montmorency, A Tale, Drake tried his hand at a story in the manner of Mrs. Radcliffe. *Ibid.*, pp. 252 ff.

[9] *Ibid.*, pp. 250; 379. Drake is of the opinion that since the gothic and Celtic superstitions are superior in "wild sublimity and sportive fancy" to the supernatural beings of ancient literature, the moderns have a distinct advantage of the ancients. *Ibid.*, pp. 380, 381.

[10] *Ibid.*, p. 379. Drake almost outdoes himself in his list of sublime English odes; a more heterogeneous group of enduring and ephemeral poets was seldom drawn up. It is too long to quote in full, but among others we find Dryden, Collins, Akenside, Smollett, Gray, Mason, Warton, Williams, Sargent, Brooke, Sayers, Hole, Rogers, and Coleridge. *Ibid.*, On Lyric Poetry.

E'en listless fair ones shall from langour wake,
And o'er the lines with pleasing terror shake,
If there the lovely tremblers may peruse
The harsh coarse horror of a German muse.
Let hideous superstition frame the base,
On which the wildly dismal tale you raise:
Let ghastliest forms, pale ghosts, and goblins grim,
Form of your verse the terrible sublime!
Paint the dire skeleton, uncloth'd with skin,
With grave-worms crawling out and crawling in,
All hell's red torches in the numbers shine,
And fiends on horseback gallop through the line.[11]

Of course Fawcett is writing with his eye on Bürger and the popular German romantic poetry, but it is obvious that the German muse cannot be blamed for the appearance of terror and the supernatural in the literature of this period. The thing is as old as English literature itself and had flourished in the poetry of melancholy, the theory of Burke, and the epics of Ossian long before England heard of the fair Leonora.

Many other curiosities of sublimity may be discovered in these closing years of the century. An anonymous essay on taste, dedicated to Mrs. Montagu, illustrates the sublime with a geometric figure. We are presented with a circle whose center is Nature, and whose circumference is common sense and common form, demonstrable beauty and truth, the utmost power of the rules, "all that is not nature and all that is not art." Superimposed on this circle is a triangle, whose sides are tangent to the circumference at the points labelled "beauty" and "truth," and whose apex, sublimity, is directly above nature, and plainly its farthest reach. This triangle represents the "region of intellectual pleasure, genius, or taste," at whose center is grace, all well above common sense and the rules, but still founded on nature.[12] Only the author's own words can do justice to this "irregular sublime," which is in truth both the logical conclusion of the Longinian tradition and the negation of the neo-classical standard of art.

Where pure grace ends, the awe of the sublime begins, composed of the influence of pain, of pleasure, of grace, and deformity, playing into each other, that the mind is unable to determine which to call it, pain, or pleasure, or terror.[13]

[11] Joseph Fawcett, *Poems* (London, 1798), pp. 262–264; 271, 272. Professor Harper has pointed out the relation of Fawcett to Wordsworth in his *William Wordsworth* (New York, 1923), I, 261–265. Another amusing skit on the terrible sublime is found in "A Curious Specimen of the Sublime and Beautiful," by George Murgatroyd Woodward, *General Magazine*, I (1787), 206–208.

[12] *An Enquiry Concerning the Principles of Taste* (London, 1785), pp. 5, 6.

[13] *Ibid.*, pp. 17, 18.

Nothing could be a clearer indication of how consistently the sublime was employed to rationalize into art elements which may properly adhere to it, but which were at least suspect in earlier theory. Pain, pleasure, grace, deformity, terror—what a hodge-podge of qualities, yet all equally at rest in the ample bosom of sublimity!

The romantic tendencies of the age come to the fore in the description of the sentiment of sublimity, which is

The mild admiration of grace raised to *wonder* and *astonishment;* to a sentiment of *power* out of *our power* to produce or control. . . . It is the pinnacle of beatitude, bordering upon horror, deformity, madness! an eminence from whence the mind, that dares to look further, is lost! It seems to stand, or rather to waver, between certainty and uncertainty, between security and discretion. It is the point of terror, of undetermined fear, of undetermined power.[14]

Although this is crude eighteenth-century romance, it nevertheless shows some awareness of that unattainable goal toward which the spirit of the new age was to strive and for which its poets were to seek. It is only fitting that such an essay should have been dedicated to the Queen of the Blues, whose circle, as we shall see when we come to consider the sublime of nature, was perhaps the most receptive audience that this curious essay could have found in all England.

Space and time permit us only to mention several other essays. In 1786 Richard Stack read to the Royal Irish Academy a paper, "An Essay on Sublimity of Writing," in which, after praising Burke and attacking Blair, he sought to reopen the question of the sublime and the pathetic, and to make a more exact distinction between Burke's terror which elevates and ordinary fear which depresses the soul.[15] He is strongly Longinian, and his essay seems strangely out of date. Another Irishman, the Reverend George Miller, in 1793, read to the same learned body a paper, "An Essay on the Nature and Origin of our Ideas of the Sublime," in which he summarized the ideas of Longinus, Burke, Priestley, Kames, and Blair, criticizing all of them, and offering his own theory which says nothing that had not been said before and which advances the problem imperceptibly, if at all.[16] Lord Monboddo's brief effort to restore the sublime to the sphere of the beautiful need not detain us,[17] but Alexander Thomson's vision of the mountain of sublimity, over whose ample sides are scattered a large and heterogeneous assembly of ancients and moderns, arranged in ascending order of merit, should not be slighted.

[14] *Ibid.*, p. 18.   [15] *Transactions of the Royal Irish Academy*, (Dublin, 1787), I, 3–26.
[16] *Ibid.*, (1794), V, 17–36.

[17] [James Burnet, Lord Monboddo], *Antient Metaphysics: or the Science of Universals* (London, 1779–1799), II, 120.

The Paradise of Taste is an allegory patterned on the medieval dream poem. In Canto VI we are conducted to the Mountain of Sublimity, whose lower clime can boast no clement charms, for the angry sky is dark and clothed by Tempest,

> in her thickest veil
> Of louring sable clouds, thro' which at times
> On livid wing the rapid lightning flew;
> Succeeding which the Thunder issued forth
> In deep tremendous tone his stern decree.

This dreadful scene, however, does not provoke unmingled terror, for pleasure, too, charms the ear which hears with "trembling joy" the war of the elements.[18]

Here we meet Statius and Young, sitting on a pyramid, for like the Egyptians they thought that "bulk was splendor." These "pompous poets" face the plain complacently, without realizing that they have not ascended the height. Slightly higher are revealed Lucan and Corneille, sitting on a tower, built by Strength, "without the necessary aid of Grace." Mounting above this lower region of sublimity, the poet finds that the sky turns to purest azure, and after a difficult journey up steep paths and through sandy country, he emerges on a verdant isle, where, in a grove, appear Plato, Demosthenes, and Longinus.

> There was the Critic too, whose hasty hand
> Essay'd in vain the fountains to disclose
> Of eloquence sublime; that ardent judge,
> Who taught his fond applause aloft to soar
> On more than critic wing; and ev'n at times
> O'ertook the flights he only meant to praise.

On the right is a verdant mount, where lies "the Pow'r of Prospect," and here we meet Lucretius, Akenside, and Thomson, "three painter Bards." Ascending to the summit over a steep and broken path along a rushing torrent, we see a car hanging "glitt'ring in mid air," which rushes by, and in this precarious chariot are Pindar, Dryden, and Gray. On the summit "enthron'd in equal majesty" sit Homer and Milton. In the Vale of Fancy on a "romantic rock" that soars higher than the Mountain of Sublimity resides Shakespeare.[19] Ridiculous as is this frigid and pompous poem, it is none the less a record of taste during the closing years of the century. The time was surely ripe for *Lyrical Ballads*.

The arrival of Gothic architecture in the fold of the sublime should be chronicled, for once this is accomplished, the sublime resembles a very full treasure box in which can be found all the paraphernalia of

---

[18] Alexander Thomson, *The Paradise of Taste* (London, 1796), pp. 93, 94.

[19] *Ibid.*, pp. 94–124.

romantic writers. The power of ruins over the imagination of the eighteenth-century poets is too well known to require exposition; from the early years of the century they had inspired reverence and awe and melancholy, and had been exploited in poetry, painting, and gardening. The anonymous author of the essay "On the Pleasure Arising from the Sight of Ruins or Ancient Structures" was certainly speaking for his age when he declared:

No one of the least sentiment or imagination can look upon an old or ruined edifice without feeling sublime emotions; a thousand ideas croud upon his mind, and fill him with awful astonishment.[20]

The gothic taste of the mid-century had, as everyone knows, brought the architecture of the middle ages into high favor. It remained to explain its æsthetic effect in terms of sublimity.

This was done by the Reverend John Milner in his "Observations on the Means Necessary for further illustrating the Ecclesiastical Architecture of the Middle Ages," a letter addressed to Mr. Taylor, the publisher of a collection of essays by Thomas Warton and others, to which it served as an introduction. Milner uses Burke's ideas in order to illustrate the sublimity of the English cathedrals. He finds that Gothic cathedrals strike with mingled impressions of awe and pleasure as buildings in the Grecian style can never do. Hence the older cathedrals are superior to St. Paul's, for they lend themselves more easily to awakening religious emotions. The reasons are four, and are all drawn from Burke. In the first place, as Burke had said, "height and length are among the primary sources of *the Sublime*," and the medieval architects strove for both; again, when length and breadth have been carried as far as possible, the mind will be impressed further by an artificial length and height, an effect that results from "the aspiring form of the pointed arches;" in the third place (and Burke is again the authority) a building can produce sublimity by suggesting infinity, an impression which the "perspective of uniform columns, ribs, arches" produces; finally, the solemn gloom of the cathedrals easily illustrates one of Burke's chief ideas. For all of these reasons, the perpendicular style (which Milner calls "florid") represents a gain in beauty and a loss in sublimity, by lowering the pointed arch.[21]

These are some of the by-products of the sublime during the last decades of the century. It is now time to retrace our steps and to consider those essays which brought the eighteenth-century sublime to its final stage of development.

[20] *European Magazine* (London), XXVIII, (1795) 184.
[21] Thomas Warton, *et al.*, *Essays on Gothic Architecture* [Second Edition], (London, 1800), xvi–xix. Milner's letter is dated February 15, 1800.

A strange book presents itself as a starting point, a book which in date belongs to the sixties, in spirit to the early years of the nineteenth century. This anachronism is a little volume called *Clio*, written by one James Usher, an Irishman, a schoolmaster, and a convert to Catholicism.[22] The first edition, printed in 1767, is an uninteresting and brief letter on taste. Between 1767 and 1769, Usher evidently gave more thought to the question, and especially to sublimity. The result is found in the "large additions" to the second edition, which contain what comes very near being a mystical interpretation of sublimity. Perhaps both by race and religion, Usher was predisposed to translate the sublime into transcendental experience, but the scantiness of material concerning him leaves us no grounds for conjecture, much less for certainty.

Usher loses no time in classifying the sublime as the "noblest source" of delight, a delight which completely absorbs our faculties in astonishment, and inspires a mixture of terror, curiosity, and exaltation. But these emotions are not to be indulged for their own sake; there is a further stage in the experience, when "our motions are suspended, and we remain some time until the emotion wears off, wrapped in silence and inquisitive horror." It is this combination of emotions which renders the sublime obscure. Fear is very distinctly an ingredient, but with a difference, for normally the soul in a state of fear, "shrinks below its usual size," but in the presence of the sublime, it assumes an unknown grandeur.

In the poet's language it flies, it soars, it pursues beauty in the madness of rapture, that words or description cannot contain; and if these expressions be extravagant and improper in the ordinary commerce of life, they exactly describe the intellectual and real state of the mind at the presence of the sublime.[23]

This, it must be confessed, is not a promising beginning. That india-rubber soul of the eighteenth-century philosopher, stretching and shrinking with a dreary monotony, certainly represents the worst rhetoric and enthusiasm of the period. But Usher means what he says, as the sequel shows, and we must forgive him his conventional language.

What is the source of this experience? His answer is not unlike Blair's in the as yet unpublished *Lectures*. He analyses the æsthetic experience of mountain scenery, with its irregularity of outline, its rocks and clouds, its rugged precipices, and the débris of ruin at its base. At first "we are terrified and silenced into awe" because all that we behold speaks of immense power, a power, be it observed, that seems to grow greater in

    [22] I[ames] U[sher], *Clio:or a Discourse on Taste*, Second Edition (London, 1769). The *D.N.B.* gives a brief account of Usher's life, in the course of which it gives 1770 as the date and Dublin as the place of the publication of the second edition. This is an error.

    [23] *Ibid.*, pp. 102–104.

proportion as "the appearance of disorder, and neglect of contrivances" is increased. But in addition to silent fear, we feel "curiosity roused from its deepest springs in the soul; and while we tremble, we are seized with an exquisite delight," an effect which association increases.[24]

So far Usher is completely of his age. Now he begins to do what none of his English predecessors had done with any success; he attempts to interpret this experience, to show its relation to human and spiritual values. Dennis had related the sublime to religion, but he had done little but speak of awe, and fear, and the "great ideas" of the Christian faith. Usher likewise merges the sublime with the religious experience.

The religious passion, attended with less tumult, but more constancy than the other passions, calls upon [the] heart in the majesty of darkness and silence, and is the source of the sublime sensation we are treating of.

This passion is obscure because its object is unknown. It arouses curiosity and hope, the source of man's eternal aspiration. Power alarms these passions (one wonders why), and at the same time it stimulates our desire to know the source of this power and its relation to us.[25]

Thus the sublime becomes a supra-sensuous experience. Its object is the infinite, reality, God, and it is felt only when for a moment we lay aside "the transitory ideas of sense" and come face to face with the power that has been always present, but not always observed. Usher denies the ability of materialistic philosophy to explain the sublime, for the very reason that it is an "impression of [an] obscure presence," which sense can never perceive. He breaks sharply with Hume, Burke, and the psychological school, preferring to base the sublime upon an intuitive and mystic recognition of the reality of the soul.

It is to meet the sublime impression undisturbed, that the poet retires to the solitary walks of the country; that he seeks for vales hid from the common eye, where silence seems to take up her dwelling; . . . there he feels with all the *certainty of intuition*,[26] the presence of the universal genius . . . [in whose presence] ideas grow brighter than the gilding of the sun can make them, and put on a strange beauty that belongs not to them. It is the beauty of a being, indistinct, and hid as it were in light, which the imagination in vain seems to lay hold of: whence you may conceive the distress, that obliges the poet to fly from image to image, to express what he finds.[27]

Call this Platonism, or pantheism, or mere moonshine, it certainly has a strange sound in mid-eighteenth-century England. Here is the foundation of a religion of nature, grounded upon a complete negation of the rationalism of the period; a vindication of intuition against the

---

[24] *Ibid.*, pp. 107–109.   [25] *Ibid.*, p. 111.
[26] A startling phrase for the year 1767. The italics are mine.
[27] *Clio*, pp. 115–119.

empirical dependence on the senses for all knowledge; one of the earliest attempts in the century to give expression to that mood which sees immanent in nature the ultimate reality for which the romantic poet was to thirst.

Indeed, Usher is a prose Wordsworth thirty years before *Tintern Abbey* was written. His belief that solitude is a prerequisite of the experience of the sublime is a foreshadowing of Wordsworth's solitary wanderings and profound imaginative experiences.[28] Usher finds that poetry draws its inspiration from a direct intuition of a supernatural reality, and he concludes that this "presence" always meets the "pensive meditative mind;"[29] and in so doing, he surely expresses Wordsworth's doctrine of "wise passiveness." His use of the supernatural light that illumines nature at the moment of imaginative insight is reminiscent of the mystic experience in all ages, and has a resemblance to familiar passages in Wordsworth.

An equally curious resemblance is found in the statement that terror is the first emotion evoked in "the solitary presence," but although most of mankind advance no further than this point, the more sensitive feel also "admiration and extasy," for in this unknown object, delight and fear, opposites by nature, are united.[30] All of this—and here is a doctrine to which Wordsworth would have been the first to assent—is a plain intuition on the part of man "of the sublimity of his own soul."[31] These are ideas that find a much more subtle expression in the first two books of *The Prelude*.

Usher is one of those people whom one cannot classify. His discussion of the sublime seems well-nigh startling when one considers it in respect to its date, for it was written in an age that was fond of proving the existence of God rather by means of deductive logic than by reliance on intuition, and that had developed a theory of knowledge based wholly on sensation and association. *Clio* strikes a note that is not often heard between 1660 and 1800. Gray had shown something of this temper in his description of the road to the Grande Chartreuse[32] but such feeling came rarely in the age of reason, and was not to find full expression until Wordsworth wrote his poetical autobiography. Blair and Ossian, the enthusiasts of terror and the devoted disciples of the sublime in nature, all spoke a totally different language. But Usher stands aside from his age, and his essay on taste demonstrates once again the surprising versatility of the sublime, which could take to itself and seek to justify

[28] *Ibid.*, p. 114. A. C. Bradley, with his customary skill and insight, has analysed the Wordsworthian mystic experience in his essay on Wordsworth in the *Oxford Lectures on Poetry*.   [29] *Ibid.*, p. 120.   [30] *Ibid.*, p. 124.   [31] *Ibid.*, p. 135.
[32] See below, pp. 210, 211.

tastes and intuitions as distinct as Burke's crude terror and Usher's romantic vision of an ultimate reality, immanent in nature but more real than nature itself.

With the next theory that calls for our attention we come again into the highway, our steps lighted by reason and our way made smooth by philosophy of a more conventional order. Thomas Reid's *Essays on the Intellectual Powers of Man* was published in 1785. Reid was the leader of the Scotch school of philosophy in the last half of the eighteenth century, when the Scotch universities were directing an attack on the scepticism and empiricism of Hume and his followers and were evolving (in the name of common sense) an idealism analogous to, though vastly different from, that of Kant. As a teacher of great popularity at Aberdeen and Glasgow, and as the chief intellectual influence on such a man as Dugald Stewart, Reid becomes a prominent figure. The *Essays*, based on lectures that were read for thirty years before they were published, represent a tendency in speculation wholly inimical to the general empirical method of Locke and Hume, and as such they were an impulse toward a view of taste and sublimity quite unlike that of the older school. In order to realize how influential they may have been, we must remember that Reid's ideas were taught from about 1755 to 1785.

The general tenor of Reid's doctrine is revealed in a letter to Alison that is quoted by McCosh. He says:

I am proud to think that I first, in clear and explicit terms, and in the cool blood of a philosopher, maintained that all the beauty and sublimity of objects of sense is derived from the expression they exhibit of things intellectual, which alone have original beauty.[33]

This conclusion is foreshadowed in his definition of taste. Refusing to consider experience as mere sensation, he sets himself boldly against the increasing subjectivism of the mid-century, and insists that objects perceived by taste have qualities that are objectively real. We must distinguish between the "agreeable emotions" and the "quality of the object which causes that emotion;" one is in the mind, the other is in the object. One is the sign of the other, but they are not to be confused. This distinction, formerly, as with Plato, held to be quite valid, Reid hopes to establish in order to counteract the doctrines of "modern philosophy."[34]

Some qualities of the object, like the secondary qualities of matter, can be known only by their effect. These are "occult qualities," none the less real because they are hidden. Others are clearly perceived and

[33] James McCosh, *The Scottish Philosophy* (London, 1875), p. 225.

[34] Thomas Reid, *Essays on the Intellectual Powers of Man* (Edinburgh, 1785), pp. 713, 714.

judged.[35] All real excellence is beauty, and beauty is of more than one kind—natural, intellectual, moral, etc. But there is one standard of beauty, despite the depraving of taste through association, custom, or a defect in the constitution of the mind, for beauty is as real as truth.[36]

Taste is no mere emotion; it is a judgment, and we judge the *object* not the emotion that the object awakens in us. We perceive an excellence in an object, or a lack of excellence, which results from the structure of the object, and we judge it accordingly.[37]

It will be seen, then, that the materialistic and sceptical implications of Locke's empiricism as developed by Hume had frightened Reid.[38] He is eager to split the universe once more into the common-sense world of mind and matter, and is quite happy to grant objective reality to matter so long as he can claim objective reality for the concepts of mind, God, truth, beauty, and all the intellectual abstractions that were the object of sceptical criticism. This distrust of the new science which had grown up from the fertile fields of pure reason is a prelude to the change of philosophical outlook that was to effect a new sort of art before the nineteenth century was many years old. It is not Kantian, of course, but it presents an interesting analogy to Kant's own efforts to eradicate the worship of reason and to establish the validity of a knowledge that the senses cannot reveal to us.

Reid's treatment of the sublime—he calls it "grandeur," adopting Addison's and Akenside's three categories—is equally reactionary and somewhat less logical than his exposition of taste. He begins with the conventional description of the effect of grandeur—an emotion awful, solemn, serious; an elevation of the mind, a kind of enthusiasm, a magnanimity that breeds a contempt of what is mean. Grandeur in an object he defines as "such a degree of excellence, in one kind or another, as merits admiration." Here is a definition thoroughly consistent with his new gospel. The object contains as a quality excellence (beauty), and this excellence is a real quality having objective reality. It is raised to so high a degree that we are struck with admiration. But Reid does not say that grandeur *is* admiration; he keeps clearly separated the quality of the object and the emotion which it awakens, and thus steers clear of the pitfall into which "modern philosophy" had fallen.[39] He rests his contention for the objective reality of "excellence" upon the

---

[35] *Ibid.*, p. 715.   [36] *Ibid.*, pp. 715–718.   [37] *Ibid.*, pp. 719, 720.

[38] In the *Essays*, pp. 727, 728, Reid gives a brief account of the rise of empiricism from Descartes to Locke, mentions Hume's reduction of truth to sensation, and expresses a desire to strike the golden mean between the extreme objectivism of Plato, Aristotle and the Peripatetics, and the modern empiricists.

[39] *Ibid.* pp. 725, 726.

common sense and the common judgment of mankind, which, like Dr. Johnson, he believes not to be at variance with true philosophy.[40]

In description or in speech of any kind—and this is important—the sublime is "a proper expression of the admiration and enthusiasm which the subject produces in the mind of the speaker," for the source of the sublime is not in art, but in the grandeur that resides in the subject and the corresponding emotion that it evokes. "A great work is a work of great power, great wisdom, and great goodness, well contrived for some important end." And now suddenly Reid takes us into the very heart of his system. These qualities of a great work are attributes of *mind* only; figuratively, we ascribe them to objects, but grandeur really inheres only in the mind that created the object. The grandeur of the universe is the grandeur of the mind of God; the grandeur of the *Iliad* is the grandeur of the mind of Homer.[41]

It is only for sake of dignifying the external world that we ascribe to it

intellectual qualities that have some analogy to those they really possess, for however excellent objects may be, they do not possess that highest grandeur save through the power of mind. Matter considered as a substance, inert, extended, divisible, movable, seems far from grand. Matter can only borrow grandeur from something intellectual of which it is the effect, or sign, or instrument, or to which it bears some analogy; . . .[42]

Finally, Reid concludes

that true grandeur is such a degree of excellence as is fit to raise an enthusiastical admiration; that grandeur is found originally and properly in qualities of mind; that it is discerned in objects of sense only by reflection, as the light we perceive in the moon and planets is truly the light of the sun, and that those who look for grandeur in mere matter, seek the living among the dead.[43]

It is impossible to escape the suspicion that Reid is attempting to have his philosophical cake and eat it too. Intent on combating the scepticism of Hume, he insists on the objective reality of qualities that become objects of taste; but when he comes to the sublime, he cannot resist the temptation to attack matter so violently that in essence he destroys it, and evolves a system which certainly indicates quite an opposite point of view from that which he professes. At the same time, it must be remembered that Reid has been a powerful influence in Scotch philosophy, and, through his influence on Cousin, on European philosophy, and that his was the first attempt to use the sublime as an integral factor of a philosophical system. Kant was to do the same thing, and it is in his *Critique of Judgment* that the sublime achieves its apotheosis into an important aspect of a philosophical system. This could be done

[40] *Ibid.*, p. 728.
[41] *Ibid.*, pp. 730, 731.
[42] *Ibid.*, pp. 735, 736.
[43] *Ibid.*, p. 736.

only when the nature of the æsthetic interpretation of experience was given a complete exposition and a rank second only to religious intuition. Reid is not sure enough of his æsthetic to achieve this, but he at least initiates the translation of the sublime into a position of far loftier significance than it could possibly have attained in the usual discussion of taste. In this respect, he may be said to approach that idealistic treatment of sublimity which Kant was to uphold in theory and which Wordsworth was to interpret in great verse.

The most purely æsthetic document of the eighteenth century appeared in 1790, when Archibald Alison published his *Essays on the Nature of Taste*, a book which set about proving Reid's doctrine of the supremacy of mind in the judgment of beauty and sublimity, but which did not scorn the older method of attacking the problem through the accepted psychology of the day. Shaftesbury and his school had confused æsthetic and ethics; the empirical school had begotten a sensationalism and an emotionalism in which the pure æsthetic experience was confounded in the complexities of practical emotions—awe, fear, admiration. Out of this blending of the practical and the theoretical no sure æsthetic knowledge could come. Alison set himself to isolate the æsthetic experience, using as his method of approach the psychology of Hartley. His book is very long and in the main very interesting, especially when he comes to consider the æsthetic of form, a section which will enter very little into the present discussion. In accordance with the thought of his day, Alison retains the categories of the sublime and the beautiful, and regards the problem of taste from both points of view.

In his preface he defines taste as "that Faculty of the human Mind, by which we perceive and enjoy, whatever is Beautiful or Sublime in the works of Nature or Art." This can be described only after a thorough experiment, based on a two-fold scheme—first, "To investigate the NATURE of those QUALITIES that produce Emotions of Taste," and second, "To investigate the NATURE of that Faculty, by which these Emotions are received." This programme shows that Alison held it necessary to distinguish the emotion of taste from the emotions of pleasure that accompany it, the first clearly expressed realization of the fact that there is a purely æsthetic experience.[44]

Alison's analysis of the effect produced on the imagination by sublime and beautiful objects rests upon the psychology of the association of ideas. There are two manners of regarding objects: one may be aware of only the object itself, or the perception of the object may be followed by a train of closely associated ideas that are somehow analogous to the

[44] Archibald Alison, *Essays on the Nature and Principles of Taste.* (Edinburgh, 1790), vii–xi.

objects themselves. In the second instance, the imagination has been engaged, and "trains of pleasing and solemn thought arise spontaneously within our minds." In the one case, we perceive only the qualities that objects present to the senses; in the other, we see the values implied, the experiences to which they are allied, their significance—in other words we see imaginatively.[45] One has to read no further to become aware of the fact that for the first time we are hearing the voice of a clearer thinker than it has been our fortune to meet so far.

Pain, grief, or habit can prevent the enjoyment of the æsthetic experience; critical analysis destroys "the flow of imagination" that is its source. Men without this "flow" (men without taste), are aware only of the useful, the agreeable, the fitting, or the convenient in objects; they are incapable of æsthetic perception, which has nothing to do with these practical relations.[46]

Associations thus increase the beauty or sublimity of objects by facilitating the flow of ideas, a statement which Alison illustrates through the whole of the third section of his first chapter. These associations often seem to have no close relationship with the object that first excited them; and "the object itself, appears only to serve as a hint, to awaken the imagination, and to lead it through every analogous idea that has place in the memory." How true this is of romantic art anyone who knows Wordsworth, Shelley, Keats, or Brahms can testify. One wonders how true it is of an art like Bach's, or (to descend in the scale) like Pope's where the primary intention is to adhere to a rigorously constructed form within which the intuitions are grouped and contrasted and set forth finally with utter clarity. Romantic art—the *Ode to a Nightingale*, a Brahms rhapsody—has quite a different structure, which is based not on outward form so much as on a steady flow of emotions and ideas that grow out of each other, and that do not aim to expose the idea in a flood of light, but to test its quality by analogy and to reveal its signicance by means of half-lights. Alison seems to belong more to the coming age than to the past. Especially interesting is his conclusion that a "powerless state of reverie" is the best for æsthetic experience, a statement that bears similarity to Wordsworth's doctrine of a "wise passiveness."[47]

The difference between the ordinary train of thoughts suggested by objects and the imaginative train produced by beautiful and sublime objects is that the latter is accompanied by a pleasure whose source lies in the fact that each one is pregnant with emotion. These Alison calls "Ideas of Emotion."[48] The two modes of thought differ again in the fact

[45] *Ibid.*, pp. 1–3.
[47] *Ibid.*, pp. 40, 41; 42.
[46] *Ibid.*, pp. 5–12.
[48] *Ibid.*, pp. 49–53.

that ordinarily there is no general principle of connection, whereas in the æsthetic experience, "however slightly individual thoughts may connect, there is a general principle pervading the whole," i.e., they are either "gay, pathetic, melancholy, solemn, awful, elevating," according to the nature of the emotion first excited, which determines the character of all succeeding images.[49] The object must first engage the attention by stimulating some simple emotion like tenderness, melancholy, elevation, etc., for although these emotions may exist without æsthetic implications, they are always found as the first movers of that train of "ideas of emotion" which form the imaginative process.[50]

Habits of thought, occupations, character, all predetermine taste by predetermining our associations—a sort of æsthetic necessitarianism, drawn from Hartley, for

every other appearance is indifferent to them, but those which fall in with the peculiar sensibility of their hearts. The gaiety of Nature alone, is beautiful to a cheerful man; its melancholy, to a man of sadness. . . .[51]

This is surely an echo from Milton, but it is none the less destined to be, in a more philosophical idiom, one of the principal ideas of the early romantics.

> Oh, Lady, we receive but what we give
> And in our lives alone does nature live.

The rest of Chapter II is taken up with fully illustrating the theory that the æsthetic experience rests on ideas of emotion suggested by objects, and that a unity of emotion pervades every such experience.[52] Alison stresses the importance of distinguishing between emotions of taste and simple pleasure; the one is æsthetic, the other practical. In the case of practical emotions, "no additional train of thought is necessary." The pleasure consequent to the exercise of taste is a compound of pleasing emotions and that peculiar pleasure which by the constitution of our nature the exercise of the imagination affords.[53] The pleasure which accompanies taste, Alison calls "delight;" simple emotions are designated "pleasure."[54]

It is thus that Alison isolates from the chaos of eighteenth-century emotion the æsthetic experience. He recognizes its complexity; he is aware that it is only *accompanied* by practical emotions. Hartley come forward as the savior of the cause, shaping through his psychology an

---

[49] *Ibid.*, pp. 54, 55.   [50] *Ibid.*, pp. 57–59.

[51] *Ibid.*, pp. 60–64. Other obstacles to perceiving sublimity or beauty are familiarity, fashion, or perceiving the "indifferent" or non-æsthetic qualities of an object. This last the rationalistic critic constantly does. *Ibid.*, pp. 68–75.

[52] *Ibid.*, pp. 77–110.   [53] *Ibid.*, pp. 113, 114.   [54] *Ibid.*, pp. 120, 121.

æsthetic that is virtually a new creation and that is strikingly similar
to the ideas on which *Lyrical Ballads* was based.[55]

The reader's patience must be requested while we examine as briefly
as possible the application of Alison's principles to the conception of the
sublime. It is important to do this since the rest of the book is given
over to an excellent summary and reinterpretation of most of the objects that had been regarded as sublime in the past.

Alison is indebted to Reid, as his introduction to the second essay,
"Of the Sublime and Beautiful of the Material World" shows, as well
as his special reference to Reid's work in his concluding remarks. Matter is unfitted to produce any kind of emotion; we know its qualities
only by means of "external senses," which cause "sensation" and not
"emotion," the *sine qua non* of our æsthetic experience.[56] That this is
inspired by Reid's doctrine is obvious. It is only when, through association, the qualities of matter—form, color, sound—come to be regarded
as *signs* or *expressions* of qualities, which *can* produce emotion—it is only
then that the external world attains through association the significance
that renders it sublime or beautiful.[57] Association with the qualities of
design, of wisdom, of skill, of power, etc., makes the form and color
(qualities of matter) capable of producing the emotions to which the
process of imagination is subsequent. "Thus Matter, through association, becomes expressive of qualities far more interesting than those it
possesses in itself."[58]

The second chapter of this essay deals with sounds. All sounds are
sublime which are associated with ideas of danger, power, majesty,
solemnity, or deep melancholy. Examples are the howling of a storm,
the murmuring of an earthquake, the report of artillery, the explosion
of thunder, the noise of a torrent, the uproar of a tempest, the sound of
a trumpet, the dashing of waves, the note of an organ, curfew, and the
tolling of a passing bell. This is a fairly old-fashioned list, and is long
enough, in all conscience, but Alison extends it. The striking of a clock
at midnight is one of the most sublime sounds, although at midday the
same sound is far from sublime.[59] Animal cries when they are the cries
of ferocious and formidable animals are sublime, for here the sound is

---

[55] For Wordsworth's knowledge of Alison see Arthur Beatty's *William Wordsworth His
Doctrine and Art in their Historical Relations*, (Madison, 1922), Part I, Chapter 3, and pp.
146 ff.   [56] *Essays*, p. 126.   [57] *Ibid.*, p. 127.   [58] *Ibid.*, pp. 128-133.

[59] *Ibid.*, pp. 138 and 149. Alison recognizes the fact that a false association can destroy
the sublime of sounds. Hence, he says, the sublime is not a natural quality of sound (*Ibid*,
p. 139). Loud sounds are generally more sublime than low ones, but again, association may
falsify this statement, as in the case of the low sound that precedes a tempest, which is
more fearful and more sublime than the storm itself, because we know what is to follow
(*Ibid.*, pp. 142, 143).

the symbol of qualities provoking strong emotion in us. The hooting of an owl at midnight or among ruins is very sublime.[60]

The sense of sight is the most fertile in producing sublime emotions. Alison's consideration of the æsthetic of form is perhaps the best part of the essay, foreshadowing, as it does, the modern interest in the same subject. He denies, as we should expect, beauty and sublimity to form *per se*, and he employs the principle of association to explain its ability to create emotion.[61] Sublimity of form has a twofold source; it arises with the quantity or magnitude of the form itself.[62] As in the case of sounds, the association is shown to be with danger or power, as well as with magnificence and splendor, awe and solemnity, magnitude in respect of height, depth, length, and breadth. Once again we are offered examples that are significant in relation to contemporary literature— trees, rocks, and a Gothic castle,[63] the throne, the diadem, the scepter of a monarch, temples, and the pomp of funerals. This list, added to that of sublime sounds, comprises much of the stock-in-trade of the gothic novelists; if Alison were consistent, he must have declared *The Mysteries of Udolpho* sublime, when, four years later, it appeared.

The point to be noticed is that much of the material that is to be used by the first generation of the romantics plays a considerable rôle in the authoritative and influential category of taste—the sublime. We have had occasion to point out instances almost from the very first years of the century. Alison seems less gothic, only because he is more philosophic and scientific than most romantic enthusiasts in his time. It has not been necessary to *prove* that the material of much romantic literature was no new thing, but a discussion of the sublime inevitably calls to mind again the fact that ideas and objects which the eighteenth century had often used clumsily and occasionally happily, were brought sharply to the fore in the closing years of the eighteenth century, and were recognized elements of the republic of letters when the romantic generation came to treat them anew, according to their own method.

When Alison tells us that a Gothic tower and a tolling bell at midnight and a raging tempest are sublime, he is expressing a view that is as old as Thomson's letter to Mallet, or the graveyard school, or Burke's *Enquiry*; a view that was held to be valid when Baillie wrote on the sub-

[60] *Ibid.*, pp. 157, 158. Alison's remarks on the sublimity of the human voice (*Ibid.*, pp. 167–177) are scarcely worth repeating. Loud and high tones and tones associated with noble passions are sublime. The sublimity of music is explained on the same grounds (*Ibid.*, pp. 194–203).

[61] *Ibid.*, pp. 221–223.

[62] *Ibid.*, p. 225.

[63] "The Gothic castle is still more sublime than all, because besides the desolation of Time, it seems to have withstood the assaults of War." *Ibid.*, p. 227.

lime and when Horace Walpole peopled his dream-projection of rococo
Strawberry Hill with ghosts of murdered men. In the *Essays on the Nature and Principles of Taste*, the sublime takes to itself, after the manner of the last half of the century, most of those elements that were
incapable of being completely at home in a strictly neo-classical art,
and there they found their final resting place until exploited and given
new significance in the poetry and novels of the rising generation.

Alison belongs to the idealistic tradition of late æsthetic thought, and
as such he is indicative of the changing *Weltanschauung* that was to
produce romantic art. He claims to be in apostolic descent from Plato
and his English followers, Shaftesbury, Hutcheson, Akenside, Spence,
and Reid, since the tenor of his essays is agreeable to the doctrine that
"Matter is not beautiful in itself, but derives its Beauty from the Expression of mind."[64] But his method of proving this fact is quite different from that of his predecessors, for he establishes it on a psychology
that was scientifically respectable in his day. With a knowledge of the
difference between actual and imaginative experience, he was able to
express the problem of taste æsthetically with more success than had
anyone before him. In regard to the sublime he is chiefly to be praised
for having gathered together the whole tradition, interpreting it finally
in the light of Hartley's teaching, and stabilizing in tradition the already
popular emotional material which was little calculated to serve the purposes of the older school of rationalistic art and which was slowly growing in power to overthrow and bury in oblivion such fashionable works
of the day as the *Botanic Garden* and the insipid and flowing couplets
of that greatest of poetic ineptitudes, William Hayley.

[64] *Ibid.*, p. 411.

CHAPTER VIII

A GLANCE AHEAD

THE last decade of the century witnessed a change in æsthetic values which can only be glanced at here. Alison is the leading spirit of the change. Despite the fact that his *Essays* did not attain a second edition until 1810 and that the heyday of his fame resulted from this edition, his influence can be detected in the chief æsthetic documents of the years that immediately precede and follow the turn of the century. His lucid style and the easily grasped tenets of his theory made naturally for the spread of his ideas, and although Coleridge might complain that Alison "explains everything and explains nothing,"[1] the psychology of his system was too palpably convenient to suffer his book to lie in neglect. The importance of his influence is not to be lightly estimated. Once established it tended to a view of art quite unlike the neo-classical code, for by translating beauty and sublimity into purely mental "emotions," it stressed the importance of the individual as opposed to the object in the æsthetic experience, and by so doing finally did away with the older objective point of view in æsthetic. It was quite impossible for Alison's disciples to write of *the* beautiful and *the* sublime. If taste is a matter of associated ideas, which are themselves largely a matter of environment and even of chance, then the wisest dictum on æsthetic judgments is clearly the adage, *De gustibus non disputandum est*, itself the very negation of absolute beauty and absolute sublimity, as well as of a critical code which based its judgments upon *a priori* conceptions of nature and beauty and truth.

"Avoid singularity," Dr. Johnson had preached, and singularity can be avoided only by staying true to the general experiences of civilized man in a well-ordered community. As long as this was the goal, there was maintained a fairly consistent balance between the poet and the object. If the poet wrote of the sea, "billowy main" would serve well enough to call up the image of the sea in its universal aspect; it was not his business to record some especially esoteric idea of the sea that he and he alone had conceived. But at the opposite extreme of neo-classic art, the poet's mind and experiences, even when they are "singular," are more important than the object. That aspect of romanticism which justifies the poet's writing of himself, of his own emotional experiences

---

[1] Samuel Taylor Coleridge, "Essays on the Fine Arts," *Miscellanies, Aesthetic and Literary*, ed. T. Ashe (London, 1885), p. 8.

rather than of the object, found its ultimate expression in the imagistic school of poetry in our own century. It is therefore not surprising to find that when H. D. writes of the sea, she actually writes of "pointed pines" and "pools of fir." In Alison's theory, we find the balance between the object and the poet's mind definitely upset; it is a prelude to romantic art, that stands midway between the neo-classicist's truth to general nature and the imagist's truth to an individual impression.

The *Essays*, then, represents the rise of a totally new attitude toward art; in it becomes definitely articulate that subjectivism which we have seen latent and dimly expressed in earlier theory. It is a far cry from the Bolevian cocksureness, from the neo-classic ideals of decorum, of the kinds, of "nature," as the basis of beauty and truth. The individual becomes of primary importance; his perception of values becomes significant, and he is left free to express them untrammelled by tradition; truth in æsthetic interpretation of objects becomes a different thing from a representation, an "imitation;" it becomes rather an individualistic *interpretation* of what the artist perceives, and self-consistency, intensity, and complete expression become the criteria for judging a work of art, not rules and faithfulness to an arbitrary tradition. In such an art there might grow up a tendency to reduce the object to its minimum importance and to emphasize above all the impression which the object makes on the artist. In its extreme phases this tendency would produce impressionism, as it did in the paintings of Turner and here and there in a poem or an image among the romantic poets, and finally as we have seen, the impressionism and imagism and other tendencies in painting and poetry that have come to birth in our own time.

It may be objected that this is to fly faster than the evidence permits; but surely, although one would hardly go to Alison for the final expression of the æsthetic of impressionism, it is not an exaggeration to find in his *Essays* the culmination of the slow growth away from neo-classic conventions and theories, as well as the beginning of a period in art in which individual perception was to set at naught tradition, even the tradition of the world as it has apparently been revealed to man through the sense of sight for half a million years. Granted that Alison would have been aghast if confronted suddenly with a painting by Matisse or a poem by H. D., it is none the less true that the implications of his theory are in harmony with those tendencies in early nineteenth-century poetry and criticism which are akin to (though vastly different from) the individualism of much of modern art.

Wordsworth, for example, might teach the duty of the poet to write with his eye on the object—a creed to which all great poets have certainly adhered; but he himself was acutely aware of the fact that the

poet does not merely represent the object. Hence his talk of the "coloring of the imagination." He is most himself when he writes not of the
object as it is, but as it seems to his imagination and as it stirs his emotions. The melody of the Highland girl's song and the joyous note of the
cuckoo ring continually through "The Solitary Reaper" and "The Cuckoo," but these poems are fine, not because they "imitate" those songs
or the singers, but because the poet has expressed their significance to
an individual and a sensitive mind; and he has done this by telling of
the associations that clustered around those sounds. The poems begin
with the physical fact of hearing, but they tell of the "old, unhappy,
far-off things" and of the "visionary hours" which the songs suggest.
This is certainly not impressionism; but it is a milestone on the way to,
shall we say, H. D.'s sea that is not a sea but a whirling forest of pines.
Nor is this to imply that Wordsworth read Alison and hastened away
from the book to write "The Cuckoo." It is merely to say that Alison's
theory has a certain kinship with the practice of the romantic generation; his book forms a convenient and an easy transition from the
eighteenth to the nineteenth centuries.

The point of view expounded by Alison continued to be prominent
in æsthetic speculation throughout the first half of the nineteenth century, finding expression and modification in Richard Payne Knight's
An Analytical Inquiry into the Principles of Taste, 1805; Edward Mangin's *Essays on the Sources of the Pleasures Received from Literary Composition*, 1809; Dugald Stewart's æsthetic in his *Philosophical Essays*,
1810; Thomas Brown's *Lectures on the Philosophy of the Human Mind*,
1820; James Mill's *Analysis of the Pleasures of the Human Mind*, 1829;
Lord Jeffry's "Essay on Beauty," contributed to the *Encyclopædia
Britannica*, 1816; and Sir Thomas Dick Lauder's *Essay on the Origin of
Taste*, prefixed to an edition of Price's writings on the picturesque, 1842.
It was not until Ruskin appeared that Alison's star began to be dimmed.

To analyse all of these essays would be to add unwelcome bulk to
this volume. It is sufficient to know Alison, in order to know in general
what was written about the sublime during the last years of its life as
an important category of æsthetic. The same objects continue to be
sublime, the same psychological point of view is maintained, the same
analysis of associations is continued. Little is added; something is taken
away, for beauty and the picturesque tend to usurp the prominent place
that the sublime had hitherto occupied in such writings. It is more
germane to this discussion to investigate briefly a curious by-product of
Burke's system that makes its appearance in the closing years of the
eighteenth century.

The paper warfare carried on between Uvedale Price and his friend,

Richard Payne Knight, through which the concept of the picturesque was evolved, has already been treated by Professor Manwaring and Mr. Christopher Hussey, and will be alluded to again in a later chapter.[2] It is therefore necessary only to sketch it at this point. At the outset, the two friends were united by the desire to reclaim landscape gardening from the style made fashionable by "Capability" Brown; but in the end, they presented a divided front, and turned their energies to the task of demolishing each other's theory of picturesque beauty.

The word *picturesque* was popularized by the Reverend William Gilpin, whose descriptive tours, published between 1782 and 1809, were devoted to illustrating his conception of picturesque scenery, a term which he defined but vaguely. Incidentally, it may be recalled, Gilpin was the prototype of Dr. Syntax, whose search for the picturesque, in order that he might write a book and add to his meager clerical income, was celebrated in hudibrastic verse by William Combe with appropriate illustrations by Rowlandson.

The term was in general use for some years before it became a subject for controversy. In 1794, Richard Payne Knight launched his attack on contemporary "improvements" in landscape gardening, by publishing his poem, *The Landscape*, addressed to the then sympathetic Uvedale Price. The aim of the crusade was to bring gardening nearer to "nature" by abolishing the artificial planting and "clumping" so much in favor with the school of Brown, and, by substituting for it gardens and parks which, by careful selection and planting, should reproduce the effect of the landscape painters.

Price gave aid to the cause by writing *An Essay on the Picturesque, as Compared with the Sublime and Beautiful*,[3] about half of which contained theory—a theory that first raised the picturesque to the dignity of a clearly defined æsthetic concept. Price's task was a relatively easy one, for he made no effort to create a new æsthetic for himself. He preferred to take Burke's and to refine on it at will.

In the phrase "picturesque beauty," Gilpin had indicated the existence of a third category, but he had been too much interested in enjoying scenery to find time for abstruse speculation. His "Essay on Picturesque Beauty," first published in 1792, had described picturesque objects as "those, which please from some quality, capable of being *illustrated by painting*," whereas beautiful objects "please the eye in their *natural state*." He quotes Burke to show that beauty has its source in smoothness, and hence he deduces that the picturesque depends on

<hr/>

[2] See below, p. 223.
[3] Published in London in 1794. I quote from the enlarged edition (London, 1796).

roughness, a quality that affords variety by contrasts of light and shade.[4] But he went no further.

Price objected to the vagueness of Gilpin's ideas, and set about converting Burke's dualism into an æsthetic trinity. While accepting Burke's theory of the sublime and beautiful, Price nevertheless had been influenced by Gilpin to think that there are "numberless objects which give great delight to the eye, and yet differ as widely from the beautiful, as does the sublime."[5] The picturesque, which bridges the gap between Burke's categories, is defined as variety and intricacy,[6] and since beauty is smoothness, and "the perfection of smoothness is absolute equality and uniformity," the two are obviously separate entities. Variety, the very opposite of smoothness, is characterized by "sudden protuberance, and lines that cross each other in a sudden and broken manner," and hence roughness and sudden variation and irregularity become the most efficient causes of the picturesque.[7]

The distinction between the sublime and the picturesque is equally clear. The sublime is usually expressed by greatness of dimension, but mere size is in no way associated with the picturesque. The sublime is founded on awe and terror, but the picturesque is equally adapted to the grandest or the gayest scenery. Infinity is sublime; it can never be picturesque, for this quality depends in large measure on shape. Uniformity is compatible with the sublime and is often its cause. "That general, equal gloom which is spread over all nature before a storm . . . is in the highest degree sublime"; such a scene becomes picturesque only when thunder rends and the wind tosses the clouds into "a thousand towering forms."[8]

It is obvious that Price is doing no more than his predecessors had done, but he is doing it with a difference. The early eighteenth century had felt certain emotions which were incompatible with the art of an age whose motto was *nil admirari* and which were associated with objects that were not beautiful according to the accepted notions of the times. They invented, or rather transformed, the sublime, and spent nearly a hundred years in enlarging that concept until it contained most of the ideas and objects and emotions which were to form the basis of a new art. By that time other objects were being appreciated, objects which appealed primarily to the eye, and which patently did not belong

[4] William Gilpin, *Three Essays*, Second Edition (London, 1794), pp. 3; 5; 6, 7; 20, 21. In the same volume is published a letter from Reynolds which sanctions Gilpin's views on the picturesque, but which restricts that quality to the "inferior schools"—Rubens and the Venetians. *Ibid.*, pp. 34–36.

[5] *Ibid.*, I, 48; 52, 53.   [6] *Ibid.*, I, 25, 26.

[7] *Ibid.*, I, 61, 62.   [8] *Ibid.*, I, 99–101.

either to the sublime or the beautiful as conceived by the late eighteenth century. The chief difference between Price and the earlier theorists is that he is concerned with the effect of objects on the eye, with light and shade, rather than with emotions and associations of ideas. It is this fact that gives to much of what he writes a modernity that earlier theories never attain. Once again, then, there is an extension of theory to include those objects and aspects of objects which were seen to have æsthetic value. And so the picturesque came into existence to satisfy the needs of a generation which was becoming increasingly subtle in its æsthetic appreciation of nature and art. A new category was welcome, for man has the delusion that if he names an object, he knows it.

The picturesque was an adaptable and convenient concept. It mixed readily with either the sublime or the beautiful, rendering beauty more captivating and sublimity less awful. It was a quality which enabled the other categories to appeal primarily to the eye trained in the appreciation of pictures. Price sums the matter up quite well:

... we may conclude, that where an object, or a set of objects, are without smoothness or grandeur [the beautiful or the sublime], but from their intricacy, their sudden and irregular deviations, their variety of forms, tints, and shadows, are interesting to a cultivated eye—they are simply picturesque; such, for instance, are the rough banks that often inclose a bye-road, or hollow lane: Imagine the *size* of these banks, and the *space* between them to be increased, till the lane becomes a deep dell—the cones, large caverns,—the peeping stones, hanging rocks, so that the whole impress an idea of awe and grandeur;—the sublime will then be mixed with the picturesque, though the *scale* only, not the *style* of the scenery, would be changed.[9]

Evidently Price considers size to be productive of terror, for these are the concomitants of the imagined scene in which the sublime is mingled with the picturesque, which latter excites the eye to curiosity, the effect of the picturesque, as terror and love are the effects of the sublime and beautiful.

Thus Burke, in his old age, could see the culmination of his system in the æsthetic of a new generation. Once and for all he had stamped on the minds of his countrymen a belief in the categories of the sublime and the beautiful. But the yeast of his doctrine did not cease to work until a new æsthetic had been created. The favor in which scenery and gardens were held and the quarrels which followed the publication of Price's *Essay* went far toward giving the new concept a popularity greater than the sublime possessed. The picturesque became the fashionable catchword, and as such was satirized by Jane Austen in her pleasant way when Catherine Morland learned to her surprise that, despite Mrs.

[9] *Ibid.*, I, 106, 107.

Radcliffe's tutelage, she knew pitifully little about the correct appreciation of landscape.[10]

But if Burke felt any satisfaction on realizing that he was the begetter
of the picturesque, only his death spared him the knowledge that his
system was totally antiquated. Price was soon made to feel the difficulty
of his position as the expounder of an æsthetic that was out of date.
Alison and the new psychology had caused Burke to seem hopelessly
passé, and far less philosophical than he had seemed to his own generation. Price soon found that he was attacked, and the vulnerable point
at which his enemies aimed was his allegiance to Burke. One does not
realize until one follows this controversy how much Burke's star had
waned. From the first he had been blamed for being too specific in attempting to limit the sublime to terror alone, but so late as 1786,
Richard Stack had nothing more to urge against Burke's system than
this fact,[11] and in his general acquiescense he is representative of all
thinkers who did not know Alison.

In 1795, however, George Mason launched the attack on Price. His
chief objection was that Price was sneering at Brown, but he spared
time to criticize the Burkean æsthetic upon which the doctrine of the
picturesque was erected. He says:

I have heard, indeed, that the well-known Enquiry into the origin of these ideas
was in highest estimation with the deep philosophers of France. It may possibly
have its advocates too in some fashionable circles, where the merit of a book depends on the circumstances of its author's being fashionable. But the majority
of thinking and of learned men, whom it has been my lot to converse with on
such subjects, are as well persuaded of terror's being the cause of *sublime*, as that
Tenterden steeple is of Goodwin sands.[12]

Knight goes even further, declaring that, except for Price, he had

never met with any man of learning, by whom the philosophy of the *Inquiry
into the Sublime and Beautiful* was not as much despised and ridiculed, as the
brilliancy and animation of its style were applauded and admired.[13]

If Knight's *Analytical Inquiry into the Principles of Taste* is particularly ruthless in attacking Burke, the reason is to be found in the fact
that Knight was seeking to demolish Price's conception of the picturesque by destroying the foundations on which it rests. The title of

[10] Jane Austen, *Northanger Abbey; and Persuasion* (London, 1818), I, 249, 260-264.

[11] *Transactions of the Royal Irish Academy*, I, 4.

[12] [George Mason], *An Essay on Design in Gardening*, First Published in MDCCLXVIII.
Now Greatly Augmented, etc. (London, 1795), p. 201. He returned to the attack in *An
Appendix to an Essay on Design in Gardening* (London, 1798), pp. 5-7, where he replied
to the answers that Price had introduced into the edition of the *Essay* (1796), I, 109-122.

[13] *Analytical Inquiry*, p. 371. This edition, according to the advertisement, is more
pointedly directed against Burke than the first had been.

Knight's book indicates a broader view of the subject than his friend
and antagonist had taken. Taste is Knight's theme, and in treating it he
develops a new æsthetic idea. He maintains that there is a "merely
visible beauty, abstracted from all mental sympathies or intellectual
fitness," which consists "in harmonious, but yet brilliant and contrasted
combinations of light, shade, and colour; blended, but not confused;
and broken, but not cut, into masses." This visible beauty is sought
principally in such objects "as display to the eye intricacy of parts and
variety of tint and surface."[14] Thus beauty attains an abstract reality,
independent of association (which Knight uses to explain beauty in
general), based on "colours and forms . . . so far as they exhibit pleasing
masses of light and shadow to the eye."[15] As Hussey has shown, this is
a new departure. Alison had displayed a comprehension of the existence
of a purely æsthetic experience, but he had soon buried himself in the
usual analysis of emotions. Knight perceives the æsthetic value of pure
light and color, undiluted with emotional associations, and at this point
æsthetic takes another step toward impressionism.[16] The rest of Knight's
discourse of beauty is based on associationism, with a quite new insistence on sex. We must look only at the sublime.

Chapter I of Part III, Of the Sublime and Pathetic is, one comes to
believe, the least important part of Knight's book. If he writes at great
length on sublimity, he does so mainly to undermine Price's position;
and the result is that most of this long section is given over to ridicule
that reaches its height in the ludicrous picture of Edmund Burke causing astonishment and terror, but not sublime emotion, by walking down
St. James's Street without his breeches and carrying a loaded blunder-
buss.

Knight found poking fun at Burke's system all too easy. As a matter
of fact, the temptation is irresistible to anyone who does not study the
Enquiry in its historical relation to æsthetic thought in general. Knight
saw quite clearly what Burke had never seen—that in the Philosophical
Enquiry there is a hopeless confusion between the æsthetic and the practical. Art can never rest on purely practical emotion and passion. Knowing this (Price should also have been aware of it) Knight had little
difficulty in annihilating Burke's theory.

He goes back, oddly enough, to Longinus, whose elevation and ecstasy make his starting points. All sympathies excited by just and appropriate expressions of energetic passion are sublime, since they "tend
to expand and elevate the mind; and fill it with those enthusiastic rap-
tures, which Longinus justly states to be true feelings of sublimity."[17]

[14] Ibid., pp. 67, 68.   [15] Ibid., p. 83.
[16] The Picturesque, pp. 16, 17.   [17] Analytical Inquiry, pp. 331–333.

This view leads Knight to claim that the pathetic is always sublime, since for him the term evidently denotes an *energetic* expression of passion. All sublime feelings, "whether they be excited by sympathy with external objects, or arise from the internal operations of the mind," exalt and expand the mind. Thus, in grasping at infinity, the mind exercises the power "of multiplying itself without end; and, in so doing, it expands and exalts itself, by which means its feelings and sentiments become sublime."[18] This principle is the source of the sublimity of all vast objects in nature and in works of art, and is the true source of the sublimity of darkness, vacuity, and silence, which share with infinity a lack of definite boundaries.[19]

As for the sublimity of such "terrific" objects as storms and earthquakes, terror exists, but energy is the source of the sublime emotions that they evoke. The distinction is drawn clearly in the following:

As far as feeling or sentiment is concerned, and it is of feeling or sentiment that we are speaking, *that* alone is terrible which impresses some degree of fear. I may *know* an object to be terrible; that is, I may know it to possess the *power* of hurting or destroying: but this is *knowledge,* and not *feeling* or *sentiment;* and the object of that knowledge is *power,* and not *terror;* so that, if any sympathy results from it, it must be a sympathy with power only. That alone is actually terrible to me, which actually impresses me with fear: for though I may know it to be dangerous, when I am beyond its reach, I cannot feel that sentiment which danger inspires, till I either am, or imagine myself to be, within it; and all agree that the effect of the sublime upon the mind is a sentiment of feeling, and not a result of science.[20]

Thus Knight says, in his own inadequate vocabulary, that Burke had not distinguished between the practical and the æsthetic, and thus he seeks to extricate the sublime from the confusion in which it had labored throughout the whole century. His perceptions are keener than his vocabulary is expressive. He illustrates his point by showing that there are two points of view from which a storm may be regarded. To the man who sees danger in the storm and who does not fear, the phenomenon is sublime; but the moment that it becomes terrible, the moment that fear comes into the experience, "all sympathy with the cause that produced it, and consequently, all relish for the sublimity of it, is at an end."[21] Practical considerations have destroyed the capacity of regarding the tempest æsthetically.

This is Knight's contribution to the question. It is of value in showing how far æsthetic thought had progressed since the days of Burke. Knight may not add much to the analysis of the sublime, but he at least knows enough about such matters to perceive to what extent Burke had failed

[18] *Ibid.*, pp. 354; 361; 362.   [19] *Ibid.*, pp. 362–364.
[20] *Ibid.*, pp. 364, 365.   [21] *Ibid.*, p. 367.

to deal with fundamental problems. The reactionary note, the harking back to Longinus, is significant also. Is it not a tacit confession that the century of discussion had done little to solve a problem by theory? that the intuitional method of the Greek critic had perhaps as much value as all the "science" that the Age of Reason could muster up? In other words, does it not imply that only art can catch the full significance of that intense and (for all the boasting of the Blues) rare experience which has been called "sublime?" The inferiority of Knight's chapter on the sublime, when one remembers his shrewd remarks on beauty and the picturesque, also has its meaning for us. The eighteenth century had set itself a task that was beyond its powers. It was not imaginatively equipped to deal with ultimates in art, and it failed. But to the fact that it did not hang back because its reach exceeded its grasp we owe much of the advance in æsthetic theory which served to clear the ground for what we hope is the more mature and penetrating thought of today.

CHAPTER IX

THE SUBLIME IN PAINTING

THE state of painting in eighteenth-century England offers no exact parallel to that of the other arts. In architecture, in the drama, and in poetry the English genius and a well-established national tradition tended, in varying degrees, to modify continental influences, but until Sir Joshua Reynolds came into his fame in the latter half of the century, English painting was definitely immature, and English artists were content to go to school to the Italians, the French, or the Dutch. Hogarth it is true, had struck out for himself both in theory and in practice, but his is the lone instance of independence in the earlier years of the century. Then came the Royal Academy and Reynolds, and British painting, hitherto tentative and uncertain, rapidly developed into a self-conscious national school, with a body of principles, as expressed by Reynolds in his *Discourses*, that were to crystallize into a tradition which continued, despite Blake and the impressionistic work of Turner, long after it had lost its vitality, and until the Pre-Raphaelites worked out a new theory of composition which they practiced with meretricious vulgarity to the no small detriment of Victorian art.

It is true that another art—landscape gardening—took its rise in the eighteenth century, but in this instance the case is quite different. England led the way; France and Germany merely followed, and were happy to imitate the "English garden." Both in the theory and the practice of landscape gardening England asked advice of none, save, of course, in the case of the pseudo-Chinese garden, popularized by Sir Willian Temple and others.[1] A different tone is heard in the early writ-

---

[1] See Arthur O. Lovejoy, "The Chinese Origin of a Romanticism," *JEGP*, XXXII (1933), 1-20. Since gardening has been mentioned, one might expect some account of the part that the sublime played in that popular art. That it exerted some influence seems certain, but it is not easy to deduce that that influence was important. The conventionally sublime objects could scarcely be created where they did not exist, and when they were ready at hand they could not be manipulated, although they might be used effectively in certain scenes. Thomas Whately, in his *Observations on Modern Gardening* (London, 1770) —a typical work of the period—suggests that rushing streams and lofty or fantastic rocks may be used to evoke terror, which, as he says, "is so nearly allied to sublimity" (pp. 62, 99, 106); but throughout his book he shows that he realizes that the materials with which the gardener works preclude much that went to the making of the sublime.

Terror played its part also in the emotional Chinese garden of Sir William Chambers, as the familiar description of scenes of terror in his *Dissertation* (pp. 35-37) proves. But it is not evident that we have the right to assume that wherever we find terror in the last

ings on painting, which are characterized on the one hand by a querulous jealousy of France, sometimes not querulous, but jingoistically and disagreeably patriotic,[2] and on the other by a naïve respect for the authority of the ancients and the dicta of continental critics.

The respect for authority that is evident in the literary criticism of the century fostered this attitude in the devotees of an art that was admittedly new in England. Poetry had its ancients and its rules, and by dint of the example of the one and the guidance of the other, Englishmen could compete on even terms with their continental neighbors. Painting, the sister art of poetry, lagged far behind, and those who were eager to see all the arts flourish in England set busily to work to cultivate a taste for painting in their fellow countrymen and to lay the foundation of theory on which could be erected a national school. In harmony with the spirit of the age, they naturally turned to the ancients, and to the example of the inheritors of the glory of the ancients, the Italians, especially as they were interpreted by the French Academy; and it was the ideas borrowed from these sources that were compiled into a body of rules and judgments for the guidance of painters and connoisseurs.

Little if anything of Greek painting had survived, and Roman painting was known in even smaller fragments than it is known today, but Pliny had written fully of the artists of the ancient world and Roman and Greek sculpture was always at hand to suggest something of the æsthetic aims of the ancients.[3] The Italian Renaissance had bequeathed not only paintings, but treatises on the art, of which Leonardo's and Lomazzo's were the most important. Vasari's *Lives* provided much anecdotal material and many judgments that appear with all too great frequency in the writings of the eighteenth century. Various Frenchmen had written treatises on the art of painting, analogous to Boileau's *L'Art Poétique*, codifying rules and categorizing taste; that English crit-

---

half of the eighteenth century we find the sublime, although the chances are that the two were never entirely unrelated in the popular mind. It is certain, however, that the terrific Chinese garden was imitated only with great restraint, except in the case of the well-known garden of Mr. Tyers of Vauxhall, where the theme of death was used to evoke terror. See *The Scot's Magazine*, XXIX (1767), 456.

[2] The spirit of Hogarth's *Dover* and *Calais* is clearly expressed in the preface to W. Brown's translation of Dolce, in which the decadence of French painting is exultantly announced on the grounds that the exhibition at the Louvre in 1769 contained no historical paintings. *Aretin: A Dialogue on Painting* (London, 1770), pp. ix–x. See also the translator's dedication of de Piles' *Art of Painting* (London, 1706).

[3] A good idea of what the first half of the century might have known of ancient painting may be had from a study of Turnbull's anonymous *A Curious Collection of Ancient Paintings* (London, 1741). The fifty plates are all after Roman paintings, of which the *Nozze Aldobrandine* and many single figures make up the whole.

ics found them useful need not be stated. It was largely out of this material that the earlier English treatises on painting were constructed. Thus it came about that until Reynolds offered in his *Discourses* a re-interpretation of theory that was characterized by clear and independent thinking, good taste, and an ability to take over the best of the classical and neo-classical tradition, and until Richard Wilson and Gainsborough began almost unconsciously to develop the manner which was to be called "picturesque," criticism of painting offers on the whole, though not entirely, the rather depressing spectacle of men who repeated the dicta of Pliny on the ancients (discussing *ex cathedra*, for example, the works of Apelles as if they were familiar with them), of Vasari, and of the French critics, until many of their phrases become as hackneyed as the *clichés* of Dick Minim.

Of these authorities the most important was the French Royal Academy, whose influence was dominant in France and extremely important in England. Founded in 1648, the Royal Academy had occupied itself during the last half of the seventeenth century with the creation of a body of rules and æsthetic ideas that rival the works of Boileau as a perfect summary of French neo-classicism. To sketch in here the ideas of the Academicians, and the controversies that, toward the end of the seventeenth century, began to modify those ideas, would be to commit the double sin of being garrulous and being needlessly garrulous. The precepts and practices of the Academy during the ascendency of Le Brun have been studied many times. The deification of the ancients, the pursuit of ideal beauty as the true imitation of nature, the search for general truth and the consequent distrust of the particular or acci-dental (resulting in the preference of form to color), and other principles of these seventeenth-century legislators are well known, and are obvi-ously expressions of ideas that are familiar in the criticism and creation of poetry. Their ultimate derivation from Raphael through the paint-ings and æsthetic dicta of Poussin and their relation to the philosophy of Descartes have been admirably set forth in Louis Hourticq's *De Poussin à Watteau*.[4]

Since our interest is with academic thought only as it manifests it-self in theories of the sublime in painting, it will be enough to quote here M. Hourticq's admirable summary of the character of the art that the Royal Academy sought to create.

[4] Published in Paris, 1921. The similarities of Poussin's ideas to some of Descartes' are striking, and the book emphasizes anew the relation between Cartesianism and the æsthetic of the age of Louis XIV. Mr. Lovejoy's article, "The Parallel of Deism and Classicism," already referred to, throws light on the prevalence of these ideas in other spheres of thought, and affords an interesting insight into the homogeneity of thought in the neo-classical period.

To be academic is, above all, to see in painting, as Poussin expresses it, "the imitation of human actions;" to put on the canvas a certain number of personages who express passions, reflecting by their attitudes and by their facial expressions the drama that they are acting . . . ; to seek a conventional type of humanity, inspired by antique sculpture and the painting of Raphael; to love . . . noble attitudes, simple and well-balanced lines; but it is also to scorn the living human body, to see only deformity and ugliness in that which is particular and typical; to rectify anatomy by memories of the Antinous or of the Laocoön; . . . to love the simple folds of Roman togas and Greek tunics, but to be indifferent to the material of the draperies . . . ; to compel color to express, like stone, only the forms of objects . . . ; to turn painting, by a taste for things moral and a superstitious veneration for antique sculpture, away from the effects which its own nature demands; to make of it an understudy of literature and sculpture; briefly, it is to ignore the proper resources of oil. . . .[5]

It was these ideas and tastes, derived from the Italians through Poussin, and spread abroad by Du Fresnoy, Le Brun, and the *Conférences* of the Academy, that form the basis of English writings on painting during the first half of the eighteenth century. They were implicit in all that was written, and though they were modified here and there, they were familiar enough, and were accepted for several decades. The controversies over the the relative importance of color and form which resulted in the canonization of Rubens and the recognition of the Venetians, and the constant discussions of the *beau idéal* came to modify in the eighteenth century the purer classicism of the Academy, and these changes in point of view were echoed in England. We shall refer specifically and more fully to whatever ideas bear on the sublime; for the present it is enough to recall that in England, as in France, the Academy was the fountain head of ideas on painting.

In the writings of the Academicians and their followers, several painters figure with considerable prominence. They are Raphael, Michelangelo, Leonardo, Claude, Salvator, and Nicholas and Gaspar Poussin. After the controversy over color had been concluded, Correggio, Guido Reni, Van Dyck, Rubens, and Rembrandt take their share of praise. It is the first group that is important in all treatises on the art, but all of them will not appear in our discussion, since we are concerned only with the "sublime" painters.[6] Raphael and Michelangelo are the only artists who consistently attain to the reputation of sublimity, and the changing estimate of these rival gods will provide some insight into the general change in taste that we have traced in the preceding chapters.

---

[5] *De Poussin à Watteau*, p. 78.

[6] It is for this reason that the Dutch painters will not figure in this chapter. Only Rembrandt could occasionally claim a place among the sublime artists, for the minute literalness in manner, the faithfulness to everyday life, and the lack of profound imagination, so apparent in the Dutch schools, were felt from the first to be incompatible with sublimity.

Vasari's *Lives of the Painters* served for many years as a source of information on, and of tastes concerning, the Italian painters. Anecdotes and dicta from this storehouse of information were repeated with wearisome frequency. But in one important respect the neo-classic period in both France and England dissented from the judgment of the disciple of Michelangelo. Vasari had declared that his master was the greatest of all painters, and by inference at least had reduced Raphael to a secondary position.[7] The eighteenth century had a great deal to learn and had to undergo an æsthetic metamorphosis before this opinion could be tolerated.

The eminence of Poussin had been sufficient to impress upon the Royal Academy the superiority of his master, Raphael. In composition and in coloring the French artist derived from the frescoes in the Stanze, and it was in those paintings that the neo-classic period found the finest expression of what it sought to enjoy and to create in art. Something of the militance with which the Academy espoused the cause of Raphael against that of Michelangelo is reflected in the opinion of Freart de Chambray, who declares that although Michelangelo's reputation is sustained by the vulgar,

Raphael Urbino, the most excellent of the *Modern* Painters, and universally so reported by those of the *Profession*, is the *Person whose Works* I shall propose as so many *Demonstrations* of the absolute necessity of exactly observing the *Principles* which we have establish'd in this *Treatise*. And on the contrary, *Michael Angelo*, superior in *Fame*, but far inferior to him in *Merits*, shall by his extravagant *Compositions*, amply furnish us to discover the *Ignorance* and *Temerity* of those *Libertines*, who, trampling all the *Rules* and *Maximes* under their feet, pursue only their own *Caprices*.[8]

It was the individuality and "capriciousness" of Michelangelo that made it impossible to fit his most characteristic works into the formulæ of the academic rules, and the irritation that the neo-classicists felt in the presence of his works was natural enough in the light of their æsthetic. Even Roger de Piles, who was the champion of color (a quality for which Raphael was never famous), declared in his *Art of Painting*,

---

[7] Giorgi Vasari, *Lives of the Painters*, etc., tr. A. B. Hinds (London, 1900). See the lives of Raphael and Michelangelo, *passim*.

[8] Freart de Chambray, *An Idea of the Perfection of Painting*, tr. J[ohn] E[velyn] (London, 1668), Preface. Any number of similar dicta could be quoted. See for example: Du Fresnoy, *The Art of Painting*, tr. Mr. Dryden, Second Edition (London, 1716), pp. 225 and 288; [André Félibien], *Des Principes de l'Architecture*, etc., Seconde Edition (Paris, 1690), p. 397; P. Monier, *History of Painting*, etc. (London, 1699), pp. 118-122; [William Aglionby], *Painting Illustrated in Three Diallogues* (London, 1686), pp. 76, 123, 80, 82, 125; de Piles, *Principles of Painting*, tr. by a Painter (London, 1743), pp. 294-300. Dolce had early upheld the superiority of Raphael to Michelangelo. See *Aretin*, *passim*.

which included an abridgment of Vasari's *Lives*, that Raphael is superior
to Michelangelo and Leonardo, and that his genius is sublime.[9] That
there should have been such a reaction from Michelangelo's art was
inevitable. His influence had been disastrous to the high renaissance
tradition in painting. As Wölfflin puts it: "All beauty was measured by
the standard of his works, and an art that had been created under ex-
clusively individual conditions became universal."[10] In the presence of
the enormously energetic genius of Michelangelo and the rather inco-
herent turbulence of his imitators, the seventeenth century, "shocked
with license, shuddered into rules," and turned to the more human and
serener art of Raphael as its criterion of beauty.

It is not difficult to deduce why Raphael found favor in the eyes of
the neo-classicist. His paintings (and for our period the frescoes and the
cartoons are his important work) are more generalized, more normal,
more urbane than Michelangelo's, and hence seemed truer to nature.
Noble, ideal, dignified, his figures came to appeal to an age that was
tiring of eccentricities and was seeking repose in the calm and security
in the universal. The neo-classicist could perceive, although he might
not justly value, the extremely individualistic genius of Michelangelo,
and since he distrusted the individual and the particular, as the exception that proves the value of the rules, he very naturally felt perturbed
before the fierce genius that contorted and seemed to mar the nature
that it wished to depict.

Raphael's thoughts, says de Piles, like those of the ancients, are simple, sublime, and natural, and he goes on to speak of

. . . the beauties of *Design*, the fine choice of the *Attitudes*, the delicacy of the
Expressions, the fair order of the *Foldings*, and a *sublime Stile* to which the
Ancients raised Nature, and the Moderns after them in the beginning of the
sixteenth Century.[11]

Not only does he excel in propriety and in attaining the taste of the
ancients, but he is also rich in invention, and "to the Justness, the
Grandeur and Elegance of the Antique, he added the simplicity of Nature without affecting a particular Manner."[12] In his preface on "the
idea of painting" it is tacitly assumed in all that is said that Raphael
has no peer. He is "the model of all perfection" and he "excelled more
in all the parts of his art, than any other painter."[13]

De Piles expresses well enough the qualities which endeared Raphael

[9] *Art of Painting* (London, 1706), pp. 27 and 126.
[10] Heinrich Wölfflin, *The Art of the Italian Renaissance* (London, 1903), p. 195.
[11] *Art of Painting*, pp. 128 and 393.
[12] *Ibid.*, p. 127.
[13] *Principles of Painting*, pp. 14, 15.

to the academicians. He was valued because of his expression,[14] because of the versatility of his invention, because of his nobility, and most of all because it was assumed that in his paintings one found an approximation, at least, of the style of the ancients, a style that was the exact imitation of nature. "A Painter must be judged," says Aglionby, "by his approximation to antique beauty."[15] Now it was known from Vasari that Raphael had studied the ancients earnestly, and it was held that to follow nature was to follow them. Respect for the ancients extended to their imitators, and the monumental figures and the grand style of Raphael harmonized with the dream that the neo-classicists had of what Greek painting had been.

The theory of nature, also, played into Raphael's hands. De Piles once again speaks for his age when he directs the painter to form an image of nature "not only as he happens to see her in particular subjects, but as she ought to be in her self, and as she would be, were she not hinder'd by certain accidents."[16] The painter should reproduce real nature, which is perfect, not the actual, which is thwarted and imperfect. As de Piles says:

'Tis visible the Ancient Sculptors sought after this natural simplicity, and that *Raphael* borrow'd from them those natural strokes, which he has every where spread over his Pieces with good *Gusto*.[17]

Thus art is above nature, and aims to perfect her imperfectly fulfilled intentions. It was the way of the ancients, and consequently it must be good; and it became the way of Poussin and of neo-classical painting generally. It was only in this manner that the generalized truths which the period sought in art could be attained.

Thus in painting as in the other arts the ancients held sway and ruled through a Vice-Roy—in this instance, Raphael. One would imagine that whole galleries were filled with Greek paintings, so often are the qualities of individual painters described. In every early treatise statements taken from Pliny are offered with due pomp and solemnity to the reader. Histories of painting, such as Henry Bell's and George Turnbull's,[18] repeat age-old platitudes, and in the case of the latter, even compare long-perished Greek masters with the Italians in a ludicrously serious manner. A sceptical eighteenth-century reader has asked in a marginal comment on Aglionby's praise of the antique as "the best of Nature"

[14] This term meant an ability to depict the passions. De Piles describes Raphael's expression as "Just, Elevated, and Touching." *Art of Painting*, p. 127.

[15] *Paintings Illustrated in Three Diallogues*, p. 104.

[16] *Art of Painting*, p. 1.   [17] *Ibid.*, pp. 14, 15.

[18] Henry Bell, *An Historical Essay on the Original of Painting* (London, 1728), and George Turnbull, *A Treatise on Ancient Painting* (London, 1740).

how these dicta could be made. The answer is first of all that the age had an almost unlimited respect for authority. But Félibien gives a more cogent reason. He argues by analogy that if the sculptors achieved excellence the painters must have done so too.[19] Raphael therefore could attain, through the study of medals and statues, the same beauty and the same manner that distinguished Apelles.

The generalizing and the idealizing of nature that were observed in ancient sculpture became, then, the criterion of the late seventeenth century, and of course it was labelled with the supreme epithet—sublime. De Piles, writing of "the Grand Gusto," demands that the painter must avoid mediocrity, since

. . . in Painting there must be something Great and Extraordinary to Surprize, Please and Instruct, which is what we call the *grand Gusto*. 'Tis by this that ordinary things are made Beautiful, and the Beautiful, Sublime and Wonderful; for in Painting, the *grand Gusto*, the Sublime, and the Marvellous are one and the same thing.[20]

The influence of Boileau's *Réflexions* on this passage need not be labored. Longinian ideas are obviously present and are being applied to an art that Longinus scarcely mentioned.

But this was not the only quality that enabled Raphael to become sublime. He was famous for his grace, and grace had a special significance which de Piles makes clear in an important passage.

A Painter has it from Nature only, and does not know that he has it, nor in what degree, nor how he communicates it to his Works. It surprises the Spectator, who feels the effect without penetrating into the true cause of it; . . . We may define it thus, *'Tis what pleases, and gains the Heart, without concerning itself with the Understanding.* Grace and Beauty are two different things, Beauty pleases by the Rules only, and Grace without them. What is beautiful is not always Graceful; but Grace join'd with Beauty is the height of Perfection.[21]

Jonathan Richardson was to talk a great deal of "grace and greatness," and the phrase is current in the criticism of painting throughout the first part of the eighteenth century. It conveys, as we see, the qualities that are to be associated with sublimity in all the arts—the *je-ne-sais-quoi*, the wonderful, the surprising, the marvellous, and, more important, those indefinable beauties that lie beyond the rules and that form the nucleus of the rebellion against the rules themselves.

[19] [André Félibien], *Entretiens sur les Vies et sur les Ouvrages des Plus Excellens Peintres Anciens et Modernes*, Seconde Edition (Paris, 1685), I, 78.

[20] *Art of Painting*, p. 19.

[21] *Ibid.*, pp. 8 and 129. It is difficult not to believe that Pope was versifying this very passage when he wrote his famous lines on the grace beyond the reach of art. Du Fresnoy speaks of the same quality in the same terms, *Art of Painting*, pp. 31, 32, as does Turnbull in his *Treatise*, p. 89.

All of this Raphael was thought to possess, and when eighteenth-century England took up the criticism of painting, Raphael, the sublime, was one of their data. And sublime he was to continue throughout the century. The case is different with Michelangelo. Vasari had praised him above all other artists, but the neo-classical age could not so think of him. Aglionby stoutly maintains that "for all Vasari commends him above the Skies, he was a better Sculptor than a Painter."[22] This is undoubtedly true, much truer than the belief that Raphael was the perfect painter, but the grounds for this belief were peculiar to the age in which it was uttered.

De Piles points out the quality in the works of Michelangelo which was certainly the basis of the disapproval of the academicians and their followers. He did not "neglect the antique"—Vasari was witness to this fact; "but he was not willing to be indebted for his art to any thing but himself."[23] In other words his art is too individualistic to permit the generalization, in terms of the simple and the normal, that the neo-classical interpretation of ancient art and of nature demanded. Hence, while unable to escape the power of Michelangelo, the neo-classicist tended to remain puzzled by his art. It tended too much to express the particular, it was too complex, it lacked the simple dignity of Raphael and the ancient sculptors. It seemed to be "capricious."

His *Attitudes* are, for the most part, disagreeable, the *Airs* of his *Heads* fierce, his *Draperies* not open enough, and his *Expressions* not very natural; yet, as wild as his productions are, there's Elevation in his Thoughts, and Nobleness in his Figures . . .[24]

In all forms of art the neo-classicist preferred the obvious to the subtle, the urbane to the violently expressive, the general to the particular. But even a generation whose vision was likely to be distorted by *a priori* prejudices derived from the rules could not remain impervious to the grandeur of the Sistine Chapel. If it failed to see in Michelangelo's work the expression of a thwarted spirit, whose bafflement was all the more tragic because of the ferocity of its energy, the age was none the less impressed by some of the more obvious qualities of his work—its elemental grandeur, ability to startle, treatment of the human body.

In one aspect of his art Michelangelo was recognized as supreme; that is, in design, by which was meant the drawing of figures.[25] The eighteenth century never wearied of repeating this opinion. Michelangelo was

---

[22] *Painting Illustrated in Three Diallogues*, p. 82.
[23] *Art of Painting*, p. 161.   [24] *Ibid.*, pp. 160, 161.
[25] Aglionby explains the word: "Design is the Expressing with a Pen, or Pencil, or other Instrument, the Likeness of any Object by its out Lines, or Contours. . . . " *Painting Illustrated*, etc., p. 8.

a "mighty *Designer*," says Aglionby, uttering the opinion held alike by Félibien, Du Fresnoy Richard Graham, Monier, etc.[26] But Du Fresnoy expresses the usual doubts. He was "fantastical and extravagant in his Composition and Bold even to Rashness, in taking Liberties against the Rules of Perspective."[27] An age that relied on rules for the appreciation and the construction of works of art could but regard with suspicion an artist who made his own rules and expressed his thoughts in his own style. As Aglionby said, Michelangelo is not "universal."[28]

Such was the general state of taste and theory when the eighteenth century opened. As was the case with poetry and the drama, the rules were already established and more or less accepted. But the course of theory and the progress of taste in regard to painting do not follow exactly the same line of development that we have observed in the other arts. The reason is plainly the existence of the Royal Academy, founded at about the same time that painting came into its own in England. There was no national tradition in painting as there was in poetry and drama, and theories and criticism prior to 1769 were likely to be imitative of ideas already expressed on the continent, and after that time to follow Reynolds's ideas with remarkable fidelity. The retarding influence of organized academic thought is readily seen in the unduly slow progress made in the theory and criticism of painting during the last half of the century. Reynolds for many years was delivering his sound *Discourses* before the Academy. No one could compete with him during his lifetime, and his successors followed in his footsteps with undue care. It is thus that Reynolds becomes the focal point of a discussion of eighteenth-century painting. No one spoke so well as he and no one's words carried such influence.

In following our theme throughout the century, we shall find one significant change—Michelangelo comes steadily into greater favor after 1750. This seems worth recording, since the same taste that condemned let us say John Donne and praised John Dryden valued Michelangelo less that it did Raphael. The gradual rise of Michelangelo to the rank of the greatest painter is indicative of a change in taste which fits in with the general changes that this study has sought to follow out, but which is likely to be obscured by the apparent continuity of critical thought from the mid-seventeenth to the nineteenth century.

Although the translations of De Piles, Monier, Freart, and others bear witness to a steady interest in painting in England during the closing years of the seventeenth and the early decades of the eighteenth centuries

[26] [Aglionby], *Ibid.*, p. 125; Félibien, *Entretiens*, I, 214; Du Fresnoy, *Art of Painting*, 224 and 283; Monier, *History of Painting*, p. 152.

[27] *Art of Painting*, p. 224.   [28] *Painting Illustrated*, etc., p. 125.

little of importance appeared from the pens of Englishmen before Jonathan Richardson began to write. Shaftesbury sums up briefly what the first decade of the century thought on the art. To him, of course, Raphael (and "Carache") is a model of perfection, and he tells how he could believe a picture by Raphael to be done by angels.[29] Michelangelo, in his opinion, "erred on the side of Greatness;" the remains of the art of the ancients he holds to be the key to the fundamentals of art; and he finds the noblest kinds of artists to be those who "paint history, and actions, and nature," the orthodox opinion of an age that considered epic the loftiest of the *genres*.[30]

A painter, he says, becomes unnatural when he follows nature too closely, copying strictly from life. Only in the general can the truth of nature be perceived, and the painter must avoid particulars, and make all subservient to the general design.

> Now the Variety of Nature is such as to distinguish every thing she forms, by a peculiar original Character; which, if strictly observ'd, will make the Subject appear unlike to any thing extant in the World besides. But this Effect the good Poet and Painter seek industriously to prevent. They hate *Minuteness*, and are afraid of Singularity; which would make the Images, or Characters capricious and fantastical. . . . 'Tis from the *many* Objects of Nature, and not from *a particular one*, that [the better sort of painters] form the Idea of their Work. Thus the best Artists are said to have been indefatigable in studying the best Statues: as Knowing them a better Rule, than the perfectest Human Bodys cou'd afford.[31]

At the outset, then, we find, as we should expect, the idea of an eclectic style as the best method of "correcting" the imperfections of nature and attaining to an expression of truth. It is natural enough that Shaftesbury's tastes should be orthodox, for until a different conception of nature could be held, Raphael was certain to occupy the highest place in the esteem of the connoisseur.

But it was Jonathan Richardson, friend of Pope and himself a painter, who contributed the most complete of the early discussions of painting. His first publication, *An Essay on the Theory of Painting*, 1715, was subsequently enlarged in the second edition. It will be best to consider this later edition, together with *Two Discourses*, which was published in 1719. In these two volumes one learns all that Richardson had to say concerning his art.

Following the lead of the French theorists, Richardson is careful to found painting on nature, which must

---

[29] Advice to an Author, *Characteristicks*, I, 338; Miscellaneous Reflections, *Ibid.*, III, 230.

[30] Sensus Communis, *Characteristicks*, I, 144, note; Advice to an Author, *Ibid.*, I, 206; *Letters* [London] (1746), p. 21.

[31] Sensus Communis, *Characteristicks*, I, 142–145.

be Rais'd; and Improv'd, not only from what is Commonly seen, to what is but Rarely, but even yet higher, from Judicious, and Beautiful Ideas in the Painter's Mind, so that Grace and Greatness may shine throughout . . .[32]

Richardson would carry this function of art—the expression of ideal form—to such length that it becomes permissible to raise a portrait above the nobility of the subject,[33] a curious example of his tendency to regard painting as the idealizer of nature. Such a view of art ruled out the Dutch painters from any consideration as lofty artists and played into the hands of those who found Italian painting of the high renaissance to their tastes. As Richardson says: "What gives the *Italians*, and their Masters the Ancients the Preference, is, that they have not servilely follow'd Comon Nature, but Rais'd and Improv'd, or at least have always made the Best Choice of it." He goes on to state that "Comon Nature" has no place in art and that the painter must "form a Model of Perfection in his own Mind which is not to be found in Reality."[34] This Raphael and the ancients had done, in the one case through the Olympian idealizations of the Greek and Roman sculptures, and in the other through the stately dignity and nobility of the figures in the frescoes and the cartoons. In these works, more than in any others, the eighteenth century found the expression of the Aristotelian view of nature as a force seeking to work out perfection through the refractory medium of matter, and as a reality whose general laws are harmonious and perfect, whose ultimate essence is unmarred beauty and truth. Hence Richardson is able to state that the ancients, Michelangelo, and Raphael constantly practiced this idealization, which he recommends, and to devote several pages to illustrations from the cartoons of Raphael.[35] This view of painting obviously brought the art into close relations with sublimity, or in Richardson's words, with the "Grand Style," the "Grand Gusto," "Grace and Greatness," a theme of which he writes at length, analysing and formulating with no lack ot skill.

Raphael is distinguished for grace and greatness, is allowed to have surpassed even the ancients, and is said to be "Vastly Great and Sublime." Of Michelangelo it is said:

His Style is his Own, not Antique, but He had a sort of Greatness in his utmost Degree, which sometimes ran into the Extream of Terrible; though in many Instances he has a fine seasoning of Grace.[36]

[32] Jonathan Richardson, *Two Discourses*, etc. (London, 1719), p. 30.

[33] *An Essay on the Theory of Painting*, Second Edition (London, 1725), p. v.

[34] *Ibid.*, pp. 171, 172.

[35] *Essay*, pp. 175–178. I am aware that the cartoons are not from the hand of Raphael, but since the eighteenth century considered them authentic, it is necessary to treat them as if they were his work.

[36] *Ibid.*, p. 204, and *An Account of Some of the Statues, Bas-Reliefs, Drawings and Pictures*

Although the neo-classicist preferred the majestic calm of Raphael, he could not avoid being impressed by the titanic energy of Michelangelo, nor could he be blind to the vivid impression that the Sistine Chapel gives of the gloomy, tragic element in the painter's own character. The age enjoyed more the statuesque calm of Raphael's compositions, the deep repose, the balance and harmony of line and mass—all of this indicated an art that struck in with the tastes of the time; it had helped to create that taste through the influence of Poussin and the French Academy. Michelangelo's experiments in the anatomy of the human body, his grandly imagined God and Prophets, the terrors of his Last Judgment—these were too vivid to be ignored, and they shattered the neo-classic calm. But while they perturbed, they fascinated, and Michelangelo was always to be reckoned with.

Up to this time no really serious effort had been made to introduce the Longinian sublime into the theory of painting. Greatness was known of course; the Italians had written of the grand style long before Longinus and Boileau joined forces. De Piles was one of the first to write of *the* sublime and to express himself in the language of Longinus, whom he quotes.[37] Richardson studied the question of sublimity in literature quite carefully, formulated a really excellent statement from the stricter neo-classical view, and applied his conclusions to painting.

The influence of Longinus and Boileau on Richardson's critical system is manifest from the outset. In the preface to the second edition of the *Essay*, he declares the superiority of "a fine Thought, Grace, and Dignity" to the "Lesser, to the more Mechanical Parts of a Picture."[38] He defines the sublime rather generally as "the most Excellent of what is Excellent, as the Excellent is the Best of what is Good;" but he becomes more specific, giving a formal definition. The sublime in writing is "the Greatest, and most Noble thought, Images, or Sentiments, Convey'd to us in the Best chosen Words," and he adds, "the Admirable, the Marvellous,"[39] thereby showing that he had studied Boileau, who,

---

in Italy, etc. (London, 1722), p. 173.—Grace and greatness are obtained by having a care to the air of the head; by so treating the figures that they seem to do what is proper and to do it as men of sense and breeding would do it; by using contours "Large, Square, and Boldly pronounc'd to produce Greatness; and Delicate, and finely Waved, and Contrasted to be Gracious;" by using simple ornaments, avoiding lace, embroidery, and gold; by dressing the figures in Greek and Roman robes; by contrasting the noble and the ignoble. Last of all, and this is Longinian, the mind must be stored with noble images. *Essay*, pp. 190–201.

[37] *Principles of Painting*, 70–72; 74. In his *Réflexions Critiques*, Abbé Du Bos had defined the sublime of poetry and painting in terms of emotion, and had sought its source beyond regularity and elegance, II, 1, 2.   [38] *Essay*, pp. vii, viii.

[39] *Ibid.*, pp. 226, 227. The first edition contained only a brief discussion of the sublime,

it will be recalled had used *la merveilleux* as an alternative to *le sublime* in the title of his translation.

He distinguishes on the next page excellence of thought from excellence of language. A sublime thought must be great; it must fill the mind. Strict truth and justness of thought are not essential to the sublime, but (and here the neo-classicist shows himself) a great and useful truth is preferable to one that is great and either untrue or useless. Richardson frowns upon "wit," and following Boileau, condemns the ornate and upholds the simple in style and diction, although he is prepared to admit that there are occasions when florid language may best express a sublime thought. Milton, Shakespeare, and Genesis i. 3, provide illustrations of both styles.[40]

Richardson's summary of his views shows him to be a follower of Boileau despite his assertion that he had evolved a new theory.

. . . it appears that my Notion of the Sublime differs from Some others; I confine it to Sense, and give a Latitude as to the Style; They are for a certain Style, and allow That a separate Sublimity, whatever the Thought be.[41]

By applying this theory to painting, Richardson concludes that the sublime is "the Greatest, and most Beautiful Ideas, whether Corporeal, or not, convey'd to us the most Advantageously." These ideas seem to be conveyed by "Grace and Greatness, whether from the Attitude, or Air, of the Whole, or the Head only." Invention, expression, and composition are mentioned as contributing to sublimity, and histories and portraits are regarded as the sublime *genres* of painting. Richardson's selection of Milton and Shakespeare as sublime poets was happily in accord with the taste of the period, but when he chose Rembrandt and Zuccaro as exemplars of the sublime in painting, he spoke only for himself, and not for his age.[42]

The confining of the sublime to histories and portraits is of a piece with the view that the loftiest form of poetry is the epic. History paint-

---

and the chapter on that subject in the second edition is the fruit of diligent study, as references to Longinus, Boileau, Huet, and Le Clerc bear witness, and as the numerous examples of sublimity taken from Milton and Shakespeare suggest. The essay was edited and reprinted with other pieces in 1773 by the painter's son, Jonathan, as *The Works of Jonathan Richardson*, "all corrected and prepared for the press." Some of the "corrections" seem to be additions from the pen of Jonathan, Jr., as well as arbitrary omissions. In 1792, *The Works* was reprinted at Strawberry Hill, as a supplement to Walpole's *Anecdotes of Painters* and the chapter on sublimity was abridged and restricted to the sublime in painting.

[40] These statements are a summary of *Essay*, pp. 230–246.

[41] *Ibid.*, pp. 246, 247.—In a footnote Richardson identifies "the others" as Longinus, Boileau (in the *Twelfth Reflection*), Le Clerc, and Huet, and he takes pains to point out contradictions between Longinus and Boileau.

[42] *Essays*, pp. 248, 249; 252–254.

ing, especially, gave opportunity for the heroic treatment of figures, for the expression of passions, for the telling of a story and the pointing of a moral that were dear to the neo-classic period. It is noticeable, however, that Richardson has nothing to say of the pathetic. In this respect he differs from all the critics of his time who attempted to write with any degree of fullness on the sublime. Raphael's cartoons were regarded as the models for histories, and were especially valued as studies in the expression of the passions. They were of course also sublime, as well for their subjects as for the dignity of their figures, and the lofty passions that they express.[43]

If Richardson neglects the pathetic it is because he concentrates on nature, and it is in his conception of the nature that painting represents that we find his views on sublimity. Sublimity comes into painting through the idealizing of nature which it is the business of all serious artists to accomplish; it consists in a heightening, a selection of great details from many objects and a combining them into one perfect whole. The mere copying of nature can never produce sublimity; that quality can come only from the expression of an exalted idea that, arrived at through a careful selection of great details, goes beyond nature itself and treats more perfect forms than can be found in common experience. Richardson admits that it is rare that the painter can so dominate his medium as to express his conception as perfectly as can the poet. But Longinus is brought to the rescue of the painter, by quoting his assertion that defects are of little consequence where sublimity exists.

But the Sublime, as the Crown in the State hides all Defects; it fills and satisfies the Mind, nothing appears to be wanting; nothing to be amiss, or if it does 'tis easily forgiven. All Faults die and vanish in the presence of the Sublime, which when it appears is as *the Sun traversing the Vast Desert of the Sky*.[44]

Richardson does not progress beyond Boileau in his conception of sublimity, but the fact that he attempted to apply the Longinian sublime to painting is significant. Perhaps if he had followed out the suggestions of Boileau's words (which he quotes) "it ravishes, it transports,"[45] he might have come nearer to evolving an original theory. As it is, he is worthy of notice chiefly as an innovator.

The second considerable book that treated of sublimity in painting is, one might hazard, virtually unknown today. *A Treatise on Ancient Painting* was written by George Turnbull, whose greatest fame is that he was the chief influence on Thomas Reid when that philosopher was

[43] See Benjamin Ralph, *The School of Raphael: or, The Student's Guide to Expression in Historical Painting* (London, 1759). The cartoons are discussed from a series of engravings that display the "passions." *Paul Preaching at Athens* is said to be Raphael's sublimest achievement.   [44] *Essay*, pp. 37 ff.; 248–250; 255–257; 259–260.   [45] *Ibid.*, 256.

a student at Marischal College. McCosh has pointed out that in *Beer Street* Hogarth shows us a porter who has deposited on the ground five folios directed to the trunkmaker, one of which is Turnbull's treatise.[46] This expresses vividly enough the oblivion into which Turnbull had fallen; and yet, as an item of historic interest the volume has some worth.

Two influences are evident throughout the book—that of Hutcheson and his mild associationism in explaining beauty, and that of Longinus, the very present help of all neo-classicists in trouble. Of course the doctrine of *Ut pictura poesis* is the very groundwork of the book, and all the other neo-classic ideas find a place in the treatise.

The comparison of the golden ages of Greek and Italian painting with which the volume opens offers much to him whom the curious spectacle of the eighteenth-century mind in action interests and amuses. With a solemnity that is as irritating as it is ludicrous, Turnbull draws a thorough parallel between the two ages, finding a parallel in Italy to each one of the Greek painters, whose works he had never seen.

Thus Apelles and Raphael are carefully compared. Their persons and their characters were similar; they are the two greatest painters that ever lived, distinguished alike for beauty, sweetness, spirit, freedom, grace, greatness. They are to painting as Homer and Virgil to poetry.

They both excelled in a fine Taste and Choice of Nature; an Idea of Beauty and Grace beyond the power of Words to express; a copious, rich Invention, a refin'd Imagination, a correct Judgment, and an elegant, sweet and gracious, yet bold, sublime, and masterly Manner of Painting.

And moreover, both idealized nature, taking various perfect parts to form a perfect whole.[47]

That part of the volume which deals with taste and imitation offers us a clear idea of the neo-classic creed in painting, despite the fact that it is somewhat colored by the ideas of Hutcheson. The doctrines of the internal sense, the equating of beauty and goodness, the view of nature as an orderly scheme of laws with which the ethical and the æsthetic strive to harmonize are all set forth and amply supported by argument.[48] The whole doctrine is thus summed up:

. . . if the Perfection of Nature consists in working unerringly towards the Beauty and Good of the Whole by simple consistent Laws; and the Perfection of Life and Manners consists in acting in concert with Nature, and in pursuing steadily the Good of Mankind by well-poised, regular and generous affections;

[46] *The Scottish Philosophy*, p. 95.   [47] *Treatise*, pp. 18, 19.   [48] *Ibid.*, pp. 129–138.

then must the Perfection of the imitative Arts consist in like manner in making regular and beautiful Systems, in which every part being duly adapted and submitted to what is principal, the Whole hath a great, noble, and virtuous Effect upon the mind. . . .[49]

Into this narrow world of neo-classical harmony and order the sublime must of course intrude, but it comes with none of the thunder that is to characterize it twenty years later. Like Richardson, Turnbull writes of the sublime in painting only as it relates to writing, and, as we may expect, he does so with Longinus as his guide. Those paintings are sublime which represent great subjects with greatness of manner; "which by exhibiting sublime Objects in the proper Light, that is, with all their natural Strength and Loftiness, inspire(d) great Sentiments into the Minds of Beholders, and mightily move(d) and elevate(d) them." This opinion is substantiated and its important element emphasized by an appeal to Longinus and his stressing of "noble Conceptions, which by leaving more behind them to be contemplated than is expressed, lead the Mind into an almost inexhaustible Fund of great thinking." In other words the conventional alliance of poetry and painting enables the critic to measure each by the same standards. Turnbull draws a long comparison between the two arts, finding the usual parallels, such as that between color and words. For both the painter and the poet the chief source of sublimity is to be able to think sublimely.[50]

All of this Turnbull had previously illustrated in his discussion of Timanthes, who was chiefly renowned, not for mechanical, but for poetical beauties. As Turnbull puts it, he was admired because of

that masterly way he had, of awakening great Thoughts and Sentiments, by his ingenious Works, in the Breasts of Spectators; his wonderful Talent of spreading their Imaginations, and leading them to conceive in their own Minds more than was expressed by his Pictures.[51]

With true academic taste, Turnbull selects Raphael and Nicholas Poussin as the sublimest of the modern painters, since they have a force and energy that "wonderfully erects and ennobles the Mind, inflames the Imagination, and lights up the Understanding, calling up great and elevated Conceptions," which the spectator imagines to be his own.[52] We are here in the realm of Longinus, and the emphasis is thrown very properly on the quality of imagination that a work of art possesses. Certainly Turnbull's description of the effect of Raphael's paintings seems more suitable to the frescoes in the Sistine Chapel, but although Michelangelo is approved for his "bold, aspiring, masterly Genius" and his "noble and elevated" thoughts, the current interpretation of nature

<hr />

[49] *Ibid.*, p. 137.   [50] *Ibid.*, pp. 83, 84.   [51] *Ibid.*, p. 26.   [52] *Ibid.*, p. 27.

and of the rules prevents his complete acceptance in the upper reaches of the hierarchy of great painters.[53]

The concluding pages on the sublime repeat most of the old saws. The sublime comes only from a great mind, and is "its Image or Soul reflected;" this greatness of mind is "original or from Nature," but study and art can add to and strengthen native sublimity; the sublimest paintings are those which display generous sentiments and actions, and which tend to inculcate virtue.[54]

As there is a sublime style in oratory and in poetry, so there is in painting. Greatness of manner, which will render the most familiar objects great, consists in producing surprise by variety, in artful contrast, and in concealing bounds; this last is explained as "giving a very large and as it were, unbounded Prospect to the Eye." The eye dislikes being confined, and the imagination is "wonderfully charmed by wide expanding Views." Hence a sense of space in sky and landscape, the presence of noble pieces of architecture, of "huge Mountains, Rocks, and other towering, awful Objects" are concomitants of the sublime in painting.[55]

A considerable distance seems at this point to separate Turnbull from Richardson. His list of sublime objects is the familiar one of the 1740's. Moreover, Richardson valued the landscapes of Salvator Rosa and of Claude because they were idealizations of nature;[56] Turnbull is making an attempt to discuss the æsthetic of space. In the interim between the publication of the *Essay on the Theory of Painting* and the *Treatise on Ancient Painting*, the landscapes of Claude and Salvator were beginning to come into favor and *The Seasons* had appeared at least in part. It is probable, too, that Turnbull is thinking of *Spectator* 412, in which Addison had celebrated the pleasure that the imagination takes in the contemplation of space, a pleasure that Englishmen were beginning to experience for themselves.

But in practice the unbounded vista, the mountains, and the rocks were too likely to degenerate into merely rhetorical devices, used to punctuate and to italicize the painter's efforts to achieve sublimity. Not that this must necessarily be true—one has only to think of Perugino and Claude to know how exciting space can become; but the eighteenth-century critic, and after him the artist, tended to treat them as such. It was easy enough to label mountains, towers, space, "sublime;" the next step was to attempt to attain the sublime simply by introducing a mountain, a tower, or a vista of apparently infinite space, regardless of its imaginative quality. This was done time and again by the descriptive poets of Turnbull's own decade. But the eighteenth century seems at

[53] *Ibid.*, p. 30.   [54] *Ibid.*, p. 84.

[55] *Ibid.*, pp. 84–86.   [56] *Essay*, p. 172.

times to be peculiarly blind to the deeper significance of what it beheld. In Shakespeare it found a great dramatist, capable of evoking and "describing" emotions; and this aspect of his genius overshadowed his greatness as a poet and an interpreter of human nature. In nature it sought and found certain obvious emotive qualities; it almost missed her "healing power" and the purely æsthetic effect of color, line, and contour. In painting it sought sublimity and found it, not in the deeply personal and grandly dark visions of Michelangelo, but in the happily expressed passions of Raphael's histories, in his obvious dignity and stately calm, in his idealization of nature, and in the forests and mountains and banditti of Salvator. All of this is not to be so absurd as to say that the paintings of Raphael and of Salvator have no æsthetic value; the point is that in the majority of instances one comes to feel that the neo-classical connoisseur admired these works for everything except their æsthetic value—for the story they told, for the passions they expressed, for the shiver of awe that they produced.

The principal document on painting in the eighteenth century, one need scarcely say, is Reynolds's *Discourses*, delivered as part of his Presidential duties at the Royal Academy during the years 1769–1790. These lectures occupy, in the history of British painting, a position analogous to that of the dicta of Johnson in the history of literature; they summarize broadly, sanely, and wisely the traditional views, and at the same time they show signs of the changes that were beginning to overtake neo-classic art. The casual student of the century too often regards Dr. Johnson as the incarnation of conservatism, the reactionary upholder of an almost defunct order, forgetting that it was he who gave the *coup de grâce* to the dramatic unities, thus smoothing the way for a radical alteration in theories of art. A much less dramatic and more subtle change is evident in the *Discourses*, a change that William Blake could not have noticed when he wrote on the title page of his copy of Reynolds's *Works*, "This Man was Hired to Depress Art." In the President's opinion Michelangelo is the supreme painter; Raphael is deposed, and the un-neo-classical Florentine takes his place at the pinnacle of art. This change in taste heralds a more general change in art; it shows the beginning of a preference for individuality, for the concrete, rather than for generalization and the *beau idéal;* for strong emotion rather than for the placid composition of Raphael's painting. But it is not to be assumed that Reynolds faced about and opposed his age; his *theory* of the sublime is, by and large, that of the past, but his *taste* is for the sublime of Michelangelo, not of Raphael.

This change was inevitable once the theory of original genius began to diminish the power of the rules. It is not surprising that the decades that admired Ossian and elevated terror to the height of the sublime should begin to see more in the paintings of Michelangelo than the Augustans had seen. Thus, although in 1770, Pilkington's *Gentleman's and Connoisseur's Dictionary of Painters* records that Raphael is a "Sublime genius" and that Michelangelo, despite the frequent sublimity of his thoughts, does not always afford pleasure, we find Dr. John Armstrong declaring in the next year that in the Sistine Chapel one finds "a prodigious display of sublime, melancholy, and dreadful Imagination," that the Last Judgment is "magnificently terrible," and is the sublime production of an extraordinary genius.[57] Martin Sherlock, at the end of the same decade, makes the inevitable comparison between the boldness of Michelangelo and the imagination of Shakespeare, and a tour, taken in 1786–87, convinced James Edward Smith that Raphael, for all his greatness, had been overrated and that Michelangelo's was a sublime genius.[58] And these are only a few of those who praise the Florentine. The significance of this new taste will become apparent as we meet the more complete criticisms of the Royal Academicians.

In 1759 Reynolds contributed a series of papers on painting to the *Idler*, joining Johnson in his war on imitation. Thus early he shows evidence of the paradox that can be found in all his writings on his art. The earlier critics had been logical; their conception of sublimity could find one supreme example—the frescoes and the cartoons of Raphael. Reynolds holds to their theories, but he finds his illustrations in the work of Michelangelo. Now the sincere admiration of Michelangelo was an admiration of "subjective" art, of power and force of genius, of depth of feeling, of stormy emotions, and of profound perceptions of the riddle of human destiny. The sincere admiration of Raphael was an admiration of a more impersonal art, of a stately, an Olympian calm, of a painter's sure taste rather than of a poet's deep feeling, of emotions that could be expressed usually in rhetorical gestures and postures,[59] and of a happy nature that, however convinced it was of the dignity of man and the sublimity of the mysteries of the Church, has obviously never been profoundly perturbed by the ways of God to man. Thus the setting up of Michelangelo in Raphael's place was certain to affect eventually the theories and the practice of art.

[57] M. Pilkington, *The Gentleman's and Connoisseur's Dictionary of Painters* (London, 1770), pp. 499 and 11, 12; "Launcelot Temple" (Dr. John Armstrong), *A Short Ramble through Some Parts of France and of Italy* (London, 1771), pp. 23–25.

[58] Martin Sherlock, *Letters from an English Traveller* (London, 1780), p. 61; James Edward Smith, *A Sketch of a Tour on the Continent* (London, 1793), II, 6–11; I, 298 and 306. He was especially impressed by the Medici tombs.

[59] The shrieking youth in the cartoon of the death of Ananias is a case in point. The figure was much admired in the eighteenth century.

True to the canons of criticism in his time, Reynolds repeats, in *Idler*, 76, the platitude that the rules can lead a critic "but a little way towards the just estimation of the sublime beauties in works of Genius," for any part of an art that can be executed by rules is not a work of genius.[60] After insisting that *imitation* does not mean reproduction, and that painting no less than poetry exercises its power over the imagination, Reynolds turns to the grand style. The Dutch and the Italian schools are his text. Minute imitation, i.e., reproduction, of nature, the characteristic of the Dutch school, is inimical to the grand style. Not literal truth to nature, but a poetic interpretation of nature, imagination, is the desideratum of great art, and this the Italians give, for they "attend only to the invariable, the great, and general ideas which are fix'd and inherent in Universal Nature." Michelangelo, "the Homer of Painting," is the practicer of this "sublimest style," which has nothing to do with common nature.[61]

In the longer and more labored *Discourses*, Reynolds continues to set forth the connection between the sublime in painting and the idealized nature of the academic tradition. The sublime is constantly equated with the "general and invariable ideas of nature" which neo-classicism had always upheld as the end of art.[62] In his third discourse, "The Leading Principles of the Grand Style," Reynolds develops fully his theory of the sublime in painting, an excellency that goes beyond mere nature and presents the ideal perfection toward which nature strives. This ideality rests not upon technique, nor even upon mere eclecticism, but upon the grandeur of a painter's ideas, his ability to seize our imagination, his "intellectual dignity."[63] This is a sure indication of the influence of Longinus. As the Greek had recognized the value of technique, but had stressed the greater value of the orator's own mind and genius, so Reynolds insists that rules, imitation, or eclecticism are not enough to make a great artist. Although his pedagogical duties forced him to deprecate mere "enthusiasm," lest the doctrine of inspiration and imagination smash the academic art which he was founding,[64] we should not lose sight of the fact that in principle Reynolds's sublime lies beyond nature and in the realm of poetic truth. His pedestrian and common-sense conception of genius (whether firmly held or adopted for the purpose of encouraging young students) as an infinite capacity for taking

---

[60] Reynolds, *Works*, II, 221.   [61] *Ibid.*, II, 229–233.

[62] *Ibid.*, I, 9. This statement, from the first discourse, infuriated Blake, whose marginal comment, "Minute Discrimination is Not Accidental. All Sublimity is founded on Minute Discrimination," shows how violently his view of art was opposed to that of the preceding age. See also his comment on I, 53.   [63] *Ibid.*, I, 52, 53 and 55.

[64] *Ibid.*, I, 55, 56. Blake's marginal comments on this passage are full of violent invective.

pains is really out of harmony with his own definition of the sublime, however harmonious it was with Johnson's own views on the subject.

This ideality which springs from the greatness of the painter's mind and which is the essence of the grand style is attained by getting "above all singular forms, local customs, particularities, and details of every kind." At this point Reynolds turns to practical questions. Granting genius and granting inspiration, the painter attains this ideal by a careful comparison of the forms of nature, so that accidental blemishes and defects are corrected and the universal and true perfection remains.[65]

As we have seen, this idea of the supreme beauty in art was inherited from the French Academicians and was current in neo-classical thought in England throughout our century. It was explicit in the histories of ancient art, it underlay the conception of nature, it found its best illustration in the paintings of Raphael, and it was given full expression several times during the course of the century.[66] It is the beauty which transcends nature and which can be attained only by transcending rules, and once it is attained it enables a painting to "warm and ravish."[67]

Simplicity of effect, complete unity, is also a characteristic of the grand style, as Reynolds shows when he treats of the Venetians in his fourth discourse. Veronese and Tintoretto lack that "simple, grave and majestical dignity" which are its essentials, and which the Roman school alone consistently achieved; for "the Sublime impresses the mind at once with one great idea." Even the subtle coloring of the Venetians militates against the sublime, for it is "too harmonious, to produce that

[65] *Works*, I, 58, 59. This passage, as well as the following, is strikingly similar to Johnson's view of the relation of poetry to nature, as expressed in the tenth chapter of *Rasselas*: " . . . [the painter] must divest himself of all prejudice in favor of his age or century; he must disregard all local and temporary ornaments, and look only on those general habits which are every where and always the same, he addresses himself to every country and every age, he calls upon posterity to be his spectators, and says with Zeuxis, *in aeternitatem pingo*." *Ibid.*, I, 67.—Blake questions these views. He asks: "What is General Nature[?] is there such a Thing[?] what is General Knowledge[?] [is] there such a thing[?] . . . all Knowledge is Particular," *Works*, I, 60.

[66] Mr. Roger Fry, in his edition of the *Discourses* (London, 1905) briefly indicated the derivation of these ideas from Aristotle and the Latin, Italian, and French critics (p. 44). They are found frequently in our period, not only in Richardson and Turnbull and De Piles, but also in Félibien's *L'Idée du Peintre Parfait* (London, 1707), Chapters III and IV; Bouffier's *First Truths and the Origin of our Opinions, Explained* (London, 1780), Chapter XIII; and Lambert Hermanson Ten Kate's *Beau Idéal*, written in 1724, and twice translated into English, in 1732 and 1769, in which the idea is illustrated from the works of Raphael and the ancients. As important for Reynolds was probably the tenth chapter of *Rasselas*, already mentioned. William Jackson, himself a painter, equates this "something beyond nature" with the sublime style. *Thirty Letters* (London, 1783), I, 35.

[67] *Works*, I, 59. It is curious to see the long survival of the Longinian and Bolevian vocabulary.

solidity, steadiness, and simplicity of effect, which heroick subjects require, and which simple and grave colours only can give to a work."[68] This was the opinion of the French Academy, and Reynolds holds to it despite his own debt to the Venetians and Rubens.

Without arguing the sublimity of the Venetians, it may nevertheless be observed that this statement shows the persistent inorganic view of art in the eighteenth century. There is no intrinsic reason why subtlety of color should diminish grandeur; indeed, painting being what it is, color should play an important part in whatever effect the art produces. Reynolds and his predecessors, however, were prone to divide painting into "parts" which roughly corresponded to the parts of poetry—words, versification, thoughts, imaginative feeling. Now color corresponded to words, and mere language, since the time of Boileau, had been given only a secondary part in the creation of sublimity. By a parallel course of thought, Reynolds obscures the organic effect of color in aiding expression, and insists on treating it as if it were a mere ornament.

Such is Reynolds's theory of sublimity in painting, and it was orthodox enough to arouse the sacrilegious ire of William Blake. All signs point to Raphael as the model from whom these rules were deduced, but when we examine Reynolds's dicta on Raphael and Michelangelo, we observe one of those inconsistencies that seem to indicate that the President's taste was not quite at one with his theory. In a letter written to Barry in 1769, Reynolds urges the young painter, who was at Rome as a pensioner of Burke, to study the Sistine Chapel, which he declares to be the work of the greatest genius that was ever employed on the arts,[69] and in his third discourse he says that Michelangelo's drawing is "executed with more truth, spirit, and science, than anything that has appeared since the resurrection of the arts." Jonas is sublime, and the figure of God creating the sun and the moon is far superior to anything of Raphael's, even to his best work, *Ezekiel*.[70]

Nevertheless, when he comes to compare Raphael and Michelangelo, the President gets the better of the private individual, and one perceives that Reynolds thinks that he should give the advantage to Raphael. These two painters, together with Giulio Romano, worked in the grand style. The comparison of Raphael and Michelangelo is similar in method to Johnson's comparison of Dryden and Pope in the *Lives of the Poets*. Though our *judgment* must decide in favor of Raphael, yet "he never takes such a firm hold and entire possession of the mind as to make us

[68] *Ibid.*, I, 95 and 97.

[69] The letter is undated, but a reference to the first discourse and Barry's answer, dated May 17, 1769, leave no doubt as to the date. See Reynolds, *Letters*, ed. F. W. Hilles (Cambridge, 1929), pp. 16–20.   [70] *Works*, I, 423.

desire nothing else"—in other words, he is less sublime, though he is a greater, or at least a better, painter. The effect of the best work of Michelangelo is compared to the effect of Homer on Bouchardon: ". . . his whole frame appeared to himself to be enlarged, and all nature which surrounded him, diminished to atoms."[71]

Raphael had more taste and fancy, Michelangelo more genius and imagination; the one excelled in beauty, the other in energy. Beauty, taste, fancy as opposed to genius, imagination, energy—there is no doubt as to which set of qualities Reynolds's own age would prefer. Moreover, continues Reynolds, Michelangelo has more poetical inspiration, his ideas are vast and sublime, his people are a superior order of beings; and Raphael's imagination is not so elevated, his figures are less titanic. Michelangleo's works have a strong, peculiar, and marked character, and "they seem to proceed from his own mind entirely." Raphael borrowed much of his material, and his excellence lay in "the propriety, beauty, and majesty of his Characters, the judicious contrivance of his Composition, his correctness of Drawing, purity of Taste, and skillful accomodation of other men's conceptions to his own purpose." This, in Pope's time was "true wit;" but Reynolds is not so sure. Which is to be preferred? he asks. If the standard is "a greater combination of the higher qualities of the art," certainly Raphael; but if, "as Longinus thinks, the sublime being the highest excellence that human composition can attain to, abundantly compensates the absence of every other beauty, and atones for all other deficiencies, then Michelangelo demands the preference."[72]

There is no doubt here as to Reynolds's own opinion, although his pedagogical conscience led him to hold up the safer model, Raphael, to the students whom he was urging to imitate great masters. But Michelangelo, bearing the qualities of original genius and the true sublime, obviously figures in the President's taste as the ultimate in the painter's art. It is interesting to observe how Reynolds focuses in his criticism of these two painters the two views of art which were current in the whole century—the rules and decorum, as opposed to the grace that is snatched beyond the reach of art. Pope had harmonized the two views in his *Essay on Criticism*, but during the decade preceding the founding of the Royal Academy, Joseph Warton had been insisting on the supreme value of *acer spiritus ac vis;* Young had written enthusiastically of originality; Hurd had vindicated individual imagination; and Johnson had carried on an attack against imitation. The new point of view manifests itself here in a juster evaluation of the genius of Michelangelo, which was similar to the new favor with which the Elizabethans were coming

[71] *Ibid.*, I, 128.   [72] *Ibid.*, II, 128–130.

to be regarded. The appeal to Longinus in an effort to gloze over the obvious faults of Michelangelo and to emphasize the value of his energetic and individual genius is characteristic of an age that habitually turned to *Peri Hupsous* for authority when its tastes were heterodox.

In his final discourse Reynolds returns to Michelangelo, the object of his youthful enthusiasm, and speaks out more boldly than he had done eighteen years earlier. Michelangelo is the source of all grandeur in modern art; he had "the most poetical and sublime imagination;" before his sublimity the correct judgment and purity of taste that distinguish Raphael disappear; the style of Michelangelo is the "language of the gods;" his faults are not the faults of a mean or a vulgar mind; they flow from the same source as his beauties.[73] Finally:

I feel a self-congratulation in knowing myself capable of such sensations as he intended to excite. I reflect, not without vanity, that these Discourses bear testimony to my admiration of that truly divine man; and I should desire that the last words which I should pronounce in this Academy, and from this place might be the name—MICHAEL ANGELO.[74]

The fact that Reynolds stressed the sublimity of Michelangelo is of some significance in the history of eighteenth-century taste, which is by no means to say that it was a revolutionary doctrine, for it certainly was not. It is undeniable, however, that a taste that finds in Raphael's frescoes the supreme art rests upon quite a different set of æsthetic values from that which turns instinctively to the Sistine Chapel. A parallel may be found in the contrast between a taste for the scenery around Windermere and an enthusiasm for Switzerland; or for the *Aeneid* and *Macbeth*. "Within that circle none durst walk but he," Dryden had said of Shakespeare, and the succeeding age had often repeated the dictum. Reynolds applies the *cliché* to Michelangelo in warning students against the danger of imitating the Sistine Chapel.[75] And if the willingness to recognize that the genius and art of Shakespeare were a law unto themselves is of importance in our period, the same is true of the Florentine.

The presidential approval of Michelangelo indicates a greater interest in an individualistic and potentially emotional art than had hitherto been possible. It is one more instance of the habit of grouping under the category of the sublime forces which were at variance with the stricter neo-classicism of Augustan theory. It also coincides with a change in the character of the sublime itself. Michelangelo had been famed in post-renaissance Italy for his *terribilità*. Now theories of the sublime in painting before Burke could easily turn to Raphael as an exemplar, for where can one find a happier illustration of the Longinian sublime than in the cartoons? But Michelangelo could best illustrate the sublime that

---

[73] *Ibid.*, II, 195–209.   [74] *Ibid.*, II, 217, 218.   [75] *Ibid.*, II, 205.

Burke made popular. Certain passages in *Paradise Lost, Macbeth,* Ossian, Michelangelo, to the undiscriminating eye of most eighteenth-century connoisseurs, could be grouped together as representative of the sublime which not only transcends rules and displays imagination, original genius, and energy, but which also has as its basis terror. Thus the perfection of Raphael, while always valued, came to seem less satisfying than the "dynamics" of Michelangelo or (God save the mark) of Ossian. And this change indicates the disintegration of the neo-classic system.

Something of this is shadowed forth in an anonymous letter to James Barry which was sent to him in 1783, shortly after he had completed his ambitious frescoes in the Great Room of the Society of Arts, Manufactures, and Commerce at the Adelphi. The letter warns the painter not to confuse greatness of size with greatness of manner, or mere extent of canvas with the sublime, which is not attained by painting gigantic and monstrous figures. The unknown critic deplores the taste for the false sublime that is current among artists, and that he attributes to "interested prejudices" and "credulous ignorance." The public is too ready to admire pompous vacuity, a weakness that accounts for the success of "those miserable rhapsodies by MacPherson under the name of Ossian," which have become "standards of true taste and sublimity." A true understanding of Homer would reform taste, for he shows that the "true sublime is always easy and always natural, that it consists more in the manner than the subject, and is to be found by a good poet and good painter in almost every part of nature."[76]

Although Barry had confessed to Reynolds that he thought himself "rather reprehensible as a furious enthusiast of Michael Angelo,"[77] the frescoes in question show nothing that is really Michelangelesque, unless it be the huge figures of the athletes at the Olympic games. The paintings as a whole are certainly frigid, dull works (if one can judge from contemporary engravings), a fact which does not prove that Barry was not working with the Sistine Chapel in mind. Except for the nudes, one thinks instinctively of a feeble imitation of Raphael when one sees

[76] James Barry, *Works* (London, 1809), I, 263–267. Barry's biographer conjectures that Burke was the author of this letter, but this is doubtful. There was no apparent reason why Burke should have written anonymously to Barry.

[77] *Ibid.,* I, 104. Despite Barry's avowal of an enthusiasm for Michelangelo, his other letters do not display him in the guise of a blind adorer. He finds the standard of beauty to reside in ancient art, and considers Raphael nearer that standard than Michelangelo (*Ibid.,* I, 99, 100). In his Observations on the Different Works of Art in France and Italy, he says, "One sees in Raphael and the antique the same things, but not in the same degree of perfection," and he holds that Michelangelo attains to this "degree," but "misses the correctness of the antique" (*Ibid.,* II, 11). He protests against the cant idea that Michelangelo is an original genius who scorned art and exactness, a refreshingly realistic view for 1774 (*Ibid.,* II, 249).

these paintings. But the protest is none the less interesting as bearing testimony to the change that was overtaking sublimity; the classic calm of Homer and Raphael was giving way to the energy and terror of Ossian and Michelangelo.

When, in 1809, Martin Shee attempted to uphold the claims of Raphael against those of Michelangelo, he felt it necessary to apologize for his presumption, since he was contradicting high authority.

The Discourses of the late President of the Royal Academy, and Lectures of an eminent Professor (mr. Fuzeli), appear to have effected a revolution in favour of Michael Angelo and to have invested him with that supreme dignity in the empire of Arts, which Raphael had so long enjoyed.[78]

Shee was certainly not mistaken in attributing the dethroning of Raphael to Reynolds and Fuseli. The Professor of Painting at the very end of the century took up Reynolds's work, and carried out the Michelangelesque both in theory and in practice.

Indeed, although he does not lie within our period, strictly speaking, he nevertheless so well sums up the vogue of Michelangelo that we must quote from him. Fuseli claims that even Michelangelo's admirers have not understood him, that he was something more than a correct designer or a genius who wrought in three arts. Michelangelo founded epic painting by building on "Nature's everlasting forms and those general feelings of humanity, which no time can efface, no mode of society obliterate."[79] This was exactly the claim that had been made for Raphael. What has happened? There has been a change either in the interpretation of Michelangelo or of nature. Fuseli's lectures will help to determine which is the case.

He distinguishes three *genres* of painting, the epic or sublime, the dramatic or impassioned, and the historic or circumscribed by truth. The first astonishes, the second moves, the third informs.

The aim of the epic painter is to impress one general idea, one great quality of nature or mode of society, some great maxim, without descending to those subdivisions which the detail of character prescribes: he paints the elements with their own simplicity, height, depth, the vast, the grand, darkness, light; life, death; the past, the future; man, pity, love, joy, fear, terror, peace, war, religion, government: and the visible agents are only engines to form *one* irresistible idea upon the mind and fancy. . . .[80]

There follows a study of the Sistine Chapel as the chief illustration of this kind of art.

It is obvious, therefore, that a change has taken place in the inter-

[78] Martin Shee, *Elements of Art* (London, 1809), pp. 188, 189, note.
[79] "A History of Art in the Schools of Italy," *Life and Works*, ed. John Knowles (London, 1831), III, 216–218.   [80] *Ibid.*, II, 156, 157.

pretation of Michelangelo. In earlier times, Raphael was the great generalizer, the man who attained sublimity by painting the *beau idéal* of nature, and Michelangelo was blamed for being too individualistic. It would seem that a new norm has arisen for nature; it is no longer a case of following the ancients to nature—Raphael had done that—but of being true to one's own vision of the great abstractions that Fuseli has named. Michelangelo becomes the painter of the genuine forms of nature; Raphael "drew forms and characters of society diversified by artificial wants." Fuseli sums up the matter as follows:

We find therefore M. Agnolo more sublime, and we sympathize more with Rafaello, because he resembles us more. When Reynolds said that M. Agnolo had more *imagination*, and Raphael more *fancy*, he meant to say, that the one had more sublimity, more elementary fire; the other was richer in social imagery, in general conceits, and artificial variety. Simplicity is the stamen of M. Agnolo; varied propriety, with character, that of Rafaello.[81]

It is this "elementary fire," expressed through titanic forms, that Fuseli values as the sublime of Michelangelo, and that fills him with awe.

The sublime mind of M. Agnolo, soaring beyond the idea of decrepitude and puny formality, strove to form a type in the elemental energy of the Creator of Adam, and darted life from his extended hand . . .[82]

And again the "breadth" (Fuseli defines this term as "uninterrupted unity") of Michelangelo is compared to "the tide and ebb of a mighty sea," which impress only with the image of power that directs them.[83] This is certainly a sublime substantially different from that of Raphael, the calm, the serene. The elevation of Michelangelo to the first place among painters has resulted in a new taste and a new sublime, a sublime that is at one with the sublime of Ossian and of wild, rugged nature, that is perceived not in ideal form, but in the intensity and depth of feeling that produced the work of art in which it resides.

In his painting, no less than in his lectures, Fuseli illustrates this new taste. Certainly he does not "follow nature" any more than he follows the ancients. One is impressed by the energetic imagination which made his technique faulty, but which manifests itself in his terrible subjects, his visionary forms, and his distorted figures. Such curious paintings as his *Witch*, *Weird Sisters*, *Nightmare*, or *The Lazar House*, *Satan Calling His Legions*, and *Satan Starting from the Touch of Ithuriel's Spear*, the last three from Milton, will admirably illustrate his qualities. All show in one way or another a fondness for distorted bodies that is probably borrowed from the Sistine Chapel and that does suggest a certain energy. Chiaroscuro is heavily used to heighten the terrible ef-

[81] *Ibid.*, III, 27.   [82] *Ibid.*, II, 205.   [83] *Ibid.*, II, 250.

fect, and wild gestures or storm-tossed garments show an effort to express strong emotions. All of these paintings aim at evoking terror, and
one of their weaknesses is that they say too much. Fuseli represents
almost the *reductio ad absurdum* of the conception of genius that the
century derived from Longinus.

That these paintings were connected with sublimity in the public mind
there can be no doubt. "Anthony Pasquin," in his scurrilous satire on
contemporary painters, *The Royal Academicians*, put into the mouth of
Cosmetic (Cosway) the following praise of his wife Maria (famous as a
painter of miniatures): ". . . She's as well acquainted with the sublime
as the immortal EDMUND or the great FUSELI;"[84] and whether he actually considered Burke and Fuseli to be authorities on the sublime, his
words suggest that they were popularly associated with that quality.
As a matter of fact, in his *Memoirs of the Royal Academicians*, ten years
later, he compares and condemns Fuseli and Ossian in the same breath,
but admits that Fuseli approaches the sublime in his ideas.[85]

If Fuseli's satirist found something of the sublime in his work, one
is not surprised to learn that his friends were not blind to his greatness.
John Knowles includes in his *Life and Works* a laudatory appendix containing both a reasoned criticism and poetical panegyrics. William
Young Ottley considers Fuseli the first painter in England to succeed
in the highest department of painting—the "poetic or epic;" and he
characteristically excuses his "wildness" by hinting that his genius was
unincumbered by mere technique, and that his exaggeration was due
to his desire to soar to the sublime regions of poetry. Moreover, Michelangelo, Raphael, and Giulio Romano were prone to exaggeration.[86] The
loftier his subject, the more easily did Fuseli rise; the proof of this remarkable opinion is found in the Milton Gallery.

The magnificent imagery of this poem, the beautiful, the sublime or the terrific
of the personages represented in it, and of the actions described, all combined
to fit it for the display of the artist's surprising genius in its fullest force; besides
which, the style of Mr. F. was here exactly suited to his subject.[87]

William Roscoe's "Verses to Henry Fuseli, Esquire, R. A., on his Series
of Pictures from the Poetical Works of Milton" goes even further, daring
to equate the geniuses of Michelangelo and Fuseli.[88]

---

[84] [Anthony Pasquin], *The Royal Academicians, A Farce* (London, 1786), p. 21.

[85] Anthony Pasquin, *Memoirs of the Royal Academicians; being an Attempt to Improve
the National Taste* (London, 1796), pp. 116, 117.

[86] *Life and Works*, I, 421–423.   [87] *Ibid.*, I, 426.

[88] *Ibid.*, I, 428. The *Analytical Review* found sublimity in Fuseli's contributions to
the Shakespeare Gallery (IV, 111). The painting singled out for especial praise was the
illustration of *Macbeth*, I, 3, which depicted the meeting of Macbeth and Banquo with the

And so the century which had begun with Raphael ends with his Florentine rival. It is noteworthy that implicit in this change in taste is a shift in emphasis from the value of correctness to the value of those more subjective elements that Wordsworth's age called "imagination." Robert Bromley's compendious history of the fine arts reflects this interpretation. Like Fuseli he appreciates Michelangelo not only for his technical skill, but also for the "poetical part" of his design.

> In this latter view of his talents in design we see him rising from the eye to the mind, from the address which engages the senses to the instruction which seizes the imagination. This is indeed the divine exercise of the art, which rises above all that is common, and leaves behind it all that is tame or simply correct. It opens to the sublime, and carries us into new regions of intellectual entertainment.[89]

This passage looks backward, through the eighteenth-century sublime to Longinus, but it also gives a hint of the criticism of the age of Wordsworth with its suggestion of a contrariety implied between the senses and the imagination.

There were other manifestations of sublimity in the painting of the century. When Gray was in Italy he made a list of subjects which various painters might have successfully executed. A subject for Salvator Rosa was "Hannibal passing the Alps; the mountaineers rolling down rocks upon his army; elephants tumbling down the precipices."[90] We could find no clearer indication of what the eighteenth century found in Salvator Rosa than this suggestion. If Raphael and Michelangelo were sublime in history painting, Salvator was sublime in landscape by virtue of the "wildness" of his imagination, which impelled him to select terrific scenes. Terror was his domain as it was Shakespeare's; hence a

---

witches. It was one of Fuseli's most extravagant works, characterized by the most theatrical use of chiaroscuro, wild gestures, distorted postures, and horrific and grotesque witches. Knowles found the painting of the ghost of old Hamlet sublime on the somewhat vague grounds of its "light, shadows, and general tone." *Life and Works*, I, 78.

[89] Robert Anthony Bromley, *A Philosophical and Critical History of the Fine Arts* (London, 1793), II, 373, 374; 423.

[90] Thomas Gray, *Poems, to Which Are Prefixed Memoirs of his Life and Writings*, ed. W. Mason (York, 1775), p. 307. It has perhaps not been noticed that this picture was painted in words by England's literary Salvator, Mrs. Ann Radcliffe, when she described Emily's crossing of the Alps. For no apparent reason, Montori and Cavigni dispute concerning the point at which Hannibal crossed the mountains, and Emily imagines the scene. Among other details the following suggests Gray: "She looked with horror upon the mountaineers, perched on the higher cliffs, assailing the troops below with broken fragments of the mountain; on soldiers and elephants tumbling headlong down the lower precipices; . . ." *Mysteries of Udolpho*, II, 15. John Cozens exhibited a "Landscape with Hannibal, in his March over the Alps" in the exhibition of the Royal Academy, 1776.

mountain scene displaying "elephants tumbling down the precipices" was felt to be suitable to his "dashing" pencil.

But such landscapes were not harmonious with the severest neo-classical taste. Lairesse's *Art of Painting* may be accepted as giving a fairly representative conception of what academic taste admired in landscape. A "Painter-like" landscape must display straight-grown trees, spacious grounds, gentle ups and downs, clear and still rivers, well-ordered colors, a blue sky with small clouds, magnificent houses, "disposed according to the rules of architecture" and peaceful animals. Nothing but scorn is given to the sort of landscape that Salvator had delighted to paint:

But a Piece with deformed Trees, wildly branched and leaved, and disorderly spread from East towards West, crooked-bodies, old and rent, full of Knots and Hollownesses; also rugged Grounds without Roads or Ways, sharp Hills, and monstrous Mountains filling the Offskip, rough or ruined Buildings with their Parts lying up and down in Confusion; likewise muddy Brooks, and gloomy Sky, abounding with heavy Clouds . . . such a Piece . . . is not to be called a fine Landskip.

The whole of the seventeenth chapter is given over to satirizing the taste for rocks, ruins, and storms.[91] Pure neo-classical taste demanded an orderly garden for its delight, and it took the influence of Salvator Rosa and Burke, together with Ossian and the sensibility of later decades to produce the taste that impelled Joseph Pott to describe a sublime landscape as one containing "rocks or ruins, castles, mountains, precipices, waterfalls."[92]

It is unnecessary to summarize the criticism of Salvator in our century. Miss Manwaring has made it familiar in the third chapter of her *Italian Landscape in Eighteenth Century England*. From the time of Richardson Salvator had found admirers as a depictor of "Wild and Savage Nature," and as a practicer of a "Great and Noble" style.[93] After the distinction between the sublime and the beautiful was firmly established, Salvator's landscapes became the example of the one and Claude's of the other. By virtue of his character, the legend of his association with banditti, his interpretation of the wild and energetic aspects of nature, and his "dashing pencil," which was supposed to have scorned correctness in its attempt to attain the higher beauties, Salvator appealed strongly to the romantic taste of the eighteenth century. His rocks and mountains, blasted trees and waterfalls, storms and gloom (already dubbed sublime by the theorizers of the 1730's and 1740's)

[91] Gerard de Lairesse, *The Art of Painting*, etc., tr. J. F. Fritsch (London, 1738), pp. 330, 331; 338–342.   [92] [Joseph Pott], *An Essay on Landscape Painting* (L., 1782), p. 81.
[93] Richardson, *Account of Some of the Statues . . . and Pictures in Italy*, p. 187.

were happily suggestive of aspects of the external world which were to
become popular with lovers of nature during the last half of the century.
Uvedale Price draws the conventional contrast between Claude and
Salvator: the one delights the eye and mind, the other alarms and ter-
rifies the imagination; the figures in a Claudian landscape suggest ideas
of peace, security, and happiness; in a Salvatorial landscape we see

> Each figure boldly passing into life,
> And breathing blood, calamity, and strife;

a Claudian scene suggests repose and love, a Salvatorial scene suggests
death, gloom, and destruction.[94]

William Parsons finds Salvator "cull'd each dreadful grace" and was

> Fond with imperious arts, that scorned controul,
> To pierce, to rouse, to terrify the soul.[95]

Here are the Burkean sublime and the Longinian idea (quite exaggerated) that sublimity is opposed to the rules. Salvator's art scorned
control, just as Shakespeare's did. The grace beyond the reach of art
that Pope thought might be "snatched" is deliberately achieved by
simply refusing to be bound.

Salvator thus became associated with certain literary original geniuses
and their divine right to go beyond the rules. Ossian, Shakespeare, and
Salvator were felt to be in important respects similar. Miss Manwaring
quotes Mason's dictum that only Shakespeare, who was "fancy's child'
is the equal of the Neapolitan painter, and Walpole's opinion that Salvator could have painted "up to the horrour" of the first stanza of
The Bard.[96] Lady Morgan's life of the painter is full of literary analogues
to her favorite—Milton, Shakespeare, Byron.[97]

It was not only his choice of subjects that raised Salvator to the sublime, although the material in which he dealt became traditionally sublime; but this of course was the chief cause of his reputation. His
technique was considered to be that of an original and a sublime artist;
in other words he seemed not to rely on rules and careful academic
building up of effects. He worked rapidly, as if inspired, resting content
with "bold" expression, a sort of rudimentary impressionism. Robert
Strange indicates this view when he says that one of Salvator's charac-

---

[94] Uvedale Price, A Dialogue on the Distinct Characters of the Picturesque and the Beautiful
(Hereford, 1801), pp. 154, 155.

[95] [William Parsons], "Epistle from Naples to Bertie Greatheed," A Poetical Tour in the
Years 1784, 1785, and 1786 (London, 1787), p. 140.

[96] Elizabeth Manwaring, Italian Landscape in Eighteenth Century England (New York,
1925), pp. 46 and 53.

[97] Lady Morgan (Sidney Owenson), Life and Times of Salvator Rosa (London, 1824), I,
175, 220, and 329, 330.

teristics is "a spirit and freedom of pencil,"[98] and William Hayley expresses it completely in his familiar lines:

> Untrodden paths of art SALVATOR tried,
> And daring Fancy was his favourite guide.
> O'er his wild rocks, at her command, he throws
> A savage grandeur, and sublime repose: . . .
> His bold ideas, unrefin'd by taste,
> Express'd with vigour, tho' conceiv'd in haste,
> Before slow judgment their defects can find,
> With awful pleasure fill the passive mind.[99]

Defects these are, but they are the endearing defects of original genius.

By the time the artists of Britain began to hold annual exhibitions, a taste for wild scenery and natural sublimities was growing up in England. This taste manifests itself in painting at about the same time that it does in literature. A reading of the catalogues of the exhibition reveals how early landscape, particularly if "romantic," began to be treated.

In 1760 Richard Wilson exhibited his *Niobe* in the Great Room of the Society for the Encouragement of Arts. There are several versions of this famous painting, all of them interesting from the point of view of the treatment of emotion. In this picture, Wilson is certainly in the region of the sublime; his materials are all conventionally sublime, and his subject impels him to break through the classic calm that one generally associates with his landscape.

At the Victoria and Albert Museum is preserved the study for the *Niobe*. In it we see the landscape background, but none of the figures that tell the story of Niobe in the completed version. The study, then, is helpful in showing us Wilson's aims. The story of the destruction of Niobe's children is one of violent emotions in which terror predominates. Wilson's landscape setting is full of the emotions which the story evokes. On the right rise high and massive rocks, down which pours a torrent; a rock is perched on the edge of the waterfall and seems about to be dashed down by the violence of the water. This part of the scene is dark and gloomy, showing nature in a violent and threatening mood. Obviously the figures will be grouped here, at the point of highest emotion. This concentration of emotion is carried off, *diminuendo*, through a sort of rocky promontory, and a castle, over which lightning flashes, to distant mountains, but it is resumed in heavy clouds at the left, from which Apollo is to shoot his darts. Here is a fitting natural setting for the dire events of the story; it is nature at her most melodramatic and

[98] Robert Strange, *A Descriptive Catalogue of a Collection of Pictures*, etc. (London, 1769), p. 114.

[99] William Hayley, *An Essay on Painting* (London, 1771), pp. 24 and 25.

sublime, but the calm sublimity of the distant landscape toward the left effects a sort of spatial catharsis.

In the version in the Tate Gallery, the rocks are diminished in size, the waterfall is more hidden, but a tree tossed in the storm keeps up the emotional pitch at the right, where the figures of Niobe, who expresses grief in her gestures, and of her children, calm and resigned, endure the arrows of the god. Even the distant landscape is dark and threatening, thus depriving the scene of the catharsis found in the study, and adding to the force of the terrible emotions which center on the human figures.

In the Bridgewater House *Niobe*, the figures, instead of expressing resignation, are animated by violent emotions, expressed in tossing of arms and strained postures. As if to intensify these passions, the vast open landscape behind, which was found in the study, is eliminated by the introduction of a tree, dead trunks, and clouds. The gloomy landscape presses in upon the victims of the gods. On the right, the waterfall has been entirely removed, and a huge, solid rock, surmounted by a ruined castle, takes its place. Lightning flashes in the sky. The landscape is ponderously sublime; the violence that had been expressed by waterfalls and storm-tossed trees is now expressed in the figures, fleeing in terror from the arrows of the offended god.[100] One can understand Fuseli's saying, "Wilson's grandeur is oftener allied to terror, bustle, and convulsion than to calmness and tranquility;"[101] and it is not difficult to find the reason for Reynolds's attack on the *Niobe* in his final discourse.

It has seemed permissible to write at such•length of the *Niobe* because in these paintings Wilson is speaking the language of Salvator and of eighteenth-century sublimity. His space, rocks, waterfalls, ruins, lightning, violent wind, etc., all became commonplace symbols of the sublime, whether in painting, or poetry, or descriptive prose. If one would understand what the latter half of the century meant by the word *sublime*, let him go to the *Niobe*.

Wilson's *Atalanta and Meleager* and *Celadon and Amelia* are representative of the same sort of painting—the telling of a tragic story, highly emotional, to the accompaniment of moods of nature that emphasize the emotions involved in the incident depicted. Both deal in the same conventionally sublime material that we have observed in the *Niobe*. In his more personal landscapes Wilson is less sublime; the influence of Claude is apparent. When sublime objects occur they are not

---

[100] A fourth version, bought by Linford in 1928, is less interesting.

[101] Quoted by M. H. Grant in his *A Chronological History of the Old English Landscape Painters* (London, 1925), I, 53.

treated rhetorically as in histories, but steeped in classic composure.

Landscape painting begins, properly, about the sixth decade of the century, at a time when the interest in gardens was high, and when a taste for natural scenery was just becoming fashionable. Although by far the majority of the pictures exhibited in the Great Room of the Society for the Encouragement of Arts was made up of portraits and histories, landscapes appeared more and more frequently, and from the first they often depicted subjects that were at least potentially sublime. *A Storm and Shipwreck*, by J. Leigh, was shown in 1761, and 1762 brought forth *A View of Corly in Cumberland* by William Bellers, *Large Landscape with Ruins* by Augustin Brumias, *View in Wales*, by Anthony Devis, *A Storm*, by John Hood, and William Woolett's landscape setting for a scene from Otway's *Orphan*. Of course it does not follow that all or any of these paintings were "sublime." Bellers' was certainly topographical,[102] and Brumias' was probably an imitation of Claude or Poussin. In the same year the Society of Artists exhibited at Spring Garden, where ruin-pieces by Dall and Lambert were hung; and in the next year similar pieces by Dall, Marlow, Pugh, and Richards made their appearance.

It would be impossible and not very profitable to discuss fully the subjects of the paintings that were exhibited at the Royal Academy from 1769 to 1800. Many of them have perished, and many have not been photographed. A reading of the catalogues of these exhibitions is interesting, if exhausting. Conventionally sublime subjects from nature and from literature, and histories (a *genre* that was traditionally associated with sublimity) crowd the pages of the catalogues. A brief discussion will indicate the nature of these works.

Sandby's topographical paintings of ruins and scenes in the United Kingdoms, for his *Virtuosi's Museum*, were being exhibited as early as 1769. There is seldom an attempt to poetize these scenes, to make them "sublime" as Wilson had done with his *Niobe*. Sandby is usually content to record rather literally what he sees; but his efforts are important, as were those of all the topographical artists, in helping to create a taste for romantic scenes and sublimities. They help to indicate the growth of taste for natural beauties that ultimately set the traveler on the road to Wales, Cumberland, and the Highlands.

Another landscape artist who was a prolific contributor was Edmund Garvey, whose first exhibition at the Royal Academy, in 1769, *A View of Rome, Waterfall near Chamberie in Savoy, Two Views from Piercefield*,[103]

---

[102] The painting was one of seven scenes in the Lake District.

[103] This was one of the famous "sublime" seats of the century. See [Arthur Young], *A Six Weeks Tour*, pp. 131 ff.

Tintern Abbey, and *Waterfall in the Alps*, is fairly representative of his work for a number of years. He follows the fashion in scenery, recording from year to year the popular scenes that filled the travel books of the period. Switzerland, Italy, Britain, and the Rhine occupy his pencil until well into the 1790's.

George Barrett, though often almost purely topographical, could none the less poetize his subjects and attempt the sublime. His *Melrose Abbey* (1769) is an example of his less literal treatment of ruins. The moon casts mysterious shadows on the building, its ivy and its tombs. The elegiac mood is expressed in the two figures who posture near the graves, obviously declaiming on such sublime themes as fill Blair's *Grave* and Young's *Night Thoughts*. The contrast between this piece and Barrett's *Classical Ruins* is instructive. The mood of the latter is entirely different. The scene is flooded with light, there is no mystery, no elegiacal feeling; the figures are animated. In *Melrose Abbey* the gothic mood prevails—all is mystery, gloom, shadowy terror; in *Classical Ruins* it is the light, not the ruins, that is important. By and large the latter half of the eighteenth century came to prefer the gothic mood to the simpler "ruins of Rome" subjects. North Wales and the Lakes were frequently the subject of Barrett's art. In 1781 he exhibited *Winandermere Lake . . . the Sun Beginning to Appear in the Morning, with the Mists Breaking and Dispersing*. An anonymous reviewer of the exhibition says of this picture that Barrett has been "successful in the highest degree in the presentation of his sublime choice of Nature."[104]

As the years passed, many, almost innumerable, paintings of sublimities were exhibited. Some of the names of the artists who did this sort of work are William Pars, "Michael Angleo" Rooker, P. J. de Loutherbourg, S. H. Grimm, Joseph Farington, Joseph Wright, the Reverend J. Gardnor, J. Rathbone, W. Marlow, J. C. Ibbettson, T. Walmsley, and the water colorists, the two Cozens and Francis Towne; these among others. And they presented to the public views of the Highlands, of Wales, of the Lakes, of Switzerland, and of the Rhine. In the main their pictures are not full of dramatic emotion as was the case with the *Niobe*. When they painted Ullswater they seldom dressed it up with storms or blasted trees by way of emphasizing its sublimity. Often, too, the sublime objects are seen *through* a tranquil scene of grazing cattle, which prevents the "terrible graces" from overwhelming the beholder. This is not always the case, however. J. More's *Cascade of Terni*, 1783, for example, is full of patent emotion. A foaming waterfall, huge, "impending" rocks, and a wide spacious view above the fall—the proper

[104] *The Ear-Wig: or an Old Woman's Remarks on the Present Exhibition of Pictures at the Royal Academy* (London, 1781), p. 8.

emotional effect of all this is indicated by the rhetorical gestures of the small figures, which express amazement and horror.

Perhaps the water colorists come as near expressing the eighteenth-century sublime as do any of these painters. Towne deletes all human figures, and gives us a sensitive interpretation of mass and line. He has no occasion for the rhetorical irrelevancies of Wilson and More. Whether he paints *The Top of Splügen Pass*, or *The Vale of St. John*, or *A View of Llyngwellyr*, or *Lake Como*, his eye sees the same thing—towering mass, sweeping lines, sharp declivities, light and shade, all composed into grand scenes. No exclaiming human figures were necessary to underscore what Towne was saying. The rocks and mountains and space become articulate and speak for themselves. The same is true of Alexander Cozens (see for example his *Among the Mountains*), and it is even more true of the greater John Robert Cozens.

Other sublimities appear from time to time in the Academy exhibitions. The relation between painting and literature was close, both in theory and in practice. We find many "sublime" passages in literature illustrated by the artists of the century. The Shakespeare Gallery of Alderman Boydell and Fuseli's Milton Gallery are illustrations on the grand scale of the tendency to force canvas and pigment to do what the words of a poet had done.

Of course Ossian is a frequent subject for the Royal Academicians. In 1771 James Barralet led the way with two drawings from *Fingal;* Angelica Kauffman followed in 1773 with *Trenmor and Imbaca;* Alexander Runciman, in 1774, exhibited a scene from *Fingal*, Book IV. Maria Cosway, ever eager to achieve fame in historical painting, offered in 1782 *Darthula . . . discovers herself to Cairbar, her lover*, and in the next year, an illustration of the passage, "Althan stood in the woods alone, and saw a ghost in the darkening air, his stride extended from hill to hill." One would give much to see it. C. R. Ryley painted *Ossian and Colman delivering Calthorn* for the exhibitions of 1789; Richter hung two scenes from Ossian in 1792; Singleton did a famous sublime scene in 1794—*The Spirit of Cathmor appearing at Cloumel's Cave;* Westall's *Fingal and the Spirit of Loda* in 1796, depicted an equally famous incident, which Halls repeated in 1798. The number is not large, but it is sufficient to indicate that painting followed the literary fashion.

Shakespeare and Milton are also frequent indirect contributors to the exhibitions. Paul Sandby left topography long enough to paint *A Storm from the Winter's Tale* in 1774; Alexander Runciman, in 1773, exhibited *Satan Starting from the Touch of Ithuriel's Spear*, a subject that was to be treated by Fuseli in 1780 and by Westall in 1793; John Mortimer's *Satan and Death* was hung in 1779; West's *Battle between Michael and Satan*, in 1782; Fuseli's *Weird Sisters*, in 1783, and *Lady Macbeth Walking in her Sleep*, in 1784; Freman's *Satan at the Court of Chaos*, in 1784; Fuseli's *Witches Cavern*, in 1793; Lawrence's *Prospero Raising a Storm*, in 1793; Mequignon's *Macbeth Consulting the Witches*, in 1793; Braine's *Satan Rising from the Court of Chaos*, in 1793; West's *Macbeth and the Witches*, in 1793; Howard's *Satan Awakening in the Burning Lake*, in 1795; Singleton's *Four Subjects from Paradise Lost*, in 1796; Howard's *Sin and Death Passing through the Constellations*, in 1797; Lawrence's *Satan Calling his Legions*, in 1797; Fuseli's *Richard III in his Tent*, in 1798; and Singleton's *Four Subjects from Macbeth*, in 1799. This is a sufficiently long list to show how the sister arts united to provide the British public with illustrations of its two favorite poets.[105]

Terrific subjects from other works were occasionally painted. Thomson provided Mullins with a subject in 1772—*A Cataract, a rude scene;* William Williams depicted *A Thunderstorm, with the Death of Amelia*, in 1788; and Wilson had painted the same scene. Gray's *Bard* was drawn by Saunders in 1778 and painted by Westall in 1798, and Singleton did the *Odin* and the *Prophetess* in 1793. Other miscellaneous sublimities were *The Ghost of Clytemnestra Awakening the Furies* by Downman, in 1782; *Eolus Raising a Storm*, 1782, by Maria Cosway; Beechey's *The Witch of Endor*, 1785; Westall's *Surprise Mixed with Terror*, 1791, and *Furies Turning the Tide of Battle*, 1794.

In 1794 gothic terror made its appearance at the Royal Academy, and remained there for many years. William Hodges exhibited *The Abbey*, from Mrs. Radcliffe's *Romance of the Forest*. Singleton did a scene from *Udolpho* in 1797; Fairbone chose *Caleb Williams* in the same year; and in 1798 Lloyd took a subject from *Udolpho*, Flaxman from *The Children of the Abbey*, and Nixon, two scenes from *The Italian;* in 1799 Drummond selected a scene from *Udolpho*, Van Assen from *The Castle of Otranto*. About the same time Lady Di Beauclerk was deserting her cupids in order to adorn a *de luxe* edition of Bürger's *Leonora* with extremely horrid illustrations.[106] Ryley's *The Banquet* and *The Vengeance*, 1797, both subjects from *The Monk*, are excellent examples of this kind of painting—sensational subjects, skulls, heavy chiaroscuro, obviously expressed emotions, all combine to show the weaknesses of this highly

[105] There were other subjects from these poets, but they do not suggest the sublime.

[106] A. Bürger, *Leonora*, tr. W. R. Spencer (London, 1796). The illustrations are worth looking at as examples of how horrid even Lady Di could become under the impulse of fashion.

dramatic and terrific type of painting, and its relation to the far-from-subtle terror of the popular fiction of the 1790's.[107]

All of this has led us a long distance from Raphael, the French Academy, and the *beau idéal*. But it has shown us how emotion and the sensational elements of the late-eighteenth-century sublime swept into painting as they did into literature and theory, and, as we shall see, as they did into the appreciation and interpretation of nature. It should be remembered that these "sublime" paintings were hung along with many that were more traditional in subject-matter and in treatment— the portraits of Reynolds and the highly academic histories of Benjamin West, for example. These paintings are typical of the pre-romanticism of the century. But Turner had begun to exhibit before the turn of the century, and the way was being prepared for his genius to establish the romantic tradition in English landscape.

[107] Something of the sublimity of *The Monk* is hinted in Dermody's satire on the price of Lewis's books:

> Yet wisely (and, I wot, by shrewd advice)
> Thou sell'st thy tome at an enormous price.
> How few can read it in this troublous time!
> For now a guinea touches the sublime.
>   Thomas Dermody, *The Harp of Erin* (London, 1807), I, 117.

CHAPTER X

THE SUBLIME IN NATURAL SCENERY

IT is no part of the scheme of the present work to trace throughout the eighteenth century the growth of what is usually spoken of as "a feeling for nature"; that subject has been touched on in every volume that deals with the history of romanticism, and more than once has been made the subject of special study. Dr. Myra Reynolds's dissertation, *The Treatment of Nature in English Poetry between Pope and Wordsworth* (1896), though superseded by more recent works, still affords a useful index to the subject. Professor Manwaring's *Italian Landscape* is an animated and instructive study of taste, particularly in respect to the popularity of Claude and Salvator and their influence on English arts; more recently, Mr. Christopher Hussey has traversed the same ground in his volume *The Picturesque* (1927); and although Mlle Engel's *La Littérature Alpestre en France et en Angleterre aux 18 et 19 Siècles* (1930), is not very well synthesized, it also contains much information both old and new on the subject of the cult of mountain scenery in our era. It would seem, then, that little remains to be said on the subject; and yet a history of the sublime would scarcely be complete did it not devote a chapter to the taste for the sublimity of nature.

Professor Manwaring has made clear the influence of Italian painters in forming among Englishmen an ability to appreciate the beauties of the natural world. She has distinguished between the nature poetry of Milton, truthful as it is, but none the less essentially uncomposed, and the descriptions in *The Seasons*, made with the eye on the object, but also evaluated and composed by a taste formed on the paintings of Claude Lorraine. This habit of seeking in nature scenes suitable both to the poet and to the painter, fortified as it was by the æsthetic of *ut pictura poesis*, dominated England until well into the nineteenth century, and finally created an æsthetic of its own—the picturesque. The cult of nature was strong from the moment when *The Seasons* achieved its prodigious popularity; it was reinforced in the mid-century by Rousseau and Ossian, and it grew in power during 1770–1800, decades which produced the picturesque traveler and his innumerable books.

Though Nature was a cult to many Englishmen during this period, she did not become a religion. She was a goddess, to be sure, and an elaborate ritual was built up through which she must be approached.

The ritual, however, often tended to obscure the goddess who had evoked it. Nature, one sometimes believes, was sought, not so much for what she was, as for what she was not. The picturesque traveler approached her with his head full of vistas and lights and foregrounds and points of view and side-screens; and he stayed to commend when she could offer to "Taste" a scene which in some way resembled the compositions of those Gemini among landscape artists, Claude and Salvator. In a sense it is true that throughout the picturesque phase nature was frequently scarcely seen at all, for the lover of the picturesque was bent upon discovering not the world as it is, but the world as it might have been had the Creator been an Italian artist of the seventeenth century. Shut up in the Palace of Art, he could look out only through stained-glass windows which falsely colored the natural world.

 Wordsworth most effectively broke the spell that Italian landscape had woven over English taste, and taught his contemporaries to hear Rotha's voice aright. The result was a new ability to see and love the natural world for its own sake, a care for the expression of what the eye saw and the imagination decreed to be significant. Whatever else nineteenth-century romanticism may have been, it was certainly in one of its manifestations a vindication of the imagination as an interpreter of experience; and this is the burden of Wordsworth's doctrine and the revolutionary aspect of his practice. A landscape may or may not resemble a painting; at best such a fact is irrelevant. It may or may not be suffused with a Claudian light; the important thing for Wordsworth was to see and to reveal the light that never was on sea or land.

In *The Prelude* he records the struggle between the physical eye and the eye of the poet's imagination, between sight and insight.[1] It was necessary for him to break the tyranny of the bodily eye before he could "see into the heart of things." This is the key to the difference between the "romantic" and the "picturesque" approach to nature. As Mr. Hussey says, ". . . the picturesque interregnum between classic and romantic art was necessary in order to enable the imagination to form the habit of feeling through the eyes."[2] The picturesque traveller, in search of Claudian beauty or Salvatorial sublimity, was busy *seeing;* Wordsworth had to teach him not only to see, but to interpret in terms of personal intuition. And in so doing he expressed, as no one else has, the romantic religion of nature that is so different from the natural religion which immediately preceded it in time. He congratulates himself some-

---

[1] *The Prelude*, XII, 121–139. All references are to Professor de Selincourt's edition (Oxford, 1926).

[2] Christopher Hussey, *The Picturesque, Studies in a Point of View* (London and New York, 1927), p. 4.

what loftily on never having given himself over to the cant terms of the picturesque.[3] But his scorn savors of ingratitude, for essentially superficial as the picturesque view of nature was, it was none the less one more example of how the eighteenth century was, in Macaulay's phrase, "indispensable." Romantic nature poetry, endowing as it does the natural world with spiritual content and values, is unthinkable without the long transition which the cult of the picturesque effected between the Cartesian appeal to reason and the romantic appeal to imagination. In the period which we are studying, English taste goes to school to Italian painters, and, if men are at all a product of their times, it is perhaps little exaggeration to say that Wordsworth would never have seen God through nature, had not the generations which preceded him seen nature through Claude and Salvator.

So much by way of generalization. The task before us is to discover what part the sublime played in the picturesque appreciation of nature, and what happened to the concept, hitherto discussed only in theory, when it was transposed into the sphere of the practical. The way will lead through emotion to Salvator, and thence to the approximation of an æsthetic of form in the writings of Gilpin.

The sublime from its beginning had been connected with the natural world. Longinus, in crying up man's inherent nobility as witnessed by his inborn love of the great, had cast a hurried glance at natural scenery. Nature, he says, "inclines us to admire, not a little clear transparent rivulet that ministers to our necessities, but the *Nile*, the *Ister*, the *Rhine*, or still more, the *Ocean*." By the same token, we wonder at and admire Etna. "And from hence we may infer, that . . . whatever exceeds the common size, is always great and always amazing."[4] True to the Greek tradition, his interest is centered not on nature, but on man, and so he passes on to dilate on the dignity of his species, not the sublimity of the external world. But the hint had been given, and future ages were to develop it far beyond the Greek critic's ken. Mountains, because of their height, and the ocean, because of its size, were ready and apt symbols in the physical world of the moral greatness to which Longinus attributed the sublime in art.

It is a significant fact that Boileau and Silvain have nothing to say of the sublime in nature. Longinus gave to each man what he wanted, and never pressed his wares on those who came to him. France, in 1700, was not ready to become enthusiastic about natural scenery. In England the case was somewhat different. Her poets had always been closer to nature than had the French poets. The author of *Beowulf*, in his description of the lair of Grendel's dam, had recorded the mystery and the

---

[3] *The Prelude*, XII, 109–121.   [4] *On the Sublime*, pp. 146, 147.

terror of nature; the Wanderer and the Seafarer had expressed in their
lays something of the power of the ocean over the imagination of a sea-
going race; Chaucer, Spenser, Shakespeare, and Milton had each, in his
different way, written intimately of the natural world. Once again we
see that Longinus was peculiarly fitted to awaken a sympathetic response among the dwellers in England's green and pleasant land. To
Boileau, Longinus's passage on the sublimity of nature quite possibly
meant little; to an Englishman of the early eighteenth century, it might
very possibly come as a reminder of something which, if not experienced
keenly, was nevertheless familiar to readers of, let us say, *King Lear*.

Moreover, as Mr. Hussey has said, the love of nature that is so obvious
in Elizabethan literature, submerged but not destroyed during the Com-
monwealth and Restoration, was soon to be manifest again as a result
of the Grand Tour. The gentlemen who went to Italy saw sights that
were calculated to reanimate that native taste for natural beauty—the
Alps and Italian paintings.[5] The slow and painful passage of the Alps
gave ample opportunity to those who were so inclined to enjoy the wild
and the grand in mountain scenery, and the picture galleries of Italy
were waiting to show how the artist interpreted landscape. Salvator
Rosa, soon to become a favorite with the English connoisseur, was
easily associated in the mind of the English tourist with the vivid experience of the Alps, and always there was Longinus in the background
to act as intermediary between nature and art and to supply the word
that described both natural and painted mountains.

Professor Manwaring and Mr. Hussey have collected the recorded
impressions of early travelers among mountains. Perhaps most seventeenth-century travelers agreed with James Howell, who could find
nothing better to say of the "Pyraneans" than that they were "uncouth
huge monstrous excrescences of Nature."[6] Certainly John Evelyn found
in the Alps "the rubbish of the earth" swept up in order to clear the
plains of Lombardy, and Gilbert Burnet inclined to the theory that the
Alps were not the "primary productions of the Author of nature," but
were the ruins of an older world, irrevocably spoiled by the deluge.[7]
Others were doubtless simply indifferent, believing, as Johnson was to
say many years later, that their "business was with men and manners."
A third, and much smaller group, finding themselves face to face with the

---

[5] *The Picturesque*, p. 12.

[6] James Howell, *Epistolae Ho-Elianae, Familiar Letters Domestic and Forren*, The Third
Edition (London, 1655), I, 67. The first edition appeared in 1645.

[7] John Evelyn, *Diary*, ed. Austin Dobson (London, 1908), p. 137. The trip was made
in 1646.—Gilbert Burnet, *Some Letters, Containing, An Account of what seemed most remarkable in Switzerland, Italy*, etc. (Rotterdam, 1686), pp. 7 and 14.

wild and stupendous, saw freshly and felt naïvely, and perhaps even made an effort to analyse their feelings, which were strong enough to overcome the current prejudice against the formless, the wild, the uncouth, so much at variance with the neo-classical and urbane taste that began to prevail about the time of the Restoration.[8]

This group became vocal toward the end of the seventeenth century in the writings of John Dennis, whose account of an Alpine journey is one of the earliest recorded æsthetic experiences of mountain scenery that the age of Dryden and Pope affords. He describes his danger amid "the impending Rock," "the dreadful Depth of the Precipice," the roaring torrent, the "craggy Clifts,"a scene "altogether new and amazing." Then follows the analysis: "The sense of all this [danger and beauty] produc'd different motions in me, *viz.* a delightful Horrour, a terrible Joy, and at the same time, that I was infinitely pleas'd, I trembled."[9]

A passage more characteristic of the eighteenth century as a whole could hardly be found. In 1693 Dennis said almost all that the later enthusiasts were to say, until Gilpin created the picturesque and intimated that mountains might be enjoyed apart from their emotive qualities. The sublime, as we have seen, began its career in partnership with the pathetic, and was to be associated throughout the century with delightful horror, the most obvious example of a strong emotion, that, despite its nature, is capable of being enjoyed. In view of this fact, it is interesting to find that in a naïve experience the same emotion was suggested by mountains. Dennis's testimony is valid because it is honest and spontaneous, and is not elicited by respect for cult or fashion.

One would like to be sure that Dennis associated this experience at once with Longinus's observations on the vast in nature. He does not use the word *sublime*, but he does borrow a comparison from the Greek critic. If the Alps were designed by nature, he says, "only as a Mound to inclose her Garden *Italy:* Then we may well say of her what some affirm of great Wits, that her careless, irregular and boldest Strokes are most admirable."[10] Moreover, it is not impossible that he recalled this experience when, several years later, he classified terror as a sublime emotion. Addison, too, was shortly to feel "an agreeable kind of Horror" in the presence of the Alps[11] and it is perhaps not without significance

---

[8] The appreciation of mountain scenery, if not general and enthusiastic, was at least not unknown in the early years of the Italian Renaissance, as Jacob Burkhardt has shown in his *The Civilisation of the Renaissance in Italy* (London and New York, 1926), pp. 298–307.   [9] John Dennis, *Miscellanies in Verse and Prose* (London, 1693), pp. 133, 134.

[10] *Ibid.*, p. 138.

[11] [Joseph Addison], *Remarks on Several Parts of Italy*, etc. (London, 1705), p. 455. Similar emotions had come to James Brome at Wokey Hole, although he was obviously

that Dennis and Addison, the first Englishmen to attempt to formulate an æsthetic theory of sublimity, had experienced, quite naïvely, the power of mountain scenery over the imagination.[12] If, coming from England, they had conventionally regarded mountains as simply disagreeable necessities, and if, in the midst of danger and labor, they felt certain agreeable emotions arising from objects that were clearly unbeautiful, they might well have been impelled to speculate on the æsthetic problems implied in this new observation. But mere conjecture cannot serve to establish a link between the experiences of these men in the Alps and their æsthetic writings.

Thus, from the very outset in England, the sublime tended to become the all-inclusive category for those objects and those emotions which the strict neo-classic doctrine could not admit as beautiful, but which Englishmen were traditionally and constitutionally ready to accept as of æsthetic value, until finally, in Burke's *Enquiry*, the ugly itself came to play its part in æsthetic. In respect to natural objects, as in theory, the sublime is found aligned on the side of the more romantic element in eighteenth-century taste.

Between the publication of Dennis's theories and Addison's *Pleasures of the Imagination*, Shaftesbury had contributed the weight of his influence to the cause of the enjoyment of natural scenery. *The Moralists*, 1709, is given over to a vindication of enthusiasm as a positive moral force, the impulse that lies behind the active as well as the contemplative life, behind great deeds as well as great thoughts.[13] Theocles, who conducts the dialogue, is an enthusiastic admirer of nature, and one of his rhapsodies includes an apostrophe to a scene composed of mountains and rocks and torrents and hanging forests. Mankind is pictured, giddy with horror, in the midst of these mountains, and eventually becoming thoughtful and contemplating the incessant changes of this earth's surface. "Here Space astonishes; Silence it-self seems pregnant; whilst an unknown Force works on the Mind, and dubious Objects move the wakeful Sense."[14]

Shaftesbury, in his *Miscellaneous Reflections*, 1711, returns to the subject of enthusiasm, commenting on his earlier *Letter on Enthusiasm*. This

not impressed by the Highlands; and Berkeley was to commend mountain scenery to Pope as a necessary element in a poet's education. James Brome, *Travels over England, Scotland and Wales*, etc. (London, 1700), p. 33, and George Berkeley, *Works* (London, 1784), I, xxxiv. The letter is dated from Leghorn, May 1, 1714.

[12] Addison once recorded his susceptibility to the sublimity of the ocean. In a calm it produced in him a "pleasing Astonishment," in a storm, "agreeable Horrour." *Spectator*, No. 489, III, 229.

[13] [Anthony Ashley Cooper, Third Earl of Shaftesbury], *Characteristicks of Men, Manners, Opinions, Times*, etc. [London] (1711), II, 400. [14] *Ibid.*, II, 389, 390.

exalted state of the soul arises from a perception of beauty that has a power "which naturally captivates the Heart, and raises the Imagination to an Opinion or Conceit of some thing *majestic* and *divine*." It raises us above ourselves; it is the basis of virtue itself.[15] In view of the fact that Shaftesbury had an enormous vogue as a philosopher, these passages must have served as an incentive to the appreciation of the wild and savage in nature, that is, of objects that were to become conventionally sublime. In the first place they recommend an enthusiastic enjoyment of *all* natural beauties as a philosophically justifiable method of perceiving the perfect wisdom and goodness of the Creator, which is revealed in his harmonious universe, and as such they became the model for Thomson's *Hymn* and for much bad poetry of the same sort.[16] In the second place they are obviously a description of that state of mind which eventually came to be regarded as one of the sources of sublime thoughts and emotions. Shaftesbury himself equates enthusiasm with the *furor poeticus;* the source of the highest art with the source of the highest virtue.

. . . all sound *Love* and *Admiration* is ENTHUSIASM: "the Transports of *Poets*, the Sublime of *Orators*, the Rapture of *Musicians*, the highest Strains of the *Virtuosi;* all mere ENTHUSIASM! Even *Learning* it-self, the Love of *Arts* and *Curiosity*, the Spirit of *Travellers* and *Adventurers; Gallantry, War, Heroism;* All, all, ENTHUSIASM!"[17]

In the third place the stupendous in nature, that order of the physical world which clearly lay beyond the conventional formulæ for beauty, is shown to be capable of evoking this lofty state of the soul. Surely it is no wonder that, taught by Italian artists, and urged to feel by Shaftesbury, Thomson and Dyer and Mallet and Akenside were soon to flood England with their descriptive poetry and to form a taste for scenery that was to continue, changed of course into something finer and truer, long into the nineteenth century.

But the limitations of these men should not be overlooked. Their appreciation is essentially crude, for as yet they record in the main only such emotions as any naïve person might feel in the presence of objects that represent forces beyond his control. It was not until about 1738[18] that landscape painting and natural scenery actually came together and that the picturesque phase of English art began. Then and only then was it possible for scenery to be valued generally for its composition and not primarily for its ability to awaken emotions; and even when, at the

---

[15] *Ibid.*, III, 30.

[16] For a discussion of the influence of Shaftesbury on the nature poetry of Thomson and his imitators, see Amy Louise Reed, *The Background of Gray's Elegy* (New York, 1924), pp. 140–187.   [17] *Characteristicks*, II, 400.   [18] *The Picturesque*, pp. 93, 94.

end of the century, this happened, there was little regard for masses and contours and rhythms of line, for an æsthetic of pure form came late. In this respect theory and practice went hand in hand. As we have seen, emotion dominated theories of the sublime until Burke attempted to employ psychology as the handmaid of æsthetic. Until that time came, philosophers were content, by and large, to feel and to record their feelings. But Dennis, Addison, and Shaftesbury were prophets of what was to come, and Thomson ushered in the long era of descriptive writing. It was he who gave to the eighteenth century the useful *cliché:*

> Whate'er Lorrain light-touched with softening hue,
> Or savage Rosa dashed, or learnèd Poussin drew.

And it was under the influence of "savage Rosa" that *The Seasons* revealed the sublimities of nature in storms and earthquakes and terrifying wild beasts and all the other popular horrors of the natural world. As we have observed, few indeed were the theorizers who, writing on the sublime, failed to analyse the effect of the visible world on the emotions of man, and by analogy to transfer these effects to the sublime in art. It would be mere redundancy to repeat their remarks, or to name again all the writers who illustrated theories by appeals to the experience of the individual in the face of the vaster powers and objects of the natural world. For the rest of the century, the æsthetic of the sublime and the æsthetic of nature go hand in hand. It is no wonder, in view of the extensive cult of terror and its association with natural scenery in the works of the descriptive poets, that young Burke was misled into regarding that emotion as the sole source of sublimity.

The taste for mountain scenery and the habit of associating it with paintings is well illustrated in the letters of Thomas Herring, who visited Wales in 1738. He found the landscape grand, and recorded that it "enlarged" his mind in a manner similar to the effect of the stupendousness of the ocean. Moreover, scenes that reminded him of the paintings of Poussin, "agreeably terrified" him, and he enjoyed contemplating them "in pleasure, mixed with horror."[19] If this is not purely an æsthetic response to natural beauty, it none the less indicates how sublime scenery was beginning to draw the attention of men other than poets and artists.

In 1739 Walpole and Gray visited the Grande Chartreuse on their way to Italy. Both wrote of their experience to their friend West, and the contrast is instructive, for in these two letters is indicated the two divergent paths that the treatment of nature in English literature was to take. Walpole, ever a child of his age, thrilled to the scene and apologized

---

[19] Thomas Herring, *Letters to William Duncombe, Esq.* (London, 1777), pp. 39, 40; 42· 50, 51. Letters XI and XII.

for his description which "sounds too bombast and too romantic to one that has not seen it, too cold to one that has." But his enthusiasm found expression in words that were soon to become conventional. "Precipices, mountains, torrents, wolves, rumblings, Salvator Rosa," he exclaims,[20] and his use of the painter's name is a prophecy of much in the future. The picturesque phase has begun, and Salvator is becoming the interpreter to men's eyes of the wild, the savage, the sublime. Walpole has been criticized for his "superficial" enjoyment of this scene, but perhaps it is unfair to blame a man for speaking the language of his age. Doubtless he saw and appreciated as much as does the average tourist who goes to the Alps today; his use of Salvator's name would argue that he enjoyed in the scene its wildness, its vastness, and its energy, for the phrase "savage Rosa" was a sort of shorthand for saying all this. At any rate, Walpole was at one with the vast herd of travelers who were content to seek in nature no more than a not-too-great Italian painter had expressed on his highly prized canvases.

Gray, on the other hand, stood aside from his age in this, respect.

Not a precipice, not a torrent, not a cliff, but is pregnant with religion and poetry. There are certain scenes that would awe an atheist into belief, without the help of other argument. . . . You have death perpetually before your eyes, only so far removed, as to compose the mind without frightening it.[21]

There is no reference here to pictures, but rather an imaginative interpretation of mountain scenery that shows a quality of mind similar to that which finds expression in *The Prelude*. Such passages are rarely found before Wordsworth. They are indicative of that submerged stream of romantic feeling that ever and anon makes its presence known in the midst of neo-classicism. A curious sight this, those young men feeling and expressing so clearly the different, though not totally opposite, tendencies of the years that were to come; Walpole, the typical Georgian gentleman; Gray, as ever, like Wordsworth, a solitary.

But it would be a mistake to infer that Gray stood eternally apart from his age. The evidence of his writings would not sustain this point of view, and the image of the poet in later life, moving among the mountains and lakes of Cumberland or of the Highlands of Scotland, taking "scenes" with his Claude Lorrain glass, looks sufficiently like Dr. Syntax to cause some slight confusion. It is only when one reads his journals of these tours, written to his friend Wharton, that one realizes that in truth no one in his age observed so subtly or recorded so delicately as did Gray. He avoids the adjective *sublime* as much as possible, but the blend

[20] *Correspondence of Gray, Walpole, West and Ashton*, I, 247 and 244.
[21] *Ibid.*, I, 259, 260.

of terror and beauty which he found in mountain scenery is amply expressed, though with little apparent effort to investigate the sources of the pleasure which it caused.[22]

To carry this inquiry step by step into the age of the picturesque traveler would be to confess a lack of conscience and of a proper sense of proportion. The letters of the Countess of Pomfret, written in 1741, show that at that date a lady of fashion, though not insensible to natural beauty, did not feel it incumbent on herself to be overwhelmed with mountain scenery,[23] but Dr. Dalton's famous poetic description of "Keswick's Vale," and "Estimate" Brown's equally celebrated prose effort on the same subject, both of which circulated in manuscript during the last few years of the next decade, are harbingers of the passion for sublime scenery that was soon to come to life in England.[24]

Enough has been said of Ossian and Blair to show what effect Mac-Pherson had on theory; it is perhaps not a mistake to attribute to him some causal relationship with the sudden burst of sublimities that is apparent in the sixth decade of the century. The way had been prepared, as we have seen, and doubtless the age of feeling would have discovered, of its own accord, that mountains and storms and heaths are possessed of powerful emotive qualities, but Ossian came to facilitate an otherwise normally slow process.

The new taste finds expression first among a group of learned ladies, who seem to have lived a considerable part of their erudite lives wrought up to the high pitch of the sublime. One does not wonder at the constant headaches of Mrs. Elizabeth Carter when it is found that to the arduous task of becoming "the learned translator of Epictetus," she added "a passion for the sublime" that kept her ever on the alert for storms, the Kentish substitute for mountains. And we cease to wonder at the strength of body and mind that enabled the Swan of Lichfield to maintain her, one would think, bankrupting correspondence throughout a very long life, when one sees the extent of her "taste for the terrific," which impelled her to seek out ocean storms on nights when people of less fine sensibilities were content to remain at home.

[22] See *The Works of Thomas Gray*, ed. Edmund Gosse (London, 1884), I, 244; 251; 254; 256; 261; 276, 277; II, 36; III, 223.

[23] See particularly her verse epistle to the Countess of Hartford, in which she describes her enjoyment of the Apennines. Most of the pleasure seems to depend upon her sense of security. Her account of the Tyrol shows a plentiful lack of enthusiasm, although no decided indifference or aversion. *Correspondence between Francis, Countess of Hartford and Henrietta Louisa, Countess of Pomfret* (London, 1805), III, 158; 252; 254, 255; 264.

[24] John Dalton, "A Descriptive Poem Addressed to Two Ladies," etc., Pearch's *A Collection of Poems*, etc. (London, 1770), I, 36–41. Brown's letter is printed as a note, I, 36–39. These descriptions were also printed in West's *Guide to the Lakes* (London, 1778).

Looking back to her childhood, Miss Seward is able to account for her susceptibility to the charms of nature.

The first scenic objects that met my infant glance, and impressed me with their lovely and romantic grandeur, were the mountains, the rocks, and the vales of Derbyshire. Nursed in their bosom till I was nine years old, and often passing the summer months there through my youth . . . , poetic descriptions and pencilled resemblances please me best when they take the Salvatorial style. This early-acquired predilection steeps my eyes in the dews of pensive transport, when they stray over the pages of Ossian.[25]

And since she was fond of pensive transports and equally addicted to the pages of Ossian, one can imagine that she frequently indulged her "not unpleasing melancholy" (the phrase is Mrs. Radcliffe's). Ossian often appears in her letters, and always as a sublime poet. The elements in his poetry that afforded her "a poignant thrill of pensive transport" were the "lonely scenery of a barren and mountainous country," the stormy seas, the rocks, and "the majestic and melancholy graces" of the warriors and their mistresses, not to mention the machinery, which "at once awes and delights."[26] No better example could be found of the ability of the Ossianic poems at once to feed and to stimulate a taste for natural and supernatural sublimities.

In literature Ossian is not her only instance of the sublime, a quality that she sought in books as zealously as she did in nature. Indeed, so often does she use the word, that it comes to be no more than a term of approbation. One cannot take very seriously her opinion that Coleridge's *Ode to the Departing Year* is sublime, when one finds that her own poems and those of William Hayley ("Dear Bard"), Bürger's *Leonora*, *The Mysteries of Udolpho*, *Caleb Williams*, and the Bible, to name no others, are also examples of the same literary quality.[27] If one can wring any meaning from her use of the word, it would seem always to refer to content and not to method of expression or intensity of feeling—the introduction of any ghost or any mountain scene or any stormy sea suggesting Ossian, who suggests Salvator, who is the sublime made flesh.

If one knew no more of Miss Seward than what these letters on books and nature reveal, and if one were less painfully aware of her precious

---

[25] Anna Seward, *Letters Written between the Years 1784–1807* (Edinburgh, 1811), III, 131, 132. See also, *Poetical Works*, ed. Walter Scott (Edinburgh, 1810), I, cliii.

[26] *Ibid.*, III, 129. For other references to Ossian's sublimities, see *Ibid.*, I, 263; III, 129 and 265; and the apologetic foot-note to her versification of the episode of Crugal's ghost; *Poetical Works*, III, 15, 16.

[27] *Letters*, V, 189 and 211; IV, 213 and 287 and 314; III, 390; IV, 211; II, 352, 353; I, 355. These statements are made on the assumption that when Miss Seward speaks of "the terrible graces" she is referring to the sublime, an assumption that is amply borne out by the most casual reading of her letters.

style, she might seem a very bold, not to say savage spirit, so much does she revel in the more overwhelming aspects of the natural world. With what evident joy does she piece together a poem from the descriptions of Switzerland furnished her by her friend Whalley.[28] She visits the romantic and renowned Ladies of Llangollen, and besides composing a poem on the subject, she writes her friends ecstatically of the Salvatorial graces of their mountain retreat.[29] This is her everyday mood; but the following incident shows her at her best in epicurean pursuit of sensation.

The scene is Scarborough; the date, July 29, 1793. The Swan had spent the preceding week invoking "the sublimity of the sea,"[30] and an east wind had come at last to gratify her "taste for the terrific." "Last night, at eight o'clock, as we walked upon the cliff, we saw the waves of a sublimely agitated sea dashing and bounding up the sides of the fort, their spray flying over the parapets." She proposes to her friends a walk on the beach, but because of their less heroic natures, she is reduced to going alone,

resolved to taste, amidst the incumbent gloom of a very lowering night, a scene congenial to my taste for the terrible graces. Requesting the stout arm of Mr. Dewes's servant, I began with him my sombre expedition. As I passed along the sands, the tide twice left its white surf upon my feet; and the vast curve of those fierce waves, that burst down with deafening roar, scarce three yards from me, sufficiently gratified my rage for the terrific.[31]

Miss Seward's letters almost convince one that the heroines of Mrs. Radcliffe's novels, who also possess a "taste for the terrific," may not be mere unreal creatures of a sentimental imagination. Equip her with beauty, a lute, and a lover, and Anna Seward could act a part in *The Mysteries of Udolpho* as feelingly and as delicately as did Emily St. Aubert. But the power of "the petrifying wand" of the terrible graces was on one occasion more than even Miss Seward's rage could endure. She confesses rather ingenuously to a sleepless night, the result of a storm. Her maid came to her at once, knowing her terror, but despite this comfort, she was unwell next day. "Hope you do not suffer, like myself, both in body and spirit, from an inflamed and pealing horizon," she adds sorrowfully and euphemistically.[32]

The correspondence of Mrs. Elizabeth Carter, less stylized, though no less voluminous, than Miss Seward's, makes us acquainted with another fine soul, equally Ossianic and equally avid of sublimity. Mrs. Hester Chapone speaks of her relish for "horrible beauty," which was apparently obvious at the early date, April 28, 1759, and she later writes

[28] "Alpine Scenery," *Poetical Works*, II, 352–373.   [29] *Letters*, IV, 97 and 98–107.
[30] *Ibid.*, III, 277.   [31] *Ibid.*, III, 289, 290.   [32] *Ibid.*, IV, 116.

Mrs. Carter from Scotland, whither she had gone with Mrs. Montagu, of the sublime beauties of the landscape there. ". . . I am wild that you and all my romantic friends should see it; for even a Milton's pen, or a Salvator Rosa's pencil, would fail to give you a complete idea of it."[33] The reference to Milton (it might just as well have been to Shakespeare or to Ossian) and to Salvator comes with depressing conventionality.

Mrs. Carter is a rather more interesting person than Miss Seward, despite the pathological tone of her correspondence. An incurable romantic, she expresses the orthodox Longinian view that Homer's deities never "arrive at the sublime," and she holds the opinion that the "Celtic superstitions and Druidical ceremonies" (Ossian) have "contributed much to the sublime of modern poetry."[34] In a letter thanking Mrs. Montagu for a copy of Hurd's *Letters on Chivalry and Romance*, she refers to herself as a "Goth," and laments the dominance of Homer and the Romans, who cannot rival "the productions of the Gothic Muse" in sublimity, an opinion with which the Queen of the Blues certainly agreed. From Lambeth Palace she writes to the same friend, "I always consider the sublime as the characteristic of Gothic architecture. . . ."[35] To Mrs. Vesey, who was evidently equally romantic and gothic, she describes the pleasure which she derived from passing a stormy night in the ancient part of Lambeth Palace. The letter creates perfectly the atmosphere of the gothic novel, with its talk of Gothic arches, pale lamps, whistling winds, and "the hollow sound of the closing doors"—all suitable stage settings for the sublime of the storm.[36] Although she agrees that reason and humanity would rejoice at the spread of civilization and culture in Scotland, she nevertheless admits that for the satisfaction of the imagination, "the lone majesty of untamed nature is better."[37]

These opinions have long been labelled and classified as "romantic;" certainly they would have been incomprehensible to a lady of the court of Charles II—Mistress Anne Killegrew, for example. They were generally accepted by the group of Blue Stockings with whom we are dealing, and they explain adequately enough why natural sublimity became the passion of this coterie. A love of Ossian, of ghosts, of Gothic architecture, and of blasted heaths and stormy seas are all symptoms of the same state of mind, and usually at this period they appear together. It may be well to ask why it is among women that these tendencies are

---

[33] Hester Chapone, *Posthumous Works*, etc. (London, 1807), I, 107 and 155.

[34] *Letters to Mrs. Montagu*, II, 271. See also, III, 18.

[35] *Ibid.*, II, 311, 312, and I, 302.

[36] *A Series of Letters between Mrs. Elizabeth Carter and Miss Catherine Talbot, from the Year 1741 to 1770*, etc., ed. Rev. Montagu Pennington (London, 1808), II, 101.

[37] *Letters to Mrs. Montagu*, I, 316.

at first most clearly marked. Mrs. Carter, Mrs. Montagu, Mrs. Vesey, Mrs. Chapone, Miss Seward, Mrs. Radcliffe—all profess themselves possessors of the same taste. The reason is perhaps almost wholly one of education. The hold of the classics on English taste was not natural; it was the product of early training in school and university. Normally women did not get the thorough grounding in the classics that the educational system provided for men. They were therefore, by virtue of their sex, somewhat outside the tradition, and if they had intellectual tastes, they might be able to criticize more independently than could men, whose minds were filled with and whose tastes were formed on a prejudged partiality to the classics.

Moreover, these women, with the exception of Mrs. Carter, could not have known much Greek, if any at all. They therefore could read Homer only in Pope's un-Homeric version, and thereby would miss much of his finest poetry. Ossian, on the other hand, they could read, and his typically eighteenth-century sensationalism and sentimentality would naturally appeal to them. Thus would grow up a taste for Ossianism as contrasted to the pure classicism of the ancients, and out of Ossian much that is "romantic" could be taken. The gothicism of these ladies, then, is not surprising. Nor is it unworthy of notice that Mrs. Montagu, by far the best educated of the group,[38] was also the least ardently gothic, notwithstanding her essay on the "praeternatural beings" of Shakespearean tragedy.

But to return to Mrs. Carter. As befits the translator of Epictetus, she is philosophical in regard to the sublime, as Mrs. Radcliffe or Miss Seward never are. The gentle Kentish landscape offered her the sea, and "Shakespeare's cliff," and storms. These Mrs. Carter thoroughly enjoyed and occasionally moralized about, and on one occasion she analysed her emotions in the face of a truly sublime scene into an experience remarkably similar to Kant's conception of sublimity.

The first impression it gave me was a sense of my own littleness, and I seemed shrinking to nothingness in the midst of the stupendous objects by which I was surrounded. But I soon grew more important by the recollection that nothing which my eyes could survey, was of equal dignity with the human mind, at once the theatre and spectator of the wonders of Omnipotence.[39]

Translate this into the terms of the German transcendental philosophy, and you have the outline at least of Kant's ideas.

It was not often that Mrs. Carter reflected thus. Normally, like her fellow Blues, she merely enjoyed, and like them, when she gave herself

---

[38] She spent most of her girlhood in the home of Dr. Conyers Middleton at Cambridge.

[39] *Letters to Mrs. Montagu*, I, 167–169. Cf. *A Series of Letters*, II, 107.

over to emotion, she was usually amusing. Once, when she was being
"entertained" by a noble storm, not "without some mixture of terror,"
she was forced to give only half her attention to the spectacle, because
of her mother's fears, which the dutiful daughter sought to soothe by
reading aloud "some of the noblest passages of Dr. Young."[40] It is an
expressive scene—the mother, good Augustan, finding nothing of the
beautiful in terror and disorder; the daughter, sharing the new taste,
extracting what pleasure the old lady's fears will permit her, and yet
both united in their attention to the pompous platitudes of the *Night
Thoughts on Death*, rolling out their "vanity of vanities" amidst the
uproar of the tempest. Even an earthquake could not totally overpower
Mrs. Carter's love of the terrific; she managed to find it sublime and by
that token to enjoy it, considering it as "the voice and hand of Omnipotence."[41] Mrs. Carter at her best is perhaps revealed in the following rather delicious extract.

We returned home beneath a sky the most awfully sublime that can be imagined.
The deep gloom of the clouds was rendered the more dismal by a mixture of sul-
len light. The rapid whirlwind, the rolling thunder, the rattling hail, and all the
dreadful enginery of heaven, seemed collecting its forces, to burst in some tremendous explosion over our heads. Miss Sharpe for all her passion for the sublime, which is very strong, was so overpowered by the terrifying scenery, that she
could not bear to look at it. I could not resist such a spectacle. . . .[42]

By what name shall we call Mrs. Carter's enthusiasm for sublimity if,
in comparison to it, Miss Sharpe's strong passion was so puny?

The last of our enthusiastic ladies is Ann Radcliffe, who carried over
into fiction the love of terror, in her characters, the incidents of her plots,
and the scenery which she so delighted to create. In only one other
novel—if novel it may be called—had landscape been used extensively.
Thomas Amory's *Life of John Buncle, Esq.*, 1756, is full of descriptions
of Westmoreland, whose scenery, he says, contains "an amazing mixture
of the terrible and the beautiful."[43]

It remained for Mrs. Radcliffe to establish herself as the landscape
novelist of all time and to create that wonderful fairyland which she
called Southern France, with its beauties and its sublimities that evoked
from the Tilneys a smile at the expense of Catherine Morland. Like the
Blue Stockings, Mrs. Radcliffe is intent on revealing the emotional effect
of the scenes which she described. Seldom, if ever, does she fail to relate
the scene to the individual who beholds it, telling exactly what passions

[40] *A Series of Letters*, I, 520.   [41] *Ibid.*, II, 308.   [42] *Ibid.*, II, 344, 345.
[43] [Thomas Amory], *Life of John Buncle, Esq.* (London, 1756), I, 100, 101; 164; 165; 287;
II, 54.

it stirs in his sensitive heart. But unlike her learned predecessors, she is also picturesque, and her landscapes show a conscious effort on her part to compose and group her objects and to flood them with light or darken them with shadows after the manner of Claude or Salvator. Thus, the two streams of tendency, the purely emotional response to the grand and the terrific, and the picturesque appreciation of nature, flow together in these truly remarkable books.

Mrs. Radcliffe, one is sure, was working on a definite theory of sublimity, was never far removed from that lofty state of the soul about which her century had said so much and had thought so constantly. If her scenes often aim at the sublime, no less do her novels as a whole. She had read Burke[44] and in common with her age she was convinced that intense terror can produce sublime emotion. Her contemporaries seem aware of the relation between her novels and the sublime. We have seen that Anna Seward considered *Udolpho* worthy of this adjective; but there is better evidence than that of the rather catholic-minded Swan.

Richard Payne Knight, conducting an offensive against Burke's *Enquiry*, speaks with hearty disapproval of the debasing influence that "this seducing author" has had on British taste. In England this influence has been "in great measure, confined to harlequin farces, pantomime plays, romances in prose; for, except for Fingal and Temora, I know of no entire poem written upon the principle of the *sublime and beautiful*."[45] Knight is beyond question referring to the so-called gothic novel and gothic drama of his own and the preceding decade, and he is beyond question correct in attributing some influence to Burke, who is certainly responsible for much of the popularity of terror during the last half of the century. No idea that became attached to the sublime failed to become popular. Terror enjoyed almost half a century of prominence, thanks to Burke, and out of the conviction that terror is sublime, came some, though not all, of the impulse that brought into existence the tale of terror.

It would be a mistake to assume that Mrs. Radcliffe ever claimed to be sublime, but she did not lack admirers to make that claim for her. The author of the "Life and Writings of Mrs. Radcliffe," prefixed to the posthumously published *Gaston de Blondeville*, discussing the use of terror as the mainspring of the action of a novel, justifies Mrs. Radcliffe's constant use of apparently supernatural events by urging that fear based on "things unseen" is not degrading; on the contrary, it "tends to elevate and ennoble our feelings" and to "become sublime

---

[44] Ann Radcliffe, *A Journey Made in the Summer of 1794*, etc. (London, 1795), p. 421.
[45] *Analytical Inquiry*, p. 393.

when inspired by a sense of the visionary and immortal."[46] Walter
Scott, who surely understood such matters, declares:

In working upon the sensations of natural and supernatural fear, Mrs. Radcliffe has made much more use of obscurity and suspense, the most fertile source,
perhaps, of sublime emotion . . .[47]

If the romances of Mrs. Radcliffe are in general expressions of Burkean
sublimity, they are certainly so in detail, particularly in their scenery.
The heroines of these amazing stories have a passion for sublimity
equalled only by Miss Seward's and Mrs. Carter's. On the sixteenth
page of the first volume of *Udolpho*, we are told that Emily loved the
wild wood walks, "and still more the mountain's stupendous recesses,
where the silence and grandeur of solitude impressed a sacred awe upon
her heart, and lifted her thoughts to the GOD OF HEAVEN AND EARTH."
For a volume and a half she is put through her paces as a lover of scenery, a device that enables Mrs. Radcliffe to display her virtuosity as a
literary Claude or Salvator. No heroines were ever such puppets as are
Mrs. Radcliffe's; they exist to be harrowed by the incidents of melodramatic plots and to stand as the author's proxy in the midst of romantic scenes, showing a sensibility that is equalled only by their
strength of mind. Supernatural terror alone can overcome their rage
for the terrific in nature.

Emily is sent to Italy for two reasons—to be the victim of the re-
incarnation of the Elizabethan Italianate villain, of whom Mrs. Radcliffe was so fond, and to indulge the author's enthusiasm for the Alps
and the Apennines, which she was destined to know only in the books
of travel that must have formed a large part of her reading. Nothing
more could be said of Mrs. Radcliffe's conception of the power of sublime
scenery over the human heart than to point out that in the Alps "Emily's
mind was even so much engaged with new and wonderful images, that
they sometimes banished the idea of Valancourt."[48] Or again, the unfortunate and fair Ellena, abducted at Schedoni's orders, is carried off,
into the mountains. It is necessary to cross a bridge, suspended over a
frightful chasm through which dashes a mountain torrent. Ellena
ascends the steep, "not with indifference, but with calmness; she experienced somewhat of a dreadful pleasure in looking down upon the
irresistible flood." And finally, when she crosses the bridge, so great is
her emotional response to the scene, that she almost forgets her mis-

[46] Ann Radcliffe, *Gaston de Blondeville*, etc., *To Which is Prefixed a Memoir of the Author,
with Extracts from her Journals* (London, 1826), I, 107.

[47] Ann Radcliffe, *Novels*. Ballantyne's Novelist's Library, x (London, 1824), xxiii.

[48] Ann Radcliffe, *The Mysteries of Udolpho, A Romance* (London, 1794), II, 7.

fortunes.[49] Rescued finally by Vivaldi, Ellena flees from her pursuers. But what are life and safety when compared with the necessity of enjoying the beauties of nature? The fugitives pause:

"This cool and balmy air revives me," said Ellena; "and what a soothing shade prevails over the scene! How softened, yet how distinct, is every near object; how sweetly delicious the more removed ones; while the mountains beyond character themselves sublimely upon the still glowing horizon."[50]

Apparently the service of Claude was no mere lip-service; his disciples must risk life and happiness if chance presents them with a scene such as he might have painted.

The Emily-Ellenas of Mrs. Radcliffe's novels are never too harrowed to compose a sonnet on evening or some other romantic subject, or to indulge, as did Ellena while she waited outside the convent that was to be her prison, "that luxurious and solemn kind of melancholy, which a view of stupendous objects inspires."[51] The relationship between the Radcliffean heroine and nature consists of a sort of emotional coquetry, the reward, so far as the sublime is concerned, being that the unfortunate young lady enjoys an enlarging of her mind, a feeling of awe and astonishment, and occasionally receives such cold consolation as this:

Here, gazing upon the stupendous imagery around her, looking, as it were, beyond the awful veil which obscures the features of Deity, and conceals Him from the eyes of His creatures, dwelling as with a present God in the midst of His sublime works; with a mind thus elevated, how insignificant would appear to her the transactions, and the sufferings of this world! How poor the boasted power of man, when the fall of a single cliff from those mountains would with ease destroy thousands of his race assembled on the plains below![52]

Space does not permit quotations from Mrs. Radcliffe's descriptions. Mountains, glaciers, streams, space, storms, crags, and precipices appear with Salvatorial regularity, often well enough composed, always bristling with emotional significance, and in general, as Coleridge did not hesitate to say,[53] fatiguing because of the prodigal liberality with which they are introduced, to the no small detriment of the plot.

Nothing more remained to be said of nature considered as a storehouse of emotion, but mention might be made of the Honourable Mrs. Murray, whose hobby-horse, as she put it, was "the simple love of

[49] Ann Radcliffe, *The Italian* (London, 1797), I, 156, 157.
[50] *Ibid.*, II, 93.   [51] *Ibid.*, I, 160, 161.
[52] *Ibid.*, I, 230, 231. Nathan Drake's praise of Mrs. Radcliffe as "the Shakespeare of Romantic Writers," and his opinion that in tales of terror one finds sublime emotion has already been recorded. It is well to recall them at this point.
[53] See the review of *Udolpho* in the *Critical Review*, XI, Second Series (1794), 361–372. This review is ascribed to Coleridge by Garland Greever, in *A Wiltshire Parson and His Friends*, London, 1926.

nature,"[54] and who equipped herself with a special chaise, very much resembling a modern caravan, and went off to the Highlands for an emotional orgy. She knew little of the picturesque, and not much of the theory of the sublime, but that she thoroughly enjoyed herself no one can doubt who reads her amusingly naïve volumes. Who can resist the charm, or fail to see the symbolical significance, in the picture that she gives of herself, lying flat in the mud at the foot of the Falls of Fyres, "to admire, and I might say, almost to adore?" It is the *reductio ad absurdum* of the cult of nature in the eighteenth century.

The picturesque tourist offers us another view of the matter. We have seen that the early travelers recounted their emotional experiences in the presence of mountain scenery, and that sublimities were enjoyed with increasing frequency as the century progressed, but it should be remembered that it was always possible for a traveler to ignore nature altogether, as in the case, say, of Sacheverell Stevens, who, in 1756, though finding Switzerland "charmingly romantic," could achieve the almost unique exploit of not finding Vesuvius sublime. Even the *Letters from Snowden*, written on the eve of the picturesque era, neglect mountain scenery for the sake of sentimentalizing about the joy of the pastoral life. The relative indifference of Johnson to the scenery of Scotland and of Mrs. Piozzi to the beauties of Italy is a welcome witness to the incorruptibility of the human heart.[55]

The time soon came, however, when journeys were undertaken for the purpose of discovering picturesque scenes, and when this happened, the purely emotional effect of the sublime began to be neglected, although it was not soon completely lost sight of. Pictures were always regarded, of course, as depositaries of latent emotion, but the picturesque traveler was not so intent on *feeling* as does a savage, as he was on *seeing* as does a cultivated man.

Arthur Young, while primarily intent on recording the state of agriculture, nevertheless acted as herald to the new age, for he was seldom too absorbed in the state of a man's field to fail to notice the view that could be "taken" from it. The picturesque traveler set out with a preconceived idea of what he would like to find. Landscape was divided into two parts—the Claudian and the Salvatorial (occasionally "learned

[54] The Hon. Mrs. Murray, *A Companion and Useful Guide to the Beauties of Scotland*, etc. (London, 1799), I, 244, 245. These falls impressed Johnson by their "gloom and grandeur." See *Journey to the Western Islands*, p. 69.

[55] Sacheverell Stevens, *Miscellaneous Remarks Made on the Spot in a late Seven Years Tour*, etc. (London, 1756), p. 367. The *Letters from Snowden* were published anonymously in London in 1770. Mrs. Piozzi's *Observations and Reflections Made in the Course of a Journey*, etc., appeared in London in 1789.

Poussin" made a third in the party), the beautiful and the sublime. The object of the tour was to find and enjoy such scenes as these artists might have delighted to paint, to classify and name them, and then, perhaps, to write a book about them. William Combe and Rowlandson have brilliantly caricatured the whole tribe of picturesque tourists in the first tour of the worthy Doctor Syntax, 1809–1811.

Since the theorizers, themselves, were never agreed as to the exact meaning of the terms *beauty* and *sublimity*, it is no wonder that the travelers attained no very clear notion of the categories in which they dealt, but contented themselves with generalities, labelling all savage, huge, and barren scenery sublime. Such is certainly Young's method. His books are plentifully salted with footnotes describing collections of pictures in the houses of noblemen and sublime and beautiful scenes that he had chanced to discover. He does not often compose his scenes successfully, but he shows clearly his allegiance to the Burkean sublime. Persfield, for instance, on the "river Why," possesses "a point of the rocks which . . . is pendent over the river, and may be called a situation full of the terrible sublime." But, looking at the scene *through* the technicalities of painting, Young finds cause for complaint.

There is a want of contrasts; for the general emotions which arise on viewing the rocks, hanging woods, and deep precipices at *Persfield*, are all those of the sublime; and when that is the case, the beautiful never appears in such bewitching colours, as those it receives from contrast . . .[56]

The complaint is lodged because the owner of the estate has failed to make nature conform to standards that never were and never will be nature's. This tone is dominant in the descriptive writings of the rest of the century. Scenes are labelled with damnable iteration, and nature is blamed for not conforming to the tastes of Claude and Salvator. It all seems rather queer.

A scene of rocks, hanging trees, a swift river, all together tending "to impress upon the mind an idea of awe and terror," wins Young's approval because the "wild imagination of *Salvator* has scarce pictured anything more striking . . .;" and the vastness and implied energy in the mountains and broken contours of the terrible and horrible scenery of Derwentwater call forth at once the adjective *sublime*.[57]

During the decade 1770–1780, William Gilpin was taking his famous tours and writing the books that were to be the basis of a new æsthetic idea. In the meantime, picturesque travel was growing in public favor.

[56] [Arthur Young], *A Six Weeks Tour, through the Southern Counties of England and Wales*, etc. By the Author of the Farmer's Letters (London, 1768), pp. 132 and 143.
[57] Arthur Young, *A Six Months Tour Through the North of England*, etc., Second Edition (London, 1770), III, 33 and 113–133.

In 1775 was published Wyndham's *A Gentleman's Tour through Monmouthshire and Wales*, with its insistence on the sublimity of the landscape in those parts, as "tremendous" and as "bold" as any idea that ever fired the "romantic imagination" of Salvator Rosa. In the next year Richard Cumberland published his "Ode to the Sun," with its enthusiastic account of the Lakes,[58] and Thomas West's *Guide to the Lakes* enables us to date the rise to favor of that celebrated section of England. West reflects the picturesque taste by saying that the scenes vary

from the delicate touches of *Claude*, verified on *Conniston* lake, to the noble scenes of *Poussin*, exhibited on *Windermere-water*, and from these, to the stupendous romantic ideas of *Salvator Rosa*, realized on the lake at *Derwent*.[59]

Enthusiasts were setting off to the mountains; Gilpin stepped forward to instruct them in what they were to see.

All of Gilpin's tours bear the accurately descriptive subtitle, "Relative chiefly to Picturesque Beauty." He traveled over the three kingdoms, taking sketches of scenes which naturally lent themselves to the manner of Claude and Salvator. His books, appearing periodically after 1782, are thorough expositions of his ideas on the picturesque. In his opinion the picturesque is simply some quality in an object that is capable of being illustrated by painting, and beauty is that quality in an object that enables it to please in its natural state.[60] The very quality, then, that Gilpin sought in nature, was not nature, but an accidental element of art, a sufficient reason for Wordsworth's condemnation of the whole jargon of the picturesque.

It will be observed that in its original usage, the term *picturesque* does not exclude the sublime. Price was to borrow the word to describe the æsthetic category which he set up to mediate between the Burkean sublime and beautiful, but Gilpin knows nothing of these refinements. He is content to distinguish picturesque sublimity and picturesque beauty, which appeal chiefly to the eye, from mere sublimity and mere beauty, which appeal chiefly to the imagination; and always the technicalities of painting control his vision. Thus, of a scene at the seat of the Duke of Athol, he says: "This whole scene and it's accompaniments, are not only grand; but picturesquely beautiful in the highest degree. The *composition* is perfect. . . ."[61] His books abound in sublimities, but

[58] Richard Cumberland, *Odes* (London, 1776), pp. 3–7.

[59] [Thomas West], *A Guide to the Lakes*, The Second Edition (London, 1780), p. 10. Later the mountains on Conniston are said to be "great, noble, and sublime, without anything that is horrid or terrible"; those on Windermere are "sublime and vast"; Borrowdale is "sublimely terrible" (pp. 53, 64, and 95).   [60] See above, p. 157.

[61] William Gilpin, *Observations Relative Chiefly to Picturesque Beauty, Made in the Year 1776, On Several Parts of Great Britain, Particularly the High-lands of Scotland* (London, 1789), I, 122.

with a difference. They are always seen with the composing eye of a painter, and the naïve emotionalism of a Seward or a Radcliffe finds no place in his comments. This change is important in the history of the sublime, for it foretells the death of the older and cruder views, represented in theory by a Burke or a Blair, in practice by the Blue Stockings. One illustration of this process will suffice.

At Ferney we had a grand scene of mountain-perspective. It is not often that these elevated bodies coincide with the rules of beauty, and composition—less often indeed than any other mode of landscape. In a level country the awkwardness of a line is hid. But the mountain rearing it's opakeness against the sky, shows every fault both in it's delineation, and combination with great exactness. These mountains however had fewer faults to show. They were both well-formed, and well-connected; and showed also in great perfection the beauties of gradation—gradation in form—gradation in light—and gradation in colour.[62]

Here is no talk of horror and terror, whether pleasing or displeasing; Gilpin refuses to be impressed by mere size or by imagined dangers, or to look on mountains as a terrifying symbol of the might of the Creator. On the contrary he seems to be approaching an æsthetic of form. In another place he admits that a scene is sublime, but he is simply not interested in it, because it is too formless to suggest a picture.[63] It is in this new emphasis that Gilpin's innovation consists. While never denying the existence of a sublimity other than picturesque sublimity, he simply ignored it, and concentrated his attention on line and form and perspective. If this marks an advance in sophistication on his part and on that of his followers (and they were legion as one can infer from the existence of Dr. Syntax), it also represents a temporary loss of interest in the immediate emotional relationship between man and nature, a relationship that the boy Wordsworth, in the fastnesses of Cumberland, was at this moment being prepared to strengthen anew, in a literature of nature that was to be free from mere sensationalism as well as from the affectation of the picturesque.

There is a long passage in the volumes on the Lake Country that shows Gilpin's willingness to admit the existence of the older sort of sublimity, and even his awareness of the influence of natural objects on the imagination. It contains the conventional reference to the "wild sallies of untutored genius," and it expresses doubts as to whether, however much art might render such a scene pleasing to the *eye*, it could ever please the *imagination* as it does in its wild chaos.[64] It pleased him

---

[62] *High-lands of Scotland*, I, 51, 52.

[63] *Ibid.*, I, 172. Cf. also the view of the Forth from Sterling Castle. "It is not indeed picturesque; but it is exceedingly grand and amusing." *Ibid.*, I, 83.

[64] William Gilpin, *Observations Relative Chiefly to Picturesque Beauty Made in the Year*

to throw the weight of his influence on the side of the eye and to leave to a greater man the vindication of the imagination.

Gilpin's clearest description of this ocular sublimity is introduced anent Dr. Johnson's strictures on the repellent aspect of the "hopeless sterility" of Scotland. The Lexicographer, it is explained, was incapable of finding attraction in the great and sublime in nature, because he had accustomed himself to see beauties only in "*flowery pastures*, and *waving harvests*." Now the very "poverty in objects, or simplicity" which injures the beauty of the Scotch landscape, is the source of sublimity.

Simplicity, and *variety* are the acknowledged foundations of all picturesque effect. Either of them will produce it: but it generally takes it's tone from one. When the landscape approaches nearer *simplicity*, it approaches nearer the *sublime;* and when variety prevails, it tends more to the *beautiful*. A vast range of mountains, the lines of which are *simple;* and the surfaces broad, grand, and extensive, is rather *sublime* than *beautiful*.[65]

Here is that total ignoring of the emotive quality of landscape that is characteristic of the picturesque school. It is true that pure form and mass and line have been considered in recent years as possessing emotional significance. But Gilpin has no such theory to express; his sublime is for the eye alone, and even when he borrows Burke's ideas as to the value of obscurity in creating the sublime, it is not, in Fawcett's words, because

> Screen'd by the wainscoat, e'en a scratching mouse
> May spread alarm throughout a coward house . . .[66]

but because obscurity increases the apparent size and the simplicity of objects.[67] To measure the advance that such a view indicates one has only to recall some of the dicta on the beauty and sublimity of scenery that were uttered by theorists in the first half of the century. David Hartley is a case in point. Not even his psychological system could help him to extricate his thought from the morass of emotionalism through which æsthetic had to pass for so many years. Indeed, it was because of the associationistic tendency of his thought that he could not abstract the æsthetic experience. In considering the pleasures and pains derived from the external world he declared:

1772, On Several Parts of England, Particularly the Mountains and Lakes of Cumberland and Westmoreland (London, 1786), I, 121, 122.

[65] *High-lands of Scotland*, I, 120 and 122. Cf. *Ibid.*, I, 171.

[66] Joseph Fawcett, "The Art of Poetry," *Poems*, p. 27.

[67] *The Mountains and Lakes of Cumberland and Westmoreland*, II, 18. It should be stated, however, that Gilpin is too good a student of Salvator and too much a man of his age not to believe that "greatness, wildness, or ferocity" all touch on the sublime. *Ibid.*, II, 45–47.

If there be a Precipice, a Cataract, a Mountain of Snow, etc. in one Part of the Scene, the nascent Ideas of Fear and Horror magnify and enliven all the other Ideas, and by degrees pass into Pleasures, by suggesting the Security from Pain. In like manner the Grandeur of some Scenes, and the Novelty of others, by exciting Surprize and Wonder, i.e., by making a great Difference in the preceding and subsequent Stages of the Mind, so as to border upon, or even to enter the Limit of Pain, may greatly enhance the Pleasure.[68]

The chief service of the picturesque was that it helped to point the way out of the confused paths of practical emotion to the more abstract consideration of æsthetic problems.

Thus Gilpin created the picturesque, and those tourists who traveled under his protection and with his passport tended naturally to seek what he had sought. The picturesque view, in these cases, tends to supplant the older desire to discover "beauty sleeping in the lap of horror," and to indulge in the emotions consequent to such a sight. The stage was set for the final scene, and by way of interlude, we had best return to Mrs. Radcliffe, who, in 1794, after the publication of *Udolpho*, made her first acquaintance with sublime scenery in her tour of the Rhine and the English Lakes.

The journal of this tour shows Mrs. Radcliffe viewing with great appreciation the sublimity which she had hitherto been compelled to imagine, and taking hints from Burke and, one would hazard, from Gilpin. The Seven Mountains, near Bonn, interest her as sublime objects, "broken, rocky, and abrupt towards their summits" and obscured by mists; "Drakenfells" causes her eye to ache in attempting to scale its height; and at one moment during her trip down the Rhine sublimity is found in terror and at another, in gloom.[69] All of this is pure Burke.

At the Lakes, Mrs. Radcliffe takes the usual tourist route, and now she feels awe, now elation, now horror as the mountain scenery unfolds before her delighted eyes. Ossian comes to her mind at one spot; another scene appears to be a proper stage-setting for the incantations of Shakespeare's weird sisters. But at Derwentwater a strange thing happens. Ullswater had seemed the epitome of the sublime; Derwentwater, in comparison, seemed scarcely interesting. West, it will be remembered, has declared that Ullswater was inferior in sublimity to Derwentwater.[70] What has happened? The answer is that Gilpin had appeared on the scene. The reasons that Mrs. Radcliffe gives for her disappointment are instructive. The lake is too small for its "accompaniments"; it is round, and hence "leaves nothing for expectation to pursue . . . or fancy to transform within the gloom and obscurity of the receding fell; and thus

[68] David Hartley, *Observations on Man* (London, 1749), I, 419.
[69] *Journey*, pp. 119, 146, 294, 310.   [70] *Guide to the Lakes*, p. 154.

it loses an ample source of the sublime." Nor is it large enough to occupy the eye, and it presents a mixture of beauty and sublimity, whereas Ullswater possesses the simplicity necessary to sublimity.[71]

No better instance could be found of the discrimination produced by the cult of the picturesque. Mrs. Radcliffe, testing nature by standards to which nature never conformed, failed to see the really great beauty and magnificence of the scenery at Keswick. It is thus that the picturesque intervened between the individual and the object. The time had come for Wordsworth to free England from

> the rules of mimic art transferred
> To things above all art.

This task he was peculiarly fitted to perform. By nature he was all his life extremely sensitive to impressions from the natural world, and his early childhood, passed among the fastnesses of Cumberland, had left on his remarkable memory the recollection of many moments when nature had spoken to him directly, startling him into a vivid realization of his own consciousness and individuality, and revealing to him the very quality of her moods and the very personality of her scenes. Unthinkingly, he had grown up nourished by natural beauty and dependent, to a degree not to be realized by him for years, on her "healing power," an enthusiastic lover of nature in her gentle as well as in her grand and wild scenes.

He grew up without becoming aware to what an extent his deeply religious nature had found its focal point in the external world. It was only with the help of Coleridge, after his disillusioning experiences in France and London, that he came finally to understand that his life, from the time of his leaving Cambridge until the moment of his retirement to the Lake District, had been merely an aberration from the path that he was destined to follow. His revolutionary period had completely severed him from orthodox and respectable religion. It was only the older Wordsworth, saddened and shaken by life, who could find in the Anglican Church a satisfactory formula for his religious impulses. But his attempt to find satisfaction in Godwinism soon proved impossible, and the London period, during which Wordsworth was at sea, was sufficiently bitter for the young radical. None the less, although neither Godwinism nor Christianity could satisfy him, he did not cease to be a profoundly religious man. And it is no wonder that his religious instincts found in nature an object of worship, and that he began, with the help of Coleridge, to interpret the external world in terms of his own religious experiences.

[71] *Journey*, pp. 449–451.

If one contrasts Wordsworth with any or with all of the enthusiastic admirers of nature in the last decades of the eighteenth century, he will observe that the basic difference between them is that while the Blue Stockings and the picturesque travelers strongly resemble faddists, and were concerned in the one instance with the theatricality of nature and in the other with the resemblance of natural scenes to paintings, Wordsworth was mainly interested in his æsthetic experience of nature as it offered support for his religious intuitions of the reality of the One in the Many. The earlier seekers after sublimities or "scenes" never approached scenery with the high seriousness that characterizes every moment of Wordsworth's communion with nature. His interest was in the thing itself, and in its relation to and effect upon his own mind, and in its value to his religious instincts as a symbol of an abiding Reality. And it was because nature had first awakened him to a consciousness of his own individuality and of the closeness of Reality to a sensitive mind that he could afford not to analyse, but to synthesize and interpret.

From one point of view Wordsworth seems to be the inheritor of the eighteenth-century cult of nature. In his tour of Switzerland with Jones he seems at first glance to be merely another picturesque traveler. The Lake District, in which he grew up, was becoming fashionable during his youth, and his enthusiasm for mountain scenery seems on the surface to be merely an expression of the *Zeitgeist*. But such a view of Wordsworth would be too inadequate to call for serious discussion. If Wordsworth went over the beaten track of the tourist, he went with a different equipment and he came back with different memories. Instead of holding to a theory of how nature should appear, he humbly accepted her as she is; instead of having a head full of Claude and Salvator, he carried with him a sensitive sensuous organization and a synthesizing imagination— i.e., a faculty for perceiving the unseen spiritual reality and for interpreting his perceptions in terms of a religious symbolism. It was because of his religious aspirations that he was able to pierce through the veil of the senses and to read into nature spiritual values that the enthusiasts of the preceding decades never discovered. To him the external world was no series of inorganic scenes, but the ever-present symbol of a spiritual Reality, and the world of nature and man was an organism, pulsating with spiritual life which flowed from the transcendent Being that he sought and found.

It is obvious, then, that, despite superficial resemblances, an enormous gulf separates Wordsworth from the picturesque tourists who wrote before and during his maturity. Coming to his poems through the eighteenth century, one is impressed by the difference between the conventional vocabulary of the writers of travel books and the sincere and direct language of Wordsworth. To the former, at their best, nature offered certain æsthetic pleasures; to Wordsworth the æsthetic pleasures afforded by the natural world had importance chiefly because they offered a foundation for a religious interpretation of nature. In *The Prelude* Wordsworth speaks with impatience of the jargon of the picturesque. To him, such analysis as that in which a Gilpin indulged must have seemed another·example of the use of "that false secondary power by which we multiply distinctions." His nature poetry, in a sense, is as much a critique of pure reason, as was Kant's system of philosophy. To both, the two chief realities were God and the mind of man, and both could turn to account the intuitions and the adventures of the mind as it explored the universe. And so Wordsworth dismissed from his mind the vocabulary of his fellow enthusiasts.

Although he deals with scenes and emotions that were traditionally considered sublime, he gives us no such descriptions as we find in the writings of Anna Seward, Anne Radcliffe, or William Gilpin. Labelling and categorizing were no part of his task. And yet one wonders whether he would have formulated the religious interpretation of nature that he gives in *Tintern Abbey* and *The Prelude* if the fashionable cult of the picturesque had not existed to call vividly to his attention the deeper significance of his own perceptions. It is a truism to remark that the youth Wordsworth did not perceive the philosophical implications of the experiences that the man Wordsworth so carefully and painstakingly set forth. It was on his recollections of early childhood, interpreted in the light of a mature philosophy, that the poet, in 1805, built up his great nature poem. And it was in the light of this philosophy that Wordsworth saw how different his own communion with nature had been from that of a Gilpin or a Radcliffe. It was his reaction against his own indulgence in the fashionable cult (a cult that later seemed to him to be traitorous to nature) that helped to crystallize his more personal apperceptions into a creed. Hence his contempt for that "feebleness" in man that shows itself in

> presumption, even in pleasure pleas'd
> Unworthily, disliking here, and there,
> Liking, by rules of mimic art transferr'd
> To things above all art.

And he gives thanks that he has escaped the picturesque.

> Although a strong infection of the age,
> Was never much my habit, giving way
> To a comparison of scene with scene,
> Bent overmuch on superficial things,
> Pampering myself with meagre novelties
> Of colour and proportion, to the moods

> Of time and season, to the moral power
> The affection, and the spirit of the place,
> Less sensible.[72]

His dislike of the picturesque approach to nature lay chiefly in the fact that it submitted the external world to the power of the eye, the "most despotic of our senses," and the one most the suppressor of the "visionary gleam," which comes only when one is "laid asleep in body," when the imagination is left free to create from the properly subordinated evidence of the senses. The votaries of the picturesque were nearer to the creation of an abstract æsthetic than Wordsworth ever came, and this was because to him the æsthetic of nature was primarily a first step to the state of ecstasy in which he felt a presence that disturbed him with the joy of elevated thoughts.

And yet Wordsworth could not wholly escape the æsthetic ideas of his age. Burke's dualism survived in his mind and became one of the basic ideas in his theory of nature as a positive moral force in his own early education. Nature for him partakes of the Burkean sublime and beautiful, and through the consequent emotions of fear and love she seemed to him to have drawn him to herself and to have built up his moral being. "I grew up," he says, "Foster'd alike by beauty and by fear."[73] The gentler aspects of the Lake District represent the beauty and the love of Burke; the grander aspects are sublime and evoke fear. The lonely, the grand, the dark, and the mysterious in nature spoke to the youth through fear, startling him into a realization of his own consciousness and awakening in him emotions that he never forgot and that seemed to him in later life earnests of the grandeur of the soul.[74] It was by such a "discipline of fear" that nature impressed on him an awareness not only of her own power, but a sense of the soul's infinitude.

> Thence did I drink the visionary power.
> I deem not profitless these fleeting moods
> Of shadowy exultation: not for this,
> That they are kindred to our purer mind
> And intellectual life; but that the soul,
> Remembering how she felt, but what she felt

[72] *The Prelude*, XI, 105–121. I quote from the text of 1805–1806.

[73] *Ibid.*, I, 305, 306.

[74] The episode of the theft of woodcocks (I, 309–332) and of the stolen boat (I, 372–427) are familiar instances. So also in other parts of the poem we hear how "the characters of danger and desire" were impressed upon all forms (I, 490–510); and again,

> How Nature by extrinsic passion first
> Peopled my mind with beauteous forms or grand.
>
> (I, 572, 573.)

> Remembering not, retains an obscure sense
> Of possible sublimity, to which,
> With growing faculties she doth aspire,
> With faculties still growing, feeling still
> That whatsoever point they gain, they still
> Have something to pursue.[75]

That Wordsworth was a sharer of that experience which the eighteenth century had called "sublime" cannot be questioned. It should only be wondered at that he shook himself so free from the language and the fads that constantly tended to burlesque the profound and valid responses of the heart of man to the grandeur of the external world. Moreover, despite the vestigial remains of the Burkean æsthetic in his own mind, Wordsworth escaped completely the materialistic implications of Burke's theory. The opposition between matter and spirit is a theme that runs through the whole of *The Prelude*, as witness the passage in which he declares that he never accepted the world of the senses, "a universe of death," as being ultimately real.

> To fear and love,
> To love as first and chief, for there fear ends,
> Be this ascribed; to early intercourse,
> In presence of sublime and lovely forms,
> With the adverse principles of pain and joy,
> Evil as one is rashly named by those
> Who know not what they say. By love, for here
> Do we begin and end, all grandeur comes,
> All truth and beauty, from pervading love,
> That gone, we are as dust.[76]

This is the Burkean antithesis, but a creative mind has taken the old idea and has transformed it to new uses and given it a new significance.

It is with Wordsworth that the experience that lay behind the eighteenth-century sublime reached its apotheosis. All that had been written in theory or in enthusiasm during our period seems to be a darkening of wisdom with counsel in contrast to Wordsworth's concrete expression of his imaginative interpretation of the enduring spiritual values of the external world. The tentative and groping efforts of the Blue Stockings are incompetent to give full utterance to the effect of grand scenery on their minds. Wordsworth succeeded where they failed, because he recognized that in his imaginative experiences,

> when the light of sense
> Goes out in flashes that have shewn to us
> The invisible world, doth greatness make abode,
> There harbours whether we be young or old.

---

[75] *Ibid.*, II, 330-341.   [76] *Ibid.*, XIII, 143-152.

> Our destiny, our nature, and our home
> Is with infinitude, and only there;
> With hope it is, hope that can never die,
> Effort, and expectation, and desire,
> And something evermore about to be.[77]

It is in the aspirations of the human mind toward the infinite that Wordsworth finds the sublime. The power of sublime scenery to evoke into
consciousness the apperception of the infinite and to become an adequate
symbol of the infinite has nowhere been given finer expression than in
the familiar description of the descent from the Simplon Pass.

> The immeasurable height
> Of woods decaying, never to be decay'd,
> The stationary blasts of water-falls,
> And every where along the hollow rent
> Winds thwarting winds, bewilder'd and forlorn,
> The torrents shooting from the clear blue sky,
> The rocks that mutter'd close upon our ears,
> Black drizzling crags that spake by the way-side
> As if a voice were in them, the sick sight
> And giddy prospects of the raving stream,
> The unfetter'd clouds, and region of the Heavens,
> Tumult and peace, the darkness and the light
> Were all like workings of one mind, the features
> Of the same face, blossoms upon one tree,
> Characters of the great Apocalypse,
> The types and symbols of Eternity,
> Of first and last, and midst, and without end.[78]

Beyond this, the eighteenth-century sublime did not go.

---

[77] *Ibid.*, VI, 534–542.   [78] *Ibid.*, VI, 553–572.

CHAPTER XI

CONCLUSION

IT has not seemed feasible to record all that was written on the subject of sublimity. Names of writers both important and unimportant have been omitted, and every reader will probably think of titles of books or essays which in his opinion should have been discussed. But if such books as Daniel Webb's *Inquiry into the Beauties of Painting*, 1760, and Anthony Raphael Mengs's *Works* (translated in 1796) find no place in this discussion it is merely because in the opinion of the writer their remarks on sublimity have merited nothing more than a mention in the bibliography of a volume already long. So much was said on the sublime, and so often, that many fragments have necessarily been neglected.

In looking back over the century of speculation, one is struck with the diversity of opinions that must always have lain behind the word *sublime* whenever used in criticism. No single definition of the term would serve in any single decade for all writers, for such unanimity was never attained; but the word naturally expressed high admiration, and usually implied a strong emotional effect, which, in the latter years of the century, frequently turned on terror. "I shall read Longinus as long as I live," said Joseph Warton; "it is impossible not to catch fire and rapture from his glorious style. . . ."[1] It was certainly "fire and rapture" that the eighteenth century sought and found in the sublime, and the phrase, vague as it is, will serve to suggest the literary qualities that evoked this word of high praise so often during the century. Æsthetically the term is also vague, though it grew more and more into a catch-all for elements in art that the Cartesian æsthetic had suppressed or had not accounted for. J. W. Bray, in his study, *The History of English Critical Terms*, can give only the most general definition of *sublime*, though he points out the importance to the concept of lofty thought and the frequent recurrence of the idea that pain can give æsthetic pleasure. Perhaps the greatest service that the sublime did for æsthetic speculation was to focus so much attention on the importance in art of the unbeautiful and the normally painful, as well as on ecstasy and "transport."

As a general interpretation of the eighteenth century this study probably has nothing new to offer, but it has sought to show from its own point of view the slow and unconscious growth of English art away from the orderly garden of the Augustan age to the open fields (the jungle, if you will) of the romantic period. The sublime has offered a useful vantage point from which to survey the change that overtook English

[1] Quoted by Bosker in his *Literary Criticism in the Age of Johnson* (The Hague, 1930), p. 188, note 4.

art and theory in the pre-romantic period. The romantic art of the
eighteenth century is often crude and always tentative; the same is true
of its æsthetic. For the purposes of this study the last half of the eighteenth century could be aptly labelled "pre-æsthetic," but for the student
of the period the often awkward attempt to philosophize taste has value
independent of its worth (or lack of it) to the philosopher, for it reveals
even more distinctly than an orderly philosophy could do what its
writers and their contemporaries most valued in the arts.

Throughout the eighteenth century Longinus was esteemed not only
as a critic but as a rhetorician. We have followed his influence on critical
and æsthetic thought to the neglect of the long survival of his dicta in
the manuals of rhetoric that were taught to schoolboys until well into
the nineteenth century. It was in rhetoric that the passions were of chief
importance, and it was by the transfer of the rhetorical values of the
pathetic and the sublime to the sphere of art that Boileau gave impetus,
in the Augustan age, to the consideration of the æsthetic value of emotions. The acceptance of a rhetorician as a literary critic was made easy,
not only by the fact that Longinus was, momentarily, a penetrating
critic, but also by reason of the close alliance that existed between
rhetoric and poetry. One has only to think of heroic tragedy to recall
how rhetorical art could become; of the amazing antitheses of *Eloisa to
Abelard* and of the courtly address to Bolingbroke at the conclusion of
the *Essay on Man* (which, it will be recalled, Warburton considered an
illustration of Longinus's five sources of sublimity) to realize how Pope
could use rhetorical devices to embellish his poetry; and the high value
attached to Raphael's cartoons, by reason of their "expression," bears
witness to the hold that the orator's art held on English taste.

The sublime was divorced from considerations of style by Boileau,
and attention was fixed upon its emotional effect. When Dennis tried
to establish sublime poetry upon enthusiastic emotion, he was not aware
that he was beginning a type of speculation that would eventually grow
into a force hostile to the good taste of his age, for he would have certainly echoed Johnson's opinion: "Enthusiasm has its rules." But the
eighteenth century was not the prophesied period in which the lion and
the lamb would lie down together, and by the mid-century, when the
downfall of the neo-classic system was at hand, the sublime emotions
which the Augustan age had been willing to experience occasionally and
to discuss theoretically were to align themselves, still with the authority
of Longinus, on the side of original genius and rulelessness.

The determination of English poets to revel in emotions showed itself
in the melancholy poets of the graveyard as well as in the theories of
Dennis, Jacob, and others. Between the *Essay on Criticism* and Burke's
Enquiry, the æsthetic experience was broken down into the two cate-

gories of the beautiful and the sublime, and while the first remained true to neo-classic taste, the latter became more and more associated with aspects of the external world which could not be approved by orthodox taste, but which the younger generation was determined to enjoy, and with the strongly pathetic, which still enjoyed a theoretical respectability by virtue of its Longinian origin. The opposition between the sublime and the beautiful is symbolic of the opposition between the art of the enlightenment and that of the mid-century, which was bent upon escaping the formalism and restraint of the neo-classic and which definitely moved in theory and in practice toward the romantic.

Longinus's declaration that the sublime lay beyond the reach of the rules prepared the way for the alignment of the sublime on the side of original genius. It was a mere matter of deduction from this premise (sanctioned by every neo-classical critic) to the conviction that the rules were inimical to great art. And as the case that Pope had made out for the ancients and the rules began to seem insufficient, as *nature* came to signify not the orderly, rational truths read into it by the enlightenment, but the imaginative truth of which Hurd wrote, as the century came to care more for emotion than for intellect, for enthusiastic spontaneity than for urbane regularity, the sublime, with its long-possessed respectability, became an æsthetic and critical concept of major importance.

In the meantime the sublime as an æsthetic concept had grown apace. By Addison, Hume, and Baillie, with the help of Locke, Shaftesbury, Du Bos, and Hutcheson, a psychological investigation was being undertaken to explain the pleasures that art affords, and under the category of the sublime were discussed objects, ideas, and emotions which neo-classicism had recognized but had tended to throw into the background. The growing popularity of the sublime of terror, of mountains, storms, and space, and the association of the loftiest art with the non-traditional work of original genius were bringing sharply to the fore æsthetic pleasures that were more typical of what was to come than of what had been.

This process reached its first synthesis in the *Enquiry* of Burke, who established the æsthetic of terror and pain, found a physical explanation for the æsthetic experience, broke, to some extent, with the canons of Augustan art, and opened the way for the widespread æsthetic discussions of the last four decades of the century. In the 1760's the rising tide of emotionalism and the new taste for the gothic and for natural sublimities for the first time threatened the neo-classic serenity. Hurd's vindication of gothic taste and his enunciation of the doctrine that truth to nature and truth to imagination are synonymous phrases; the sweeping success of the Ossianic poems; the noticeable growth of a fashionable craze for the sublime in nature, go hand in hand with the emergence of Michelangelo as the sublimest of painters. The first change

represents a break with the ancients, the rules, and the neo-classical conception of nature; the second offered to the eye an example of what an
original genius could do in the sublime, especially in the more gloomy
and terrible sublime that Burke had made popular and that the gothic
novel was to exemplify; the third is a prelude to the religion of nature
that contrasts so vividly with the natural religion of the deists, and that
Wordsworth was to treat with so much dignity; the fourth sums up all
the others, showing, in the deposing of Raphael, how completely the
new æsthetic standards had turned from the art of the neo-classicists
to an art that was at the same time intense, individual, and original.

At the same time Kames and Priestley were carrying on the analysis
of the æsthetic experience and were broadening its significance by a
closer adherence to psychology. The old critical and objective method
of discussing art was destined to lose out as such speculation became
general. Once it was seen that the sublime is a state of mind evoked by
objects and ideas, the objective criteria of the rules were gradually in-
validated and the perceptions of individuals, together with their personal emotions and their independent imaginative interpretation of
experience could usurp the place of the older truth to nature. By his
thorough use of association to explain beauty and sublimity (in which
he was followed later by Alison), Priestley foreshadowed the complete
abandonment of the rules, and the romantic emphasis on the subject
rather than the object. Moreover the same decade produced the enthusiastically approving estimate of Ossian that converted Blair into a
momentary enemy of the old order and an apostle of original genius,
terror, sublime scenery, and the sublimity of darkness, ghosts, and
savage energy—all an exaggerated instance of the transforming influence
of Ossian on English taste. In the criticism of Ossian by Blair, the
sublime, which had been a convenient safety-valve for the neo-classic
system, became a weapon which could be turned against the theories of
art that had been dominant when it appeared in 1674.

The difference between pre-romanticism and the romantic is largely
a matter of subtlety, the measure of which can be taken by contrasting
the terrors of the gothic novel and of *Christabel*, or the enthusiasm of
the Blue Stockings for mountain scenery and Wordsworth's treatment
of the same theme. The hectic and sensational literature of which Wordsworth complained in the Preface to *Lyrical Ballads*, 1800, was the expression of the crude emotionalism that the sublime had nourished and
vindicated. In theories of the sublime during the last half of the century
there can be found much of the material, many of the emotions, and
numerous special instances of points of view in æsthetic, all of which
were to be turned to something finer than the eighteenth century could
produce, when the first generation of romantic poets came into its own.

BIBLIOGRAPHY

(Titles marked with an asterisk are not referred to in the preceding pages. Miscellaneous titles, referred to only in passing, are not included.)

* *An Account of a Series of Paintings, in the Great Room of the Society of Arts.* London, 1783.

* *The Artist; A Collection of Essays,* etc., ed. Prince Hoare. London, 1810.

[Review of Burke's *Enquiry*], *Critical Review: or Annals of Literature* (1757) III, 361–374.

[Review of Burke's *Enquiry*], *The London Chronicle, or Universal Evening Post,* (1757), I, 556–558; 580, 581; 595, 596; II, 26, 27; 50–53.

A Catalogue of the Pictures, Sculptures, Models, Drawings, Prints, etc. of the Present Artists. Exhibited in the Great Room of the Society for the Encouragement of Arts, Manufactures, and Commerce. [London, 1760–1769.]

"A Catalogue of the Pictures in the Shakespeare Gallery," *Analytical Review,* IV (1797), 107–112.

"A Catalogue of the School Books Now in General Use," *A Complete Catalogue of Modern Books Published from the Beginning of this Century, to the Present Time.* London, 1766.

A Description of the Series of Pictures Painted by J[ames] B[arry], etc. L. 1792.

"Du Sublime," *Le Pour et Contre* II (1733), 284–288.

The Ear-Wig: or an Old Woman's Remarks on the Present Exhibition of Pictures at the Royal Academy. London, 1781.

An Enquiry Concerning the Principles of Taste, and of the Origin of our Ideas of Beauty. London, 1785.

"Enquiry whether Philosophy is not capable of receiving the Ornaments of Poetry," *Gentleman's Magazine: or, Monthly Intelligencer,* V (1735), 252, 253.

The Exhibition of the Royal Academy. London, MDCCLXIX-MDCCC.

[Review of *Fingal*], *Annual Register, or a View of the History, Politicks, and Literature of the year 1761,* IV, 276–286.

[Review of Hickey's *History of Painting and Sculpture*], *Anal. Rev.* (1792), XIV.

Letters from Snowden, etc. London, 1770.

* [Review of Courtney Melmoth's *The Sublime and Beautiful of Scripture*], *Critical Review: or Annals of Literature,* XLIII (1777), 252.

* "Observations on the Tragedy of Othello," *British Magazine or Monthly Repository for Gentlemen and Ladies,* VIII (1767), 451.

* "Observations upon the Tragedy of Macbeth," *Ibid.,* 514–516.

"On the Pleasures Arising from the Sight of Ruins or Ancient Structures," *European Magazine, and London Review,* XXVIII (1795), 183–184.

[On Rhyme], *Gentleman's Magazine: or, Monthly Intelligencer,* V (1735), 358–360.

"On the Sublime," *Ibid.,* V (1735), 461–463.

[Review of Mrs. Radcliffe's *Mysteries of Udolpho*], *Critical Review, or Annals of Literature,* XI (1794), Second Series. 361–372.

"Response à l'Advertisement qui a été ajoûté à la nouvelle Edition des Œuvres de M. des Preaux," *Bibliothèque Choisie,* XXVI (1733), 64–82.

Rhetoric; of the Principles of Oratory Delineated, etc. London, 1736.

[Abstract and critique of Silvain's *Traité du Sublime*], *Memoires pour l'Histoire des Sciences et des Beaux Arts,* etc. (September, 1733), pp. 1802–1826.

"Critique du Traité du Sublime de M. Silvain," *Le Pour et Contre*, XI (1733), 74–85.

[The Taste of English Audiences for Sensation], *Ibid.*, I (1733), 71, 72.

A Tour from London to the Lakes. . . . Made in the Summer of 1791. By a Gentleman. London, 1792.

Traité de l'Eloquence Dans Tous les Genres, Paris, 1752.

[Addison, Joseph], *Remarks on Several Parts of Italy*. London, 1705.

———, *Works*. London, 1903. Bohn Standard Library.

———, *The Spectator*, ed. H. Morley. London, 1891.

[Aglionby, William], *Painting Illustrated in Three Diallogues, Containing Some Choise Observations upon the Art.* London, 1686.

Aikin, J. and A. L., *Miscellaneous Pieces, in Prose*. London, 1773.

Akenside, Mark, *The Pleasures of Imagination*. London, 1744.

Alison, Archibald, *Essays on the Nature and Principles of Taste*. Edinb., 1790. Anonymous. See above.

[Armstrong, John], *Taste: an Epistle to a Young Critic*. London, 1753.

Augustine, Aurelius, *Works*, ed. Rev. Marcus Dods. Edinburgh, 1871–1876.

Avison, Charles, *An Essay on Musical Expression*, London, 1753.

Bailey, N., *Dictionarium Britannicum*, etc., Second Edition. London, 1736.

Baillie, John, *Essay on the Sublime*. London, 1747.

*Bayly, Anselm, *The Alliance of Musick, Poetry, and Oratory*, etc. L., 1789.

Baldwin, Charles S., *Ancient Rhetoric and Poetic*. New York, 1924.

———, *Medieval Rhetoric and Poetic*. New York, 1928.

Barry, James, *Works*. London, 1809.

Basch, Victor, *Essai Critique sur l'Esthétique de Kant*. Paris, 1927.

Batteux, Charles, *Principes de la Littérature*, Cinquième Edition. Paris, 1774.

Beattie, James, *Dissertations Moral and Critical*. London, 1783.

*———, *Essays*. Edinburgh, 1776.

Bell, Henry, *An Historical Essay on the Original of Painting*, etc., London, 1728.

Bennett, John, *Letters to a Young Lady on a Variety of Useful and Interesting Subjects*. Warrington, 1789.

Berkeley, George, *Works*. London, 1784.

Blackmore, Sir Richard, *Essays upon Several Subjects*. London, 1716.

Blackwell, Anthony, *The Sacred Classics Defended and Illustrated*, etc. L., 1725.

[Blair, Hugh], *A Critical Dissertation on the Poems of Ossian, the Son of Fingal*. London, 1763.

———, *Lectures on Rhetoric and Belles Lettres*. London, 1783.

Blount, Thomas, *The Academie of Eloquence, containing a compleat English Rhetorique*. London, 1653.

[———], *Glossographia: or a Dictionary. Interpreting all Such Hard Words . . . as are now used in our refined English Tongue*, etc. London, 1656.

Boileau-Despréaux, Nicolas, *Œuvres Complètes*, ed. A. Ch. Gidel. Paris, 1873.

Bosanquet, Bernard, *History of Aesthetic*, Second Edition. London, 1922.

Bouffier, Claude, *First Truths, and the Origin of our Opinions, Explained*, etc. London, 1780.

Bouillier, Victor, "Silvain et Kant, ou les Antécédents Français de la Théorie du Sublime," *Revue de Littérature Comparée* VIII (1928), 242–257.

* Boyle, Hon. Robert, *Some Considerations touching the Style of the Holy Scriptures*. London, 1661.

Bray, René, *La Formation de la Doctrine Classique en France*. Paris, 1927.

Brome, James, *Travels over England, Scotland, and Wales*, etc. London, 1700.

Bromley, Robert Anthony, *A Philosophical and Critical History of the Fine Arts.* London, 1793.

Brown, Joseph E., *The Critical Opinions of Samuel Johnson*. Princeton, 1926.

Brown, Thomas, *Lectures on the Philosophy of the Human Mind*. Edinburgh, 1820.

[Brown, Isaac Hawkins], *An Essay on Design and Beauty*. Edinburgh, 1739.

Brunetière, Ferdinand, "L'Esthétique de Boileau," *Revue des Deux Mondes*, XCIII (1889), 662–685.

Bürger, Gottfried Augustus, *Leonora*, tr. W. R. Spencer, with Designs by the Right Honourable Diana Beauclerk. London, 1796.

[Burke, Edmund], *A Philosophical Enquiry into the Origin of our Ideas of the Sublime and Beautiful*. London, 1757.

——, *A Philosophical Enquiry into the Origin of our Ideas of the Sublime and Beautiful*, Second Edition. London, 1759.

Burnet, Gilbert, *Some Letters. Containing an Account of what seemed most Remarkable in Switzerland, Italy*, etc. Rotterdam, 1686.

[Burnet, James, Lord Monboddo], *Antient Metaphysics: or, the Science of Universals*. London, 1779–1799.

Candrea, Georg, *Der Begriff des Erhabenen bei Burke und Kant*. Strassburg, 1894.

Carter, Elizabeth, *Letters to Mrs. Montagu between the Years 1755 and 1800*, ed. Rev. Montagu Pennington. London, 1817.

——, *A Series of Letters between Mrs. Elizabeth Carter and Mrs. Catherine Talbot, for the Years 1741 to 1770*, ed. Rev. Montagu Pennington. L., 1808.

* Castel, A. P., "Reflexions sur le Nature et la Source du Sublime dans le Discours," *Memoires pour l'Histoire des Sciences et des Beaux Arts* (October, 1733), pp. 1748–1762.

"Castor," "Essay on Ossian," *European Magazine, and London Review*, XXIX (1796), 302–305.

Chambers, Ephraim, *Cyclopedia, or, An Universal Dictionary of Arts and Sciences*, Second Edition. London, 1738.

Chambers, William, *A Dissertation on Oriental Gardening*. London, 1772.

Chambray, Freart de, *An Idea of the Perfection of Painting*, tr. J[ohn] E[velyn]. London, 1668.

Chapone, Hester, *Posthumous Works*, etc. London, 1807.

Cobb, Samuel, *Poems on Several Occasions, To which is prefix'd a Discourse on Criticism, and the Liberty of Writing*, Third Edition. London, 1710.

Coleridge, Samuel Taylor, *Anima Poetae from the Unpublished Note-Books*, ed. E. H. Coleridge. London, 1895.

——, *Miscellanies, Aesthetic and Literary* ed. T. Ashe. London, 1885.

——, *Table Talk, and Omniana*, ed. T. Ashe. London, 1884.

* Constable, John, *Reflections upon Accuracy of Style*. London, 1734.

[Cooper, Anthony Ashley, Third Earl of Shaftesbury], *Characteristicks of Men, Manners, Opinions, Times*, etc. [London], 1711.

——, *Letters*. [London], 1746.

* Coxe, William, *Travels in Switzerland, In a Series of Letters to William Melmoth, Esq*. London, 1789.

Crousaz, Jean Pierre, *Traité du Beau*. Amsterdam, 1724.

Cumberland, Richard, *Odes*. London, 1776.

Cunningham, Peter, "James Thomson and David Mallet," *Miscellanies of the Philobiblon Society*. (London, 1857–8), IV.

Dalton, John, "A Descriptive Poem Addressed to Two Ladies," Pearch's *A Collection of Poems* (London, 1770) 1, 36–51.

Demetrius, *On Style*, ed. W. Rhys Roberts. London, 1927.

Dennis, John, *The Advancement and Reformation of Modern Poetry*. L., 1701.

——, *Miscellanies in Verse and Prose*. London, 1693.

——, *Remarks on a Book entituled, Prince Arthur, an Heroick Poem*, etc. London, 1696.

——, *Select Works*. London, 1718.

Dermody, Thomas, *The Harp of Erin*. London, 1807.

Dionysius of Halicarnassus, *On Literary Composition*, ed. W. Rhys Roberts. London, 1910.

Dodridge, Philip. *A Course of Lectures on the Principal Subjects of Pneumatology, Ethics*, etc. London, 1763.

Dolce, Lodovico, *Aretin: A Dialogue on Painting*, tr. W. Brown. London, 1770.

Drake, Nathan, *Literary Hours or Sketches Critical and Narrative*. London, 1798.

Dryden, John, *Essays*, ed. W. P. Ker. Oxford, 1900.

Du Bos, Jean Baptiste, *Réflexions Critiques sur la Poésie et sur la Peinture*. Paris, 1719.

Du Fresnoy, Charles Alphonse, *The Art of Painting*, tr. John Dryden, Second Edition, Corrected and Enlarged. London, 1716.

Duff, W., *Critical Observations on the Writings of the Most Celebrated Original Geniuses in Poetry*. London, 1780.

[——], *An Essay on Original Genius*, etc. London, 1767.

* Elmes, James, *A General and Bibliographical Dictionary of the Fine Arts*, etc. London, 1826.

Engel, Clair-Eliane, *La Littérature Alpestre en France et en Angleterre aux 18 and 19 Siècles*. Chambéry, 1930.

Evelyn, John, *Diary*, ed. Austin Dobson. London, 1908.

Fawcett, Joseph, *Poems*. London, 1798.

[Félibien, André], *Des Principes de l'Architecture, de la Sculpture, de la Peinture, et des Autres Arts qui en Dependent*, etc., Seconde Edition. Paris, 1690.

[——], *Entretiens sur les Vies et sur les Ouvrages des Plus Excellens Peintres Anciens et Modernes*, Seconde Edition. Paris, 1685.

——, *L'Idée du Peintre Parfait*. London, 1707.

Felton, Henry, *A Dissertation on Reading the Classics and Forming a Just Style*, Fifth Edition. London, 1753.

Fénelon, François de la Mothe, *Dialogue Concerning Eloquence in General*, tr. Wm. Stevenson. London, 1722.

Fielding, Henry, *Miscellanies*. London, 1743.

Folkierski, Wladyslaw, *Entre le Classicisme et le Romantisme*. Paris, 1925.

* Formey, M., *Elementary Principles of the Belles-Lettres*, tr. Sloper Foreman. London, 1766.

* Freeman, Sir William, *Letters on Several Occasions*. London, 1758.

Fuseli, Henry, *Life and Works*, ed. John Knowles. London, 1831.

Gerard, Alexander, *An Essay on Taste*, Second Edition. Edinburgh, 1764.

Gibbon, Edward, *Journal to January 28th, 1763*, ed. D. M. Low. London, 1929.

Gibert, Balthasar, *Jugemens des Savans sur les Auteurs qui ont traité de la Rhetorique*, etc. Paris, 1713.

——, *Réflexions sur la Rhetorique, ou l'on repond aux Objections du P. L'Amy*. Paris, 1705.

*Gildon, Charles, *Complete Art of Poetry*. London, 1724.

———, *The Laws of Poetry as lai'd down by the Duke of Buckinghamshire*, etc. London, 1721.

*Gilpin, William, *Observations on the River Wye and Several Parts of South Wales Relative Chiefly to Picturesque Beauty, Made in the Summer of the Year 1770*. London, 1782.

* ———, *Observations on Several Parts of the Counties of Cambridge, Norfolk, Suffolk, and Essex. Also on Several Parts of North Wales; Relative Chiefly to Picturesque Beauty, in Two Tours*, etc. London, 1809.

———, *Observations Relative Chiefly to Picturesque Beauty Made in the Year 1772, on Several Parts of England; Particularly the Mountains and Lakes of Cumberland and Westmorland*. London, 1786.

———, *Observations Relative Chiefly to Picturesque Beauty, Made in the Year 1776, on Several Parts of Great Britain, Particularly the High-Lands of Scotland*. London, 1789.

———, *Three Essays: On Picturesque Beauty; on Picturesque Travel; and on Sketching Landscape*, etc., Second Edition. London, 1794.

Goldsmith, Oliver, *The Bee*. London, 1759.

[———], [Review of Burke's *Enquiry*], *Monthly Review: or Literary Journal*, XVI (1757), 473–480.

———, *Works*, ed. J. W. M. Gibbs. London, 1884.

[Gordon, John], *Occasional Thoughts on the Study and Character of Classical Authors*. London, 1762.

Gray, Thomas, *Corrspondence of Gray, Walpole, West, and Ashton*, ed. Paget Toynbee. Oxford, 1915.

———, *Poems, to Which Are Prefixed Memoirs of his Life and Writings*, ed. William Mason. York, 1775.

———, *Works*, ed. Edmund Gosse. London, 1884.

[Greene, Richard Burnaby], *Critical Essays*. London, 1770.

Hartford, Countess of, *Correspondence between Francis, Countess of Hartford and Henrietta Louisa, Countess of Pomfret*. London, 1805.

Hartley, David, *Observations on Man*. London, 1749.

Hayley, William, *An Essay on Painting*. London, 1771.

Helvetius, Claude Adrien, *A Treatise on Man, his Intellectual Faculties and his Education*, tr. W. Hooper. London, 1777.

Hendrickson, G. L., "The Origin and Meaning of the Ancient Characters of Style," *American Journal of Philology*, XXVI (1905), 249–290.

Herring, Thomas, *Letters to William Dunscombe, Esq. deceased; from the Year 1728 to 1757*. London, 1777.

* [Hickey, Thomas], *Storia della Pittura e la Scultura*. Calcutta, 1788.

Hofmann, H. J., *Die Lehre vom Erhabenen bei Kant und seinen Vorgängern*. Halle, 1913.

Hogarth, William, *Analysis of Beauty*. London, 1753.

Holmes, John, *The Art of Rhetorick Made Easy: or, the Elements of Oratory*, etc. London, 1739.

[Home, Henry, Lord Kames], *The Elements of Criticism*. Edinburgh, 1762.

Q. Horatius Flaccus, *Epistola ad Augustum, with English Commentary and Notes. To which is added, A Discourse concerning Poetical Imitation*, by [Richard Hurd]. London, 1751.

———, *Ars Poetica. Epistola ad Pisones. With an English Commentary and Notes*, ed. [Richard Hurd]. London, 1749.

Hourticq, Louis, *De Poussin à Watteau*. Paris, 1921.

Howell, James, *Epistolae Ho-Elianae, Familiar Letters Domestic and Forren*, etc., Third Edition. London, 1655.

Huet, Pierre Daniel, *Demonstratio Evangelica*, etc., Tertia Editio, Paris, 1690.

———, "Examen du sentiment de *Longin*, sur ce passage de la Genese, etc.," *Bibliothèque Choisie*, x (1706), 211–260.

Hume, David, *Philosophical Works*, ed. Green and Grose. London, 1874.

Hurd, Richard, *Letters on Chivalry and Romance*, ed. Edith Morley. L., 1911.

[———], *Letter to the Rev. Dr. Thomas Leland*. London, 1764.

[———], *Works*. London, 1811.

Hussey, Christopher, *The Picturesque, Studies in a Point of View*. London and New York, 1927.

[Hutcheson, Francis], *An Inquiry into the Original of our Ideas of Beauty and Virtue*. London, 1725.

[Jackson, William], *Thirty Letters on Various Subjects*. London, 1753.

Jacob, Hildebrand, *Works*. London, 1735.

Jaucourt, Louis, Chevallier de, "Le Sublime," *Encyclopédie ou Dictionnaire Raisonné*, (Neufchastel, 1765), xv.

Jeffry, Francis Lord, *Essay on Beauty; and Essays on the Nature and Principles of Taste, by Archibald Alison*. London, 1817.

[Johnson, Samuel], *Journey to the Western Islands of Scotland*. London, 1775.

———, *Works*. Oxford, 1825.

Kant, Immanuel, *Beobachtungen über das Gefühl des Schönen und Erhabenen*. Königsberg, 1766.

———, *Critique of Aesthetic Judgement*, tr. J. C. Meredith. Oxford, 1911.

Kate, Lambert Hermanson Ten, *The Beau Ideal:* tr. from the French by J. C. Le Blon. London, 1732.

———, *Ideal Beauty in Painting and Sculpture Illustrated by Remarks on the Antique*, etc., London, 1769.

Knight, Richard Payne, *An Analytical Inquiry into the Principles of Taste*, Second Edition. London, 1805.

* ———, *The Landscape, A Didactic Poem*. London, 1794.

* Knox, Vicessimus, *Essays Moral and Literary*. London, 1779.

Lairesse, Gerard de, *The Art of Painting*, tr. J. F. Fritsch. London, 1738.

Lamotte, Charles, *An Essay upon Poetry and Painting, with Relation to the Sacred and Profane History*, etc. London, 1730.

* Lamy, Bernard, *La Rhetorique ou l'Art de Parler*, Cinquième Edition. Amsterdam, 1712.

Lanson, John, *Lectures Concerning Oratory*, Second Edition. Dublin, 1759.

Le Clerc, Jean, *Parrhasiana*. London, 1700.

———, "Remarques sur la X Réflexion sur Longin," *Bibliothèque Choisie*, xxvi (1713), 83–112.

Leland, Thomas, *Dissertation on the Principles of Human Eloquence*, The Second Edition. Dublin, 1765.

Leslie, Henrie, *A Treatise of the Authority of the Church*. Dublin, 1639.

Longinus, Dionysius, *Peri Hupsous, or Dionysius Longinus of the Height of Eloquence rendred out of the originall by J*[ohn] *H*[all], *Esq*. London, 1652.

———, *An Essay on the Sublime: Translated from the Greek*. Oxford, 1698.

———, *On the Sublime*, tr. from the Greek by William Smith, Fourth Edition, Corrected and Improved. London, 1770.

———, *On the Sublime*, ed. W. Rhys Roberts. Cambridge, 1899.

——, *A Treatise of the Loftiness or Elegancy of Speech*, tr. by J. P. L., 1680.

——, *The Works of . . . On the Sublime: or, a Treatise Concerning the Sovereign Perfection of Writing. Translated from the Greek with Some Remarks on the English Poets*. By Mr. Welsted. London, 1712.

Lovejoy, Arthur O., "The Parallel of Deism and Classicism," *Modern Philology*, XXIX (1932), 281–299.

Lowth, Robert, *Lectures on the Sacred Poetry of the Hebrews*, tr. G. Gregory. London, 1787.

McCormick, Charles, *Memoirs of the Rt. Honourable Edmund Burke*, Second Edition. London, 1798.

[Mangin, Edward], *Essays on the Sources of the Pleasures Received from Literary Compositions*. London, 1809.

Manwaring, Edward, *Institutes of Learning, Taken from Aristotle, Plutarch, Longinus*, etc. London, 1737.

Manwaring, Elizabeth, *Italian Landscape in Eighteenth Century England*. New York, 1925.

Marguetel de St. Denis (St. Evremond), *Works*. London, 1700.

[Mason, George], *An Essay on Design in Gardening, First Published in MDCCLXVIII Now Greatly Augmented*, etc. London, 1795.

[——], *An Appendix to an Essay on Design in Gardening*. London, 1798.

Melmoth, Courtney (S. J. Pratt), *The Sublime and Beautiful of Scripture*. London, 1777.

* Mengs, Anthony Raphael, *Works*. London, 1796.

Michiels, Alfred, "La Théorie de Kant sur le Sublime Exposée par un Français en 1708," *Revue Contemporaine*, III (1852), 447–465.

Middleton, Conyers, *Works*, Second Edition. London, 1775.

Mill, James, *Analysis of the Phenomena of the Human Mind*. London, 1829.

* Miller, George, "An Essay on the Origin and Nature of our Ideas of the Sublime," *Transactions of the Royal Irish Academy*, [1794], V.

Milton, John, *Prose Works*, ed. J. A. St. John. London, 1848.

Mirabent, Francisco, *La Estética Inglesa del Siglo XVIII*. Barcelona, 1927.

Monier, P., *The History of Painting, Sculpture, Architecture, Graving*, etc. London, 1699.

[Montagu, Elizabeth], *An Essay on the Writings and Genius of Shakespeare*, etc. London, 1769.

Montesquieu, C. de S., *Pensées et Fragments inédits*. Bordeaux, 1899–1901.

* Moore, John, *A View of Society and Manners in France, Switzerland, and Germany*, Third Edition. London, 1780.

Morris, Robert, *Lectures on Architecture*. London, 1734.

[Murphy, Arthur], [Review of Burke's *Enquiry*], *Works of Johnson*, ed. Sir John Hawkins (London, 1787) X, 199–219.

Murray, Hon. Mrs. S., *A Companion and Useful Guide to the Beauties of Scotland*, etc. London, 1799.

[Newberry, John?], *The Art of Poetry on a New Plan*. London, 1762.

[——], *The Circle of the Sciences*, Fourth Edition. Dublin, 1770.

* Nichols, G. T., "The Gift of Sublimity," *General Magazine and Impartial Review*, II (1788), 153, 154.

* Northall, John, *Travels through Italy*, etc. London, 1766.

Ogilvie, John, *Philosophical and Critical Observations on the Nature, Character, and Various Specimens of Composition*. London, 1774.

* Opie, John, *Lectures on Painting*, etc. London, 1809.

Ossian, Son of Fingal, *Works, Translated from the Galic Language by James Mac-Pherson*, Third Edition. London, 1765.

Owenson, Sidney (Lady Morgan), *Life and Times of Salvator Rosa*. London, 1824.

* [Papon, J. P.], *L'Art du Poete et de l'Orateur*, etc. Lyon, 1768.

Parnell, Thomas, *Essay on the Different Stiles of Poetry*. London, 1713.

[Parsons, William], *A Poetical Tour in the Years, 1784, 1785, and 1786*. L., 1787.

"Pasquin, Anthony" (John Williams), *Memoirs of the Royal Academicians; being an Attempt to Improve the National Taste*. London, 1796.

[————], *The Royal Academicians, a Farce*. London, 1786.

Paul, H. G., *John Dennis: His Life and Criticism*. New York, 1911.

Pemberton, Henry, *Observations on Poetry, Especially on the Epic*, etc. London, 1738.

Perrault, Charles, "Reponse aux Réflexions Critiques de M. Despréaux sur Longin," *Mélange Curieux des Meilleurs Pièces Attribuées à M. De Saint-Evremond*. Amsterdam, 1726.

Phillips, Edward, *A New World of English Words*, etc. London, 1658.

Piles, Roger de, *The Art of Painting, and the Lives of the Painters*, etc. L., 1706.

————, *Principles of Painting*, etc. London, 1743.

Pilkington, M., *The Gentleman's and Connoisseur's Dictionary of Painters*, etc. London, 1770.

Piozzi, Hester Lynch, *Observations and Reflections Made in the Course of a Journey through France, Italy, and Germany*. London, 1789.

[Plumer, F.], *A Letter from a Gentleman to his Nephew at Oxford*. London, 1772.

Pope, Alexander, *Works*, ed. Elwin and Courthope. London, 1886.

————, *Works*, ed. William Warburton. London, 1751.

[Pott, Joseph], *An Essay on Landscape Painting*, etc. London, 1782.

Price, Sir Uvedale, A *Dialogue on the Distinct Characters of the Picturesque and the Beautiful*. Hereford, 1801.

————, *An Essay on the Picturesque, as Compared with the Sublime and Beautiful*, etc., Second Edition, enlarged. London, 1796.

————, *On the Picturesque: With an Essay on the Origin of Taste*, etc., by Sir Thomas Dick Lauder, Bart. Edinburgh and London, 1842.

Priestley, Joseph, *A Course of Lectures on Oratory and Criticism*. London, 1777.

————, *Hartley's Theory of the Human Mind*. London, 1775.

Quintilianus, Marcus Fabius, *Institutio Oratoria*, tr. H. E. Bell, Loeb Classical Library. London and New York, 1922.

Radcliffe, Ann, *Gaston de Blondeville, etc., To Which is Prefixed a Memoir of the Author, with Extracts from her Journals*. London, 1826.

————, *The Italian*. London, 1797.

————, *A Journey Made in the Summer of 1794, through Holland and the Western Frontier of Germany, with a Return down the Rhine*, etc. London, 1795.

————, *The Mysteries of Udolpho, A Romance*. London, 1794.

————, *Novels*, Ballantyne's Novelist's Library, x. London, 1824.

Ralph, Benjamin, *The School of Raphael: or, the Student's Guide to Expression in Historical Painting*, etc. London, 1759.

[Ralph, James], *The Touchstone: or historical, critical, political, philosophical, and theological essays on the reigning diversions of the Town*. London, 1728.

Rapin, René, "Réflexions sur l'Usage de l'Eloquence de ce Temps en Général," *Œuvres*. La Haye, 1725.

Reid, Thomas, *Essays on the Intellectual Powers of Man*. Edinburgh, 1785.

Reynolds, Sir Joshua, *Discourses Delivered to the Students of the Royal Academy*, ✓
    ed. Roger Fry. London, 1905.

――――, *Letters*, ed. F. W. Hilles. Cambridge, England, 1929. ✓

――――, *Works*, ed. Edmond Malone, The Second Edition. London, 1798.

Reynolds, Myra, *The Treatment of Nature in English Poetry between Pope and* ✓
    Wordsworth. Chicago, 1896.

Richardson, Jonathan, Senior and Junior, *An Account of Some of the Statues,*
    Bas-Reliefs, Drawings, and Pictures in Italy, etc. London, 1722.

Richardson, Jonathan, *An Essay on the Theory of Painting*, Second Edition, ↙
    Enlarged and Corrected. London, 1725.

――――, *Two Discourses*. London, 1719.

――――, *Works*. London, 1773.

Rollin, Charles, *De la Manière d'Enseigner et Etudier les Belles Lettres*, Séconde
    Edition. Paris, 1728.

Rosenberg, Alfred, *Longinus in England bis zur Ende des 18. Jahrhunderts.*
    Weimar and Berlin, 1917.

Ruffhead, Owen, *Life of Pope*. London, 1769.

* [Ruskin, John], *Modern Painters*. London, 1846–1860.

Samuels, A. P. I., *The Early Life, Correspondence and Writings of Edmund*
    Burke. Cambridge, 1923.

Schasler, Max, *Kritische Geschichte der Aesthetik*. Berlin, 1872.

* [Seran de la Tour], *L'Art de Sentir et de Juger en Matières de Goût*. Paris, 1762.

Seward, Anna, *Letters Written between the Years 1784 and 1807*. Edinburgh, 1811.

――――, *Poetical Works*, ed. Walter Scott. Edinburgh, 1810.

Shee, Martin, *Elements of Art, A Poem in Six Cantos*. London, 1809.

Sherlock, Martin, *Letters from An English Traveller*. London, 1780.

* ――――, *Letters on Several Subjects*. London, 1781.

Silvain, *Traité du Sublime*. Paris, 1732.

Smith, Gregory, *Elizabeth Critical Essays*. Oxford, 1904.

Smith, James Edward, *A Sketch of a Tour on the Continent, in the Years 1786 and*
    1787. London, 1793.

[Smollett, Tobias George], *The Adventures of Ferdinand Count Fathom*. L., 1753.

――――, *Travels through France and Italy*. London, 1766.

* South, Robert, *Forty-Eight Sermons and Discourses on Several Subjects and Oc-*
    casions. London, 1715.

Spingarn, Joel E., *Critical Essays of the Seventeenth Century*. Oxford, 1909.

Stack, Richard, "An Essay on Sublimity of Writing," *Transactions of the*
    Royal Irish Academy (Dublin, 1787) I, 19–26.

[Stedman, J.], *Laelius and Hortensia; or, Thoughts on the Nature and Objects of*
    Taste and Genius; in a Series of Letters to Two Friends. Edinburgh, 1782.

* [Steele, Sir Richard], "On the Sublime," *Tatler*, 43 (July, 19, 1709).

Stein, Heinrich von, *Die Entstehung der Neuern Aesthetik*. Stuttgart, 1886.

Steinke, Martin W., *Edward Young's Conjectures on Original Composition in*
    England and Germany, Americana Germanica 28. New York, 1917.

Sterne, Lawrence, *Works*, London, 1823.

Stevens, Sacheverell, *Miscellaneous Remarks Made on the Spot in a late Seven*
    Years Tour through France, Italy, etc. London, 1756.

Steward, Dugald, *Philosophical Essays*. Edinburgh, 1810.

Stockdale, Percival, *An Inquiry into the Nature and Genuine Laws of Poetry*
    Including a particular Defense of the Writings and Genius of Mr. Pope.
    London, 1778.

* ———, *Lectures on the Truly Eminent English Poets*. London, 1807.

Strange, Robert, *A Descriptive Catalogue of a Collection of Pictures*, etc. London, 1769.

Sulzer, Johan Georg, *Allgemeine Theorie der Schönen Künste*. Leipzig, 1786.

[Swift, Jonathan], *On Poetry: A Rhapsody*. London, 1733.

"Temple, Launcelot," (Dr. John Armstrong), *A Short Ramble through Some Parts of France and Italy*. London, 1771.

———, *Sketches: or Essays on Various Subjects*. London, 1758.

Thomson, Alexander, *The Paradise of Taste*. London, 1796.

Thomson, James, *The Seasons*, ed. Otto Zippel, Palaestra LXVI. Berlin, 1908.

Trapp, Joseph, *Lectures on Poetry Read in the Schools of Natural Philosophy at Oxford*. London, 1742.

[Turnbull, George], *A Curious Collection of Ancient Paintings*, etc. L., 1741.

———, *A Treatise on Ancient Pinting*. London, 1740.

U[sher], I[ames], *Clio: or, a Discourse on Taste*, Second Edition. London, 1769.

[Villiers, George, Second Duke of Buckingham], *The Rehearsal, as it was Acted at the Theatre-Royal*. London, 1672.

* T. W., "Remarks on the Beauty of Simplicity in Writing," *The British Magazine or Monthly Repository for Gentlemen and Ladies*, V (1764), 565, 566.

Warburton, William, *The Doctrine of Grace*. London, 1763.

Ward, John, *A System of Oratory, Delivered in a Course of Lectures Publicly used at Gresham College*. London, 1759.

[Warton, Joseph], *Essay on the Writings and Genius of Pope*. L., 1756 and 1782.

———, "Translation of a Manuscript of Longinus," *The Adventurer*, 51 and 57.

Warton, Thomas, et al., *Essays on Gothic Architecture*, 2 ed. London, 1800.

———, *Observations on the Faerie Queene of Spenser*, Second Edition. 1762.

* Webb, Daniel, *An Inquiry into the Beauties of Painting*, etc. London, 1760.

[———], *Observations on the Correspondence between Poetry and Music*. L., 1769.

———, *Remarks on the Beauties of Poetry*. London, 1762.

[West, Thomas], *A Guide to the Lakes*, The Second Edition. London, 1780.

Wicheln, Herbert A., "Burke's Essay on the Sublime and its Reviewers," *Journal of English and Germanic Philology*, XXI (1922), 645–661.

Woodward, George Murgatroyd, "A Curious Specimen of the Sublime and Beautiful," *The General Magazine and Impartial Review* (London, 1787) I, 206–208.

Wordsworth, William, *The Prelude*, ed. Ernest de Sellincourt. Oxford, 1926.

* [Wyndham, Henry Penruddocke], *A Gentleman's Tour through Monmouthshire and Wales, in the Months of June and July, 1774*. London, 1775.

Young, Arthur, *A Six Months Tour through the North of England*, etc., Second Edition. London, 1770.

[———], *A Six Weeks Tour, through the Southern Counties of England and Wales*. London, 1768.

[Young, Edward], *Conjectures on Original Composition*. London, 1759.

———, *Conjectures on Original Composition*, ed. Edith Morley. Manchester and New York, 1918.

INDEX